BARKSDALE'S CHARGE

Barksdale's Charge

The True High Tide of the Confederacy at Gettysburg, July 2, 1863

PHILLIP THOMAS TUCKER, PH.D.

CASEMATE
Philadelphia & Oxford

Published in the United States of America and Great Britain in 2013 by
CASEMATE PUBLISHERS
908 Darby Road, Havertown, PA 19083
and
10 Hythe Bridge Street, Oxford, OX1 2EW

Copyright 2013 © Phillip Thomas Tucker

ISBN 978–1-61200–179-1
Digital Edition: ISBN 978–1-61200–180-7

The maps in this book are courtesy of Bradley M. Gottfried from his work
The Maps of Gettysburg, Savas-Beatie Publishers, 2007.

Cataloging-in-publication data is available from the Library of Congress
and the British Library.

10 9 8 7 6 5 4 3 2 1

Printed and bound in the United States of America.

For a complete list of Casemate titles please contact:

CASEMATE PUBLISHERS (US)
Telephone (610) 853-9131, Fax (610) 853-9146
E-mail: casemate@casematepublishing.com

CASEMATE PUBLISHERS (UK)
Telephone (01865) 241249, Fax (01865) 794449
E-mail: casemate-uk@casematepublishing.co.uk

Contents

Introduction

ACCORDING TO CONVENTIONAL wisdom, "Pickett's Charge" has been long seen as the climax of Gettysburg, the largest and most important battle fought on American soil. But contrary to traditional assumptions, the failure of "Pickett's Charge," despite all its tragic majesty and heroic grandeur, was not the decisive event that condemned the Army of Northern Virginia and the Confederacy to an early death. In truth, Gettysburg was decided not on the famous third day of the battle, but on the previous afternoon. Indeed, Thursday, July 2, 1863 was the most important day in the Confederacy's short lifetime and the most decisive of the three days at Gettysburg. And the defining moment of that Second Day was the repulse of the most successful Confederate attack, which came closer to toppling the Army of the Potomac than any other Rebel offensive effort of the war. It was the charge of General William Barksdale and his 1,600-man Mississippi Brigade on the afternoon of July 2, which one Union observer described as "the grandest charge that was ever made by mortal man."

Unfortunately, the mythical qualities and romantic dimensions of the most famous assault in American history, "Pickett's Charge," has left a far more successful Southern attack—one that swept through and routed much of a veteran Union Corps, captured nearly 20 artillery pieces, and penetrated more than a mile to drive a deep wedge into the Union army's left-center—in the historical shadows, and often only in obscure footnotes of books about the Battle of Gettysburg. In truth, however, Barksdale's attack—as the foremost spearhead of Longstreet's offensive on July 2—came closer to achieving decisive success and winning it all for the Confederacy than any other assault of the battle.

In America's fabled national Iliad, the relatively slight, ever-so-brief penetration of the Union center by the courageous attackers of General

1

George Edward Pickett's Virginia Division on July 3 has been long celebrated as the "High Water Mark" of Gettysburg and the Confederacy. But only a relatively few men of a depleted band of attackers ever reached the little copse of trees on the Union right-center along Cemetery Ridge, and once there could only fall to Union fire or be captured. In terms of achieving the greatest gains and coming closer to achieving decisive success, the "High Water Mark" of Gettysburg has long been located in the wrong place.

After the war, United States government historian John Bachelder "officially" established—or rather invented—the "High Water Mark" at the copse of trees along Cemetery Ridge. Influenced by powerful veteran groups from both sides, especially Pickett's Virginians, Bachelder's designation became the established "High Water Mark" that has forever commemorated the geographical and military zenith of Confederate fortunes during the four years of war. Therefore, "Pickett's Charge" has been widely seen as Lee's best chance to have won the battle, which was not the case. Propelled by the tide of popular history based upon the much-embellished Virginia version of the story, generations of historians and popular writers have long celebrated the Rebel zenith on the incorrect day and place.

The true "High Water Mark" of the Battle of Gettysburg took place farther south of the famous clump of trees, near Cemetery Ridge's southern end on the Union left-center, where Barksdale struck with his brigade. In terms of its overall success, gains reaped, and closeness to achieving a decisive victory, "Pickett's Charge" was neither the most successful nor most important Confederate attack at Gettysburg. In fact, it never came close to achieving what had been accomplished and gained by the Mississippi Brigade's sweeping attack the day before.

Unlike when Barksdale's men smashed through the Union left-center, at a time when it was most vulnerable, General Robert E. Lee's decision to target the Federal right-center on July 3 was made when it was far too strong—in terms of the number of defenders, both front-line and reserve, excellent elevated defensive terrain, and high-quality Union commanders—to overcome. Quite unlike Barksdale's Charge on July 2 when the fate of the American nation was decided, "Pickett's Charge" never really had a chance of succeeding.

Seldom before and afterward would Lee and his Army of Northern Virginia come closer to achieving decisive victory than when Barksdale's Charge came so tantalizing close to cracking the Union line on the late afternoon of July 2. Under Barksdale's inspired leadership, the Mississippi Brigade's success in smashing everything in its path, including the Peach Orchard salient and the Emmitsburg Road defensive line, was remarkable by any measure. A single regiment of Barksdale's Brigade (the 21st Mississippi) captured more artillery pieces than any regiment on either side at Gettysburg. As never before, Barksdale went for broke in personally leading his brigade's onslaught in an attempt to win the war in a single afternoon. And he nearly succeeded.

But in one of the great inequities of American history, Barksdale's Charge has long remained in the shadow of "Pickett's Charge," thanks largely to the dominance of the Virginia School of history. The general obscurity of Barksdale's effort, despite its tactical success, has resulted from the sheer power of myth, traditionalism, and romance in both popular and academic history. As fate would have it, the Mississippians' attack was never promoted, embellished, or celebrated by generations of historians after the Civil War. Southern writers favored the gallant effort of the Virginians, while Northern writers preferred to celebrate their clear triumph over Pickett's men rather than the moment when their line was barely hanging by a thread, and elements of four corps were forced to converge to stop the onslaught of Barksdale's Mississippians.

Pro-Virginia propagandists early rewrote the dramatic story of Gettysburg's Third Day to conform to a chivalric and heroic tale dominated by layers of Victorian Era values and romance. They succeeded in transforming the folly of "Pickett's Charge" into the most romanticized saga of the Civil War. The aggressive advocates and prolific writers of the Virginia School, which glorified Virginian leaders, troops, and accomplishments, decisively influenced generations of latter-day historians, popular writers (ironically including Mississippi's own William Faulkner), documentaries, and films for generations to come. Unlike Pickett, whose enduring romantic image was largely the product of the writings of his well-connected Virginia wife, the Deep South general, William Barksdale, who led the far more successful charge at Gettysburg, was forgotten.

Unlike Barksdale, who fell to rise on more on July 2, Pickett ideally fit the overwrought image of a romantic Virginia cavalier in the popular imagination. In the historical memory, the enduring image of the West Point-trained Pickett cast a giant shadow over the more homespun, less attractive Barksdale, an outspoken Mississippi politician, newspaper editor, and self-made leader. Barksdale's death on the field likewise contributed to the obscurity of his attack, so that the authentic "High

Tide" at Gettysburg has been generally overlooked.

Unlike the soldiers of Pickett's Virginia Division, which was not a battle-hardened command, Barksdale's veterans possessed an early and well-deserved reputation for repeatedly achieving the impossible during some of the war's most important battles. In fact, reaping dramatic battlefield gains was the hallmark of Barksdale's rough-hewn brigade of combat troops by the time of the battle of Gettysburg. In key roles the Mississippi Brigade had repeatedly fought against great odds in vital battlefield situations, revealing that Barksdale's command was possibly the best fighting brigade in Lee's Army.

While Pickett was neither in command of the overall July 3 assault (only his Virginia Division) nor led the charge all the way to Cemetery Ridge, and his men were not the majority of attackers, Barksdale personally led Lee's most successful attack in terms of coming closer to achieving a decisive victory at Gettysburg. Ironically, the widely celebrated twin dramas of "Pickett's Charge" (primarily a romanticized product of the Nineteenth Century) and the battle's most famous small-unit action, when the 20th Maine garnered recognition in the struggle for Little Round Top (primarily an equally romanticized product of the Twentieth Century) have together obscured the *real* "High Water Mark" of Gettysburg."

Compared to Pickett's men, Mississippi's veterans, mostly illiterate farm boys from a remote frontier-like region located far from leading eastern centers of population and influence, possessed little clout, political connections, and literary machinery to garner recognition for their supreme effort at Gettysburg. Therefore, despite the importance of Barksdale's steamrolling attack in nearly winning it all, this remarkable story of the most successful offensive effort at Gettysburg has been a forgotten chapter of history.

Most of all, the Mississippi Brigade's unsurpassed success on July 2 marked the true zenith of the Confederate offensive effort during the three days of Gettysburg. The closest that the Army of Northern Virginia ever came in its long storied history to reaping a truly decisive success in vanquishing the Army of the Potomac was when Barksdale's assault overran nearly twenty field pieces and demolished one brigade after another, while gaining hundreds of yards during the relentless push to gain Cemetery Ridge's strategic crest at any cost.

In an attempt to finally set the historical record straight and to overturn a host of longstanding assumptions and myths about Gettysburg, this is the first time that the full story of the most successful Confederate offensive effort at Gettysburg has been told to reveal just how close Barksdale's crack Mississippi Brigade nearly came to winning the most decisive success of the Civil War. Clearly, Barksdale and his Mississippi soldiers saw their finest hour on Thursday July 2, rising to the supreme challenge by almost winning the war in a single afternoon.

But more important, Barksdale's Charge should be remembered today as one of the most dramatic and memorable chapters of not only the battle of Gettysburg but also the Civil War. Few examples in the annals of American military history have more thoroughly revealed the courage, fighting prowess, and heroics of the American fighting man than the unforgettable story of Barksdale's Charge. When the shattered remains of the Mississippi Brigade, after having lost half its strength, retired along the bloody path they had made and fell back in the fading light of July 2, Barksdale's repulse also marked the Confederacy's sunset: the South was now on the road to extinction and there was no detour or exit.

For the millions of people from around the world who have toured Gettysburg's hallowed ground each year to marvel at the majesty of the stately Virginia Monument, where the Old Dominion men of "Pickett's Charge" began their lengthy march from Seminary Ridge, over the open fields toward the famous copse of trees on Cemetery Ridge, where the doomed attack finally ended in its inevitable bloody climax, has long drawn the greatest gatherings of any spot on the Gettysburg battlefield. In a classic irony and in striking contrast, relatively few visitors of Gettysburg today are even aware of Barksdale's Charge or how the Mississippians' sweeping attack of more than a mile actually came closer to achieving victory. Consequently, almost all visitors to the pastoral fields and seemingly haunted hills of the battlefield drive by the forgotten but true "High Water Mark" of the Confederacy, oblivious to its importance.

Therefore, it is now time to take a fresh new look at the truths, myths, and realities of the battle of Gettysburg and its relatively forgotten culminating moment, beyond the romantic stereotypes and unchallenged conventional wisdom that that have flourished for the last 150 years. It is now time to tell the story of the true Confederate High Tide, Barksdale's Charge, when the fate of the American nation was decided.

Dr. Phillip Thomas Tucker
Washington, D.C.
May 23, 2013

ᴄ— 1 —ᴐ

"We have never been whipped and we never can be!"

DURING THE THIRTEEN months after General Robert E. Lee took command on the first day of June 1862, the Army of Northern Virginia compiled a record of battlefield successes second to none in the annals of American military history. The names of victories at the Seven Days, Cedar Mountain, Second Manassas, Fredericksburg, and Chancellorsville now adorned Southern battle-flags. This is even as it can plausibly be said that Antietam (Sharpsburg), where the army fought a Federal force twice its size to a standstill, might have been the Rebels' most impressive fight. By the summer of 1863, the Army of Northern Virginia, characterized by its "very democratic equality," in one Georgia soldier's words, represented the aspirations of not only its seemingly invincible commander and the fighting men in the ranks but also the infant Southern nation.[1]

These Confederate successes stemmed from Lee's aggressive and skillful employment of the army's most highly efficient combat unit: the brigade. The best of these tactically flexible, hard-hitting brigades possessed the capability to function independently to achieve victory on their own on the battlefield. And one of the foremost of these crack units by the time of the Gettysburg campaign was General William Barksdale's Mississippi Brigade, which was composed of some of Lee's hardest fighting veterans.

Earning a well-deserved reputation for hard-hitting offensive capabilities since the war's early days, the 13th, 17th, 18th, and 21st Mississippi Infantry Regiments of Barksdale's Brigade played prominent roles in each of their battles. Most Magnolia State soldiers had received their baptismal fire at First Bull Run on July 21, 1861, contributing to that rout of Union forces. Then, barely three months later, at Ball's Bluff, the

Mississippi Rebels reaped a one-sided success with a fierce bayonet charge that annihilated a sizeable task force under a close friend of President Abraham Lincoln, Colonel Edward D. Baker, who had made the fatal mistake of crossing the Potomac from Maryland to Virginia on a bloody October 21, 1861.

Lincoln had named his son, Edward Baker Lincoln, in his friend's honor. Having introduced president-elect Lincoln during his inaugural address, the handsome, gentlemanly Baker, a U.S. Senator from Oregon, whose political ambitions and flowery quotations of classical poetry were limitless, led his men recklessly into a Confederate trap. He was killed when a Mississippi bullet tore through his brain, just before the Rebels' bayonet charge literally drove the Yankees off the 100-foot-high river bluff and into the Potomac. Private Ezekiel Armstrong, 17th Mississippi, penned in his diary how the Mississippians "whipped five times our number in a fair fight."

With early successes like these, Barksdale's Mississippi Brigade early became the pride of the Magnolia State and well known across the Confederacy. Lee consistently relied upon the brigade as one of his shock units that could be depended upon in a crisis situation. One aristocratic officer of the Richmond Howitzers, Lieutenant Robert Stiles, emphasized that "Barksdale . . . was my general, commanding the infantry brigade I knew and loved best of all in Lee's army."[2]

Presenting insight into those key qualities that made them elite fighting men, Lieutenant Stiles explained how his artillerymen from the Confederacy's capital "were closely associated with these sturdy fellows and became strongly attached to them. This Mississippi brigade was, in many respects, the finest body of men I ever saw. They were almost giants in size and power. In the color company of the 17th Regiment, when we first met them, there were thirty-five men more than six feet one inch high [when the average height of a Civil War soldier was around five foot, five inches], and in the 21st there was one man six feet seven inches in height, and superbly formed, except that his shoulders were a trifle too square and too broad in proportion. They were healthy and hardy, even ruddy, which was surprising, coming as they did from a region generally regarded as full of malarial poison. They were bear hunters from the swamps and canebrakes and, naturally enough, almost without exception fine shots . . . as a body, they were very young men and brimful of irrepressible enthusiasm, equally for play and for fight. The laugh, the song, the yell of the rebel charge burst indifferently from their lips; but in any and every case the volume of sound was tremendous. . . . At times they seemed about as rough as the bears they had hunted, yet they were withal simple-minded and tender-hearted boys . . . how could I help loving these simple, brave, great-hearted fellows?"[3]

But the Virginian's analysis was more colorful than accurate. Most of these young men and boys were middle-class yeoman farmers, who had been toughened by swinging the ax and plowing the fields. But they were familiar with hunting, which went hand-in-hand with everyday life in rural Mississippi, for sport and to put food on the table. A young farm boy of Barksdale's Brigade, Private Joseph A. Miller, who was destined to lose his life in this brothers' war, reflected on better times in his diary on April 18, 1863: "How gloriously I would enjoy [to be] either out fishing, or with my little shot gun on my shoulder, roaming the grand old botom [sic] of Tuscalossa in quest of game. I wish I was at home today and down in the bottom hunting squirels [sic]."[4] And with the white-tailed deer of Mississippi's dark forests in mind, Private Pickney M. Lewis, 17th Mississippi, described in a letter how his brother Private Benjamin Lewis, known as "Benny," "is as hearty as a buck."[5]

Hailing from a yet untamed frontier region just east of the Mississippi River, these "bear hunters," in Lieutenant Stiles' estimation, were indeed tough and durable. Many of the men experienced difficult lives on small farms carved out of the thick pine, oak, and cypress forests along the dark-hued rivers that led either south to the Gulf of Mexico, or west to the Mississippi. General Barksdale's men were products of distinctive cultural and geographic regions known as the Gulf Coast Meadows, the Piney Woods, the Mississippi River lowlands, and the Central Prairie. They came from rural communities with Choctaw Indian names like Alamuthca, located near the Alabama border, and others with more conventional names such as Columbus, located on a site known to the Indians as Possum Town, and small agricultural communities with unique names like Sunflower, which was on the fertile Mississippi River plain about halfway between Vicksburg and Memphis.

Barksdale's soldiers were molded by iron discipline imposed by capable officers, who were also mostly community leaders. With a sense of admiration, one Confederate officer explained how the Mississippi Rebels were indeed the "splendid soldiers that they were, they obeyed orders, held their own fire [to ensure that] Almost every man struck was killed, and every man killed shot through the brain [and later] their comrades had gone into the woods as soon as it was light, brought out the bodies and laid them in rows, with hands cross upon the breast, but eyes wide-staring." By the time of the dramatic showdown at Gettysburg, Barksdale's Mississippians were seasoned experts at vanquishing large numbers of their opponents with considerable tactical skill, business-like efficiency, and superior marksmanship. They had perfected their bloody trade on the gory battlefields of Virginia and Maryland, where lethal skills were refined at the expense of a good many Union soldiers. The high-spirited Rebels of the Mississippi Brigade, in one Confederate soldier's words, "were ready to fight anything, from his Satanic Majesty down; but they were a very poor set indeed as to judging when not to fight, or when to stop fighting."[6]

Another factor that explained the Mississippi brigade's elite quality was the burning desire to save their threatened home state. By June 1863, Mississippi had been invaded and Vicksburg was under siege by President Lincoln's favorite western commander, Ulysses S. Grant. Grant's invaders, economic hardship, and the Confederate government's neglect led to a severe crisis situation across Mississippi. Ironically, thousands of Mississippi troops, including Barksdale's men, had been early shipped east to defend Richmond, leaving the Magnolia State vulnerable. Few Mississippians ever imagined that the war would meantime descend upon their home state with such unbridled fury.[7]

Consequently, by the time of the Gettysburg Campaign, Mississippi Brigade members were eager for revenge, itching to strike a blow to redeem their invaded homeland. In a late October 1862 letter to his mother Maria, Lieutenant William Cowper Nelson, 17th Mississippi, wrote, "I feel uneasy about letters [because] they bring intelligence that the hateful invaders were once more in our country."[8] Then, in a January 15, 1863 letter to Maria, a worried Lieutenant Nelson admitted how, "I am afraid our beautiful home has been desolated by the ruthless hands of the vile invader. I wonder if ever I shall be" home again.[9]

Despite being a political general without formal military training, therefore often subject to close scrutiny from professional soldiers, especially West Pointers, William Barksdale contradicted negative stereotypes. He became the 13th Mississippi's commander during the 1862 Peninsula Campaign. More like a father than a commanding officer to the men, Barksdale was the very heart and soul of the Mississippi Brigade by the time of the battle of Gettysburg. Standing straight and tall, the large-boned, bulky general possessed a distinguished bearing and inspirational command presence that paid high dividends on the battlefield. Like a zealous Crusader waging righteous war in the Holy Land, Barksdale's sheer size and shoulder-length white hair gave him an almost regal appearance.

One secret of Barksdale's success was his distinctive personal leadership style distinguished by a sense of egalitarianism and democratic tendencies. He was on familiar terms with the common soldier in the ranks, treating them fairly. The popular general often intimately mingled freely with his men. A respected Mississippi Congressman who had ensured that Mississippi was the second Southern state to secede from the Union, he interacted with his boys with an easy familiarity. Barksdale, consequently, early endeared himself to his men of all origins, ranks, and classes.

Most of all, Barksdale was a resilient, hard-nosed fighter and resourceful battlefield commander. He was naturally aggressive, especially when his fighting blood was up or when on the verge of success. Mirroring the qualities of his elite brigade, Barksdale's chief characteristics—aggressiveness, a hard-hitting style, and tactical flexibility—contradicted the stereotype of the incompetent, almost useless, political general in gray.

Barksdale was distinguished by sharp, typically Scots-Irish features and a face that displayed strong character and determination. One Mississippi soldier emphasized the importance of Barksdale's leadership style, describing him as "brave, patriotic and kind. He felt a personal interest in every man in his brigade; he was proud of his men, and never doubted them. He believed they would follow him, nor was he mistaken." Barksdale placed his faith in the importance of discipline and seemingly endless drill to create an elite soldiery and instill tactical flexibility at the brigade level to meet any battlefield emergency. His hard-fighting brigade became a lethal tool in his hands and one that could overcome the odds and achieve gains far out of proportion to its size.

Born on August 21, 1821 in Smyrna in Rutherford County, Tennessee, of Virginia-born parents, William Barksdale, Jr., persevered through a life that early presented him with a host of challenges. He was born at the same farm, just southeast of Nashville, from which his father had marched off to the War of 1812. Hence, unlike many of Lee's aristocratic, upper-class generals, nothing had come easy for Barksdale. As a youth he struggled with the drudgery of farm life, scratching out a meager existence. Personal qualities that made him a resourceful, unorthodox, and flexible commander, such as a deep-seated stubborn streak, penchant for independent thought and action, and a deeply-imbedded streak of defiance toward authority were early evident.

In many ways, the free-thinking Barksdale was a natural Rebel long before the sectional crisis so cruelly tore America apart. "Quick to rebel against an encroachment upon what he considered to be his personal rights," he had often clashed with an authoritarian teacher. Barksdale grew up independent and self-reliant after his parents died (mother Nancy Harvey Lester in 1825 and his father, William B. Barksdale, Sr., ten years later). As an orphan, he was left on his own "to work out his own destiny," after the family's hardscrabble Tennessee farm was sold to pay off debts. But Barksdale made the most of his misfortunes by trying harder to succeed, transforming setbacks into positives. As on the field of Gettysburg, he seemed to perform better when the odds were stacked against him. Most of all, Barksdale was determined to overcome adversity, defying cruel twists of fate.

Knowing what it took to succeed in the harsh frontier world of mid-Tennessee, Barksdale understood that a decent education was the key to a better life. Therefore, he attended Clinton College and then Union Seminary near Spring Hill, Tennessee, located just south of the state capital of Nashville. A lively interest in the military also developed in Barksdale, who relished his father's and grandfather's wartime stories. Grandfather Nathaniel B. Barksdale, a Virginian born in 1760, fought in the American Revolution before settling in Tennessee in 1808. His own father, William Sr., had helped to defeat the assaulting formations of British regulars while serving with General Andrew Jackson at Chalmette, just south of New Orleans, in January 1815. At age sixteen and along with brothers Harrison, who was killed in battle at Tupelo, Mississippi, Fountain, and Ethelbert, he attended the University of Nashville, gaining more knowledge from a high-quality education.

Barksdale then studied law in Columbus, Mississippi, and soon became a promising attorney. Intelligent and flexible in thought, he possessed a fine legal mind, and before age twenty-one, earned his license to practice law. He then opened up a legal practice in Columbus, the county seat of Lowndes County. Here, at this busy commercial town located near the sluggish Tombigbee River in east central Mississippi, Barksdale's law firm became "one of the ablest in the South." The young lawyer earned a widespread reputation for an eloquent command of language, while demonstrating considerable finesse in the courtroom. More important, Barksdale was also known for his egalitarian sense of justice and fairness across Mississippi and the South.

A strong advocate of states' rights of the Thomas Jefferson mold, Barksdale also gained recognition as the hard-working editor of a popular newspaper, the *Columbus Democrat*, in 1844. This experience transformed him into an artful writer and later a masterful orator as a Southern spokesman. Also a Mason and a civic leader, Barksdale became a respected member of the Columbus community.

As one Mississippian recalled, Barksdale was "no ordinary citizen. As a citizen, his manly frankness and sterling virtues won him friends; as a lawyer, his genial nature and commanding talents secured audiences." Not long after the Mexican-American War's outbreak in April 1846, Barksdale departed Columbus for what was initially seen as a grand adventure south of the border with his friends and neighbors in uniform. He served capably as the Inspector of the Second Brigade, Fourth Division of the Army of the State of Mississippi.

After enlisting as a private but gaining a captain's rank, Barksdale then became a staff officer of the Second Mississippi Infantry Regiment. Another equally tough-minded Mississippi politician, Colonel Jefferson Davis, led the First Mississippi Regiment (First Mississippi Rifles) during a dramatic showdown against a powerful army commanded by Antonio Lopez de Santa Anna, the victor at the Alamo in March 1836. Here, at the battle of Buena Vista, Davis played a key role in saving Zachary Taylor's Army amid the mountains of northern Mexico. With the American left collapsing before Santa Anna's onslaught on February 23, 1847, Colonel Davis boldly took the initiative and led a spirited counterattack. Davis thwarted the Mexican onslaught with only a relative handful of Mississippi riflemen, whose marksmanship rose to the fore. Ignoring a wound, Davis then formed his troops in a V-shaped formation to repulse a large number of Mexican lancers. Consequently, Taylor's less than 5,000 men escaped what appeared certain defeat at the hands of Santa Anna's 15,000 troops.

In Mexico, Barksdale was often "seen coatless, with a big sword, at the very front when fighting was promised."[10] In a letter to his wife, Varina Howe Davis, the Confederacy's future president wrote modestly—in the tradition of a Southern gentleman planter—how the "Mississippians did well" at the battle of Buena Vista.[11] After the war ended, Barksdale returned to Columbus to resume the practice of law. He then embarked on a political career, running for a seat in the state legislature. Barksdale rose to prominence during the emerging sectional crisis amid the heated debates of the Compromise of 1850, after he won a landslide election to a congressional seat.

Barksdale initially sought a permanent settlement to the sectional crisis without war. He was anything but the stereotypical fire-eater, swollen with the blindness of sectional pride. He resisted regional and nationalist fantasies (especially the idea of an easy victory over Northerners if it came to war) that consumed a generation of Southern leaders, thanks partly to his humble origins that kept him solidly grounded. Following his moderate convictions despite their unpopularity in antebellum Mississippi, he early served as a Union Democrat. Barksdale, nevertheless, won election to the state convention of 1851. During these debates, he declared that "no occasion for the exercise of the right [of secession] existed." But Barksdale's often unpopular opinions created a good many enemies, thanks partly to the chivalric code of ethics of a hypersensitive Southern male culture. The inevitable physical clashes resulted, including violent deaths, in the name of honor, politics, and personal pride. When Barksdale accidently encountered one political opponent, Reuben Davis, who had been his former Mexican War regimental commander, in a Vicksburg hotel, a violent clash ensued on July 1, 1853. An unarmed Barksdale was stabbed nearly a dozen times in the melee. He survived the vicious attack only by knocking Davis unconscious with one blow.

Barksdale first journeyed to Washington, D.C. in 1852 to enter the stage of national politics. Here, at the nation's capital he served with distinction in the House of Representatives, becoming a leading Southern spokesman for states' rights. Mississippi Congressman Barksdale served his people faithfully from 1853 to 1861, turning reluctantly to secession —while preferring a peaceful exit from the Union—as the South's best recourse. After learning his painful lesson from the Vicksburg altercation with Davis at the Hotel Washington and with sectional passions reaching new heights, Barksdale prudently armed himself with a Bowie knife, a weapon carried by Colonel Davis' men at Buena Vista and later by Barksdale's Mississippi Brigade soldiers.

Barksdale's fighting spirit became evident in the halls of Congress. Here, he maintained his reputation first earned in the Mexican War and from the wild brawls on the Mississippi frontier. Embracing the traditional cultural values of Southern antebellum society, he was known to never turn away from an insult, which led to at least one duel. Barksdale's fiery temperament gained publicity on a national level. One Mississippian recalled how Barksdale "was as prompt to resent any [attack on the South] as a personal injury to himself." Indeed, Barksdale acted as a personal guardian to Congressman Preston A. Brooks of South Carolina, when "Bully" Brooks caned the unfortunate Massachusetts Senator Charles Sumner in the famous 1856 incident on the Senate floor. And on February 6, 1858, Barksdale played a prominent role during a wild melee among at least a dozen Congressmen in a physical confrontation over "Bloody Kansas." Congressman Galusha Grow of Pennsylvania landed a blow to Barksdale's head during the melee. The blow knocked off the Mississippian's wig, revealing not only his bald head but also his vanity. Undeterred, Congressman Barksdale instantly replaced the hairpiece on his head before continuing the fistfight.

When not battling fellow Congressmen in the House of Representatives or political rivals on the dusty streets of Mississippi towns, Barksdale came to passionately embrace the Southern dream of an independent nation. A Northern writer described how Barksdale "had done much to bring on the war." He declared how, "the army that invades the South to subjugate her will never return; their bodies will enrich Southern soil." Ironically, it was Barksdale himself who would never return from an invasion of northern soil.

Barksdale was not only successful professionally but also in his personal life. He lived in Columbus with wife Narcissa Saunders Barksdale, who hailed from neighboring Louisiana. He had married the pretty young woman in 1849, and Narcissa was a loving wife.

Days after Mississippi seceded from the Union, on January 9, 1861 (the second state to do so after South Carolina), Barksdale resigned from Congress. Embracing the new revolution like his forebears back in 1775, Barksdale had known Jefferson Davis on intimate terms since the Mexican-American War. At Davis's insistence, Barksdale was chosen as the quartermaster-general of the Army of Mississippi, which was organized by John J. Pettus, Mississippi's governor, before the state's troops enlisted in Confederate service. But this position was only a desk job, and not to the liking of the ambitious Barksdale, who was eager for action.

Barksdale was clearly ill-suited for the bureaucratic duties of a meticulous quartermaster-general, shuffling papers at a desk all day. He consequently departed his prestigious position to enlist as a humble private in the 13th Mississippi Infantry Regiment, when newly elected President Davis called for volunteers to join the Confederate Army. He was shortly elected the 13th Mississippi's colonel on May 14, 1861 by a landslide vote. Stout of build, tall, and barrel-chested, Colonel Barksdale commanded respect, which was needed to tame unruly, independent-minded

Mississippi volunteers. At a solid 240 pounds, the bulky general knew how to throw his weight around both on and off the battlefield. But beyond the rough exterior and sharp tongue, well-honed to a cutting edge in Congressional debates, Barksdale was also a compassionate commander. He was early concerned about his men's welfare, and did whatever he could to assist the common soldiers in the ranks: a redeeming quality that endeared him to his troops, who were willing to follow him to hell and back if necessary. During exhausting marches in hot summer weather, Barksdale often sacrificed his own comfort to help sick or exhausted privates. He allowed these flagging men to ride behind him on horseback to prevent them from falling behind.

At First Manassas just west of Washington on July 21, 1861, not long after the 13th Mississippi was dispatched to Virginia, Colonel Barksdale led his troops from a reserve position and entered the battle on the left in the early afternoon. As part of the final offensive effort, he led a successful bayonet charge that scattered the Federals, pushing them off their perch on Henry Hill, initiating the Federal Army's rout. More recognition came for Barksdale when he led his 13th Mississippi in the surprising victory in the battle of Ball's Bluff, Virginia, thanks to yet another frontal assault with the bayonet. Spying a tactical opportunity since the Unionists were vulnerable with the Potomac River to their backs, Barksdale launched an assault that carried everything before it. Thus Barksdale's name, as a promising military leader, was early known across the South. Fawning Southern ladies even penned flowery poems about Colonel Barksdale and his Mississippi "saviors" after the Ball's Bluff victory. Southern journalists wrote in detail about Colonel Barksdale's hard-hitting attack that drove the Yankees into the Potomac during the near annihilation of the Federal task force.

Additional bloody fighting for Barksdale's Mississippi Rebels followed in the spring of 1862, when General George B. McClellan's Army of the Potomac launched a massive offensive to capture Richmond by advancing up the Virginia Peninsula. Barksdale's 13th Mississippi first came under fire at Yorktown, where George Washington and his French allies won the most decisive victory of the American Revolution. On June 29 the Mississippi Brigade's commander, General Richard Griffith, fell at the battle of Savage's Station, the fourth of the Seven Days battles, when "at least half a shell" struck him in the groin. A handsome, darkhaired leader of promise, Griffith went down to rise no more. Like Barksdale, a Mississippi politician and a close friend of the Confederacy's president, Griffith had served in Jefferson Davis' First Mississippi Rifles during the Mexican-American War.

Barksdale, the senior colonel, became the Mississippi Brigade's commander. Under his steady leadership, this roughhewn command of backwoodsmen and yeomen farmers of the 13th, 17th, 18th, and 21st Mississippi Regiments gained a lofty reputation. The Mississippi Brigade then suffered heavily during the attack on Malvern Hill, where McClellan's troops made their last stand before the James River, on July 1, 1862. In his first battle as brigade commander, Barksdale led the attack. When a color bearer was cut down, Barksdale grabbed the flag of one Mississippi regiment and then inspired his cheering troops onward into murderous artillery fire pouring off the high ground. In this assault, which also came under fire from Union gunboats in the James, one third of the Mississippi Brigade was either killed or wounded—the highest loss of any brigade at Malvern Hill.

After the brutal Seven Days fighting, Lee declared that Barksdale demonstrated the "highest qualities of the soldier." Continuing to gain respect throughout the army (a relative rarity for a Southern politician without formal military training), Barksdale gained a hard-earned brigadier general's rank on August 12, 1862. He then took official command of the Mississippi Brigade, though having led the unit since the fight at Savage's Station.[12]

Most of all, Barksdale worked hard to transform his Mississippi Brigade into a lethal fighting machine second to none in the Army of Northern Virginia, in part by instilling the value of drill and discipline into the very fiber of his troops. Exemplifying the general's determination to create the best soldiers possible, Private Robert A. Moore, Company G (Confederate Guards of Holly Springs), 17th Mississippi, described in his diary how "Gen. Barksdale generally closes the drill with the bayonet charge." His unorthodox leadership style made Barksdale not only a popular, but also a highly effective commander. As Private John Saunders McNeily, 21st Mississippi, explained: "of the comfort of his men he was most considerate, would tolerate no neglect or denial of their rights, or imposition on them from any one."[13] But from beginning to end, perfection in drill and discipline was always Barksdale's foremost priority in creating a crack brigade. Having enlisted to "do his bit," Sergeant Major Charles C. Cummings, 17th Mississippi Infantry, recalled how "We were taught to drill with hands placed tight to the seams of pants."[14]

Even in bad weather, including in wintertime, when other brigade commanders cancelled drills and inspections, Barksdale focused on the task at hand. Private Joseph A. Miller, Company K (Magnolia Guards), 17th Mississippi, who was fated to be killed in battle, described in his diary how Barksdale conducted one inspection on "a cold windy, disagreeable day. I thought I would freeze before they got through, Old Barksdale inspected us."[15]

Most of all, Barksdale exemplified the feisty, combative nature and fighting spirit of the Mississippi Brigade. He possessed "a thirst for battle glory," wrote one Mississippian, who got his personal wish for a fighting general. Inspiring by example, Barksdale was a leader who dared to go where many other high-ranking officers would not go in a crisis situation. He gained popularity by taking the same risks and enduring the same dangers as the common soldiers in the ranks, and especially in leading a charge.

Before the great clash of arms at Gettysburg, Barksdale's pluck and fighting spirit was most convincingly demonstrated at Fredericksburg on December 11. The Mississippi general ignored the orders of his division commander, burly General Lafayette McLaws, to disengage and retire from his advance position along the river to rejoin the main army on the heights behind the town. Instead, the stubborn Barksdale refused to budge, ordering his troops to continue to fight on and delay the attackers as long as possible. At Fredericksburg it was as if the Mississippian was waging his own private war. However, Barksdale's defiance of orders earned admiration—instead of arrest—from his corps commander, General James Longstreet. Clearly, these combative fighting men from Mississippi were just the kind of never-say-die soldiers who could win a victory in a key battlefield situation, such as at Gettysburg.[16]

～ 2 ～

"To lay my life on the altar of my country"

BY 1863, THE forty-two-year-old General Barksdale commanded some of the first Mississippi troops of the Army of Northern Virginia. The 13th, 17th, and 18th Mississippi regiments were placed in the same brigade after First Bull Run, while the last regiment, the 21st Mississippi, joined the brigade in November 1861. Therefore, the first action in which three of the four Mississippi Brigade regiments served together was at Ball's Bluff on October 21, 1861. In his diary, Private Ezekiel Pickens Miller, of the Magnolia Guards (Company K), 17th Mississippi, penned how the regiment "drove the enemy at the point of the bayonet headlong down a steep bluff into the river [and only] Night came on in time to save the enemy from utter annihilation."[17]

They charged to the war cry of "Drive Them Into Hell or the Potomac River," smashing the over-confident Union task force and hurling it into the water.[18] The Marshall County boys of the Mississippi Rangers (Company B), 17th Mississippi, laid claim to the brigade's first captured Union artillery piece, "a small howitzer," in the lopsided victory.[19]

Private Miller, age 23, and his brothers of Company K, 17th Mississippi, provided a good representative example of the sturdy fiber of the fighting men in the brigade. Along with his Lafayette County brothers, William T. Miller, age thirty, and eighteen-year-old Joseph A. Miller, Lieutenant Ezekiel Pickens Miller was dead by the time of the epic clash at Gettysburg.[20] Private William T. Miller was the first brother to die, succumbing to disease on June 24, 1862. Before the year's end, Lieutenant Ezekiel Miller, was killed in Fredericksburg's defense on December 11. Then, Private Joseph A. Miller was killed on May 3, 1863 in the Mississippians' tenacious defense of Marye's Heights to protect Lee's rear to

19

buy time and an opportunity for Stonewall Jackson to unleash his masterful flank attack at Chancellorsville.[21]

The last surviving Miller brother, Joseph, penned in his diary on December 18, 1862 of his heartache upon learning of his brother Ezekiel's death: "He has gone, the brother with whome [sic] I sported in childhood days. Today he is far, far away from home and home folks [and] my own loved brother has been snatch[ed] from me, his body lies in the cold cold grave upon the banks of the Rappahanock [sic]."[22]

Then, on Sunday, December 21, 1862, Private Miller learned of the sad details of his brother's death. When lying mortally wounded in the snow after having been shot down attempting to climb over a split-rail fence during the withdrawal, after having held the Yankees at bay for so long, a felled Lieutenant Ezekiel Miller told another wounded soldier lying nearby "that he could not live long [and] to tell me not to grieve for him, that he was going to a better world, and for me to send his uniform coat home, and write to father and mother and tell them he was going to a better home. God grant that I may so live that I may meet my deare [sic] brother in heaven."[23]

Private Joseph A. Miller finally was bestowed his heartfelt wish, meeting his Maker and joining his brother by receiving his death stroke on May 3, 1863, defending the same town during the Chancellorsville Campaign.[24] Before he was killed, the last surviving Miller brother described in his diary how, "I begin to feel lonesom [sic]."[25] On New Year's Eve, the deeply religious, grief-stricken young man from Lafayette County, Mississippi, reflected: "New years eve, two of the dearest friends I had on earth have been taken from me, my brothers WT and EP who this time last yeare was alive, and enjoying good health, are now gone. WT sleeps in the cemetry neare Fredricksburge . . . God grant that we may form a family in heaven."[26]

One key to the Mississippi Brigade's success was a high-quality officer corps at the regimental level. From beginning to end, Barksdale relied upon highly qualified and seasoned lieutenants of outstanding leadership ability. By the time of the Pennsylvania Campaign, Colonel James W. Carter, age thirty, led the 13th Mississippi, Barksdale's old regiment. Carter continued Barksdale's legacy of instilling discipline. Colonel Carter first gained experience as the captain of the Kemper Legion, Company C, 13th Mississippi. Consisting mostly of yeomen farmers like the rest of the Mississippi Brigade's soldiers, the 13th Mississippi men hailed from the hard-clay territory of Kemper County.

The vast majority of Barksdale's soldiers grew up on the small farms of the Mississippi interior, rich lands drained by the Tallahatchie, Yalobusha, and the Sunflower Rivers, which all entered the Yazoo River. Mostly Methodists and Baptists, the young men of the Mississippi Brigade also came from the central prairie of a fertile limestone soil, the north-central sand-clay hills, the Tombigbee Prairie noted for its rich, black soil, and the low country of the Yazoo Delta region, simply known as "the Delta," of Mississippi. Mostly yeomen farmers of humble origins, the economic, political interests of these homespun soldiers were not historically aligned with the large, upper class cotton planters of the Southern aristocracy.

By the time of the Gettysburg campaign, Colonel Carter still carried the scars of Malvern Hill's bloodbath on July 1, 1862. This injury kept him out of action for most of 1862. With the blessings of his close friend General Barksdale, the capable Carter was promoted to colonel in August 1862, and he led the 13th Mississippi for the first time during Fredericksburg's spirited defense. Here, along the Rappahannock in the stinging cold of a wind-swept December, Carter demonstrated considerable leadership skill, inspiring his fast-firing troops to hold firm under heavy pressure. As fate would have it, Colonel Carter would not survive the bloody fighting at Gettysburg.[27] Partly because of Barksdale's hard-hitting leadership style, the 13th Mississippi early became known as "the Bloody 13th."[28] Earned at the loss of many lives, this well-deserved sobriquet could apply to Barksdale's other regiments as well.[29]

By the time of the battle of Gettysburg, Colonel William Dunbar Holder commanded the 17th Mississippi. A native Tennessean like Barksdale, Colonel Holder had been born in Franklin County in south central Tennessee. He bacame an industrious farmer of Birmingham, which was located amid the Tennessee River hills of northeast Mississippi. He began the war as the captain of the Quitman Grays (Company C) from Quitman and Pontotoc Counties, Mississippi. This rough-and-tumble company was named for the dynamic Mississippi leader and former governor (1835–36), John Anthony Quitman, who served as a volunteer in the Texas Revolutionary Army of 1836, and then as a general who won recognition during General Scott's drive on Mexico City. The versatile Quitman was also a well-known filibuster, who focused his efforts on acquiring Cuba, and then became the "father of secession in Mississippi."

Colonel Holder was not only a wealthy planter but also a distinguished community leader. He served as the Deputy United States Marshal, starting in 1850, in Birmingham and Pontotoc, a Chickasaw word meaning "the land of hanging grapes," in northeast Mississippi. Holder was elected a member of the Mississippi legislature, beginning in 1853, representing the hard-working people of Pontotoc County.

Like Colonel Carter, the thirty-nine-year-old Holder was cut down during the attack at Malvern Hill, while leading his regiment against the lengthy rows of Union cannon. His wounds required an eight-month period of hospitalization before he once again led the 17th Mississippi in action. When he finally returned to his regiment, the popular colonel still "limps a right smart yet," penned an admiring Private Joseph A. Miller in his diary in early March 1863. A scrappy fighter and strict disciplinarian, Holder was promoted to colonel in late April 1862. He soon became one of Barksdale's dependable right arms. Like Barksdale, Colonel Holder was a gifted speaker, who was often "cheered . . . enthusiastically" by the boys for saying words they wanted to hear. He also cared for the welfare of his men, as on one occasion when he found and brought his hungry boys a batch "of some sweet potatoes," as penned a delighted Private Ezekiel Armstrong in his diary. Colonel Holder led his regiment at Fredericksburg, earning additional recognition for his leadership ability. A horrible wound in the groin and stomach, which required him to hold his bloody intestines in place, during Barksdale's attack at Gettysburg ended Holder's promising future. He then served in the Confederate Congress in Richmond from 1863–65, representing the state that he loved and nearly died in defending.

Receiving their baptismal fire in July 1861, the 17th Mississippi fought with distinction at First Bull Run and then at Ball's Bluff to gain an early taste of victory. At Ball's Bluff, "one volley from our line drove them back in disorder" and the 17th Mississippi troops overran all opposition in a sweeping bayonet attack, capturing prisoners and an artillery piece. When ordered to "drive them into the Potomac or into eternity," these tough north Mississippi troops had promptly done so. The 17th Mississippi soldiers hailed from a land of upland hardwoods and short-leaf pines that was a generally poor cotton growing region.

Barksdale's soldiers remained free-thinking in the tradition of the western frontier, retaining distinctive self-reliant ways. Some defiant 17th Mississippi's boys had "even refused to be fitted out with uniforms," because they were simply not to their liking. Instead, they preferred more durable homespun apparel, as worn while hunting game in the dense pine forests back home to provide for the dinner table, which was more practical for active campaigning.

Another example of defiance of authority, or a least mockery of it, came from an Ireland-born 17th Mississippi soldier, Private Bill Day. Sergeant Major Charles C. Cummings, a popular member of the Mississippi Rangers, or Company B, described with affection how the irrepressible Day was "our Irish wit."[30] Once when General Robert E. Lee rode along the line with his staff, the lowly Day simply "could not resist the opportunity for fun" at the aristocratic Virginian.[31] The spunky Irishman yelled —so that Lee could plainly hear—to his 17th Mississippi boys in regard to the South's most revered commander: "Boys, where did you get that old bushwhacker? What has he done? He looks like a good old man. There's no harm in him. Turn him loose."[32] Not known for his sense of humor, the austere General Lee's face actually lit up in a smile. Sergeant Major Cummings never forgot how Lee's "bright smile, after half a century, haunts me still."[33] But the enlisted men's humor sometimes went too far, as when Barksdale became the butt of one soldier's good-natured joke, and the "General got mad."[34]

In terms of demographics and socio-economic backgrounds, Company G represented a typical 17th Mississippi company. Raised in Holly Springs, this fine unit was known as the Confederate Guards. Of the 150 volunteers who served in the unit, about two-thirds were yeoman farmers, 20 were students from local academies, and there were 8 railroad laborers, 4 clerks, 3 carpenters, 3 schoolteachers, 2 physicians, 2 merchants, and 1 each of the following occupations: harness maker, gin maker, wheel wright, attorney, printer, and painter. Of these 150 young men and boys of Company G, two-thirds never returned to their Mississippi homes and families. As a cruel fate would have it, some 30 Confederate Guards men were killed or mortally wounded during the war. Another 68 died of disease, while more than half fell wounded. However, such devastating losses were proportional in the other companies of all four of Barksdale's regiments: the high cost of becoming an elite combat brigade.[35]

Like Barksdale's other regiments, a high level of proficiency in drill and discipline partly explained why the 17th Mississippi performed so well on the battlefield. As Private Moore explained in his diary: I "think our Reg. as well drilled as any Miss. Regt. in the Army of the Potomac." Barksdale's requirements of drill were high and most demanding. Private Moore complained how the lieutenant colonel, who obviously enjoyed his liquor, "gets about seventy-five cents in the dollar drunk & doublequicks us nearly all the time."[36] But officers seldom displayed such alcohol-fueled lapses. From beginning to end, military discipline was quite severe: the necessary price for creating elite soldiers. Dedicated officers at even the company level, like Lieutenant Archibald T. Roane, were martinets with exacting standards that resulted in regular inspections. In his diary, Private Joseph A. Miller of the Magnolia Guards described not long before the Pennsylvania invasion, "Lt. Roan [sic] inspected our room [winter quarters at Fredericksburg], and accouterments. We were forewarned, that there will be brigade inspection."[37]

Worn down by the intense drills that had no end, Private Armstrong lamented in his diary how he "suffered considerably on account of strict discipline . . . I never shall forget how our officers bore down on us."[38] Not even the Christmas holidays stopped Barksdale from fulfilling his priority of drilling his troops to a fine-tuned perfection. In his diary, Private Miller described on December 23, 1862 how, "Had batalion drill this evning . . . just two days untill christmas, look[s like] Coln [John Calvin] Fiser intends to mak us work because it is so neare Christmas . . . ."[39]

Defying the stereotypical demographic view of the average Confederate soldier, Private Branch Murray was an African-American Rebel who served in the 17th Mississippi. Murray later applied for a pension from the State of Tennessee for his war service. Such African-American warriors as Murray were the forgotten Confederates of Barksdale's Mississippi Brigade.[40] However, slaves of Mississippi Brigade owners back home occasionally escaped to join black Union regiments. Born in Yazoo City, Mississippi, on April 9, 1837, Dr. Cyrus N. Brown, a former sergeant in the Benton Rifles (Company B), 18th Mississippi, was destined to attend the wounded at Gettysburg. Meanwhile, his slave, Silas L. Johnson, departed the Brown family's plantation named "Alterra," escaping slavery's horrors. While Brown's wife Louisiana, nicknamed Lou, managed the Mississippi plantation, Silas joined the Ninety-sixth United States Colored Troops.[41]

One of the finest 17th Mississippi companies was the Mississippi Rangers of Company B, organized at Holly Springs. These young soldiers, wrote William Meshack Abernathy, consisted of "a joyous, jolly set of boys" who first went to war in distinctive uniforms consisting of "blue flannel shirts . . . and we did not think we were 'dressed-up' unless we had that blue shirt on." Company B included a hard-fighting clan of nine Franklin boys, consisting in part of Columbus [the company's only married soldier], "Little Shack," Jesse D., and Jesse H. Franklin. This was a crack combat unit, thanks partly to its high quality leadership, such as from Captain Gideon Edward Thurmond, born in 1843. A savvy back-woods hunter who was also the best scout of the Mississippi Rangers, Thurmond "was the only man that I ever knew during the War who never tired his Company while drilling them," wrote one Johnny Reb.[42]

But it was more than simply the officer corps' high quality that made the 17th Mississippi an elite combat regiment. Battling primarily for a new nation's independence like their revolutionary forefathers, the common soldiers in the ranks were highly motivated. Two fine soldiers of Company B, 17th Mississippi were Sergeant James ("Jim") O. Ramsuer, a farmer in his twenties from Early Grove, and Private Scott Lynch. Like his comrades, Private Lynch also possessed a well-deserved reputation for his skill in stripping off the boots, pants, and blouses of dead Yankees with business-like efficiency on the battlefield at the first opportunity. Both young men, wearing parts of blue uniforms taken from the foe, were cut down during the holocaust of Gettysburg.

To pass the time and lift morale, the 17th Mississippi soldiers maintained a glee club. Private Ed Robinson provided musical entertainment as "the mockingbird of the outfit." Another popular singer was teenage Private Franklin Ross, "whose propensity to talk got him the nickname of the Mobile Gas Bag." But young Ross' fun-loving days ended forever in the nightmarish fighting at Gettysburg, where he received his death stroke like so many others. Among the favorite songs of Barksdale's men were "Maryland, My Maryland," "Carry Me Back to Old Virginny," and the "Bonnie Blue Flag," which had been first performed by an Irishman, Henry McCarthy, in Jackson, Mississippi, when the Magnolia State seceded on January 9, 1861. At least early on, not all 17th Mississippi, soldiers were enamored with Colonel Holder's leadership style, however. "We had a Martinet for our Colonel," penned one disgruntled Rebel, who failed to appreciate the value of intense drill. However, such discontent was positive proof that the time-consuming process of forging an elite fighting machine was not smooth or easy.[43]

But the endless drilling and harsh discipline paid high dividends on the battlefield, especially at Gettysburg. Symbolically, in terms of continuing a martial tradition, Company A, 17th Mississippi, was known as the Buena Vista Rifles. This company was composed mostly of Chickasaw County soldiers from the small agricultural community of Buena Vista which had been named in honor of Jefferson Davis' Mississippi Volunteers, whose exploits at the bloody Mexican War battle were legendary. Three farm boys of the Buena Vista Rifles, Privates James H. Harmon, a bachelor, Private Daniel S. King, and Private John E. Smith, a married man, received their death strokes during Barksdale's assault at Gettysburg.[44]

One of the best examples of the 17th Mississippi's fighting spirit was witnessed during the bitter street fighting at Fredericksburg on December 11, 1862. At one point a desperate Florida officer threatened to shoot down 17th Mississippi soldiers with his revolver because they refused to withdraw. Barksdale's men continued to fight back with spirit to draw concentrated Union artillery fire, which the incensed Florida officer desired to escape at any cost.[45] But this kind of fighting spirit was most costly. As early as October 17, 1862, Lieutenant William Cowper Nelson, 17th Mississippi, penned in a letter how, "Our Regiment which on the Peninsula had some 1100 men, now does not turn out more than 400 for duty."[46]

By the start of the Gettysburg Campaign, these 17th Mississippi soldiers were prepared to fight to the bitter end to secure decisive victory. Twenty-year-old Sergeant Ezekiel Armstrong of the Magnolia Guards, from a small slave-owning family in Big Creek, Calhoun County, wrote in his diary how he was "determined to lay my life on the altar of my country or see her free." Above all, Armstrong was a realist. In stoic fashion, he penned with resigned fatalism how "many of us would fall victims to disease if we did not fall by the sword." A lover of literature and the finer things in life, the young aspiring lawyer was killed at Fredericksburg.[47]

Deliberately promoted by Barksdale as part of a calculated design, a healthy rivalry existed between the Mississippi Brigade's regiments, which raised overall standards for excellence. 17th Mississippi troops possessed an especially heated rivalry with the 18th Mississippi. An angry Private William Meshack Abernathy, 17th Mississippi, complained: "I never saw that [missing] skillet any more, but the boys do say that the thieving 18th Mississippi got it . . . it was commonly true that they could steal anything in the commissary line from a red hot skillet to cold soup with tallow in it, and when we missed anything all we had to do was to go over to the thieving 18th and get somebody's there."[48]

Colonel Thomas M. Griffin led the 18th Mississippi with distinction at Gettysburg. His men had first marched off to what they thought would be little more than a frolicking adventure, first seeing "the Elephant" at

Bull Run. In October 1861, Griffin took command of the regiment after Colonel Erasmus R. Burt, state auditor of Mississippi, a large slave-owner, "Father of the Deaf and Dumb Institute of Mississippi," and respected state legislature member, was mortally wounded at Ball's Bluff. Along with Colonel Burt, 85 other regimental members were lost to Yankee fire during the Mississippians' successful action on the Potomac. Like Colonels Carter and Holder on July 1, 1862, Griffin was likewise knocked out of action in leading his troops at Malvern Hill. Anxious to once again enter the fray, he rejoined the regiment in early 1863. Born in January 1816 and age forty-seven, Griffin was half a dozen years older than Barksdale. Like Colonels Carter and Holder, Colonel Griffin was destined to be cut down in the hellish fighting at Gettysburg.[49]

One of the regiment's most unforgettable enlisted men, James, or Jimmie, Dinkins never forgot "the brave and soldierly Colonel Thomas Griffin, a model soldier, and the grandest colonel in the army."[50] For the most part, the 18th Mississippi's young soldiers were adventurous and rambunctious, which made for a high-spirited soldiery. Private Dinkins, a long-haired planter's son from Madison County, enlisted at age sixteen but he was no country bumpkin. Despite being only "a slender and apparently delicate youth" when sent to school by his parents to Charlotte, North Carolina in April 1860, Dinkins possessed a well-grounded military education gained at the North Carolina Military Institute.

Serving in the Quitman Grays of Company C, 18th Mississippi, Private Dinkins was one of Barksdale's favorites, and the general affectionately called him, "Little Horse." Dinkins described how his 18th Mississippi comrades consisted of "Southern youths [who] had, from the cradle, been plumed for just such an occasion." Jimmie's wealthy father sent a slave, "Uncle Freeman" to serve as the personal body servant for the teen-age private. If Jimmie was killed in battle, Freeman would bring the body back home to the Dinkins family. "Uncle Freeman" was "personally the friend of all the company," recalled Dinkins of his African-American companion, who shared the regiment's dangers.[51]

High quality officers and hardy common soldiers meshed well together on both the drill field and the battlefield to become a hard-hitting team. The tempered mettle of the hardened 18th Mississippi soldiers was well summarized by one ragged private. He explained with pride how "these men never skirted duty, never straggled, missed a march or a battle. They were an inspiration to the other men."[52] The combination of invaluable prewar military experience and heavy reliance on drill and discipline helped to transform the 18th Mississippi into a crack regiment.[53]

Some 18th Mississippi soldiers boasted of splendid classic educations, especially those men from leading planter class families, obtained both in Mississippi and beyond the state's borders. Wealthy planter families often hired tutors or sent their sons to the North or Europe to obtain the finest educations. Benefitting from a "private tutor" hired by their father, the promising sons of planter Colonel Oscar James Ewell Stuart, the brothers James Hardeman and Oscar Ewing Stuart, of Meadville, Franklin County, in southwest Mississippi, were educated at the University of Mississippi at Oxford. Of the three Stuart brothers who served in Company K, the Burt Rifles, 18th Mississippi, two were killed in battle. Younger brother, Edward Ewing Stuart, enlisted in Company K at age fifteen in June 1862, but Oscar Ewing Stuart, who had entered the University of Mississippi in 1859, "tried to protect him from harm by seeing that he was kept out of battles."[54]

Cousins of Lee's leading cavalryman, General James Ewell Brown (Jeb) Stuart, the lives of the three handsome young Stuart brothers, whose mother Sarah had died in 1849, revealed the overall high quality of the 18th Mississippi soldiery.[55] James Hardeman Stuart was the oldest son of the family. A scholar, he graduated first in his class (1858) at the University of Mississippi. He not only "read law" under an esteemed judge at the state capital of Jackson, but also "wooed & won the Judge's daughter [Bettie Wharton], one of the most beautiful & intelligent of Mississippi daughters."[56]

But a cruel fate intervened and the two young lovers never married. When the war came to disrupt their lives forever, James enlisted as a lowly private of the Burt Rifles and was killed at Groveton, Virginia, on August 30, 1862.[57] But Oscar Ewing Stuart became the most outstanding soldier of the family. After abruptly departing the University of Mississippi, he joined Burt's Rifles along with his brother James. Oscar was promoted to Sergeant Major in late June 1861, and also served as the regiment's acting adjutant.[58] He proved to be no ordinary officer. He was widely considered to be "the best adjutant of the Brigade, or Division."[59] But Stuart was most "particularly noted for his gallantry, & had the reputation of being the bravest & coolest man in the 18th Mississippi on the field of action."[60] Indeed, even when under heavy fire, he often stopped "to laugh & jest with the boys, although after the death of his brother James & his fair fiancee & later that of his uncle Col. Wm Hardeman, he laughed by seldom," recalled one sympathetic comrade, who felt his friend's pain, in June 1863.[61]

Indeed, Adjutant Stuart lost almost everything in America's most lethal war that destroyed so many promising lives. First, he lost the pretty young lady, to illness, who was to have been his future wife.[62] Meantime, like other 18th Mississippi soldiers, he fought the bluecoat "vandals" with all his might. He trusted in God and his strong religious faith to protect him from harm. During the bitter fighting at Fredericksburg on December 11, 1862, he wrote how, "I prayed to God for assistance to carry me successfully through the struggle . . . ."[63]

But nothing could protect Adjutant Stuart during the desperate defense of the stone wall at the base of Marye's Heights against the onslaught of the Sixth Corps on May 3. As one of his comrades wrote of the tragic loss: "After we were surrendered [and] the Col. had surrendered I was by his side [when he] fell backward pierced by three of the cowardly assassins' balls. The Col. caught him in his arms but life was already extinct. He was interred in a beautiful spot on top of Marye's heights . . . . "[64]

In a sad June 29, 1863 at Chambersburg, Pennsylvania, on the eve of the battle of Gettysburg, Captain John A. Barksdale, the Acting Adjutant General of the Mississippi Brigade, and one of the general's most reliable staff members, presented the tragic news to the father: "Your son (Adj. O.E. Stuart) was killed in the engagement at Marye's Hill. Some of the men belonging to his Regt. report that he and several others were shot after they had been compelled to surrender [but] your son died a hero—as becomes a brave man battling for his rights and his honor—must afford some consolation. He was beloved and died regretted by this entire command."[65]

Besides the Stuart boys, other University of Mississippi soldiers also served with distinction in Barksdale's Brigade, especially in the Mississippi College Rifles of Company E.[66] Among the best and brightest of the 18th Mississippi was young Sergeant Major William Blake from Holmes County. Looking too young and fresh-faced to be a hardened sergeant major, the soldier also served as the regimental courier because of his wiry frame and superior horsemanship. Young "Billy Blake" was one of the most popular soldiers in Colonel Griffin's regiment. The fun-loving, hard-riding teenager, who flew like the wind when on horseback, was "the pet of the entire regiment," wrote one comrade about "Billy." The high-spirited Sergeant Blake "was always full of mischief." However, a

cruel fate awaited Sergeant "Billy" Blake at Gettysburg, where he would
lose a leg at the hip and nearly his life in fighting for what he believed
was right.[67]

By the time of the Gettysburg campaign, Colonel Benjamin Grubb
Humphreys, age fifty-four, commanded the crack 21st Mississippi. An
endless source of Barksdale's pride, this fine regiment was organized in
the summer of 1861. From Tallahatchie, Lafayette, Claiborne, Madison,
Warren, Hinds, Union, and Holmes Counties, Mississippi, the volunteer
companies were formed independently, and journeyed to Richmond.
Here, in October 1861, they were organized into the 21st Mississippi.
Leading the Sunflower Guards of Company I, Humphreys was elected
colonel in the democratic tradition, despite being older than most of Lee's
regimental leaders and brigade commanders, who were mostly in their
early to mid-thirties. Colonel Humphreys commanded the Mississippi
Brigade's best regiment, a fact largely due to his inspired leadership and
tireless efforts. The ever-reliable Humphreys was Barksdale's senior regimental commander, but most of all he was his top lieutenant and right
arm, especially during the showdown at Gettysburg.

On August 26, 1808, he had been born at the family plantation,
"Hermitage" on the sluggish, dark waters of Bayou Pierre, located just
below Vicksburg. Benjamin was one of sixteen children from a leading
family of Claiborne County, where Grant landed his army on Mississippi
soil after crossing the river to gain Vicksburg's rear in May 1863. The
capable Colonel Humphreys was Barksdale's only regimental commander
with West Point experience, having entered the prestigious United States
Military Academy in 1825.

From an early date, Humphreys was a young man of promise with
great expectations. Like many sons of Mississippi's planter class, Humphreys received an education in the North, attending an institution that
predated the American Revolution, the College of New Jersey (Prince-
ton). He then went to school in Kentucky, before entering West Point. At
the military academy, Humphreys was in good company with such distinguished classmates as Robert E. Lee, Jefferson Davis, Joseph E. Johnston, and Albert Sidney Johnston. Humphreys enjoyed military life,
drawing upon a rich revolutionary family heritage. But although a good
student and acclimating easily to life at the nation's leading military
institution, Humphrey's promising military career appeared to end
abruptly. The high-spirited cadet from Claiborne County was dismissed
the following year for his participation in the infamous cadet riot at West

Point on Christmas Eve 1826. Along with almost 40 other cadets who were part of the largest riot in the Academy's history, Humphreys was dismissed for "breech of discipline."

Humphreys was not deterred by the setback, however, and simply returned to the family's plantation, which he operated successfully. Benjamin then married a young woman of high standing, but his wife died to again shatter his personal world. Clearly, Humphreys was no stranger to adversity and life's cruel twists of fate. As if to blot out the personal tragedy, the ambitious Humphreys then devoted himself to the legal profession. He became a lawyer of note in Claiborne County, while also thriving as a successful planter during the cotton boom. Humphreys then served as a political "independent" in both houses of the Mississippi legislature from 1839 to 1844. Throughout his career, he refused to follow the dictates of party or cronyism.

Humphreys then remarried on December 3, 1839, taking a fifteen-year-old girl who was fifteen years his junior. Mildred Hickman Humphreys was the daughter of a respected judge and from one of the leading families of Port Gibson, the county seat of Claiborne County, which was captured by Grant's invading forces on May 1, 1863. His first child, Julian Maury, was born in 1840. With his new wife, Humphreys and family lived comfortably on this sprawling plantation near Roebuck Lake in Claiborne County. With the help of slave labor he transformed an untamed wilderness into a land of plenty, as his father had earlier accomplished on his "Hermitage" Plantation. Over the years Humphreys' fortunes grew by leaps and bounds. He and his wife had three more children in the 1840s, and another child in 1856.

Ironically, fearing the grim consequences of sectional warfare, this highly respected Claiborne County legislator, not fearful of advocating contrarian positions, had boldly opposed secession. He took his unpopular stance despite owning a good many slaves and a large cotton plantation, which he affectionately called "Itta Bena," after he had moved from Claiborne County to settle on the more fertile soils north of Vicksburg. Throughout the antebellum period, the far-sighted Humphreys feared the folly of the resource-short agrarian South going to war against an industrialized giant with superior resources and far larger population. With the call to arms in the spring of 1861, Humphreys nevertheless joined the struggle along with his friends and neighbors. He became the captain of a volunteer company known as the Sunflower Guards, or Company I, of the 21st Mississippi Infantry Regiment.

In September 1861 and not long after reaching the Virginia theater, Humphreys was promoted to colonel of the regiment. Month after month, Humphreys waged a holy war, especially on the second day at Gettysburg, not only to obtain the dream of independence but also to defend, "all I held dear . . . family, friends and property [which] welded me to that soil by the strongest cement of nature."[68] Because of his outstanding leadership ability and tactical skil,l Humphreys was destined to command the Mississippi Brigade after Barksdale's death at Gettysburg, winning his general's stars in August 1863. After surviving the war's horrors, the respected Humphreys was elected Mississippi's governor.[69]

Key qualities that made Colonel Humphreys Barksdale's top lieutenant was summarized by one soldier who wrote: "By nature he was singularly fitted as an official soldier. He had courage without impetuosity; fidelity without ambition; and firmness without oppression, each soldier was his brother, and not one should suffer when it was in his power to furnish relief. He participated in nearly all the hard fought battles of the war, coming out of [Gettysburg] having had two horses shot from under him, and with nine bullet holes through his cloak within a radius of eleven inches from his collar button, and finally returned to the conflict bearing in his body four severe wounds that undermined his health and doubtless hastened his death" in 1882.[70]

The Mississippi Brigade was early employed in key battlefield situations, and never failed to rise to the challenge. During the battles of the Seven Days, the 18th Mississippi's commander calmly informed his men in preparation for meeting the enemy for the first time: "We are selected to drive [the Yankees] back to their boats [and] they outnumber us greatly, but the safety of the army requires that we whip them." Private Dinkins described how this situation was "a desperate occasion, and if it became necessary to protect the army by sacrificing the brigade, the sacrifice would be made, but we would do our duty [and] ordinarily, such desperate conditions would have filled the men with dread; but they moved to the slaughter with no apparent fear." The Mississippi Brigade's upcoming fight at Gettysburg would be no different in this regard, but the challenge would be far greater.[71]

By the time of the Pennsylvania invasion, successfully meeting formidable battlefield challenges had become almost a routine for the Mississippi Brigade. For the Mississippi Rebels, this tradition of vanquishing superior numbers developed at an early date. At Savage's Station on June

29, 1862 during the Peninsula campaign, the Mississippi Rebels cut a Vermont brigade to pieces. In those woods the Mississippians' frontier and backwoods skills rose to the fore against the hapless New Englanders, and more than 400 Vermont soldiers fell to the Rebels' fire. The next day a full third of the crack Mississippi Brigade was cut down at Malvern Hill. But these Magnolia State soldiers of companies like the Camden Rifles, Panola Vindicators, Kemper Legion, Magnolia Guards, Vicksburg Southrons, Madison Guards, New Albany Greys, Hurricane Rifles, Mississippi College Rifles, and Jackson Avengers were as resilient as they were tough.

During Lee's first invasion of the North, the Mississippians, along with Kershaw's South Carolina Brigade, stormed Maryland Heights, thus triggering the mass surrender of the Union garrison at Harpers Ferry the following morning. McLaws' Division then marched to Sharpsburg, arriving on the morning of September 17, 1862—the single bloodiest day in American history—to find the battle already raging. Barksdale's men plunged into the West Woods, just north of the famous Dunker Church, to knock back a Union division under John Sedgwick in the nick of time.

The Mississippi Brigade's gallant stand-alone fight on the riverfront at Fredericksburg that December, before the eyes of both armies, became a legend in its own time. When Ambrose Burnside finally unleashed his entire artillery of 170 guns to crush Barksdale's Brigade, onlookers in the Army of Northern Virginia held their breath. But the storm of shell did not succeed. Longstreet's artillery chief, Edward Porter Alexander, wrote, "I could not but laugh out heartily, at times, to catch in the roar of the Federal guns the faint drownded pop of a musket which told that Barksdale's men were still in their rifle pits & still defiant."

During the Chancellorsville campaign, the Mississippi Brigade was once again asked to hold the sunken road in front of Marye's Heights against attacking Federals—but this time without the rest of the army nearby save the Washington Artillery of New Orleans which supported them from the heights. After two assaults by John's Sedgwick's Sixth Corps had been repulsed, the position was finally overrun by a massive third assault, and the Washington Artillery lost some guns. The story had it that the Mississippians had unwisely granted a truce so that the Federals could collect their wounded, but Union officers used the opportunity to see how few men the Confederates really had. Sedgwick then made a supreme effort that no one brigade could resist. However, the Mississippians had bought General Lee a precious additional day to finish off

Hooker's main army, and while Barksdale's men reoccupied the heights the next day, it was Sedgwick himself who soon had to retreat across the Rappahannock.

In one bloody contest after another, Barksdale's Mississippians steadily acquired a reputation for ferocity, combat prowess, and lethality on the battlefield. No matter how many boys in gray and butternut were killed or disabled for life, the Mississippi Brigade became only stronger in moral fiber, toughness, and mettle. By the time of Gettysburg, Barksdale's soldiers were more determined to win decisive victory than ever before, so that their many fallen comrades would not have died in vain.

But even more deadly for the Mississippi Brigade's soldiers than Yankee bullets and shells were the ravages of illness, including venereal disease. Sexually transmitted diseases were spread to the men by promiscuous barefoot Virginia country girls and finely-dressed, world-wise prostitutes, such as the infamous Teeny Kid or such as Cecillia Smith, Alice Ashley, and Lizzy Winn of the Anna Thompson bordello on Richmond's row of busy whorehouses, which overflowed with lustful, drunken customers. Many bordellos were located in the notorious Screamersville section of the Southern nation's capital along the James River. Barksdale revealed his dismay, as early as July 1861, when he wrote how many Mississippi soldiers were ill because of "improper sexual indulgence." At that time, the 18th Mississippi's surgeon reported another twenty-five new cases of gonorrhea for that month alone. Then, in August 1861, the 16th Mississippi lost additional manpower with 32 new cases of gonorrhea and 11 of syphilis.

Clearly, the young innocents fresh from Mississippi's farms, woodlands, and prairies were not ready for life's temptations in a major port city like Richmond. But the epidemic of venereal disease failed to discourage enthusiasm for sexual experimentation, when the Mississippi farm boys, bolstered by a sense of youthful invincibility, were far away from home for the first time and had consumed too much cheap, rut-gut liquor. But more wholesome outlets were also available. During the fall of 1861, Private Moore, 17th Mississippi, described the high spirits of Barksdale's soldiers in his diary, "the boys are very merry, some of them have a dance nearly every night . . ." [72] And on April 20, 1863 just before the bloodletting of the Gettysburg Campaign, Private Joseph A. Miller, 17th Mississippi penned how, "We [have] taken a game of town ball [baseball] this morning [and] The boys are passing by heare [sic] with great loads of fish, They catch them with seins [sic] out of little branch

. . . near the river [and other men] are playing the fiddle so down stairs that I can neither read or write."[73]

But these Mississippians so far from home were not merely unruly hell-raisers, women chasers, gamblers, and hard drinkers of corn whisky and apple brandy, whenever the opportunity allowed. As early as the winter of 1861–62, the Mississippi Brigade's soldiers turned to God as never before, seeking spiritual comfort and salvation. Private John Saunders Henley, Company A, 17th Mississippi, revealed the widespread dedication to religious worship: "We had Sunday School on Sunday [when our captain] taught the class. We took a Chapter in the Bible, and everyone had to read a verse and comment on it."[74] This young private's words revealed yet another factor that partly explained why and how the Mississippi Brigade became an elite fighting machine: the evolution of a moral soldiery by 1863, after the horrors of war had turned more men to God than ever before.

A soldier of General Joseph B. Kershaw's South Carolina Brigade described in an April 10, 1863 letter, less than three months before the slaughter at Gettysburg, how: "The revival still continues, and several hundred of Barksdale's men have been converted, and many more are still anxious about their soul's salvation." In fact, the religious revival within the Mississippi Brigade's ranks lingered longer than in the majority of Lee's units in part because Mississippi and Vicksburg were under threat. Lieutenant Stiles described how the "religious interest among Barksdale's men began about the time of, or soon after, the battle of Fredericksburg . . . and continued with unabated fervor up to and through Gettysburg." Clearly, these religious awakenings were timely, as a large percentage of the more than 500 Mississippi Brigade members who were converted during the passionate revival became casualties at Gettysburg.[75]

Contrary to pervasive stereotypes, Barksdale's Mississippi Brigade was anything but an ethnically homogenous command as long believed by many Civil War historians. A considerable amount of ethnic diversity existed in every regiment. A good many Irish Rebels and other ethnics served in every regiment. Most of this little-known ethnic diversity—French, Scottish, German, Celtic, Swedish, Spanish, Hebrew, and Irish soldiers—was most readily evident in those units hailing from the Gulf coast region, first settled by the French, and the towns along Mississippi's major waterways, including the "Father of Waters." Especially along the

Gulf Coast, the diverse ethnicities and distinctive cultures influences were the antithesis of the Deep South cracker stereotype. Here, a mixture of languages blended together to create a distinct, "beautiful" local and regional language that seemed like a foreign tongue to northerners.

By the spring of 1863 the Army of Northern Virginia was dominated by Virginia leadership, with the commanders of half a dozen divisions and two of the three corps born in Virginia.[76] Therefore, Barksdale and his Mississippians felt that they had much to prove in the upcoming spring campaign. Once again and on past battlefields going back to 1861, Barksdale and his troops were most of all determined to demonstrate to the army's Virginia-dominated leadership corps and the press that they could perform not only as well but even better than the much heralded local men, who seemed to always reap greater recognition, even for less important accomplishments. For the Mississippi Rebels to win recognition that would make the people of their home state proud and to rival the accomplishments of Colonel Davis' regiment at Buena Vista in February 1847, they would not only have to vanquish the Yankees on the battlefield, but also overcome the bias of non-Mississippians against Magnolia State frontiersmen from the southwest.[77]

For a host of reasons, consequently, the Mississippians were highly motivated for the next challenge in a far-away northern state that they had never before seen: Pennsylvania. However, in the words of one cynical Texas soldier of John Bell Hood's Texas Brigade, the boys in gray had been only "rested up and fattened so we could stand a long hard drive to the next slaughter pen."[78]

Despite the fact that their home state was invaded by the relentless Grant, a strong sense of commitment, religious faith, and a firm resolve to "do or die" kept the men faithfully in the Mississippi Brigade's ranks. In an early 1863 letter to his beloved mother Maria and seemingly almost prophetic with the showdown at Gettysburg on the horizon, Lieutenant William Cowper Nelson wrote, "Should I fall though, Mother dear, Recollect there is a Savior who died for me and all the other sinners who believe in him. I have an abiding trust and a lively faith in the might of his power, and put my whole trust in the Lord of Hosts."[79]

The Mississippians' sense of determination was most recently witnessed in their tenacious defense of Fredericksburg in December 1862, but it came at a high price. A 116th Pennsylvania Volunteer Infantry soldier described a tragic and strangely serene sight that he never forgot: "Numbers of Barksdale's men lay where they had fallen when disputing the passage of the stream. One group had an almost fascinating interest because every one of the party was boyish and handsome. They had fought in a garden by the riverside, where they . . . had died just where they had been placed. . . . Gazing upon these brave Southern boys as they lay amid decaying flowers of the garden one's mind was apt to wander to the Southern homes where the sun was still shining and the roses still blooming, and this mournful Christmas there would be in many a far off Mississippi home whose soldier lad would never return again."[80]

But compared to the fighting at Fredericksburg, the Mississippi Brigade's devastating losses at Gettysburg were about to bring far more grief to hundreds of families across Mississippi.[81] By the time of the Pennsylvania Campaign, Barksdale's veterans were imbued with a fatalistic determination to succeed at any cost or die in the attempt. In an ominous, prophetic letter to his sister, the 18th Mississippi's philosophical, University of Mississippi-educated adjutant, Oscar Ewing Stuart, who was killed at Second Fredericksburg on May 3, 1863, caught the essence of the Mississippi Brigade's warrior spirit, which explained a stoic, never-say-die attitude that was necessary for these crusaders in gray to secure decisive victory: "I am not afraid to die! . . . Relying upon *His* arm we are *invincible* . . . our trade is in life & death, and our readiest customers are time and *eternity*. I feel like I don't 'care a straw' for my life, I have *every confidence* in the infinite mercy of my divine *Redeemer*. I will fall *doing* my duty, and will I trust have my reward. There is a testament in my pocket."[82]

Having already accepted an inevitable death on the field of strife far from home, the self-sacrificing young adjutant of so much promise concluded his letter by emphasizing in no uncertain terms, "I say again, I care not one straw for my life, it is my *country's,* & I have no *right* to it. I freely & gladly give it—& pray it may be an acceptable sacrifice. Goodbye dear Aunt [and] Farewell to all the rest."[83]

— 3 —

"We are going into Yankey land"

IRONICALLY, FOR THE young men and boys of Barksdale's Brigade, Lee's Pennsylvania invasion first evolved from developments in faraway Mississippi. After a failed offensive the previous winter, the ever-resourceful General Ulysses S. Grant had now arrived on the doorstep of the vital Mississippi River port city of Vicksburg, the most important strategic point in the western Confederacy. His was part of a triune Union thrust that season, along with Hooker's drive against Richmond and Rosecrans' impending offensive in central Tennessee. The Army of Northern Virginia had already taken care of its end of the task—defeating Hooker at Chancellorsville—so now the problem in grand strategy was how to turn back the Union offensives in the west.

During two high-level May 1863 conferences in Richmond, Lee was firmly against the idea of sending reinforcements from his own army to Mississippi in an attempt to save Vicksburg. They would arrive too late to relieve the siege and, not having their full trains via rickety Confederate rail lines, would be unable to swing the balance against Grant's rapidly growing army with its secure supply line on the river. Longstreet proferred the idea of splitting off part of the Army of Northern Virginia to effect a concentration against Rosecrans, in order not only to destroy the Army of the Cumberland but to disrupt Grant's concentration against Vicksburg by calling him to the defense of the Ohio Valley.

Lee remained convinced that another decisive victory in the east by his own army would more than offset Federal gains in the western theater. And the great victory at Chancellorsville had put him in a unique position: he had not only inflicted severe losses, if not demoralization, on the Army of the Potomac, but his army had actually grown stronger afterward with the return of Longstreet and his two divisions (Hood's and Pickett's) that had missed the battle. Combined with the fact that Hooker had just lost thousands of men to expired enlistments, Lee was now closer to numerical parity with the Federals than he had been in a year. He now saw an invasion of Pennsylvania that threatened Philadelphia, Harrisburg, Baltimore, and Washington as the best solution to the Vicksburg dilemma. Even if Vicksburg was lost to Grant, then the blow could be more than negated by a decisive success won on northern soil.[84]

When word came that Pennsylvania-born General John C. Pemberton, a Jefferson Davis crony of relatively little tactical ability, was bottled up in Vicksburg, a final crisis meeting was held in Richmond on May 26. At Davis' invitation, Lee articulated his strategic views at length to the Confederate cabinet. While Davis wanted to dispatch troops west to General Joseph Johnston's forces in Mississippi for a last-ditch attempt to relieve Vicksburg, Lee convinced the cabinet, by a resounding five-to-one vote, and even Davis himself, to embrace his strategic thinking. Forcing a crisis on the Union in the east would be the quickest, most efficient way to draw off pressure on other points in the Confederacy. Further, carrying the war to northern soil would relieve tired Virginia of the burden of supporting the contending armies, while providing a bountiful new source of supply to the Confederates. Finally, Lee made the point that the South could never hope to win the war by continuing on the strategic defensive. Every time he turned back a Federal offensive they simply withdrew behind river lines or into the fortified environs of Washington so that he could not follow up his victories. Only by taking the offensive himself could he hope to achieve a truly war-winning battle.

Thus ironically, as a strange fate would have it, the subsequent role of Barksdale's Mississippi Brigade at Gettysburg had been dictated by the crisis in their own home state.[85] Instead of attempting to save Vicksburg directly, the Army of Northern Virginia would seek to force the Federal army in the east to look to its own salvation, as the Confederates embarked on their most risky gamble to date. Lee knew that the best chance to win the new nation's independence was by reaping a decisive victory north of the Potomac, while his confident army yet possessed the capability to do so.[86] Private Nimrod Newton Nash, 13th Mississippi, and his comrades were convinced, as revealed in a June letter, that "Genl Lee is too smart to bee [sic] fooled by a Yanky."[87] With high hopes for reaping significant gains not won during the Maryland campaign less than a year before, a confident Army of Northern Virginia launched its second invasion of the North on June 4, 1863.

After Stonewall Jackson's death the Army of Northern Virginia was divided into three corps, instead of the previous two, for greater tactical flexibility. Barksdale's Brigade remained in Lafayette McLaws' Division, Longstreet's First Corps, which also included the divisiions of John Bell Hood and George Pickett. Richard Ewell was named commander of Jackson's Second Corps, for virtue of having been Stonewall's chief lieutenant during the Valley Campaign and on the Peninsula. Ambrose Powell Hill was given command of a new Third Corps that consisted of his own division (now under Dorsey Pender), Richard Anderson's Division from Longstreet's Corps, and a newly formed division under Harry Heth. Preceded on the flank by the cavalry under Jeb Stuart, thousands of Lee's Rebels, cocky and lean like hungry wolves, pushed north from central Virginia's depths. Pushing through the Shenandoah Valley, employing the towering Blue Ridge as a heavily-forested screen of green, the Confederates waded across the cold waters of the Potomac River and then moved into Maryland beginning on June 19.[88]

Confidence soared through Barksdale's ranks during the relentless push north. The veteran Private Nash, who was fated to be killed at Gettysburg, wrote to his wife Mollie in a June 7, 1863 letter, "We are going into Yankey land [and] I hope we will and that we will scare some of the blue bellies as bad, or worse, than they have scared some of our people."[89]

Foremost in Lee's mind was the painful knowledge that his increasing losses, even in victories like Chancellorsville, were leading the Confederacy down the road to certain extinction. The manpower-short South would slowly die from a lengthy war of attrition, suffering losses that could not be replaced, while the much larger North could easily replace its losses while only increasing its gigantic advantage in manufacturing. As Lee wrote to President Davis in a realistic assessment of the South's situation, "Conceding to our enemies the superiority . . . in numbers, resources, and all the means and appliances for carrying on the war, we have no right to look for exemptions from the military consequences of a vigorous use of these advantages."[90]

In short, the Confederacy needed to rely on skill and valor on the battlefield while it still could, before the arithmetic of Union material and numerical superiority overwhelmed it. And for this, Robert E. Lee needed to hold the initiative, forcing the Federal army to battle on his terms. If the Army of Northern Virginia invaded the north, the Army of the Potomac would be forced to fight it on open ground, without first securing a line of retreat for itself. If a victory could thence be won by the Confederates, it could be the decisive battle of the war.

As related verbatim by General Isaac R. Trimble, Lee's ambitious tactical plan on northern soil was based upon the sound premise that the pursuing Army of the Potomac "will come up, probably through Frederick [Maryland]; broken down with hunger and hard marching, strung out on a long line and much demoralized, when they come into Pennsylvania. I shall throw an overwhelming force on their advance, crush it, follow up the success, drive one corps back on another, and by successive repulses and surprises before they can concentrate, create a panic and virtually destroy the army."[91]

It was a good plan, providing the best formula for achieving a victory to end the war in the Confederacy's favor.[92] And Lee's vision of a decisive success on northern soil was shared by his men. In the words of one confident Virginian in a letter, "I think we will clear the Yankees out this summer."[93] And a 13th Mississippi private who waded across the Potomac River's waters, only about two feet deep on June 26, Private Nash, was convinced on June 28 that "I think we will have Capitol (Harrisburg) ere long."[94]

The invasion began with a nifty success, when Ewell's Corps nearly obliterated three Union brigades at Winchester in the Shenendoah. With fire and maneuver he forced 7,000 Federals out of their stronghold, then caught them on their retreat, capturing nearly 4,000 men plus immense stores. Any doubts that the legendary Stonewall had not properly been replaced were temporarily put on the shelf. Afterward, Ewell's Corps spread out into Pennsylvania and was soon at York and Carlisle, on the very doorstep of Harrisburg. Longstreet's Corp followed Ewell's, concentrating on Chambersburg, and then A.P. Hill's new Third Corps crossed the Potomac. Union General Hooker, who first wanted to lunge at Richmond once he sensed the Confederate army's movement away from his front, was instead instructed by the authorities in Washington to rush to follow the Rebel movements.

But then Lee's carefully laid plan began to go awry, in part by his own decision-making. With Lee's permission, General Stuart, who commanded the army's highly trumpeted cavalry corps, galloped away from the army toward Washington, D.C., on the most ill-timed of all Confederate cavalry raids. Stuart rode off with more than 5,000 veteran troopers, attempting to encircle Hooker's army, and for a week his cavalry remained absent from the Army of Northern Virginia at the most critical time. On the eve of the most important battle in American history, Lee was thus blinded, without his cavalry to inform him of Union movements.[95]

Thus the first word that Lee gained about the Army of the Potomac's whereabouts came not as usual from Stuart and his companies of experienced scouts, but from a grimy-looking actor-turned-spy named Henry T. Harrison. Some of Barksdale's men almost certainly knew Harrison, who had served in the 12th Mississippi until discharged with a medical disability in November 1861.[96] On Sunday night June 28, Harrison presented his invaluable intelligence to Lee at Chambersburg, just west of Gettysburg. Naturally, Lee was shocked by the startling news that the entire Army of the Potomac was already on the march through northern Maryland, after having crossed the Potomac on June 25–26. Not anticipating such alacrity, the news struck Lee like a body-blow, after hearing nothing about the Union Army's whereabouts for nearly a week. With much of his own army situated around Chambersburg, and with his most advanced infantry, the Second Corps, headed toward Harrisburg, Lee now knew that the Army of the Potomac was already in close proximity.[97]

At this time he also heard news that Hooker had been displaced from command of the Army of the Potomac by the former commander of its Fifth Corps, George Gordon Meade. Lee was largely pleased by Meade's ascension, even if he felt mystified by the continued fickleness of Federal authorities. A new general would need time to get his army in hand, even as Hooker had showed great acumen in some respects, and after Chancellorsville would doubtless have been out for revenge. Nevertheless, by now the non-descript Meade was known to former West Pointers on both sides as a formidable, careful fighter.

While Meade proceeded to familiarize himself with the entire Union army's whereabouts (he adopted Hooker's chief of staff, Dan Butterfield for this purpose), he continued to press Northern units onward. This rapid pursuit was surprising because Lee's Army had kept up a swift pace in surging north during this grueling campaign, which had taken a toll on Barksdale's ranks. Private Nash described the difficult trek in a June 23 letter: "We have done some hard marching since we left Fredericksburg. Our men suffered with heat as hot as we would be in Miss [and] I believe I never felt warmer weather. Many of the men were completely overcome with heat. Some fainted by the road. I was suddenly attack [by sunstroke] and fainted away for some time."[98] Not only was Lee's Army exhausted but also strewn out for miles along dusty Pennsylvania roads by the time the Union Army's whereabouts became known.

On June 28, after being informed of the danger, Lee dispatched fast-riding couriers to his far-flung commands with orders to concentrate to meet the Army of the Potomac. Thanks to finally having gained timely intelligence, a greatly relieved Lee told his top subordinates on June 29, "Tomorrow gentleman, we will not move to Harrisburg, as we expected, but will go over to Gettysburg and see what General Meade is after."[99] But former attorney Colonel Eppa Hunton, who commanded the Eighth Virginia Infantry of General George Edward Pickett's Division, who was destined to fall wounded in "Pickett's Charge," described Lee's true thinking: "the invasion of Pennsylvania would be a great success, and if so, it would end the war . . . . "[100]

On the same day that Harrison reached the army, the confidence of Barksdale's men for success continued to soar like the rising temperatures. On this day, Private Nash described in a letter to his wife Mollie how, "we are in the enemies country, and so far [it] has amply paid for the invasion. We are all liveing [sic] on the fate of the land [and] There is the finest wheat, now nearly ripe [and this is] the richest and most beautiful country I ever beheld [and] I hate to see such a fine country in the possession of such people."[101]

A mighty clash of arms among the sprawling farmlands of south Pennsylvania was now inevitable. Instead of retiring west of the mountains to concentrate his forces, Lee decided to gather his troops on the east side, where the Army of the Potomac was rapidly pushing north. A climactic meeting of two armies now moving toward each other was only a matter of time. Like many great battles which have determined the course of history, however, the Battle of Gettysburg was about to result from an accidental clash of arms. Two great armies were about to unexpectedly collide just northwest of Gettysburg on the hot morning of July 1 in what became the largest battle on the North American continent.

Contrary to one of the most persistent myths about Gettysburg, the battle was not the result of barefoot Southern troops desiring to secure shoes rumored to be stored in the town. Both armies were drawn to Gettysburg because it was a vital crossroads center, where nearly a dozen roads met from all points of the compass. With the dusty roads of Gettysburg radiating outward like the spokes of a wheel and acting like a giant magnet to the interlopers in blue and gray, it was as if fate itself was drawing the two armies together to decide America's future once and for all.[102]

Abraham Lincoln, for one, placed great faith in Meade, a competent and capable, if not brilliant, West Pointer (class of 1835) of Scots-Irish stock, who now commanded the Army of the Potomac. At age forty-seven and a Mexican War veteran, he presented the government no such problems as Hooker had, and would simply fight hard per his duty. "I think a great deal of that fine fellow Meade," proclaimed Lincoln with typical understatement.[103] Robert E. Lee's comment was: "General Meade will commit no blunder in my front."[104] However, the unassuming Meade now faced the greatest challenge of any American army commander since George Washington at Trenton in late December 1776: defeating an army, Lee's, that had never yet been beaten. And now he would have to meet it, not on ground carefully chosen by himself, but in the open terrain of Pennsylvania.

On the morning of July 1, approaching Gettysburg from the north-west and initially believing that they were facing only ragtag Pennsylvania militia, Harry Heth's Division of A.P. Hill's Third Corps smashed into two brigades of General John Buford's Union cavalry. A fast-escalating battle, with dismounted, veteran troopers in blue blasting away with fast-firing breech-loading carbines, quickly developed. The dismounted cavalrymen held Heth off long enough to stop his line of march and force him into battle lines. Thereupon John Reynolds' First Corps of the Army of the Potomac, including the renowned "Iron Brigade," arrived. Taking on a life of its own, the fighting soon spun out of control, Heth's reconnaissance turning into a major battle. Pender's Division was right behind Heth's, but the Union Eleventh Corps was right behind Reynolds. Lee was yet unready for a major engagement, not only because of the lack of intelligence from Stuart but also because Longstreet's powerful First Corps was still to the west and Ewell's Second Corps was to the north. But the showdown at an obscure college town in south central Pennsylvania, where all roads seemingly led, was already underway.

Fighting raged across the brightly colored fields, rolling hills, and woodlands northwest of Gettysburg. This was Lee's unwanted battle at a place and time not of his choosing. Worst of all, Lee was unable to ascertain if he faced the entire Army of the Potomac or only an advanced portion. However, the situation suddenly changed when two divisions of Ewell's Corps arrived from the north, striking the ill-fated Eleventh Corps, which had previously been mauled by Stonewall Jackson at Chancellorsville. Robert Rodes' initial attack was clumsy and its first onset was shredded; but then Jubal Early's division arrived and the entire Federal right flank caved in.

Together with Pender supporting Heth against the already battered First Corp, whose commander, Reynolds, had been killed, the entire Union line broke in a mad scramble to retreat through the town, thence to the formidable heights south of it. The Confederates captured upwards of 3,000 prisoners, "the number being so great as to really embarrass us," according to Early, and the Confederates thence held both the field of battle and Gettysburg itself.

The only problem was that the Federals retreated to better terrain south of the town than they had had tried to hold west and north of it. And they had kept behind part of a division plus artillery to secure it for such a contingency. The beaten Federals rallied on the position, even as a stream of reinforcements arrived. Among these the most important was Major General Winfield Scott Hancock, head of the Second Corps, who quickly took charge of the situation. The Federal line was now emplaced on the high ground of Cemetery Hill, south of Gettysburg, and heavily timbered Culp's Hill, to its right. Both elevations were located at the northern end of Cemetery Ridge, which extended south for nearly a mile and a half till ending in more formidable heights called Little Round Top and Round Top. General Lee, immediately recognizing the importance of securing Cemetery Hill, ordered Ewell to take the high ground, "if practicable," and if he could so "without bringing on a general engagement."

This has become one of the most controversial orders of the war, with partisans of the late, lamented Stonewall claiming that of course those hills would have been taken, with the Yankees on the run, if "Old Jack" had still been alive. However, Ewell, new to corps command, did not feel that he could organize a proper assault. Aside from one of his brigadiers, John B. Gordon, who had his fire up, he could not see how Rodes' Division, which had just suffered 3,000 casualties, or Early's, which due to new intelligence or rumors (another consequence of the absence of Stuart's cavalry) had to dispatch two brigades backward to watch other roads. He had no connection at all with A.P. Hill's command to his right, which had been fighting all day and was bloodied enough. And his own third division, under Edward Johnson, had yet to come up. Meantime his own units were strung out and disorganizaed, as were Hill's, while all he could see was a frowning array of artillery and infantry on the Union-held heights as the daylight slipped away.

In Gettysburg literature, Ewell has been chastised for his hestitation to take those heights ever since that day, but he received no firm order to do so, and his main support since has come from Federal officers such as Henry Hunt, who said, "Ewell would not have been justified in attacking without the positive orders of Lee, who was present, and wisely abstained from giving them." But the final verdict must go to Hancock, who said that if the Confederates could have rushed the heights in the initial hour when the First and Eleventh Corps broke, they might have been taken. But after that slim hour an attack would have been repelled with loss. Of course the Federals were initially disorganized after their retreat, but so were the Confederates after their victory, which was a typical factor in all Civil War battles. Ewell would have thrown away the July 1 victory if he had been repulsed while pushing it too far in the twilight, having no artillery of his own in position to bear against the hills, but sending his men into the face of a considerable Federal array. This is even as Hancock called the fallback Union stronghold "the strongest position by nature upon which to fight a battle I ever saw . . ."[105]

Lee won the first day at Gettysburg. In fact, he had already gotten a good start on his prediction to Trimble of smashing the lead elements of the Federal army. But now he had to think of something else, quickly. The battle was upon him, whether he wanted it at this time or not, but the Union troops were steadily being reinforced upon their newfound heights, and it was now his task to concentrate the full Army of Northern Virginia in a race for numerical advantage.

That evening, amid a cloud of dust, the reinforcing Union Twelfth Corps arrived to take good defensive positions on the 140-foot high Culp's Hill. Ewell's third division, under Johnson, arrived, weary from their much longer march. The Union Third Corps was coming onto the field, soon to be followed by the Second Corps, while Anderson's Division of Hill's Corps came up, and Longstreet's Corps was on the way.

That night, a flurry of conferences took place among the Confederate high command, to determine how to hit the Federals next. Longstreet, for one, was appalled that Lee wanted to resume the offensive at all against that position. Though a hard-hitting attacker, he preferred the tactical defensive, and thought he had come to an understanding with Lee before the invasion began that the Confederates would only maneuver to invite offensive tactics, not initiate them. Meantime, the Federal troops on their heights could be easily outflanked by a further maneuver, interposing Lee's army between Meade's and Washington. Lee would hear none of it, however, only saying, "The enemy is here, and if we do not whip him, he will whip us."

The Confederates would resume the attack the next day, and to Longstreet's chagrin, he learned that it was his own corps that would have to strike the major blow. The heights faced by Ewell's corps having finally been determined to be "impracticable," the solution was to have Longstreet's fresh troops bypass them to assault the lower ground on the Union left along Cemetery Ridge.

Another great controversy about Gettysburg has arisen over whether Longstreet was ordered to attack "at dawn," or first thing in the morning, or, as Lee might have put it, "as early as practicable." There can really be no doubt that sometime on the evening of July 1 Lee urged an attack as early as possible the next day. To this many acolytes of Lee have attested, largely for the purpose of putting blame for the next day's battle on Longstreet. However, in the absence of Stuart's cavalry, Confederate reconnaissance was pitifully poor. Longstreet was given no guides, or else faulty ones. It was not clear until the last moment where to put his men in position, and Lee's orders, "to attack up the Emmitsburg Road," displayed a complete misunderstanding of the battlefield.

It is possible, too, as many writers have claimed, that Longstreet took a "passive-aggressive" attitude toward the impending assault, not fully wishing to comply with Lee's orders, but only grudgingly doing so, and with no great speed or initiative of his own. But this hardly equates with the loyalty he must have felt to his own men, and when he finally did assault the Federal left, it was with full force and determination to succeed. And among his brigadiers were such as William Barksdale, who wanted nothing more than to end the war in one afternoon, with the greatest victory yet for Confederate arms.

The symbolically red dawn of July 2 consequently witnessed the beginning of "the most critical day at Gettysburg."[106] Shaking off their weariness, Barksdale's troops were up early in the predawn darkness of July 2. Even the blackness of 4:00 AM, when they rose, felt like a sultry, summer morning along the Mississippi Gulf Coast. They were yet sore and tired. Barksdale's men had force marched at a brisk pace from Greenwood, east of Chambersburg and around fifteen miles from Gettysburg, until halting around midnight on July 1 and encamping on Marsh Creek, several miles west of town. With muskets on shoulders, they now headed toward Gettysburg, a rendezvous with destiny, and the grim killing fields of summer.[107]

The dramatic confrontation at Gettysburg continued unabated on July 2 between Generals Meade, the homespun "tall, spare man," and Lee, the handsome, dignified Virginian, whose fighting blood was up after tasting success on July 1. While Meade was initially reluctant to accept the Confederate challenge to stake everything on a final showdown at Gettysburg, Lee felt quite the opposite. He wanted to strike a decisive blow before Meade could gather all his troops, sensing a great opportunity.

Despite its setback and heavy losses on July 1, however, the Army of the Potomac was anything but defeated. In a strange way, so many past defeats now worked as a tonic on the overall psyche of Meade's Army, having been tempered by adversity. No sense of panic or demoralization infiltrated this increasingly resilient army now fighting on its home soil. In the analysis of an observant Union officer, Captain Frank Aretas Haskell, "the Rebel had his whole force assembled, he was flushed with recent victory, was arrogant in his career of unopposed invasion, at a favorable season of the year . . . but the Army of the Potomac was no band of school-girls. They were not the men likely to be crushed or utterly discouraged by any new circumstances in which they might find themselves placed."[108] And this reality was never more true than on the second day of Gettysburg.

But Lee was determined to exploit the first day's success to the fullest, and so far, with eight of his nine divisions on or near the field, was winning the race for the build-up. He decided to resume the offensive to crush Meade's Army on the morning of July 2, before it was united and in position.[109]

But the glory days of Lee's easily vanquishing one incompetent Union general after another were no more. In a letter that was right on target, Captain Haskell described the general feeling throughout the army in regard to Meade's appointment on June 28, "The Providence of God had been with us . . . I now felt that we had a clear-headed, honest soldier, to command the army, who would do his best always—that there would be no repetition of Chancellorsville."[110] Most important, the Army of the Potomac was emboldened by the fact that Meade had decided on the night of July 1 "to assemble the whole army before Gettysburg, and offer the enemy battle there."[111]

As the early morning mists of July 2 rose higher from the low-lying areas around Gettysburg, thousands of Meade's veterans no longer fretted about what the brilliant Lee was going to do next. A quiet confidence dominated the ranks of blue. As Captain Haskell penned, "The morning was thick and sultry, the sky overcast with low vapory clouds [and] all was astir upon the crests near Cemetery, and the work of preparation was speedily going on."[112]

Therefore Lee's decision to rely upon the tactical offensive to push Meade off his high ground perch was sure to meet with stiff resistance, upon confronting highly-motivated veterans in defending home soil.[113] As revealed in a letter when a South Carolina officer quoted the words of a boastful Yankee prisoner, the Confederates would find that there was "a great difference between invading the North & defending the South."[114]

From the beginning, seemingly nothing went right for either Lee or his army on July 2. The Confederates were still without Stuart, and Meade was allowed all morning to prepare to meet Lee's assault and for his troops to arrive on the field. Barksdale's men, up since dawn, marched along the Chambersburg Road, moving east toward Gettysburg through the rising dust. While Lee planned to unleash an oblique attack with John Bell Hood's and Lafayette McLaws' Divisions, Longstreet's Corps, to roll up Meade's left flank to exploit the first day's gains, his top lieutenant, Longstreet, thought quite differently. He wanted to ease around the southern end of the Union Army's defensive line to outflank the Cemetery Ridge position.[115]

As day went on, nothing happened quickly for the Confederates. Longstreet failed to immediately march south to a position on Meade's left flank as early as Lee had anticipated. Instead hour after hour, he waited—a most "impractical decision"—for a single Alabama brigade (General Evander Law's) to come up before undertaking his flank march south, as if time was of no importance or Law couldn't have caught up to the corps by himself. In consequence, Lee's proposed attack led by Longstreet's two divisions was not launched in the morning as desired by the commander-in-chief. That morning, too, the Union Fifth Corps arrived as well as remaining brigades of the Third Corps.

Meanwhile, Barksdale's troops swiftly marched across McPherson's Ridge past the sickening clumps of bodies left from the previous day's fighting. They arrived on Seminary Ridge near Lee's headquarters, where the Chambersburg Pike gained Seminary Ridge, around 9:00 AM. Longstreet's more than 14,000 battle-hardened veterans were tardy in moving out when timeliness was vital for success. Here, the Mississippians, foot-sore and tired, at least gained a few hours of much-needed rest with the lengthy delay.

Finally, around noon, Longstreet embarked upon his much belated march south to gain an attack position beyond the Union Army's left flank. Longstreet was to deliver the knock-out blow from Lee's far right. To keep Meade distracted, A.P. Hill's Third Corps would apply pressure to Meade's center to keep Union forces there in place. And Ewell's Second Corps would demonstrate on the north before Culp's Hill and launch a full assault if a favorable opportunity presented itself.[116]

After numerous delays and counter-marching in an attempt to disguise his movement from Yankee eyes, Longstreet's Corps finally reached its designated position in mid-afternoon. With the rest of McLaws' Division, Barksdale's soldiers, dusty, hot, and sweaty, reached their assigned position to the left of Hood's Division. Because Barksdale had brought up McLaws' rear, the Mississippi Brigade fell into line on the left flank of McLaws' Division just north of Joseph B. Kershaw's South Carolina brigade, after pushing up fairly steep, ascending ground along the heavily timbered western slope of Seminary Ridge. Here Barksdale positioned his troops along Seminary Ridge in the cooling shade, but inadequate shelter, of Emanuel Pitzer's Woods around 3:00 PM. Cadmus "Old Billy Fixin" Wilcox's Alabama brigade, General Richard Anderson's Division, Hill's Third Corps, was on Barksdale's left.

By now on this scorching mid-afternoon, Confederate battle-plans were in the process of slowly self-destructing and falling apart at the seams. Longstreet's time-consuming flank march, and then countermarch (to escape detection), south to form on Lee's far right had cost far too much time. The additional hours—a reprieve of sorts—allowed Meade's Army the opportunity to establish its "operational balance," gather strength, and prepare for the upcoming attack. By now the last of its corps, the Sixth under John Sedgwick, was nearing the field.

Instead of obtaining an advantageous position beyond the Union army's left and finding no enemy before them as anticipated when Lee's plans were first formulated, McLaws and his officers were shocked to discover a good many Yankees ready for action on either side of a Peach Orchard barely 600 yards distant. Lee's overall tactical objective was to gain the Emmitsburg Road Ridge, nestled about halfway between Seminary and Cemetery Ridges, and attack up the Emmitsburg Road to roll up Meade's weak left flank. But everything had changed by the mid-afternoon of July 2. Instead, the formidable might of the entire Third Corps was now poised on either side of the high ground of the Peach Orchard beside the Emmitsburg Road, blocking the way to Gettysburg to the northeast. With a lengthy defense line pivoting on a salient angle, nearly 11,000 Yankees of General Daniel Egar Sickles' Corps were deployed along the Wheatfield Road and toward Little Round Top, and then north along the Emmitsburg Road that led to Gettysburg. The 45-degree, defensive angle's point existed where the two roads intersected on the Emmitsburg Road Ridge at the Peach Orchard of farmer Joseph Sherfy.

No one was more upset by this startling new development of thousands of alert Yankees now occupying the high ground of the Peach Orchard than Lafayette McLaws and his fellow division commander on the Confederate right, John Bell Hood. They now saw the Peach Orchard overflowing with Union troops and batteries, in a lengthy blue line extending all the way to Little Round Top, where Union signalmen were busy betraying Confederate movements. An incensed McLaws blamed Longstreet "for not reconnoitering the ground." Clearly, in regard to ascertaining the new position of an entire Union corps, Confederate leadership, staff work, intelligence-gathering, and reconnaissance had failed miserably.

Now poised on Seminary Ridge, McLaws' troops realized that they were simply not in a position from which to strike Meade's supposed vulnerable left flank. As Colonel Humphreys, commanding the 21st Mississippi, described this most perplexing tactical situation in a letter, after realizing that Lee's plan to gain General Meade's left was already checkmated: "When we arrived there it was unmistakably anything but the flank [and] it was a formidable compact line of frowning artillery and bristling bayonets."[117] Fueling his anger toward his corps commander's leadership failure, McLaws never forgot the shocking sight presented to him by the Peach Orchard position: "The view presented astonished me."[118] And Colonel Edward Alexander Porter lamented how if Longstreet's "corps had made its attack even two or three hours sooner than it did, our chances for success would have been immensely increased.[119]

In addition, a confident Major General Alfred Pleasonton, commander of the army's cavalry corps, reasoned that by this time, "We had more troops in position than Lee."[120] Therefore, in many ways, Barksdale's Mississippians shortly would be fighting against a cruel fate today because the odds, more than 10,000 Yankees poised around the Peach

Orchard and supported by plenty of artillery manned by veteran can-noneers, were stacked high against them. Clearly, the Magnolia State sol-ders would have to struggle long and hard against the odds to compensate for the many mistakes and miscalculations by the Confeder-ate leadership.

About all that Barksdale's soldiers now knew was that a little Peach Orchard stood atop a slight knoll—its high point stood at the intersection adjacent to the Wheatfield Road and only a few yards east of the Em-mitsburg Road—amid a gently rolling landscape of open fields that lay before them. And, most of all, they realized that a good many Union troops and rows of cannon were aligned across the commanding ground, patiently awaiting their next move. Nevertheless, a can-do spirit yet re-mained high among Barksdale's veterans. Private Dinkins, 18th Missis-sippi, believed that the infantry assaults of "General Lee's army [were] irresistible [and] no troops on earth, with the arms then in use, could have withstood his charges."[121] At the edge of a thin belt of woodland just west of Seminary Ridge and under the relative protection of a reserve slope position, one soldier described how the 13th Mississippi troops were first "formed . . . under a ledge of rocks along a small branch [and in] enough hill and timber to hide us from the Yankees."[122]

Gettysburg's First Day had already brought victory, and Lee's Rebels expected that the next day would be no different. Hence, Lee's soldiers felt that this small town of Gettysburg might soon become the site of the most decisive Southern victory of the war. Sir Arthur James Lyon-Fre-mantle, an astute officer of His Majesty's Coldstream Guards, sensed traces of smugness in the Confederate ranks, however. Having only re-cently run the Union naval blockade to reach the South in order to ob-serve Lee's Army, he noted its air of overconfidence, writing how, "The universal feeling in the army was one of profound contempt for an enemy they had beaten so constantly, and under so many disadvantages."[123]

Meanwhile, the sight of the Peach Orchard's high ground covered with the Third Corps' blue formations and rows of cannon was imposing. In addition, behind the Peach Orchard position to the east loomed Ceme-tery Ridge, which was distinguished by its tree-line on the distant hori-zon. Ironically, the Mississippi Brigade's last great attack was at Malvern Hill almost one year to the day. And now Barksdale's soldiers would have to do it all over again in attacking the formidable Peach Orchard sector. Hardly could Barksdale's veterans now realize that the upcoming attack on the Peach Orchard and Cemetery Ridge would far surpass the bloodletting of Malvern Hill. As Colonel Humphreys lamented in a letter, "many Mississippians perished" at Gettysburg and more so than on any other field of strife.[124]

As often before an offensive effort, some of Barksdale's troops tore up their letters from loved ones. If killed during the upcoming assault, then these Mississippi soldiers wanted no victorious Yankees to read, ridicule, or poke fun at his family members' written words, thoughts, and emotions. This was a nagging concern because they themselves had often found ample amusement in reading letters removed from Union dead.[125] Partly from necessity, Barksdale's veterans had long taken almost everything from Federal dead. After the slaughter of hundreds of bluecoats at Fredericksburg, a Virginia artilleryman, Henry Robinson Berkeley, wrote with some amazement in his diary how, "All the Yankee dead had been stripped of every rag of their clothing and looked like hogs which had been cleaned."[126] In a letter to his beloved sister Anne, Adjutant Oscar Ewing Stuart, 18th Mississippi, bragged of the spoils of war taken from Union dead, "I have a fine Yankee canteen, but could not get an overcoat."[127] Durng the march to Gettysburg, Lieutenant Colonel Fremantle, the keen-eyed British observer, wrote with some amazement how "the knapsacks of the [Mississippi] men still bear the names of the Massachusetts, Vermont, New Jersey, or other regiments to which they originally belonged."

On this scorching afternoon in Adams County, the formidable challenge of capturing the Third Corps' high ground position at the Peach Orchard, looming before the Mississippians in forbidding fashion, did nothing to sway their determination to win today at any cost. Private Dinkins, 18th Mississippi, described the typical psychology of the brigade's soldiers: "One would not suppose that in so short a time after they had fought with such desperation, and seen so many of their friends killed and wounded by their sides, men could be cheerful and hopeful, could throw off trouble, or face dangers, as occasion demanded. Merry laughter and jests could be heard at every mess fire. The men sang and danced at night, and talked of home . . . it was impossible to break or even check their spirits."[128]

Despite about to launch yet another offensive effort, the spirits among the Magnolia State soldiers remained surprisingly high this afternoon. During the long march from Virginia to this vast killing field nestled between Seminary and Cemetery Ridges, the Mississippi Rebels had sung their favorite songs as if carefree schoolboys on a lark, and perhaps some soldiers whistled or sang these tunes to now break the mounting tension. These popular tunes included old "plantation songs," and those of African-American origin, such as "I'm Gwying down the Newburg Road," "Rock the Cradle, Julie," and "Sallie, Get Your Hoe Cake Done."[129]

British Colonel Fremantle was greatly impressed by the Mississippi Rebels, having witnessed them on the march to Gettysburg: "Barksdale's Mississippians, renowned for their heroic stand at Fredericksburg, were passing—marching in a particular lively manner—the rain and mud seemed to have produced no effect whatever on their spirits. They had got hold of colored prints of Mr. Lincoln, which they were passing about from Company to Company with many remarks upon the personal beauty of Uncle Abe. One female had seen fit to adorn her ample bosom with a huge Yankee Flag, and she stood at the door of her house, her countenance expressing the greatest contempt for the bare-footed Rebs; several companies passed her without taking notice, but at length a Mississippi soldier pointing his finger, and in a loud voice, remarked, 'Take care, madam, for we Mississippi boys are great at storming breastworks when the Yankee colors is on them.' After this speech the patriotic lady beat a precipitate retreat." While spirits were high, Barksdale's men looked unlike crack troops and anything but ready for the formidable challenge which lay ahead. They were dust-covered, ragged, lice-ridden, and dirty. The Mississippi Rebels now appeared more like scarecrows in a Magnolia cornfield along the Tallahatchie than some of the army's elite combat troops.[130]

Private Dinkins described his tattered uniform as consisting of only "the rim of a hat, no top or brim to it, simply a band; the waist of an old coat (the shirt had been cut off to patch the sleeves, and for other uses); a pair of old Yankee pants, the left leg split from the knee down, and tied together with willow bark . . . mangy skin, and, what was worse than all, [I] was full of 'gray backs' [body lice and] a pair of boots, which [were] tied together at both ends and cut a hole in the middle; there were shoes [and] no socks."[131] One of Lee's men wrote how the army consisted of "two years' veterans [who] were scarcely recognizable by their own mothers as the tidy boys who had 'gone out for glory,' in resplendent uniforms," which were no more.[132]

One Confederate officer described the shocking appearance of Lee's veterans, who looked like a strange aberration of abject poverty amid the bountiful countryside of south central Pennsylvania: "Begrimed as we were from head to foot with the impalpable gray powder which rose in dense columns from the macadamized pikes and settled in sheets on men [we] had no time for brushing uniforms or washing the disfiguring dust from faces, hair, or beard [and] all of these were of the same hideous hue."[133]

In jaunty fashion and with a cockiness that betrayed their lethal prowess on the battlefield, some Mississippi veterans wore bucktails in dirty slouch hats or gray kepis. These "trophies" were taken from the dead of the famous "Bucktails," of the 13th Pennsylvania Reserves. In the beginning, these Keystone State frontiersmen had been instructed by officers to bring the trophy of a white-tailed deer tail to verify their marksmanship. At Gettysburg, the prestige of these trophies now worn by Barksdale's veterans instead verified the deadliness of Mississippi marksmanship. Giving them a devil-may-care look, the Mississippians, wearing the deer tails from Pennsylvania's mountains, displayed these badges of honor with a great deal of pride.[134]

But nothing else distinguished the Mississippians' appearance except for a shabby, lean, and threadbare look that masked a plethora of superior combat qualities. Clearly, Barksdale's men looked like the antithesis of elite soldiers. Jimmie Dinkins described himself as a "Little Confederate" with "long yellow hair, badly tangled and matted," and badly in need of a good bath and thorough delousing.[135]

Twenty-five-year-old Private Robert A. Moore, Company G, 17th Mississippi, was determined to win decisive victory at any cost "even life itself, for the liberty of our country." Like other Confederate Guards members, Private Moore believed that he was "battling for our rights & are determined to have them or die in the attempt." However, Private Moore, from a slave-owning family on a farm nestled amid the rolling hills immediately north of Holly Springs, was fated to "die in the attempt." He would survive Gettysburg, but fall to Yankee bullets at Chickamauga, less than three months later.

In his diary, Private Moore wrote with pride how he and his comrades were "determined to fight as long as their country demands." This crusading zeal among Barksdale's veterans was not fueled as much by a mindless support of slavery—since most of these Mississippi soldiers owned none—as it was in fighting to defend their young republic in a righteous struggle against a "ruthless invader who is seeking to reduce us to abject slavery," explained Private Moore. Dark-featured and handsome, the never-say-die 17th Mississippi private also scribbled in his diary that they must "let our last entrenchments be our graves before we will be conquered" by the Yankees. For Private Moore and other Mississippi soldiers, this was most of all a holy struggle "for the liberty of our country" like their Revolutionary War forefathers.

Yet another motivation was all-important in explaining why the Mississippi Brigade's soldiers would perform so well at Gettysburg: Grant's invasion of their home state. In his diary on February 5, 1863, an incensed Private Moore, 17th Mississippi, penned how "heard from home this evening [and the invading] abolitionists have left Pa an old blind mule," while taking practically everything else from his family's middle-class Mississippi farm. During the spring of 1863, Grant's western army slashed across Mississippi in a bold campaign to reduce fortress Vicksburg. A gloomy Private Moore scribbled in his diary on May 18 how, after Grant won the battles of Port Gibson and Raymond, Mississippi, "the enemy have occupied Jackson, the capitol of the State." And only four days later, he wrote in his diary how, "to-day was recommended as a day of prayer by our chaplain for our nation & particularly our native state which is now invaded by our ungenerous foe." In a letter to his wife that revealed the ironic and paradoxical situation of the Mississippi Brigade at this time, Private Nimrod Newton Nash, who was known as "Old Newt" to the boys in the 13th Mississippi, explained the burning desire of so many of Barksdale's men at this time: "I wish Gen. Longstreet's Corps was down there, and they would let us loose on old Grant. We would have him out of his den in a little time."[136] But while Barksdale's soldiers, racked by anxiety and gloomy thoughts about the welfare of their families, had marched with confidence toward Gettysburg, they eagerly awaited the news of the fate of their home state and Vicksburg, the key to the Mississippi River.

And the Mississippi Brigade's top leaders were likewise deeply affected by the fates of homes, families, and relatives in the Magnolia State, and these nagging concerns were on their minds on the field of Gettysburg. After crossing the Mississippi from eastern Louisiana in the greatest amphibious operation to date, Grant's Army had swarmed into Colonel Humphreys' own Claiborne County on May 1. Humphreys' sister, Mrs. A.K. Shaifer whose husband served in the Port Hudson, Louisiana, garrison, on the Mississippi below Vicksburg, had been driven from her home, when the battle of Port Gibson literally erupted on her property. The Humphreys' family plantation "Hermitage" was caught in the vortex of Grant's storm. Clearly, this increasingly brutal war now affected Barksdale, Humphreys and their men in the most personal of ways: a factor partly explaining why the Mississippi Delta colonel and his 21st Mississippi were so highly motivated and determined to reap a decisive victory at Gettysburg.[137] Reflecting the July 2 mood in the ranks, an anguished 13th Mississippi private scribbled in a letter how, "we have all been in an agony of suspence [sic] to hear of the final result of the conflict which has been going on in Miss."[138]

Many of the 1,620 veterans of Barksdale's Mississippi Brigade now massed in Pitzer's Woods sensed the ironic twist fate that now placed them before the Peach Orchard. By the time of the showdown at Gettysburg, Lee's Army contained more Mississippi infantry regiments than defended Vicksburg. With most of Mississippi's sons fighting and dying far away, Vicksburg was doomed. Instead of defending their home state, the four regiments of Barksdale's Mississippi and Lee's other seven Mississippi infantry regiments hoped to secure victory at Gettysburg to relieve their beleaguered homeland. While Vicksburg was slowly strangled to death, Lee's Mississippi troops were now farther away from the Magnolia State than ever before.[139] With his thoughts never far from his invaded homeland, Private Nash, 13th Mississippi, penned in a letter home, "I feel story for our boys at Vicksburg." But the worst was yet to come.[140]

Of all Longstreet's troops, the Mississippi Brigade now most directly confronted head-on the full might of the Peach Orchard position, bristling with artillery and thousands of veterans in blue coats. But this formidable appearance of Third Corps might disguised weaknesses. Quite simply, too few Union fighting men were deployed along a long, over-extended front, offering "great dangers," in the words of one tactically astute Union general. However, negating this advantage, what also lay before Barksdale's Mississippi Brigade was a natural killing field that flowed east across the open fields and gently rolling terrain that ascended up to the Emmitsburg Road. The Mississippi Brigade's opportunity to strike the most vulnerable point—the salient angle—in the Third Corps' line had developed quite unexpectedly, and to Meade's utter shock back at his Cemetery Ridge headquarters.

In a letter, Captain Haskell described what had set the tactical stage for the struggle for possession of the Peach Orchard, when the Third Corps' independent-minded commander General Daniel Egar Sickles "Somewhat after one o'clock P.M. [made] a movement to the second ridge West, the distance is about 1,000 yards, and there the Emmitsburg road runs near the crest of the ridge . . . Gen. Sickles commenced to advance his whole Corps, from the general line [on Cemetery Ridge], straight to the front, with a view to occupy this second ridge, along, and near the road. What purpose could have been is past conjecture [but] It was not ordered by Gen. Meade, as I heard him say, and he disapproved of it as soon as it was made known to him."[141]

Incredibly, because he deemed his assigned line "unsatisfactory," Sickles had moved his entire corps of two divisions forward to the west against orders. The Third Corps had been initially ordered by Meade to take a defensive position on the Second Corps' left and to extend the Union line down Cemetery Ridge southward to Little Round Top on the morning of July 2. All of a sudden, therefore, the Peach Orchard position now presented Lee with an unexpected development and a new opportunity. He now found his Third Corps opponent in an entirely new position that disrupted his original battle-plan of assaulting up the Emmitsburg Road to hit the Union left flank. To exploit Sickles' ill-advised forward thrust that created an over-extended, vulnerable salient, without support on either side, Longstreet now possessed an opportunity to crush the Third Corps with a mighty offensive onslaught.

Indeed, the Peach Orchard salient, a 45-degree angle formed by defensive line that spanned northeast along the Emmitsburg Road and southeast along the Wheatfield Road, was now vulnerable on three sides, hanging in mid-air before Meade's main line aligned along Cemetery Ridge. A perplexed Captain Haskell lamented how Sickles "supposed he was doing for the best; but he was neither born nor bred a soldier [and] we can scarcely tell what may have been the motives of such a man—a politician [and] a man after show and notoriety."[142]

However, a nervous Sickles had only abruptly responded to a vexing tactical situation and the contours of geography at Cemetery Ridge's southern end, where the ridge gradually dipped as it extended south to flatten out to reach a low point, just north of Little Round Top. He had been assigned the worst ground on all of Cemetery Ridge, low, marshy, and in his view dominated by the elevated ground at the Peach Orchard in his front. By occupying that height he would be better able to stave off an attack; just as important, he believed the Confederates could pulverize his position on Cemetery Ridge if they occupied it themselves.

Even General Henry Hunt, commanding the army's artillery, recognized the Peach Orchard's high ground as "favorable" for defense, especially artillery placement. Captain George E. Randolph, commanding the

Third Corps' Artillery Brigade, felt the same. Recalling how Confederate artillery perched atop the higher ground of Hazel Grove had severely punished his low-lying troops at Chancellorsville, Sickles had immediately viewed the higher ground along the Emmitsburg Road as well worth occupying, if only to deny its possession to Lee.[143] Coinciding with the views of his top lieutenant, General David Bell Birney, whose First Division held the Peach Orchard salient, Sickles was convinced that "to abandon the Emmitsburg road to the enemy would be unpardonable."[144]

Sickles, a leading New York City Democrat and self-promoting politician of the cut-throat Tammany Hall machine, possessed lofty White House ambitions. As suspected by Union officers who were familiar with the unorthodox, "notorious" New Yorker, the ever-ambitious Sickles knew that winning lasting fame at Gettysburg was a sure ticket to the White House.[145] Therefore, leading Union officers, including Meade, suspected that Sickles' decision to secure that Peach Orchard defensive line was more "political than military."[146]

However, it was also true that Sickles, at Chancellorsville less than two months earlier, had witnessed Stonewall Jackson's famous flank attack while it was in motion, but had misinterpreted its meaning. He assumed it was a retreat rather than preparation for the most devastating surprise attack of the war, and now at Gettysburg he refused to be caught at a disadvantage, or unawares. As the far left of the Union army he wanted the best defensive ground he could find. In fact, unlike Meade at this time, who expected a Confederate attack against his right, Sickles was fully correct that another Rebel flank attack was in the works, and that it was coming straight against his part of the line.

Captain Haskell thought that "there would be no repetition of Chancellorsville" on July 2.[147] But he also added, "This move of the Third Corps was an important one [because] it developed the battle [but] O, if this Corps had kept its strong position upon the crest" of Cemetery Ridge.[148] Indeed, the tactically astute Longstreet saw clearly that Sickles' line at the Peach Orchard "was, in military language, built in the air."[149] In addition, Sickles' advance to the Peach Orchard sector also left Little Round Top to the southeast more vulnerable, even though the southern arm of his angled line along the Wheatfield Road extended southeast toward that rocky hill.[150]

Therefore, thanks to Sickles' move west over the broad open fields to create an exposed bulge, or salient, situated about halfway between Cemetery and Seminary Ridge, and his attempt to hold the Peach Orchard salient and Emmitsburg Road Ridge with too few troops, the Mississippi Brigade was now presented with the golden opportunity to smash the exposed Third Corps salient and to "end the war in a single afternoon."[151]

Gripping their muskets in the relatively cool shade of Pitzer's Woods, Barksdale's men marveled at more than the sight of Sickles' salient.[152] Before the Mississippi Brigade's position in the thick woods, acre after acre of the finely-manicured Joseph and Mary Sherfy farm stretched eastward as far as the eye could see.

One of Lee's generals was impressed by the richness of this land of plenty, writing how Pennsylvania's "broad grain-fields, clad in golden garb, were waving their welcome to the reapers and binders [and] on every side, as far as our alert vision could reach, all aspects and conditions conspired to make this fertile and carefully tilled region a panorama both interesting and enchanting." And Colonel Edward Porter Alexander, commander of Longstreet's reserve artillery, described how "the Dutch [are] generally apparently very industrious & very prosperous [with] big barns, & fat cattle, & fruits & vegetables were every where." After all, Pennsylvania's bounty and prosperity were key factors that had originally caused Lee to decide to invade the Keystone State, where his provision-short army could be re-supplied off what was essentially a vast granary untouched by the war's wanton destructiveness.[153] Private Nash, 13th Mississippi, was amazed by the land's seemingly endless bounty. He wrote in a letter how there "has been thousands of the finest horses I ever saw taken for the use of the army besides wagons, forage and every other supply for the army."[154] In his diary, Private William Henry Hill, 13th Mississippi, was equally astounded at "their prosperity [and we] have taken a large number of horses, mules . . . cattle, sheep, forage, &c."[155]

But the sheer natural beauty of the landscape lying before the Mississippians like a naturalist's colorful painting was about to be transformed from a scene of pastoral tranquility into a vast killing field. However, the eerie calm before the storm and dream-like imaginary of the idyllic setting was abruptly shattered when Barksdale shortly screamed out orders to send skirmishers forward to protect the brigade's front. Each regimental commander hurled his best skirmish company forward from the haven of Pitzer's Woods into the expansive, sun-baked fields of farmer Sherfy. To safeguard the 17th Mississippi's front, Colonel Holder ordered Captain Gwin Reynalds Cherry and his Company C sol-

diers [Quitman Guards] forward into the broad, open fields of summer.
A former sergeant major who knew how to get the most out of his men
on the battlefield, Cherry was a reliable officer of ability and merit. With
a clatter of gear and jingling accouterments, the Pontotoc County boys
spilled out of the tree-line and into the open fields bathed in bright sunlight and intense afternoon heat.[156]

With a lengthy formation of skirmishers from the 63rd Pennsylvania
aligned in the open fields before the Emmitsburg Road Ridge, the Mississippians were immediately vulnerable when they poured out into the
field, where zipping bullets made the air sing. Therefore, experienced
skirmish captains ordered their men to take kneeing positions to minimize their vulnerability. However, after retiring closer to the ridge, the
blue skirmishers were sufficiently distant that a mounted Longstreet appeared on the skirmish line. Longstreet's micro-management of even relatively small matters to an extent seldom seen before raised the ire of the
proud McLaws, a tough leader, who saw this hands-on leadership as interference and disrespect.[157]

However, some of Longstreet's personal interference with McLaws'
Division was well-calculated and beneficial. He ordered Captain Cherry
to send two men of Company C, 17th Mississipppi, forward across the
sprawling expanse of farmer Joseph Sherfy's fields to an "unidentified"
log house, located before the Emmitsburg Road and the Sherfy House,
on a vital mission to "tear down the picket fences which stood around
the yard and garden areas," in the words of Private James W. Duke, Company C, 17th Mississippi.[158]

Aware of the mission's extreme danger, Captain Cherry turned to
the young orderly sergeant, and ordered him to read off the first two
names on the company's "duty roster." But no one answered the call.
Then, the orderly sergeant moved down the list, and shouted out the
next two names. Once again, no man stepped forward from the ranks.
Clearly, with the lengthy line of bluecoat Pennsylvania skirmishers, yet
blasting away, so near the house, this assignment appeared suicidal. A
model soldier, nevertheless, Captain Cherry became incensed by the lack
of response. "Angry and exasperated," therefore, the captain shouted
out, "I *will* make the detail!"[159] Even though this assignment was "a job
with a limited future" from which any volunteer would very likely never
return.[160]

Knowing that his two best soldiers would not fail to accept the stiff
challenge, Captain Cherry made his final decision. He said, "Jim Duke

and Woods Mears, they will go."[161] Private Archibald Y. Duke held his breath, while his brother Jim stepped forward without hesitation. Ironically, Archibald, and not Jim, was destined to receive his death stroke on this day; however, clearly, this special mission was most daunting. With a veteran's insight, Private Duke turned to Woods, and blunted out, "We will be killed."[162]

Captain Cherry made his choice not only because these two young men were not only the best Company C soldiers, but also because of their size and strength, which was necessary to tear down the fence line surrounding the house's garden and yard. Despite knowing that the mission was suicidal and after leaving muskets behind, Privates Duke and Woodson, or "Woods," B. Mears dashed forward. They then raced through the slight depression amid the open fields about halfway between Seminary Ridge and the Emmitsburg Road Ridge. While heading toward the house, the two Rebels, exposed in the open, expected the 63rd Pennsylvania skirmishers, and even their main line along the ridge to open fire. But then something entirely unexpected and strikingly surreal happened, to the surprise of everyone.

Not a shot was fired at the two young boys in gray when they neared the picket fence around the house's yard. Almost as if no one had noticed, they had been allowed to race up the open western slope of the Emmitsburg Road Ridge. In an act of chivalry, no Federal soldier fired at them from the high ground around the Sherfy House. Although they were breathless by this time, the two Quitman Guards members reached their objective. Here, in frantic haste, they tore down the fence planks, which served an obstacle to Barksdale's upcoming attack. All the while, the Pennsylvania skirmishers, situated only around "fifty paces" distant, quietly watched the two Rebels' hectic activity. The Yankees felt a sense of admiration for the daring bravery of the two Company C boys. In honor of their courage, neither the Pennsylvania skirmishers, main line soldiers, or artillerymen fired a shot, allowing Jim Duke and Woods Mears to complete their work.[163]

Miraculously, the two Mississippi boys returned safely to their comrades without a scratch after completing a dangerous job well done. Hoping to gain insights upon the strength of the Union positions along the Emmitsburg Road, Longstreet quizzed Duke and Mears, asking "What did you see there?" Then, violating military etiquette and protocol, Private Jim Duke posed Longstreet a direct question, "General, do you think we can take those heights?" Knowing that taking the high ground would only come at a frightfully high cost, a bemused "Old Pete" simply replied to the outspoken private, "I don't know, do you?"[164]

More than any other Southern unit because it directly faced the Peach Orchard, the Mississippi Brigade was now in the key position to exploit the tactical vulnerability of Sickles' salient. To bolster his defensive stance on Cemetery Ridge, meanwhile, Meade had strengthened his right around Culp's Hill at the expense of his left—exactly where Longstreet's flank attack was about to take place. Hence, by this time, Meade's left was relatively vulnerable compared to his right.

With a keen eye for choosing good terrain, General Hunt, the capable commander of the Army of the Potomac's artillery, early realized the potential of the commanding terrain of the Peach Orchard knoll for massed artillery.[165] After the overall poor performance of the Union Army's artillery at Chancellorsville, at no fault of his own since "Fighting Joe" Hooker had made an error of judgment in demoting him, Hunt was determined that the army's "long arm"—now independent under Meade—would fulfill its potential during what was shaping-up to be the most important battle on the North American continent. After the Union army's artillery arm had reached its zenith on the open ground at Antietam, Hunt now worked hard to orchestrate a repeat performance on Pennsylvania soil. Most important, he had already ordered Reserve Artillery batteries forth to bolster the Third Corps artillery at the Peach Orchard, strengthening the position based upon his own considerable expertise. Like Meade and fortunately for the Union, the brilliant Hunt was about to have his finest day. Gettysburg marked the high point of Hunt's career.

Despite the Third Corps' high ground salient angle jutting out before Meade's main line along Cemetery Ridge, the elevated position was formidable with its massive array of artillery support from both the Third Corps and the Reserve Artillery, thanks to Hunt's expert placement of guns. Several Union batteries were "tightly packed" inside the salient angle, and three more were aligned southeast along the Wheatfield Road. More than three dozen artillery pieces were supported by General Charles Kinnaird Graham's fine Pennsylvania brigade of Birney's First Division. This battle-hardened Keystone State brigade was poised in good defensive positions at the advanced point of the Peach Orchard salient angle, and all the way northeast along the Emmitsburg Road to the Abraham Trostle Lane. Most daunting, the several veteran Union batteries crammed into the salient angle promised to drop a good many attackers with a vicious fire. A close friend of Sickles, with Tammany Hall connections and a gifted civil engineer, General Graham, age thirty-nine, was the former colonel of the 74th New York Volunteer Infantry, Excelsior Brigade. He now performed as competently on this day of destiny with his brigade as when a tireless dry dock civil engineer of the Brooklyn Navy Yard.

Supporting the rows of artillery and holding the Emmitsburg Road Ridge sector, Graham's brigade consisted of half a dozen veteran Pennsylvania regiments. The brigade had launched a successful counterattack at Chancellorsville to help stem the Rebel tide that had reached new heights on one of Lee's finest days. As fate would have it, this heavy concentration of Third Corps and Reserve Artillery guns and infantry ensured that this would be primarily a Mississippi-Pennsylvania showdown for possession of the vital Peach Orchard. The struggle was guaranteed to be tenacious because the Pennsylvanians now defended their home state. In total, seven batteries (40 guns) of both the Third Corps and the Reserve Artillery, thanks to Hunt's timely efforts, bolstered the Peach Orchard salient.

The concentrated firepower of these veteran artillery units helped to make up for some of the line's tactical vulnerabilities, especially filling gaps in a defensive line of infantrymen spread too thin. A row of guns, facing south, deployed along the Wheatfield Road protected the southern arm of the angle that extended southeast down the farmer's dusty lane to protect Sickles' left. In addition, Sickles had been promised support from both the Second and Fifth Corps to strengthen his advanced position.

Graham's First Brigade and the First Division's remainder held the Third Corps' left, while General Humphreys' Second Division occupied the right of the Third Corps' line. No relation to Colonel Humphreys of the 21st Mississippi, General Andrew Atkinson Humphreys, who hailed from a distinguished Philadelphia family, was a reliable West Pointer and a veteran of the Seminole War. A distinguished ancestry included Humphreys' grandfather, who had designed the *U.S.S. Constitution*, or "Old Ironsides." Sickles' salient was bolstered by double-strength levels of support infantry in the center. Along the Emmitsburg Road and the shallow, open ridge stretching toward Gettysburg, Graham's 68th, 141st, and 57th Pennsylvania Volunteer Infantry Regiments were aligned from south to north. The dependable 68th Pennsylvania anchored the line's left along the Wheatfield Road.

Protecting the artillery, Graham's reserve consisted of the 105th Pennsylvania Volunteer Infantry, on the right of the brigade's support line, and the 114th Pennsylvania. These two regiments were aligned across the open eastern slope of the Emmitsburg Road Ridge. If the initial blue line was broken at the Peach Orchard, then these readily available reserves could advance swiftly to plug a hole in the line or reinforce any hard-pressed defensive sector.

To support the 1,515 infantrymen of Graham's Pennsylvania brigade anchoring the First Division's right, the six guns of the 15th New York Light Artillery, under Lieutenant Albert N. Ames, stood on the Peach Orchard's knoll. Meanwhile, another three Federal batteries were aligned along the Wheatfield Road near the southern arm of the salient angle to the Peach Orchard's left rear. Besides the massed array of Third Corps artillery, among the heaviest concentration of guns in the Peach Orchard sector were field pieces of the 1st Volunteer Light Artillery, consisting of the 5th and 9th Massachusetts Batteries, 15th New York Light Artillery, and Batteries C and F, Pennsylvania Light Artillery of the First Volunteer Brigade, Reserve Artillery. Meanwhile, the 3rd Maine Volunteer Infantry of Ward's Second Brigade held a position on the southern front of the Peach Orchard, just south of where the Wheatfield Road intersected the Emmitsburg Road.

North of the Peach Orchard to Graham's right, Humphreys' Division consisted of the Pennsylvania, New Jersey, New Hampshire, and Massachusetts troops of the First Brigade, under General Joseph B. Carr. This fine brigade was aligned along the Emmitsburg Road and on the road's east side north of the Abraham Trostle Lane. Meanwhile, Colonel William R. Brewster's New York "Excelsior" brigade of Humphreys' Division occupied the Emmitsburg Road line just northeast of the Sherfy house on the road's east side. These experienced New York regiments were deployed north of the Abraham Trostle Lane on the right of Graham's units that were aligned along the Emmitsburg Road. These New York troops sensed the seriousness of this key situation at the Peach Orchard salient, after Colonel Brewster ordered his troops to hold his elevated ground "at all hazards." It was clear that some very hard fighting lay ahead.

Adding more infantry muscle to the Peach Orchard salient, two additional regiments, the 2nd New Hampshire Volunteer Infantry, around 350 men, and the 7th New Jersey Volunteer Infantry, 275 men, of Humphreys' remaining infantry brigade, under Colonel George C. Burling, were sent to reinforce General Graham's Pennsylvanians along the Emmitsburg Road, after Burling received instructions from Birney to dispatch "two of my largest regiments" to reinforce Graham's Pennsylvania brigade. The 7th New Jersey, under Colonel Louis R. Francine, formed to the left-rear of Captain A. Judson Clark's New Jersey battery in protective fashion with the uniting of the Garden State's infantry and artillery. The 2nd New Hampshire would soon support these six New Jersey guns to the right-rear of Captain Clark's battery.[166]

With the keen eye of a veteran artillery commander in recognizing that the commanding Peach Orchard knoll along the Emmitsburg Road was the key to the battlefield, Colonel Alexander described the Peach Orchard sector before him in some detail. He explained how the infantry and artillery might of Sickles' Third Corps' "had taken position along this ridge [and] formed along this pike until he reached a cross road, where there was a large peach orchard, & there he turned off to the left & rested his flank in some broken ground" before Little Round Top. Most important, Colonel Alexander believed that, "now, the weakest part of Sickles' line was the angle at the Peach Orchard."[167]

With considerable insight, William A. Love indicated as much when he mockingly emphasized how "at the so-called 'high-water mark of the Confederacy' or elsewhere, no incident can surpass in grandeur the glorious achievements" of the upcoming attack of Barksdale's Mississippi Brigade on July 2. Indeed, the opportunity to exploit a key breakthrough at the Peach Orchard embraced even more potential for a truly decisive success, because the Union lines below and southeast of the Peach Orchard were relatively weak. A wide gap existed between the left of Graham's Brigade, defending the Peach Orchard, and the right of Colonel P. Regis de Trobriand's Brigade, First Division, Third Corps, on the Wheatfield's west side. And most important, to the north, the Third Corps' right on the Emmitsburg Road was not linked with the Second Corps' left on Cemetery Ridge. Nearly half a mile of undefended ground lay in rear of Sickles' left and the right of Hancock's Corps.[168]

From Seminary Ridge, meanwhile, Barksdale's Mississippians faced their high ground target as it stood forebodingly before them under the boiling July sun. If Barksdale could smash through this sector, especially at the salient, then the entire defensive front of the isolated Third Corps would cave in like a rotten apple hit with the full force by a baseball bat. Fortunately, no lengthy rows of sturdy rail fences stood erect on the gentle slope across the open ground leading up to the Emmitsburg Road Ridge. Most of these barriers already had been torn down by skirmishers in preparation for the infantry assault, except relatively near to the ridge-top: an invaluable advantage which ensured that the upcoming attack would not be impeded, and no precious time would be wasted.

Here, along the Emmitsburg Road Ridge, stood the stately, but small, two-story farm house of red brick, the Joseph and Mary Sherfy home. Almost as if dropped out of the sky and into the middle of this pristine, rolling landscape of beautiful farmlands, the Sherfy House stood prominently on the slight ridge next to the road. The modest but stylish, farmhouse, with a small front porch, was situated amid a broad expanse of flowing fields, now covered with rich crops of oats, corn, wheat, and clover. The red brick Sherfy home was located immediately beyond, or just west, of the Emmitsburg Road and just before the west-facing north side of the salient angle. Now defended by hundreds of Yankees, the north side of the defensive angle ran as far as the eye could see along the dusty Emmitsburg Road. This narrow dirt avenue offered a means of rapid redeployment for either Union infantry or artillery in case of an emergency. Positioned on both side of the Sherfy barn, the six guns of Lieutenant John K. Bucklyn's Company E, First Rhode Island Light Artillery, would give Alexander's booming guns more than they could handle this afternoon.

The red Sherfy barn, a large wooden structure resting on a sturdy stone base in the German country style, looked huge compared to the Sherfy's House, just to the north. Unlike the type of structures found in the Deep South and somewhat a puzzling contradiction of sorts to these Deep South soldiers from both a yeoman and a planter class culture, the German farmer's barn was much larger than his own house.

From Barksdale's view looking eastward, the barn offered a focal point by which to guide and target his offensive effort on the brigade's left. Along with the fact that this was the position of Bucklyn's six guns, the red barn of farmer Sherfy was a natural target for the Mississippians' attack. In launching his charge, consequently, Barksdale and the Mississippi Brigade would have an ideal central visual point to direct their advance upon: a dominant sight that would not escape their view even after they descended into the slight depression between the ridges.

And farmer Sherfy's barn stood only a few yards west of the road indicated to the observant Barksdale as the exact location of the Emmitsburg Road. After reaching the road in the Sherfy House sector, the Mississippians' assault, after surging east, could then roll northeast and strike General Humphreys' Division from the left flank. Barksdale's plan of assaulting with three regiments—the 18th, 13th, and 17th Mississippi from left to right—above the salient angle promised to neutralize the Union defenders on the salient's south side, which faced southwest, with a breakthrough. But more important for the ambitious goal of collapsing Third Corps resistance, Colonel Humphreys and his 21st Mississippi were to strike the point of the salient angle to capture the highest ground of the Peach Orchard to enfilade the salient's southern arm along the Wheatfield Road from right to left. Hence, the guns of three Union batteries positioned along the Wheatfield Road would not be able to shift northwest to fire into the rear of the Mississippi Brigade's assault barreling northeast when Barksdale attacked up the Emmitsburg Road. Also Barksdale planned to attack through the gap that existed between the widely separated Union artillery units aligned on the salient's north side, so that his three regiments would avoid the salient's south, where more Federal artillery was concentrated.

By advancing only one regiment (the 21st Mississippi) straight east toward the salient's apex, the protruding angle which lay closest to Longstreet's soldiers, Barksdale's assault with his other three regiments was calculated to avoid fire, especially artillery, from the salient's entire southern arm. Barksdale's attackers of three regiments would be hit by the fire of only one instead of both sides of the Peach Orchard salient. Here, by exploiting these weaknesses and vulnerabilities of the Third Corps line, Barksdale possessed an opportunity to crush the Peach Orchard salient, if his troops could first cross the open fields of fire as rapidly as possible to minimize casualties and the loss of momentum. Because Sickles' units of infantry and artillery were positioned at right angles to each other, the defenders' field of fire was reduced to a great extent: a fact that Barksdale, hoping to gain an edge, was determined to exploit.

But in overall terms and despite the obvious weaknesses in the Union defensive line, the task for Barksdale's Mississippi Brigade was daunting. These veteran Mississippians had already seen what awful destruction a good many well-placed Federal veterans on elevated and fortified position could do to assault formations. Memories of Malvern Hill, almost precisely a year earlier, still renovated. However, Private McNeily, Hurricane Rifles (Company E), 21st Mississippi, noted a crucial difference: "On just another such hot July afternoon the year before our command had assaulted Malvern hill, a position where the enemy had massed infantry and artillery [and] it was twice as distant as the Peach Orchard hill, which made a vast difference. One was within and the other beyond the rushing space, hence one was charged with full confidence of success, the other with little or none."

If only Barksdale's men could first make it across the long stretch of open ground before the lengthy rows of Yankee guns decimated assault formations without suffering great losses, then a good chance existed that the Peach Orchard could be overwhelmed. Such a sparkling success would certainly unhinge resistance all along Sickles' over-extended line, collapsing the salient angle and the entire Third Corps' defensive line. In this way, the Mississippians could unhinge the Union line's center and open the floodgates to a truly decisive Confederate victory, after ripping a hole in the Army of the Potomac's vulnerable mid-section.

Most important, the promise of decisive victory for Barksdale hinged upon a two-part tactical formula: first, overrunning the foremost high ground position of the Peach Orchard and along the Emmitsburg Road Ridge to set the stage for continuing the attack farther east to capture the other and most important key to the battlefield, Cemetery Ridge. And running just beyond these two parallel high-ground defensive positions lay an undefended, inconspicuous dirt artery that led straight to Washington, D.C., the Taneytown Road. This innocuous, little road led straight to the fulfillment of the most lofty Confederate dreams and ambitions: ending the war in glorious victory. Lusting at the thought, Lee later swore to Reverend J. William Jones: "A complete victory [at Gettysburg] would have given us Washington and Baltimore, if not Philadelphia, and would have established the independence of the Confederacy."[169]

Because the offensive efforts of Hood's Division to the south at the Round Tops would be frustrated this afternoon, the commanding knoll of the Peach Orchard would shortly become the key to Confederate victory on July 2. With commanding heights solidly anchoring both of Meade's flanks—Culp's Hill on the north and Little Round Top on the south—the Union left-center was now the most vulnerable Union sector, because no Federal troops stood in defensive positions on Cemetery Ridge to the Third Corps' rear. Beyond the Peach Orchard, the land was open, gently rolling in sloping down toward the little creek known as Plum Run, until rising up open ground to Cemetery Ridge. Just north of Little Round Top's rocky western face, Cemetery Ridge gradually diminished to reach a low point. Consequently, the gently sloping terrain and colorful patchwork of fields, meadows, and pastures flowing east beyond the Peach Orchard was a relatively easy and wide open avenue that now led to decisive Southern victory, if only Sickles' line could be successfully penetrated and swept aside. Then, the successful assault could be continued east all the way to Cemetery Ridge and the fulfillment of Confederate dreams.

Lee described the importance of gaining the elevated position along the Emmitsburg Road: "in front of Longstreet the enemy held a position from which, if he could be driven, it was thought our artillery could be used to advantage in assailing the more elevated ground beyond, and thus enable us to gain the crest of the ridge." Indeed, the open, elevated terrain of the Peach Orchard—even higher than some sections of Cemetery Ridge —and the Emmitsburg Road Ridge was the last geographical obstacle, before the generally open ground to the east rolled gently down toward Plum Run. If everything went according to plan, then the combined might from both Confederate infantry and artillery in this relatively concentrated sector along a narrow front might be sufficient enough to punch a gaping hole through the heart of Meade's line to spell the end of the Army of the Potomac's existence.

Consequently, the Mississippi Brigade's challenge before the Peach Orchard salient was now the best chance to win it all for the Confederacy. As fate would have it, Barksdale and his troops were about to take the lead role for achieving the most significant gains of any Confederate brigade on the Second Day at Gettysburg. Like no other Rebel troops at Gettysburg this afternoon, and as Barksdale realized, he and his Mississippi Brigade possessed the golden opportunity to win it all for the Confederacy.[170]

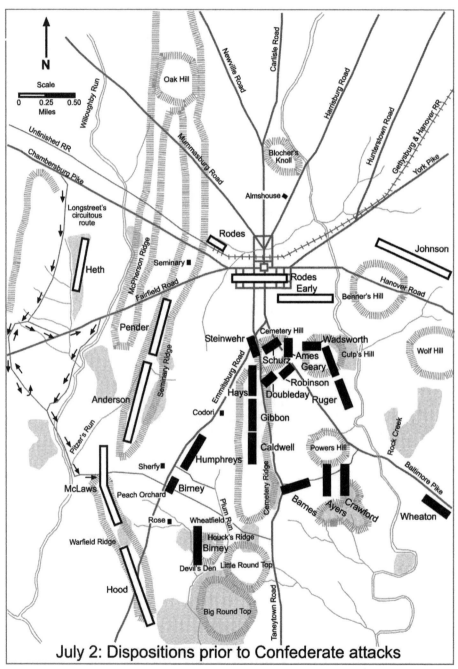

July 2: Dispositions prior to Confederate attacks

Map courtesy of Bradley M. Gottfried

4

"Exceedingly impatient for the order to advance"

BY MID-AFTERNOON on July 2, Longstreet's divisions under Hood and McLaws were in position to begin their attack, supported by 54 guns under Alexander (who kept 8 in reserve). For all the clumsiness of Longstreet's approach march, the Union high command had cooperated superbly by removing all Union cavalry from the left. Buford's brigades had been on the field the prior evening, but had been ordered to Westminster to guard the army's trains and to rest their horses. Thus Longstreet's men were allowed to march to their assigned positions without a need for Jeb Stuart to screen their flank movement, as he had Stonewall Jackson's at Chancellorsville two months earlier.

Nevertheless, if Meade still doubted the imminence of a huge Confederate attack on his left, there was no longer any doubt in Sickles' Third Corps, as they could glimpse signs of infantry formations through the trees or between rises in the ground, as well as artillery rolling into position. Federal batteries had already begun feeling the woods in order to flush out the Rebels and develop their strength.

Finally, at about 3:45 PM, Longstreet's artillery opened up. At that moment Meade had been conferring with Sickles and was about to order him to pull back his corps to the main Union line on Cemetery Ridge; however, the opening of the guns meant it was too late. According to Sickles, Meade hastily promised him support from the Second and Fifth Corps, before both men hurried back to their headquarters. By now the full Third Corps artillery had opened up in turn. In his diary, Private William Henry Hill, a seasoned member of Barksdale's 13th Mississippi, wrote, "the cannonading was the most terrific I ever heard."[171]

The Peach Orchard salient, bolstered by batteries, thousands of experienced front-line troops, and fresh reserves presented an awe-inspiring appearance. In the words of Private McNeily, 21st Mississippi, the high ground of the Peach Orchard sector now overflowed with thousands of men and dozens of cannon, and "seemed impregnable to a frontal attack."[172] Knowing that some of the most savage fighting of the war lay just ahead, Private Nimrod Newton Nash, 13th Mississippi, had attempted to reassure his wife Mollie in a June 28, 1863 letter, "Darling if I should get wounded here and left behind . . . if such befall me, for my sake don't be uneasy about me, if not for your own, though I don't fear any thing of the kind, for I have been in many hot places, and have come out safe. My trust is still in the same God that has always shielded me from harm."[173] But now in surveying the wide stretch of open ground flowing smoothly to gently ascend to the Peach Orchard and the Emmitsburg Road Ridge, Private Nash now possessed less confidence for success. He knew that no place would be as "hot" as in the upcoming struggle, an especially brutal contest in which he was to receive his death stroke.[174]

On the Confederate right, General John Bell Hood was equally dismayed. As he told Longstreet about his trepidation to advance: ". . . we would be subject to a destructive fire in flank and rear, as well as in front; and deemed it almost an impossibility to clamber along the boulders up this steep and rugged mountain, and, under this number of cross fires, put the enemy to flight. I knew that if the feat was accomplished, it must be at a most fearful sacrifice of as brave and gallant soldiers as ever engaged in battle."

Since neither side had any cavalry on that flank, Hood had sent out some of his Texas scouts to see what was behind the Round Tops, and they reported back that there was nothing but unprotected Federal wagon trains. Hood repeatedly applied for permission to go around the heights and hit the Union rear, but each time Longstreet refused, finally saying, "We must obey the orders of General Lee." For Hood, the most lion-hearted of Lee's division commanders, to protest the attack was remarkable. However, as Longstreet later explained, if Lee had been on the spot the new intelligence could have been reported to him; however "to delay and send messengers five miles in favor of a move that he had rejected would have been contumacious." This may possibly have been an indication of spitefulness on Longstreet's part since he himself had argued for a further move to Meade's right earlier in the day, only to be abruptly rejected. So if Lee wanted an attack "up the Emmitsburg road," he would get it, regardless of the consequences.

Hood's attack began around 4:00 with Evander Law's Brigade on the right, supported by Henry Benning's Brigade, and J.B. Robertson's Brigade, supported by George T. Anderson's, to their left. Immediately it was seen that holding to the Emmitsburg Road was a fantasy. They had a full Federal corps in front of them stretched to Little Round Top. Law's Brigade began climbing those heights, a key to the battlefield, only to be met by a newly arrived brigade of the Federal Fifth Corps. Robertson's Brigade attacked Ward's Third Corps brigade head-on. Hood was spared from witnessing the culmination of his fears as he was knocked out of the battle with a severe arm wound in the first minutes. But soon all four of his brigades were engaged in a horrific fight, ranging from a jumble of boulders called Devil's Den across to the Round Tops, and in particular in an open killing ground known simply to this day as the Wheatfield.

While Hood's division battled, McLaws' waited for Longstreet's go-ahead. His righthand brigade consisted of South Carolinians under J.B. Kershaw, another popular politician and attorney in gray, who like Hood, was not optimistic about the chances of success. He described how the Federal position was "heavily supported by artillery [and] the intervening ground was occupied by open fields, interspersed and divided by stone walls [and] The position just here seemed almost impregnable."[175]

Kershaw was to be supported by General Paul Jones Semmes' Georgia brigade. Semmes was the younger brother of the daring high seas captain of the Rebel raider *C.S.S. Alabama*, a former prewar Georgia militia officer, and former colonel of the 2nd Georgia Infantry. A tough-minded Catholic from southern Maryland, Semmes would soon be mortally wounded in the tempest below the Peach Orchard. Barksdale, in the front line to Kershaw's left, was to be supported by the 1,400-man Georgia brigade of William T. Wofford, who had been a captain of a volunteer mounted company during the Mexican-American War. He yet possessed a Mexican lance that he had captured from the Castilian Lancers in a contest that he considered glorious. Wofford was a Georgia politician and lawyer, who had been anti-secessionist, like Colonel Humphreys, before inflamed sectional passions led to this most murderous of wars. He first won distinction as the commander of a lone Georgia regiment, the hard-fighting 18th Georgia attached to Hood's famed Texas Brigade, and had most recently led his brigade to victory at Chancellorsville.

In preparation for the assault, Semmes' four veteran Georgia regiments stood in neat lines behind Kershaw's South Carolinians and adjacent to Wofford's brigade behind Barksdale. Since McLaws did not file an official report on Gettysburg it can only be conjectured, but the order of his brigades may have been influenced by their respective casualties at Chancellorsville. Wofford's and Semmes' men had suffered more in dead and wounded in that battle than Barksdale's and Kershaw's brigades, so for that reason may have been placed in support positions. Barksdale's losses in his solo defense of Marye's Heights during that campaign had lost largely in prisoners when Sedgwick's Corps overran the position, but not so heavily in killed and wounded.

Meanwhile, to the Mississippi Brigade's left stood the troops of General Cadmus Marcellus Wilcox's Alabama brigade of General Richard H. Anderson's Division, Ambrose Powell Hill's Third Corps.

Colonel Alexander summed up the tactical alignment among the Confederates as the attack got underway: "Each of our divisions formed a double line of battle. Two brigades in the front line & two in the rear. McLaws was on our left, & the middle of his line was opposite the Peach Orchard, where Sickles' line made a large obtuse angle back to his left. A wood enabled us here to come up within about 500 yards." This was in keeping with Longstreet's penchant for hard-hitting attacks, a technique he would perfect the following September at Chickamauga.[176] In contrast, to McLaws' left was Richard Anderson's division of A.P. Hill's Corps, which aligned its brigades in a long, single line, none of them having a supporting or follow-up unit at all.

While Barksdale's troops lay in line on the reserve slope amid the shade of Pitzer's Woods, the artillery duel between the Confederate guns along Seminary Ridge and the Peach Orchard's artillery raged. With four Union batteries of more than twenty guns defending the Peach Orchard proper, Colonel Alexander's concentration of firepower of more than 50 guns continued to hammer Sickles' lines in an effort to gain an advantage before the attack. In total, nine Federal batteries of the Third Corps and the Reserve Artillery, more than forty guns, bolstered the Peach Orchard sector, after additional Federal batteries, from the Fifth Corps and the Reserve, were rushed forward and unlimbered to counter the intense Rebel bombardment

Only age twenty-eight, Georgia-born Colonel Alexander described his tactical "long arm" objective before the Peach Orchard: "I had hoped, with my 54 guns & close range, to make it short, sharp, & decisive. At close ranges there was less inequality in our guns, & especially in our ammunition, & I thought that if ever I could overwhelm & crush them I would do it now. But they really surprised me, both with the number of guns they developed, & the way they stuck to them. I don't think there was ever in our war a hotter, harder, sharper artillery afternoon than this." The twenty-eight-year-old Alexander had been appointed on the field by "Old Pete" to command all of Longstreet's artillery over a more experienced, older officer, Colonel James Walton, whose ire was understandably raised in consequence. Alexander had done exceptionally well at both Fredericksburg and Chancellorsville, but the Gettysburg challenge was more formidable than anything he had yet experienced.[177]

Lee had originally hoped that Alexander's concentrated firepower would clear the way for a successful oblique attack up the Emmitsburg Road to strike the Union left flank. But the flank was no longer where he thought it was, if it ever was in the first place. The Union line had been designed to stretch all the way to the Round Tops, which overlooked the Emmitsburg Road, but now, thanks to Sickles, the flank was on the road itself, prepared and waiting for an attack. Thousands of veteran Third Corps soldiers were now solidly arrayed in lengthy defensive lines, withstanding the punishment delivered by Alexander's concentration of guns. Shells exploded in Sherfy's orchard, tearing off branches and thick, green leaves of the stately peach trees, but Sickles' tried veterans held firm under the pounding.[178]

Meanwhile, on the eastern fringe of Pitzer's Woods along the slope just before the ridge's crest, Barksdale's men took punishment of their own, because Union gunners out-shot their targets of Alexander's guns positioned before the brigade. Private John Saunders Henley, 17th Mississippi, described how the shells "tore the limbs off of the trees and plowed gaps through his men."[179] Positioned in the center of McLaws' line, along the ridge, and astride the Wheatfield Road, Alexander's fast-working guns continued to rake the Peach Orchard with a barrage of shot and shell, while the field pieces of Colonel Henry C. Cabell's artillery battalion, positioned along the ridge below the Wheatfield Road, bellowed in anger from McLaws' right. With the Rebel cannoneers working their guns rapidly amid the drifting low-lying clouds of sulfurous smoke, Alexander's "long arm" units suffered a steady attrition during the intensive artillery duel.

On high ground north of the Wheatfield Road, the four booming howitzers of Captain George V. Moody's Madison Light Artillery's blazed in anger before the 21st Mississippi, on the brigade's right. Manned by expert gunners, including French-speaking, dark-featured Creoles, these Pelican State cannon pounded the Peach Orchard with everything they had from their wooden ammunition chests. Moody himself was a lawyer from the picturesque community of Port Gibson, which Grant had captured on May 1, 1863, and had old scores to settle with the boys in blue.

With Rebel cannoneers falling fast to Union return fire, and two guns dismounted, Alexander was forced to find infantry volunteers to help man the guns. As he wrote, "I had to ask General Barksdale, whose brigade was lying down close behind in the wood, for help to handle the heavy 24-pounder howitzers of Moody's battery. He gave me permission to call for voulunteers, and in a minute I had eight good fellows, of whom, alas! We buried two that night, and sent to the hospital three others mortally or severely wounded." Among Barksdale's volunteers who stepped forward to serve the Louisiana guns were two young brothers from the 17th Mississippi. Moody was delighted to receive these strapping Mississippians, who could be depended upon.[180] A veteran member of the Buena Vista Rifles, Private John Saunders Henley, 17th Mississippi, described how the Union artillerymen "killed so many of our artillerymen that some of our infantrymen had to go and help them handle the guns."[181]

Alexander's cannon poured their fire into the Peach Orchard, blowing up trees, fences and unlucky defenders caught amid the storm of shot and shell. From south to north along the smooth ridge-line, Alexander's lengthy row of guns in the Mississippi Brigade's sector consisted of the fast-firing guns of Captain Parker's Virginia Battery, Captain Osmond B. Taylor's Virginia Battery, Moody's Louisiana Battery, and Lt. Brooks' South Carolina Artillery.[182]

Unlike in Chancellorsville's blinding forest, and reminiscent of the nightmarish artillery storm at Antietam, the Union artillery, manned by veteran gunners and capable young commanders, rose magnificently to the challenge. Colonel Alexander continued to be frustrated by the fact that his artillery concentration could not "crush that part of the enemy's line in a very short time, but the fight was longer and hotter than I expected." Instead, the Federal guns remained "in their usual full force and good practice" on the high ground before the Georgian, who gained a new respect for his counterparts in blue. "At last seeing that the enemy was in greater force than I had expected," he wrote, "I sent for my 8 reserve rifles, to put in the last ounce I could muster."[183]

Meanwhile, Longstreet made final preparations to hurl more troops forward. Hood's attack had stalled in the face of Union reinforcements, so that instead of readying the Federals for a knockout blow, Hood's men themselves needed help. Providing a signal for the assault to commence in McLaws' sector, the barking row of Confederate artillery on the right finally ceased firing. Kershaw's South Carolina Brigade stepped off, and though originally intended to strike Sickles' left flank at the southern end of the Peach Orchard salient, they now headed straight into the conflagration that had nearly swallowed Hood's men.

It was about 5:00 PM when, beneath their Palmetto state flags of silk, the veteran South Carolinians pushed east below the Peach Orchard salient, targeting a Union stronghold Kershaw called the "stony hill." However, his left flank was immediately assailed by a Federal gun line on his left, severely disrupting his attack. Long after the war Kershaw wrote: "When we were about the Emmitsburg Road, I heard Barksdale's drums beat the assembly and knew *then* that I should have no immediate support on my left, about to be squarely presented to the heavy force of infantry and artillery at and in rear of the Peach Orchard." This implication that Barksdale was slow to attack that afternoon has unfortunately influenced students of Gettysburg ever since. In fact, Barksdale had been appealing to both McLaws and Longstreet for permission to launch his men almost since arriving at Seminary Ridge. In his Official Report, written soon after the battle, Kershaw said that Barksdale "came up soon after, and cleared the orchard."

The delay in the Mississippi Brigade's attack was no fault of Barksdale, who had been "chafing" to launch his attack. McLaws remembered that "Barksdale had been exceedingly impatient for the order to advance, and his enthusiasm was shared in by his command."[184] He was eager to strike a blow, knowing that so much delay allowed the Yankees time to strengthen the Peach Orchard sector while reducing his chances for success. Unlike Longstreet, who remained hesitant today to embark upon the tactical offensive, Barksdale and his top lieutenant, Colonel Humphreys, were eager for the charge, sensing the opportunity that lay before them. Both of these officers were "straining at the leash" and confident that they could take the position in front of them. To add to their chagrin, the neighboring brigades to their right were already engaged in full-scale battle while the Mississippians were simply forced to remain stationary under artillery fire. With his battlefield instincts rising to the fore, an optimistic Barksdale "sensed victory" on this late afternoon.

Barksdale now had his 1,600 soldiers ready for their greatest challenge to date. All the while the Mississippi troops laid low to escape the incessant hammering that resulted from Union artillery overshooting their targets in attempting in vain to knock out Alexander's artillery. Union artillery sent shells flying through the belt of woods, though without causing any panic in Barksdale's gray and butternut ranks. But all the while, the Mississippians' casualty lists lengthened as the bombardment grew in severity during this nerve-wracking experience. For what seemed like an eternity to them, the troops, in Colonel Humphrey's words, continued to be "subjected to a terrific cannonading" from the angry Union guns.

The heightened tension and eagerness to strike among Barksdale's troops steadily mounted, especially after a shell exploded in the midst of Company F (Tallahatchie Rifles), 21st Mississippi. The explosion sent unfortunate soldiers flying in every direction, and iron fragments tore through the legs and thighs of Captain H.H. Simmons and Privates John T. Neely and John H. Thompson. Other dependable men went down in the explosion, including J.T. Worley, one of seven family members in the ranks, who was killed. Especially when unable to strike back at the Yankees, the pent-up rage among the simmering Mississippians gradually increased, while the bombardment continued unabated. And only Barksdale's ordering the charge would now release it.

Raising his anger and sense of frustration because of the long delay in receiving orders to attack, Barksdale witnessed the bloody carnage which tore through Company F's ranks, but yet spared the Benton brothers who remained close together. The white-haired general in gray became even more determined not to have his boys killed for nothing, especially without striking back at the blazing Union cannon, especially Bucklyn's Rhode Island guns that were causing so much damage. Upset at the useless loss of life among his boys without being allowed to do anything about it was too much for Barksdale to bear. He realized that the brutal punishment being delivered from the Union artillery could only be stopped if he took those lethal guns around the Sherfy House and barn himself. Barksdale's pent-up anger would soon play a role in fueling one of the great infantry assaults of the war.

Ohio-born Lieutenant William Miller. Owen, a promising Washington Artillery officer and graduate of Gambier Military Academy, described how the Mississippians under Barksdale's command "were as eager as their leader, and those in the front line began to pull down a fence behind which they were lying. "Don't do that, or you will draw the enemy's fire," barked Longstreet. At this time, "Old Pete" was yet hesitant to order Barksdale forward because he hoped that Hood's attacks on Meade's left flank would draw reinforcements from the Peach Orchard sector.

Anchoring the Mississippi Brigade's right was the ever-reliable Colonel Humphreys and his 21st Mississippi, the brigade's elite regiment. Humphreys' right was aligned next to the Wheatfield Road, which meant, appropriately for the hard fighting that lay ahead, this crack regiment was aligned more directly before the salient angle of the Peach Orchard than any other in the brigade. On this day the 21st Mississippi, numbering about 424 men, would achieve the most remarkable gains of any of Barksdale's regiments, and perhaps of any other regiment on the field, Confederate or Union. Barksdale's largest regiment was the 13th Mississippi, with 481 men, followed by the 17th Mississippi with 468, and then the 18th Mississippi, which mustered only 242 for the battle.[vii]

Under B.G. Humphreys, the 21st Mississippi was the best led and most dependable regiment of Barksdale's Brigade, with its fighting spirit demonstrated on one battlefield after another. In his diary on April 13, 1863, Private Joseph A. Miller, bestowed an indirect compliment to the 21st Mississippi's feisty qualities even off the battlefield: "There was a considerable row in the brigade [when] some of the 21st were playing ball, which was against orders on Sunday. The provost guard undertook to stop it and I supose [sic] was rather too harsh, which caused the 21st to resist the guard [until they] had to call out the whole force of the guard [but not before] a good [many] weapons were drawn, but no blood spilt."[185] The rebellious leaders were thrown into the guardhouse. However, somewhat ominously, Private Miller noted the lingering animosity that existed between the 21st and the 17th Mississippi. He scribbled in his diary how afterward, the soldiers of the "21st have been consoling themselves with breathing out threatenings against the guard today, but I hope we shall heare [sic] nothing" of another clash.[186] Clearly, the ever-combative 21st Mississippi soldiers were almost as eager to fight fellow Mississippi Rebels as the Yankees.

Now on this day at Gettysburg, young Captain Middleton of the 17th Mississippi, the unfortunate provost marshal who had become the focal point of the 21st Mississippi's wrath, now stood before his line of Panola County soldiers on this hot afternoon, perhaps yet holding a grudge against the 21st Mississippi boys for that April 12 melee. If so, any lingering animosity he harbored was about to finally come to an end, because he soon received his death stroke in the upcoming attack and would never see his beloved Batesville, Mississippi, again.[187]

Indeed, fierce regimental pride, and thus competition, had long existed between the Mississippi Brigade's regiments. During the previous winter this rivalry had played out in hard-fought snowball battles, in which maneuvering and attacks helped to fine-tune the Mississippi troops for July 2. In his diary, Private Miller described one such clash that surged back and forth over the snowy fields outside Fredericksburg on February 25, 1863: "The boys had another big fight to day with the 21st regt snowballing [and] they fought about two hours, when the 17th come off victories [sic] again."[188] Indeed, the 17th Mississippi was larger than the 21st Mississippi, which was a regiment long familiar with overcoming the odds.[189] Now with Barksdale's men sweating amid the searing afternoon heat and humidity of summer, the February snows seemed almost like a century ago to the boys in the ranks. Perhaps a few Magnolia State soldiers now realized that those sweeping mock battles in the snow had been part of a conditioning process that would assist them in reaping success on this most decisive of afternoons.[190]

While the Mississippi Brigade remained in position among the tall trees of the eastern edge of Pitzer's Woods along Seminary Ridge's southern end, Warfield Ridge, the sight before Barksdale was awe-inspiring. Under the heavy bombardment, Private McNeily described how the 21st Mississippi lay "under the crown of a low ridge, five or six hundred yards distant from the position of assault [and] open fields, fences and scattered farm houses lay between [while] parallel with our line, and at the base of the Peach Orchard hill, ran the Emmitsburg road, between two high rail fences [and] farther to the left a picket fence lay beyond the road."[191] With a gift for understatement, Private John Saunders Henley, 17th Mississippi, marveled how the "Federals were strongly posted."[192]

Even though Hood's Division, attempting to turn Meade's left flank, had initiated Longstreet's assault around 4:00 PM , the Mississippi soldiers yet remained idle for what seemed like an eternity, while the savage contest roared to the southeast at Little Round Top and the most eerie-looking spot on the Gettysburg battlefield, the Devil's Den. For an agonizing hour and a half thereafter, Barksdale's men listened to the crackling musketry of the escalating battle. Like a wildfire raging out-of-control, the slaughter flowed slowly north east and began to crisscross the twenty-acre Wheatfield sector. Here, Kershaw's South Carolina troops ran into trouble in meeting stiff opposition, and were dutifully followed it into by Semmes' Brigade, while the ever-intensifying fight raged to higher levels from right to left. As Private McNeily, 21st Mississippi, described the struggle, "The noise of battle, when Hood's division opened the fight, was heard far to our right soon after 4 o'clock [and] the resistance was most obstinate, and the wave of attack was longer in reaching us than calculated."

The Mississippians' gear included Yankee and new Confederate knapsacks (including more than 100 new ones issued to the 21st Mississippi soldiers on April 28), haversacks, mess gear, and blankets. But by this time, this cumbersome gear had been piled behind the lines in Pitzer's Woods to lessen each soldier's load for the upcoming the attack. "Well shod and efficiently clothed," Barksdale's men wore over their gray jackets, with brass Mississippi buttons, leather cartridge-boxes and wooden and tin canteens, which they needed on this scorching day, if the attack was to be continued all the way to Cemetery Ridge as planned. Mississippi canteens had been recently filled with cold creek water from Pitzer's Run or the spring that flowed north from the Sherfy House, just before they ascended the relatively steep, timbered western slope of Seminary Ridge.

Taken from the vanquished enemy on hard-fought fields in Virginia and Maryland were some of the Mississippians' favorite weapons, especially Springfield rifles. Well-known for their superior marksmanship, Barksdale's hardened veterans were experts at using rifled muskets with deadly affect. One Northerner who had felt the Mississippians' wrath wrote how these Rebels "from Mississippi . . . were more vicious and defiant" than other Army of Northern Virginia troops.[193] In addition, Barksdale's veterans wore all manner of headgear, both civilian, especially wide-brimmed slouch hats, and military, including "jaunty kepis of gray and blue." Private James J. Lampton, Company K (Columbus Riflemen), 13th Mississippi, wore a low-crowned straw hat that was relatively light and cool on hot days like July 2. Armed with an array of .577 Enfield rifles, sturdy, dependable weapons imported from England, captured .58 caliber Springfields, and .58 caliber "Richmond Rifles," these Mississippi Rebels were ready for action with well-balanced weapons so clean that they now shined brightly under the July sunlight.[194]

Most of all, and as penned by Private Ezekiel Armstrong, of the Magnolia Guards, 17th Mississippi, in his diary, the Mississippi Brigade's soldiers were now "determined to lay my life on the altar of my country or see her free."[195] Destined not to live to see his twenty-second birthday, Private Armstrong's words were not hyperbole.[196] And thirty-two-year Lieutenant Marcus D. Lafayette Stephens, a respected physician from

Sarepta in Calhoun County, emphasized how the all-consuming goal of the 17th Mississippi men was now "to set our country free."[197] And now as never before, the upcoming assault held that golden promise, if the attack could be continued all the way to Cemetery Ridge.

Some of Barksdale's men, however, began to sense that they personally would not get that far. On the Mississippi Brigade's right flank, Captain Isaac Davis Stamps was wrapped up in his own ominous thoughts. Commanding Company E, the Hurricande Rifles, of the 21st Mississippi, Captain Stamps was haunted by a dark premonition that now nagged at the fiber of his being, He was thoroughly convinced that he was going to be killed in the forthcoming assault. Nevertheless, the revered captain was bound by a deep, biding obligation to lead his troops in what he knew was to be his final attack. After all, his revered uncle, Jefferson Davis, now sat in the Confederate White House in Richmond. His mother, Lucinda, was the sister of the president, who possessed only the fondest of memories of her. And the handsome captain's father-in-law was Colonel Humphreys. Appropriately, Captain Stamps now served as one of Humphreys' top lieutenants, and his heavy burden of military, family, and moral obligations was heavy, weighing on his mind and soul.[198]

Carrying the same ornate saber that Jefferson Davis had carried at Buena Vista to win glory in Mexico in February 1847, Captain Stamps was correct in his premonition. He would not survive the upcoming attack nor see his wife, Mary Humphreys, who he had married in 1854, his two little girls, or his beloved Rosemont Plantation again. On his last furlough home, Captain Stamps had made his wife Mary, age twenty-six, promise to retrieve his body (especially from northern soil) and return it to Mississippi should he fall. Perhaps by way of a battlefield death, Captain Stamps had reconciled himself to the bliss of eventually rejoining his two deceased children, including Sallie who died in the spring 1862, when he was far from home battling for his country. To Captain Stamps' great relief, Mary had promised to have his body returned to the family's burial plot at Rosemont to be buried by Sallie's side, when killed in battle. Stamps was now peacefully resigned to his tragic fate.[199]

Private Archibald Y. Duke, of Company C, the Quitman Grays, 17th Mississippi, likewise was consumed with a dark premonition just before the attack. Consequently, he turned to his brother, Private James W. Duke, who everyone called Jim, and made a request that he had never made before. With uncharacteristic seriousness, Archy asked his brother to be sure to write a letter home after the upcoming battle. But it was not Jim's turn to write, his brother protested. Then Archibald explained with firm conviction: "Something is going to happen to-day."[200] Indeed, Private Archibald Duke, who had silently prayed that God would take him at Gettysburg instead of his brother, was about to receive a severe leg wound, which would become gangrenous and take his life.[201]

Nevertheless, despite forebodings, the Mississippians' fighting spirit today was early evident. Riding atop a bouncing Louisiana caisson that kicked up a trail of dust, Captain Charles W. Squires, Washington Artillery, was hailed by Lieutenant Colonel John Calvin Fiser, 17th Mississippi. Fiser, one of the most respected Mississippi Brigade officers, yelled out that "he would soon have some guns for me to replace those lost on Marye's Hill," during the so-called second battle of Fredericksburg in early May 1863, when the Mississippi Brigade had supported the Washington Artillery.[202] Private Dinkins, 18th Mississippi, described how Fiser "filled to a high degree the most exalted idea of a dashing cavalier, and proud as a knight of the crusades. We have seen him at the head of his regiment, on that light bay. His face would be radiant. He was always looking out for his men. He was the same courtly, elegant gentleman under fire that he was in camp, or on the march."[203]

Lieutenant Owen of the Washington Artillery described a moment when Barksdale suddenly rode up to him and yelled, "I hope we will have better luck this time with your guns than we had on Marye's Hill," where the battery position had been overrun by the overwhelming might of Sedgwick's Sixth Corps. Meanwhile, the artillery duel raged with an intensity not seen by the Mississippi Rebels since Fredericksburg. Private McNeily described how the fierce artillery exchanges resulted in "a din that was deafening [and] as fast as the gunners could load they concentrated a fire on the Peach Orchard, which must have been destructive and demoralizing."[204]

Unfortunately for the Mississippi Brigade, however, the Confederate bombardment was relatively ineffective. Thanks to the height of the Emmitsburg Road Ridge, General Hunt had correctly visualized how Union troops positioned in prone positions behind the crest would be protected from even the most intense artillery bombardment. A 57th Pennsylvania Volunteer Infantry soldier described how "our regiment was lying in a field a few rods in the rear of the Sherfy house, which stood on the opposite side of the road. The 105th Pennsylvania was on our right, and the 114th on our left. For two hours we lay here under the hottest fire of artillery we had yet been subjected to. The enemy had some thirty pieces of artillery planted on the ridge to the south and west of us, hurling their missiles toward us as fast as they could work their guns. Fortunately most of them were aimed too high to do us injury . . . ."[205]

All the while, the Mississippi officers and men grew increasingly anxious to attack, despite the Peach Orchard's formidable appearance. Barksdale's veterans knew that they were in for serious fighting today, realizing that high casualties were inevitable. With sharpened socket bayonets and clean, well-maintained muskets, the Mississippians remained under their relatively slight cover of the hardwood timber and reverse slope, knowing that there was about to be a good many more widows and orphans across the Magnolia State.

Meanwhile, with the long delay in launching the attack, the tension in the Mississippi Brigade's increased to the breaking point. A sharp increase in Union activity before the Mississippians' position seemed to indicate that the Federals were even considering a pre-emptive blow. Already, an advancing lengthy line of 63rd Pennsylvania skirmishers had swung off the high ground and onto the slope that led to slight bowl-like depression between Seminary Ridge and the Peach Orchard. Moving with crisp precision and mechanical-like ease that indicated that these men were veterans, the Pennsylvania skirmishers began to bang away in the stifling heat. Under the searing sun, the Yankee skirmishers busily loaded and fired, sending bullets through the fast-working Louisiana artillery crews of Captain Moody. Minie balls then continued on to zip over the prone Mississippians, while other lead balls struck trees and limbs with sharp cracks.

As the line of Yankee skirmishers advanced through the open fields, the ever-aggressive Barksdale became even more convinced that the best defense now called for a good offense. For all that he knew, the entire Third Corps was now preparing to pour off the dominant high ground of the Peach Orchard in an attempt to outflank the left of Hood's Division to the southeast. If such an attack succeeded, then Lee's army, over-extended for nearly six miles in sprawling exterior lines around the Army of the Potomac, would be destroyed.

Champing at the bit and with the tension as well as his temper rising, Barksdale had repeatedly ridden up to his division commander and implored: "General, let me go; General, let me charge!" But McLaws had not yet received attack orders from Longstreet. After Barksdale had approached him more than once with the same request, McLaws finally informed the "fiery impetuous Mississippian" to just be patient.

When his corps commander passed near the Mississippi Brigade, Barksdale confronted Longstreet. He begged for the opportunity to strike while the Third Corps' position remained vulnerable: "I wish you would let me go in, General and I will take that battery in five minutes." No doubt amused by the impetuous nature of the gray-haired Mississippian who was overwhelmed by impatience and frustration, Longstreet merely replied, "Wait a little, we are all going in presently."[206]

In the meantime, Private McNeily of the 21st Mississippi, for one, was galled by the heavy bombardment, writing, "While waiting their turn, Barksdale's men lay low under the fire of artillery and infantry in their front, which they were not allowed to return for an hour or more. Where they were well covered the casualties were few; but where the line was exposed the punishment was severe. The severest of all tests on troops, to receive fire without returning it, was born unflinchingly. In total the brigade would lose 133 men (19 killed and 114 wounded) in Pitzer's Woods under the artillery fire before they had an opportunity to strike back. It but increased the impatience of Barksdale and his men to get the order to move on the offensive batteries."[207]

With a far-sighted vision which shortly paid the highest of tactical dividends on this most open of battlefields yet seen by the Mississippi Rebels, consequently, Barksdale made a number of decisions to ensure the chances for greater success. First, he ordered "a detail of ten men from each company [to draw] twenty rounds of extra cartridges for the bloody fray" that lay ahead. These extra rounds hurriedly gathered from the ordnance wagons in the rear now gave the Mississippians not the usual forty, but a total of sixty rounds in their leather cartridge-boxes. The brothers Archibald and James Duke were among those who secured the vital extra rounds, which would be much needed this afternoon, for their company in the 17th Mississippi.[208]

Barksdale also issued orders for his soldiers not to place percussion caps on the nipples of their rifles. He reasoned that this would ensure that his attackers would not be tempted to halt and return fire too early in the assault. Indeed, this wise tactic would allow the charging Mississippi Rebels to cross the open stretch of killing ground and up the western slope of the Emmitsburg Ridge Road at a faster pace. Such an early unleashing of return musketry would only slow the attack, while inflicting minimal damage on the high ground defenders. After having carefully calculated the terrain and tactics, Barksdale realized that even a few minutes of wasted time might spell the difference between success and failure.

In addition, Barksdale ordered his officers, except regimental commanders (who needed to be mounted to lead their troops) and staff officers (who needed horses to communicate orders), not to go into the assault mounted as usual, but on foot. Veteran soldiers in blue, including advanced skirmishers, made sport out of shooting Rebel officers off their horses. Barksdale wanted to save as many officers' lives as possible, enhancing the chances of a successful attack. Personally, Barksdale planned to serve as an inspirational beacon while mounted, upon which the eyes of his men could follow during the attack. He would lead the assault across the open ground by example and for all to see. But, of course, this was a deliberate calculation that might have cost Barksdale his life.

So as not to slow the attack, Barksdale had already ordered his soldiers to remove excess equipment. One 18th Mississippi officer recorded how "the order was given to 'strip for the fight'. The men carried their scanty change of clothing wrapped in their blankets and thrown over their shoulders; each regiment piled these in a heap" behind the lines. Haversacks, blanket rolls, and mess gear now lay in neat piles, almost as if these young soldiers expected everyone to return from the attack unscathed. But tragically, nearly half of these men never reclaimed their belongings, including the precious ambrotypes and daguerreotypes of wives, children, sisters, and other family members.

Barksdale also issued orders to his soldiers, once unleashed upon his orders, to advance "in closed ranks." Clearly, reaching the high ground would now largely depend upon the Mississippians' discipline and the speed of their advance. Barksdale had also ordered a lengthy picket fence to be torn down before the brigade. Of course, all of these timely measures were initiated so that his troops would cross the open fields as rapidly as possible to minimize losses. If success was to be won on this afternoon, then the Mississippi Brigade must gain the Emmitsburg Road Ridge in relatively good shape for any hope of continuing farther east to Cemetery Ridge to reap far greater gains before nightfall. With a clear tactical vision of what it would take to win a decisive victory today and quite unlike either a reluctant Longstreet or McLaws, Barksdale orchestrated a well-thought-out scenario to enhance the chances for success in what other commanders might have seen as a hopeless situation.

All the while, the Mississippi soldiers listened patiently to the roaring gunfire of the battle that gradually grew louder, rolling like thunder from south to north. To the Mississippians, this escalating gun-fire told them of the continuance of Confederate attacks en echelon all along the line to their right, and that they were meeting stiff resistance from the boys in blue.

Thanks to veterans' instincts, Barksdale's seasoned warriors from the Magnolia State knew that the time to go forward was finally nearing. This intuitive sense was only additionally confirmed when they saw Barksdale meeting with his regimental commanders to give last-minute instructions. With the attack imminent, Barksdale continued to lay forth his tactical ideas and last minute instructions to his regimental officers, Colonel Carter of the 13th Mississippi, Colonel Holder, 17th Mississippi, Colonel Griffin, 18th Mississippi, and Colonel Humphreys of the 21st Mississippi. For the upcoming attack to succeed, there could be no errors, confusion, misunderstanding or miscommunication to sabotage prospects for a successful assault. Solemnly and with firmness, the former Mississippi Congressman informed his direct subordinates of the hard work that lay ahead, articulating his plans for the coming attack. Barksdale then pointed to the lengthy rows of cannon and formations of blue along the crest of the Emmitsburg Ridge and on the high ground of the Peach Orchard. In a stern voice, he emphasized, "The line before you must be broken—to do so let every and man animate his comrades by his personal presence in the front line."[209]

James Longstreet recalled how his Mississippi brigadier was yet "chafing in his wait for orders to seize the battery in his front." Barksdale's "thirst for glory was as sharp in Pennsylvania as it had been on his great day at Fredericksburg, where Lee to his delight had let him challenge the whole Yankee army," summarized historian Shelby Foote. But his motivations ran much deeper. As so often in the past, Barksdale and his troops were determined to demonstrate to Lee and the Army of Northern Virginia exactly what this crack Mississippi Brigade was capable of accomplishing. Indeed, "never was a body of soldiers fuller of the spirit of fight, and the confidence of victory," wrote Private McNeily, 21st Mississippi.[210]

Meanwhile, the roar of the Confederate artillery pieces finally ceased echoing over sun-baked Seminary Ridge, and in the day's intense heat without a wind to blow it away, the thick, white clouds of smoke lingered low over the field. The powder-grimed, sweating Rebel artillerymen of Alexander's battalion rested in exhaustion beside their smoking guns, after what they hoped had been a job well done to assist Barksdale's infantrymen in their assault. The sudden, haunting silence said everything to the Mississippi Rebels. About to charge into the teeth of the formidable Peach Orchard salient, Private McNeily and his 21st Mississippi comrades, on the brigade's right flank, now realized that when "the order was given by the battery commanders to cease firing, every man in the brigade knew that 'our turn' had come at last."[211]

At long last, the great wreaths of sulfurous smoke, whitish and thick as an early morning fog, began to slowly rise higher into the clear, hot sky. To Barksdale's Deep South soldiers, the sudden unveiling of the curtain revealed the rows of bronze barrels of multiple Union batteries, sites aimed at the open ground in front of them, and the lengthy lines of bayonets of one veteran Union regiment after another along the high ground. All of this formidable might was just waiting for Barksdale's men.

Meanwhile, Barksdale made final preparations to lead his troops into hell itself. Ironically, one of the best descriptions of Barksdale's physical appearance at Gettysburg came from a Federal surgeon who wrote how the Mississippi general was "large, corpulent, refined in appearance, bold, and his general physical and mental make up indicated firmness, endurance, vigor [and] quick perception . . ." At this time, Barksdale was not dressed in a fine, double-breasted gray uniform coat like most of Lee's generals, such as Semmes who wore a resplendent uniform for all to see. Not surprisingly, Semmes was mortally wounded in the open fields of the John W. Rose farm, southeast of the Peach Orchard, paying a high price for his pride.

Instead of committing the folly of making himself a much too conspicuous target and symbolically in a display that revealed a close identification with his men, Barksdale was now "dressed in the jeans of [the Mississippians'] choice [and] his short roundabout was trimmed on the sleeves with gold braid. The Mississippi button, with a star in the center, closed it. The collar had three stars on each side next [to] the chin [and he wore under his uniform coat] a fine linen or cotton shirt which was closed by three studs bearing Masonic emblems. His pants had two stripes of gold braid, half an inch broad, down each leg." The 13th Mississippi's capable adjutant, E.P. Harman, described how "Gen'l. Barksdale was dressed in a Confederate gray uniform and wore a soft black felt hat [and] rode a bay horse." Especially when mounted and despite his less than stellar horsemanship in a cavalier-inspired army known for its superior riders, Barksdale presented an inspiring appearance on the battlefield. Like their popular commander, the Mississippi soldiers of all ranks wore the dirty, dust-covered, and grease-stained jean uniforms, which were either dyed gray or butternut.[212]

On his finest day and one that was very nearly his last, Colonel Humphreys, Barksdale's dependable "right arm," likewise wore a denim uniform of plain brown wool. The colonel's uniform coat was double-breasted, with the three gold stars of a full Confederate colonel stitched on his collar. Like Barksdale's homespun apparel today, Humphreys' uniform possessed a distinct symbolism that indicated the close camaraderie and team spirit the existed between officers and enlisted men. The uniform had been presented to him by an aid society of patriotic Southern women from Woodville, Mississippi, during a solemn ceremony.

McLaws described Barksdale, his most aggressive lieutenant, as "the fiery, impetuous Mississippian" upon whom he could rely. Private Mc-Neily also recalled Barksdale's inspiring presence at this time, when superior leadership was never more important or timely: "General Barksdale was a large, rather heavily built man of a blond complexion, with thin light hair. He was not a graceful horseman, though his forward, impetuous bearing, especially in battle, overshadowed and more than made up for such deficiencies. He had a very thirst for battlefield glory, to lead his brigade in the charge [and] as this was destined to be my last sight of him, impressions of his appearance are indelible. Stamped on his face, and in his bearing, as he rode by, was determination 'to do or die'."[213]

After Confederate artillery ceased roaring, Lieutenant Owen, Washington Artillery, described the moment when the dignified Barksdale now "called for his horse, mounted, and dashed to the front" in a swirl of dust. Meanwhile, Mississippi drummer boys furiously beat their instruments. The pounding of the drums were those heard by General Kershaw and his South Carolina boys as they advanced around 300–400 yards to the southeast. With everyone now standing in their assigned place in line before a lengthy stone wall that ran between Pitzer's Woods and the open fields, Barksdale ordered his men to fix bayonets. The metallic ringing of hundreds of bayonets being attached to muskets echoed over the green fields and pastures bathed in bright sunlight, clanging louder than the pounding drums.[214]

One of Barkdale's young aides, who remained mounted, recalled that the Mississippi general's face was "radiant with joy," just before being unleashed, despite facing his greatest challenge to date. In the words of nephew, Captain Harris Barksdale, "the time had come when Mississippians must try their hand." Like a warrior-prophet from the pages of the Old Testament, Barksdale was confident of success in part because "he was proud of his men, and never doubted them," wrote Private Dinkins of the 18th Mississippi.[215]

In a position to reverse the war's course if successful, the young men and boys in the Mississippi Brigade ranks sensed the golden opportunity presented by the Peach Orchard salient's vulnerabilities. Most of all, these hardened veterans knew that a good many Mississippi Brigade members would die before the sunset of July 2. Because most of Barksdale's men were zealous "Christian soldiers of the grandest type," wrote Private Dinkins, 18th Mississippi, they now prayed silently to themselves, asking for God's mercy, before moving forward into the vortex of hell itself. And these elite fighting men from across Mississippi made sure that Holy Bibles were securely-placed in breast pockets for physical and spiritual protection.[216]

After finally getting word from Longstreet, McLaws belatedly dispatched his able aide-de-camp from one of Georgia's leading families, Captain Gazaway Bugg Lamar, Jr., to order Barksdale to launch his long-awaited assault on the Peach Orchard. Dashing rapidly over the open fields, Captain Lamar rode a fine horse, which had cost him $500 in Confederate money earlier in the year. Here, before the shell-torn Pitzer's Woods and the Mississippi Brigade's ranks that stretched for several hundred yards from north to south, Captain Lamar galloped up to Barksdale, who was mounted before the 13th Mississippi, his own former regiment that he had first led into battle at First Manassas. Here, on the left-center of the Mississippi Brigade's line, Captain Lamar recalled how "anxious General Barksdale was to attack the enemy, and his eagerness was participated in by all of his officers and men, and when I carried the order to advance, his face was radiant with joy. He was in front of his brigade, his hat off, and his long white hair reminded me of 'the white plume of Navarre'."

Barksdale barked out for his troops of all four regiments to advance simultaneously over the stone wall in their front at the eastern edge of Pitzer's Woods. Without the usual clattering of gear and accouterments that had been piled behind them, the Mississippi Rebels climbed over the wall that ran along the eastern edge of the timber. With the almost unbearable tension of waiting having broken, they passed out of Pitzer's Woods and into the bright sunlight of the open field.

As usual Barksdale took center stage before his elite brigade as one of the most stirring dramas of Gettysburg was about to unfold. One Mississippian long remembered "General Barksdale's appearance, riding rapidly along in rear of the line, was the signal to the respective regimental commanders to get alert." Barksdale galloped a short distance south from the 13th Mississippi's front to the brigade's center. With all eyes focused on him, Barksdale drew his saber, simply disregarding the obvious fact that he was thus about to become the most prominent target in the assault.

In a booming voice Barksdale yelled for all to hear: "The entrenchment 500 yards in front of you, and that Red Barn and that park of artillery [must be taken and] there is another 200 yards beyond which we are also expected to take. This is a heroic undertaking and most of us will bite the dust making this effort. Now if there is a man here that feels this is too much for you, just step two paces to the front and I will excuse him." No man stepped forward from the double ranks of gray and butternut.

Within the next couple of hours, the Civil War could be decided once and for all by the upcoming clash at the Peach Orchard and in the open fields beyond that stretched toward Cemetery Ridge. As the culminating blow in Longstreet's offensive against the Union left, it was Barksdale's charge more than any other that would reap the fruits of victory, or else signal the failure of Confederate strategy. Never again would the Army of Northern Virginia meet the Army of Potomac on such equal terms, in an open-field battle on Northern soil, where the impact of a decisive victory for the South could decide the entire war. Much now depended on Barksdale and his men, and they were eager to meet the challenge.

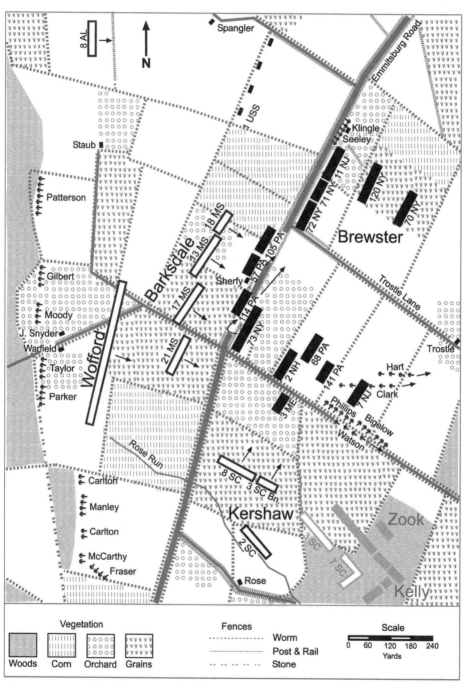

Map courtesy of Bradley M. Gottfried

⌒ 5 ⌒

"The grandest charge ever seen by mortal man!"

LIKE BARKSDALE'S MEN, the Union soldiers holding the Peach Orchard salient had listened to the swelling tumult of battle approaching from the south. They knew their turn was coming, and as a long line of Confederates stepped out of the woods to their direct front they realized it was at hand. The men holding the salient were the First Brigade of the First Division, Third Corps, under Brigadier General Charles Graham. They were six regiments of Pennsylvania troops, who for the first time in the war were defending their home state instead of trying to invade another below the Mason-Dixon Line. Never more highly motivated than today, they yet had no way of knowing that their opponents, now in sight, were the Army of Northern Virginia's Mississippi Brigade, men whose own home state was just then likewise being invaded, by Grant, in this most tragic and costly of American wars.

The Pennsylvania boys gave quick final checks to their rifles, then leveled them against the assembling Rebel host, still some 600 yards away. To fire too soon would be wasting a shot, then having to reload while the onslaught was nearly upon them. Fingers tensed on triggers and eyes squinted at the tree line as officers stalked up and down demanding, against natural instinct, for the men to hold their fire until ordered. Artillerists, who heretofore had been firing shell, now piled up their supplies of canister to fire like gigantic buckshot against oncoming infantry.

On the other side, at the fringe of Pitzer's Woods, and before his lengthy formations of veterans standing at attention and not moving a muscle, "General Barksdale gave the word, and, waving his hat, led the line forward himself and we all followed him," recalled one Confederate who never forgot the moment. As the heightened tension seemed about

95

to burst, sharp orders rang out to "dress to the colors and forward to the foe!" With more determination to reap a decisive victory than ever before, some 1,600 men of the Mississippi Brigade surged ahead in two lengthy, parallel lines that stretched across the bright green field. To encourage his troops onward over the open ground and down the gentle eastern slope of Seminary Ridge, Barksdale continued to shout and wave his saber, imploring "Forward, men, forward!"

Captain Harris Barksdale, diminutive but every-inch a fighter, never forgot the moment when "Gen. Barksdale rode to the center of his Brigade, and in a firm voice gave the command, 'Attention, Mississippians! Battalions Forward!' . . . and the line officers repeated the command 'Forward, March'." Along a 350-yard front spanning Seminary Ridge's eastern slope, Barksdale's assault waves surged across the open fields of summer with red battle-flags waving.

From the Emmitsburg Road Ridge, one bluecoat described how General "Barksdale and his Brigade had to pass over a mile of open field [sic] to get to us . . . while he was forming his men in line of battle, the missiles from the [artillery] plowed gaps through his men, yet in battle line they stood [and prepared] to traverse the mile of open field intervening [and] when our sharp-shooters and the pickets opened fire on [and] besides the mischief done by the sharp-shooters and pickets, the [artillery] was hurling missiles of death into ranks . . ." Watching in awe at the Mississippians' disciplined surge down Seminary Ridge, Longstreet remembered when his high-spirited Magnolia State brigadier went into action "with glorious bearing."[217] And an Alabama soldier never forgot how the stirring sight of the Mississippians' assault was "grand beyond description."[218]

To the steady thud of beating drums and the shrill of fifes played by young, beardless musicians in gray, no regiment advanced in Barksdale's long line with more firmness of step and resolution than the 21st Mississippi. On the brigade's right and serving as a steady anchor for Barksdale's assault, Colonel Humphreys described how, "the men sprang forward and sixteen hundred voices raised the famous 'Rebel yell' which told the next brigade, Wilcox's Alabamians, that the Mississippians were in motion."[219]

To the 21st Mississippi's left, Private Judge D. Woodruff, Winston Guards of the 13th Mississippi, described the panoramic, wide-open arena that lay before him: "The field was clover and a gradual slope up to where the Yankee lines and batteries were about six hundred yards away."[220] Meanwhile, Mississippi drummer boys, who should have been in school, continued to beat their drums in a steady cadence as if leading a Sunday parade in Jackson rather than into the maelstrom, until it seemed that their instruments would certainly burst. Archibald H. Christy, an eighteen-year-old from Holly Springs, of Company B, 17th Mississippi, was one such musician. Despite having already been wounded at First Manassas and at Fredericksburg, Christy was now advancing in the front ranks, even though he knew would receive the brunt of the Yankees' fire.[221]

By now the row of Federal guns, Bucklyn's lethal Rhode Island pieces and a section of Thompson's Pennsylvania Battery, that represented Pittsburgh, roared from the high ground along the Emmitsburg Road Ridge, hurling shells that smashed into the Mississippi Brigade's ranks. One Federal defender of the Peach Orchard described how the intense concentration of artillery fire "swept gaps through them all the way across the field, and when a solid shot tore a gap in their ranks, it was instantly closed up, and the Brigade came on in almost perfect line." Most of all, these Mississippi infantrymen felt the inspiration from what Barksdale had yelled to them just before he launched his winner-take-all attack upon the Peach Orchard: "We have never been whipped and we never can be."[222]

The expert Union gunners blasted away at the lines on the open ground that could hardly be missed. Private John Saunders Henley, 17th Mississippi, described how "all their artillery [was] firing on us [but] We went in perfect line. They would knock great gaps in our line."[223] Barksdale's neatly aligned formations pushed stolidly forward with a well-honed steadiness that told the Yankees on the high ground that hardened veterans from the South were descending upon them in a hurry. Keeping on the move, the Mississippi Rebels ignored the exploding shells that knocked down an ever-increasing number of comrades. Clearly, the dividends of Barksdale's longtime, seemingly obsessive focus on the importance of drill was now displayed in splendid fashion across the fields that stretched all the way to the Emmitsburg Road Ridge. Neither Union artillery fire nor the brisk firing of bluecoat skirmishers, banging away angrily and effectively, disrupted the flow of Barksdale's advance.

Most of all knowing that his troops had to reach the Emmitsburg Road Ridge as soon as possible to avoid being shot to pieces during a methodical, textbook-like advance, Barksdale ordered his men to double-quick when yet far from their objective. Unleashing the high-pitched

"Rebel Yell," to both "inspire and terrorize," the Mississippi soldiers raced on toward the smoke-wreathed Peach Orchard and Emmitsburg Road Ridge. Now finally unleashed with flashing bayonets that sparkled in the summer sunlight, the Mississippi soldiers neared the slight swale, located roughly halfway between Seminary Ridge and the Emmitsburg Road Ridge.

On the brigade's right, Private McNeily, 21st Mississippi, never forgot when Colonel Humphreys gave "the ringing command–'Double quick, Charge,' and at top speed, yelling at the tops of their voices, without firing a shot, the brigade sped swiftly across the field and literally rushed the goal [and] our men began to drop as soon as they came to attention, and were well peppered in covering the distance with the enemy." On the double, Barksdale's lines poured through the fields without breaking ranks, even when exploding shells blew holes in formations. All the while, the powder-grimed Confederate gunners cheered the Mississippians' attack by waving hats. These sweating artillerymen, shouting their lungs out, wanted Barksdale's boys to exact bloody revenge on those lethal Union cannon, which had outmatched the inferior Rebel guns. With battle-flags flapping, Barksdale's onrushing ranks neared the depression about mid-way between Seminary Ridge and the Emmitsburg Road.

The Mississippi veterans now felt a surge of new invigoration by having been finally "unleashed at last and eager to come to grips" with the Yankees. Leading the 21st Mississippi onward, Humphreys described how everyone "moved forward, amid the roar of cannon and the rattle of rifles [and] the work of death" was cruelly relentless to Barksdale's attackers.[224] In the 17th Mississippi's ranks, Private John Saunders Henley described the ever-escalating momentum that could not be stopped after the "regiment began to run" toward the high ground.[225]

Inspiring the soldiers onward in the first rank of gray and butternut waved the brightly colored battle-flags, while Barksdale's four regiments, the 18th, 13th, 17th, and 21st Mississippi, from left to right, surged onward. One emblem now flapping at the head of this charge was the silk banner of Company K, 18th Mississippi, which had been sewn by wives, daughters, mothers, and sisters of home communities. Presented to Company K by Miss Alice Hilzm, the Burt Rifles' battle-flag was decorated with a colorful painting of a full blooming Magnolia tree that represented their state. The Burt Rifles' banner contrasted with the standard Confederate battle-flags featuring a star-bedecked St. Andrews Cross.[226]

Due to tactical developments to the south, Barksdale's Brigade was charging alone, without connection to any units on its right, nor yet on its left. John Bell Hood's division, more fresh and ferocious on this day than most in the Army of Northern Virginia—for having missed Chancellorsville, much to its commander's dismay—had drawn upon itself the entire Union Fifth Corps, as well as a division of the Second Corps, in addition to the troops of the Third Corps it had first attacked. In addition, part of the division had been compelled to attack up the steep citadel of Little Round Top, over unspeakable terrain that broke up formations by itself. As Federal reinforcements piled into the sector, Kershaw's Brigade of McLaws' Division, followed by Semmes', had gone in to retrieve the situation. But by now the Union Sixth Corps had arrived on the field, also ready to resist the continued onslaught against the Federal left. As Hood had predicted, his attack could not succeed except at high cost. However, as Longstreet may have perceived, his initial assault had sucked in so much of Meade's strength on his far flank that an opportunity was now presented to make the true breakthrough at the Union left-center. Not by "attacking up the Emmitsburg Road," as Lee had mistakenly envisioned, but by striking due east, onto ground which by now had been denuded of troops save the forward array around the Peach Orchard. If that salient could be crushed, there was little behind it to prevent a breakthrough of the Federal line.

If one examines Longstreet's offensive actions throughout the war, it's clear that he always preferred the "one-two punch." The classic example is Second Manassas, when Stonewall Jackson held the Union army for over a day, then Longstreet delivered the knock-out blow. This technique was perfected at Chickamauga where Polk struck first, drawing in Union reinforcements, and then Longstreet launched a gigantic battering ram that obliterated Rosecrans' entire right wing. At the Wilderness the following spring, Longstreet arrived last on the field after Ewell and A.P. Hill had held off the Federals for a day, but then the arrival of his corps turned the tide completely, facing Grant with catastrophe in his first battle in the east, until Longstreet himself fell wounded and thus the Confederate effort dissipated.

At Gettysburg, Longstreet much rued the fact that the Confederate Second Corps was so far-flung that it could be of no help to him. In the new Third Corps he had little faith, and it had been largely used up on the first day of the fight, except for Anderson's Division, which had formerly been under his command and would now assist. He primarily had to devise a one-two punch with his own two divisions, but that is what he essentially did. Naturally he would have preferred Hood to drive in the enemy flank before he launched McLaws. However, if Hood only succeeded in drawing the weight of Union countermeasures on himself, Longstreet could wait, and wait longer, till he saw Meade was committed. Despite Barksdale's eagerness, he held back the Mississippi Brigade until he was certain that Meade had poured his available reinforcements into supporting his flank. Then he finally launched Barksdale against Meade's left-center. If Barksdale could only crack the Peach Orchard salient, there would be an opportunity to sever the Federals' entire left wing.

Meantime, Kershaw's South Carolinians had run into trouble during the minutes before Barksdale's launch. When Kershaw's left wing, below and within 300 yards of the southern edge of the Peach Orchard's salient angle, pushed northeast toward the Wheatfield Road sector, nearly perpendicular to Barksdale's impending advance, a row of Union cannon along the road raked Kershaw's left wing with blasts of canister, enfilading the South Carolina line. So deadly was the Federal artillery fire and so heavy were Kershaw's casualties that the left wing's advance, closest to Barksdale, was thwarted. Those South Carolina soldiers not killed or wounded fell to the ground to escape the artillery salvos, especially the murderous fire from the fast-working guns of the 9th Massachusetts Battery. The Palmetto Staters on the left were in a killing zone that reaped a grim harvest amid the ripe yellows stalks of the Wheatfield, while Kershaw's right continued to attack straight east against a hotly contested feature known as the Stony Hill.

Semmes was launched to support Kershaw, thus temporarily stabilizing that situation. Hood's four brigades still battled mightily, including in their Quixotic task of conquering Little Round Top. After the war the 15th Alabama's Colonel William Oates, foremost in the assault, said that even if the tired remnants of his infantry had succeeded in gaining the summit, they couldn't have held it anyway. Clearly, the hopes of the battle now rested with Barksdale, if he could only break through Sickles' forward salient.

All the while, Barksdale led his fast-moving troops ever-closer to the flaming Peach Orchard sector now clouded in the white haze of sulfurous smoke. Despite the lack of support to its left, right or rear, the Mississippi Brigade's attack was now, according to Noah Trudeau, "a living definition of unstoppable."[227] On through the open fields charged the Mississippians with the abandon so characteristic of elite troops in such a key situation. Around the halfway point between the two parallel ridges, the long waves of Mississippi Rebels neared the rail fence. From the ridge-top named after the Lutheran Theological Seminary, Captain Lamar, of McLaws' staff, watched the inspiring sight of Barksdale, who was leading his fast-moving Mississippians through the killing fields: "I saw him as far as the eye could follow, still ahead of his men, leading them on."[228] Before the Mississippi Brigade's advance, the wooden fence posed no impediment. Barksdale's formations packed a pent-up, natural force all of its own, after having seemingly gathered momentum with each yard passed by the surging ranks.

In the rush to reach the smoke-laced crest of the Emmitsburg Road Ridge, the Mississippi Rebels continued to push onward with the Rebel Yell and a determination to gain the high ground at any cost. A Union colonel from New England standing in the Emmitsburg Road sector swore that this "was the grandest charge that was ever seen by mortal man." Indeed, the Federal officer described with astonishment how, "nothing we could do with pickets, sharp-shooters or with cannon seemed to confuse or halt Barksdale's veterans . . . nothing daunted Barksdale and his men and nothing seemed to be in their way [for they] just came on, and on, and on . . ."[229]

Indeed, the initial blue line of skirmishers, which was almost dense enough to make Barksdale's men believe it was the first Yankee line of battle, was swept aside. Yelling louder with the exhilarating sight of the flight of so many Federals, the Mississippi veterans continued to run as fast as possible, while they closed in on the Emmitsburg Road Ridge with a renewed cheer.[230] Charging with the boys of Company A, the Buena Vista Rifles, Private John Saunders Henley described how 17th Mississippi soldiers surged ahead on the "run," after Barksdale gave the word.[231]

Before being brushed aside by Barksdale's furious onslaught, the line of 5th New Jersey and 63rd Pennsylvania skirmishers had initially fought back from behind the slight shelter of a fence, a few cedar trees and scattered underbrush around the small spring at the lowest point of the slight depression. As the Yankee skirmishers had discovered the hard way, Barksdale's countless drills month after month now paid dividends for the attacking Mississippians. A soldier recalled how, "the Magnolia State brigade sped swiftly across the field and literally rushed the goal" of the Peach Orchard, while pushing the hard-hit Federal skirmishers steadily before them as if by a giant broom.

Ignoring the hailstorm of shells and bullets dropping more good men from the ranks, the Mississippi Brigade continued to surge onward. Exploding shells wrought destruction among Barksdale's formations, but the gaps were quickly closed-up. Meanwhile, the swiftness of Mississippians' assault waves was an awe-inspiring sight not only to other Confederates but also to the Yankees. From the high ground, Sickles' men watched the iron discipline and near perfect alignment of onrushing Barksdale's soldiers. Private George Clark, a soldier of General Cadmus M. Wilcox's Alabama brigade to the Mississippi Brigade's left-rear, realized beyond a doubt that Barksdale's onslaught was "the most magnificent charge I witnessed during the war." And Captain Lamar, McLaws' faithful staff officer, described how, "I had witnessed many charges marked in every way by unflinching gallantry . . . but I never saw anything equal the dash and heroism of the Mississippians."

Captain Fitzgerald Ross, an "Austrian to the core" and an erudite observer with Lee's army, recorded how Barksdale's sweeping charge across the wide open fields "was a glorious sight [for the men] went in with a will . . . there was no lagging behind, no spraining of ankles on the uneven ground, no stopping to help a wounded comrade." Mounted on his reddish-colored charger and waving his saber amid the whizzing bullets and bursting shells, Barksdale was distinguishable to one and all by his shoulder-length, prematurely gray hair streaming over his shoulders. Barksdale also wore a bright red sash around his waist. One observer watched with a mixture of awe and admiration, estimating that Barksdale was now leading his screaming Mississippi troops some fifty yards before his surging ranks. Impressed by the martial spectacle, Lieutenant Owen of the Washington Artillery described how the Mississippians' attack "was a glorious sight."[232] Yet another fence and Yankee line of advanced skirmishers was swept away "like chaff before the wind."[233] Lamar could hardly believe his eyes, because "I was anxious to see how they would get over and around. When they reached it the fence disappeared as if by magic, and the slaughter on the other side was terrible."[234]

Meanwhile, the defenders of the Peach Orchard sector were not idle while the Mississippi Brigade surged toward them. Facing the Emmitsburg Road and in support behind Lieutenant John K. Bucklyn's Battery E, First Rhode Island Light Artillery, situated along the road just below the Abraham Trostle Lane, Graham's brigade was aligned in the open fields. Here, they made final preparations for meeting Barksdale's onslaught. During the nerve-wracking wait, Yankee soldiers said final prayers, recalled the lessons of bayonet practice, and braced for Barksdale's tempest. With lengthy ranks covering a broad front along the Emmitsburg Road, the 68th Pennsylvania anchored the left flank just south of the Wheatfield Road, the 104th Pennsylvania held the left-center amid an oat field, the 57th Pennsylvania stood on the right-center, and the 105th Pennsylvania, known as the Wildcat Regiment, was poised on the right flank, up to the Abraham Trostle Lane.[235]

After the Confederate artillery bombardment of two hours ceased, a flurry of adroit tactical adjustments were made by Graham to meet the Mississippians' assault.[236] On the double to confront the howling tide, fresh companies of skirmishers of the 57th Pennsylvania Volunteer Infantry advanced to the west side of the Emmitsburg Road to take possession of a better defensive position and higher terrain from which to deal punishment upon the onrushing Mississippians. On the double, a good many expert marksmen in blue also hurriedly filed into the Sherfy House, an ideal elevated shooting platform perched on commanding ground. Here, they took firing positions at the narrow windows—perfect firing slits—overlooking the open fields now filled with howling Mississippians. Situated atop a little knoll, the Sherfy House offered not only shelter from Barksdale's onslaught but also the most elevated spot to deliver punishment over a wide area.[237]

While rushing toward the Emmitsburg Road Ridge, the Mississippi Rebels felt that not only the battle's outcome but also the Confederacy's life depended upon them. By this time, the furious Confederate assaults to the south at Little Round Top, the Devil's Den, where one appalled Texas soldier described the bitter fighting that swirled savagely "around rocks as large as a meeting house," and the golden stalks of the body-covered Wheatfield of farmer George W. Rose, were meeting terrific resistance and sputtering from right to left. Despite Southern heroics and high sacrifices, all that was accomplished was a grim lengthening of casualty lists with each passing minute during what one horrified survivor called "a devil's carnival." The slaughter led to "Confusion [which] reigned supreme everywhere" on Lee's battered right.[238] William, "Bill," A. Fletcher, a proud member of Hood's hard-fighting Texas Brigade, lamented over so many "true and tired men being shot down like dogs."[239] Consequently, as Confederate fortunes continued to flounder to the south, it was increasingly up to the Mississippi Brigade to smash through the Peach Orchard sector and reap a decisive success for the Army of Northern Virginia.[240]

Meanwhile, Federal defenders continued to be impressed by the grand spectacle of the Mississippians' rush headlong into a murderous fire of Rhode Island and Pennsylvania artillery. The lithe and lean veterans kept surging ahead on the double without a pause. By this time, the Mississippi Rebels instinctively realized that their only chance for success called for getting across these broad, open fields of fire as rapidly as possible.[241] Atop the Second Corps sector of Cemetery Ridge to the northeast, Captain Haskell described the dramatic showdown for possession of the Peach Orchard: "We see the long gray lines come sweeping down upon Sickles' front . . .O, the din and the roar, and these thirty thousand [sic] Rebel wolf cries! What a hell is there down that valley!"[242]

Indeed, Barksdale's ranks promised to pack a mighty punch and inflict devastation on the defenders in a wide swath, if the ridge could be swiftly reached.[243] Barksdale's headlong attack, in the words of Private McNeily, 21st Mississippi, was most of all a "matchless 'rush to glory or the grave'."[244] Indeed, more than anything else, Barksdale's all-or-nothing charge was now in essence a desperate bid to reach the commanding high ground, before too many men were cut down and the attack's momentum was destroyed. In charging so swiftly up the gradually rising ground to the Emmitsburg Road Ridge, the Mississippi Rebels were in the process of fulfilling Barksdale's earlier bold promise to Longstreet that he could capture the most destructive Union battery—Lieutenant Bucklyn's six Rhode Island guns—in only five minutes once unleashed. Such a tactic was in keeping with Colonel Humphreys' conviction that his 21st Mississippi attackers were now "determined to break the line before them, or perish."[245]

All the while, Barksdale remained in advance of his troops, leading the way before his surging ranks of gray and butternut. Mounted for all to see, he continued to wave his saber, as unornate and relatively plain as his uniform, while encouraging his boys onward. The commanding figure of the forty-two-year-old Barksdale served as a shining "beacon for his brigade" during one of the greatest charges of the war.[246]

To escape the 21st Mississippi's onslaught upon the suddenly strategic Peach Orchard crossroads and salient angle, the 63rd Pennsylvania, which had screened Graham's over-extended front as skirmishes, continued to head rearward on the double, after having expended its ammunition in attempting to kill as many Mississippi Rebels as possible. Captain Harris Barksdale never forgot how his charging Mississippians "sweep the enemy's picket line before them like chaff before a whirlwind."[247]

Meanwhile, the sight of the onrushing Mississippi Brigade caused defenders to lament the absence of trenches, earthworks, or even piles of fence rails. In the words of one soldier of the 57th Volunteer Infantry, "Unlike the battlefields of Virginia where we usually fought in the woods or thickets, we were now on a field where we had an unobstructed view" of the field of strife.[248]

A hot fire, meanwhile, poured from the second floor windows of the Sherfy House, with sharp-eyed Yankees blasting away at Barksdale's attack lines on the open fields. Not only from the Sherfy House, 57th Pennsylvania skirmishers around the farm's outbuildings and trees also maintained a heavy "fire on the enemy who were within easy range."[249] However, Barksdale still resisted the temptation to halt the ranks to return fire by volley. Most of all, Barksdale knew that he had to get his troops across these open killing fields as quickly as possible. Like his comrades, therefore, a 57th Pennsylvania soldier was greatly surprised by the fact that the Mississippians "did not reply to our fire."[250]

The reliable veterans of Graham's 1,516-man brigade, with their plentiful artillery, held firm at the Peach Orchard salient and the high ground along the Emittsburg Ridge Road. The line bent at a right angle where it met the Wheatfield Road, where stood the 68th Pennsylvania under Colonel Andrew H. Tippin. No ordinary officer, Tippin was a revered hero of the Mexican War, having been the first American soldier to gain the Mexican defenses during the bloody assault at Molino de Rey outside Mexico City, on September 8, 1847. When Barksdale's attack began, the 68th Pennsylvania's was brought up to the Emmitsburg Road south of its junction with the Wheatfield Road, directly across from the Peach Orchard's rows of fruit trees. To meet Barksdale's onslaught, Graham's four veteran Pennsylvania regiments, bolstered by Bucklyn's Rhode Island guns and Thompson's section of Pennsylvania artillery, were aligned along the east side of the Emmitsburg Road, holding the strategic crest of the Emmitsburg Road Ridge. Belonging to General David Bell Birney's First Division of Sickles' Corps, these reliable Pennsylvanians proudly wore their red diamond corps badges on blue kepis with a jaunty air, feeling a great deal of pride in themselves and their hard-fighting units.

Bracing for the Mississippians' impact, the 57th Pennsylvania was led by a most capable commander. Colonel Peter Sides had demonstrated skill that had elevated him to lieutenant colonel from a captain's rank back in mid-September 1862. In the war's early days of innocence and

as if yet on the farm, these Pennsylvania men had called their commanding officer "Charley" instead of colonel. But now the 57th Pennsylvania
boys were tough, disciplined soldiers. Its Company K included a number
of Native Americans from the once-mighty Iroquois nation. Their names,
such as Levi Turkey Williams and Wooster King, reflected a distinctive
Native American culture that had failed to sufficiently distance them from
the ugly realities of the white man's civil war. These mostly Seneca warriors from New York's Allegheny Indian Reservation proved worthy of
their tribe's warrior heritage during Gettysburg's inferno.

Even after the 57th Pennsylvania's strength had been reduced by one-
fourth by the brutal ravages of bloody battles and epidemics of deadly
disease, the mettle of these high-spirited men was evident when they had
nearly mutinied upon receiving orders to consolidate with another unit.
Like Washington's Pennsylvania Line Continentals who mutinied in early
1781 and marched in protest on Philadelphia during America's struggle
for liberty, these boys in bue had threatened to march on Harrisburg
under arms in protest. Ironically, the 57th Pennsylvania's baptismal fire
had been received on the Virginia Peninsula at the "battle of the Peach
Orchard," at Williamsburg, Virginia. And as a strange fate would have
it, the 57th Pennsylvania had been positioned on the high ground at
Malvern Hill when the Mississippi Brigade attacked. Then, before the
year's end, the Keystone State regiment lost more than half of its strength,
including its regimental surgeon, during the suicidal attack on Fredericksburg's heights. And in early May 1863, another 30 percent casualties
were suffered by the 57th in Chancellorsville's dank woodlands, leaving
only a relatively small-sized regiment for the showdown at the Peach
Orchard.[251]

Nevertheless, Colonel Sides now led a well-disciplined regiment,
armed mostly with .54 caliber Austrian rifled muskets. Promising to give
Barksdale's men a tough fight, the 57th had won the hard-earned reputation for reliability. These hardy soldiers now defended the northern arm
of the Peach Orchard salient along the Emmitsburg Road around the
Sherfy House. They were yet motivated by an inspirational example that
was now part of their unit identity: their respected former commander,
General Philip Kearny, whose "pet" regiment was the 57th, who had
been killed at Chantilly, Virginia on September 1, 1862. Grieving 57th
Pennsylvania soldiers had served as the special honorary escort that took
the body of the revered Mexican-American War hero to Washington,
D.C.

The 57th Pennsylvania had been under fire from Colonel Alexander's artillery for two long hours. However, they had suffered relatively little damage. Consequently and despite having been initially positioned in the open fields on the Emmitsburg Ridge Road's east side without shelter during the intense cannonade, the 57th Pennsylvania troops were in overall good shape. Most Rebel shells had whizzed harmlessly over the prone Pennsylvanians to explode in the open fields behind them, destroying Farmer Sherfy's well-nurtured crops instead of Yankees. Federal infantry positioned near the targeted cannon suffered more than any others, but the overall damage inflicted on both infantry and artillery was insufficient. Even the 114th Pennsylvania, in support of Bucklyn's Rhode Island guns, was relatively unscathed from Alexander's bombardment.

Consequently, everything now depended on the Mississippi Brigade's fighting prowess to punch a hole through the Peach Orchard defensive sector by the standard tactics that had long ensured bloody failure in this war: a frontal assault with the bayonet launched against a high ground defensive position held by large numbers of veterans and artillery.[252] And defenders like the 57th Pennsylvania had earned the reputation as "men that won't run."[253]

To the 57th Pennsylvania's left and deployed along the Emmitsburg Road to protect the six guns of the First Rhode Island Artillery stood the 114th Pennsylvania. Bucklyn's six guns stood defiantly in the 150-yard open space of high ground situated between the Sherfy House and the John Wentz buildings just to the southeast and immediately north of the Wheatfield Road. While the battery's left and center sections blasted away from good high ground firing positions between the Wentz House and the Sherfy barn, the right section fired at the attacking 18th Mississippi from a dominant, elevated position in the garden near the Sherfy House.

Holding the line near and immediately south of the Sherfy barn to protect Bucklyn's booming guns, the 114th Pennsylvania was yet another fine regiment of Graham's Pennsylvania brigade. Symbolically providing an indication of the close relationship existing between Union artillery and infantry, because each depended so much upon the other for mutual survival against attacking Rebels, these Pennsylvania infantrymen had rescued Captain Randolph's guns at Fredericksburg. The memory of that timely intervention now set the stage for a comparable timely support role of these Pennsylvania infantrymen, who had been specifically chosen by Graham to support the Peach Orchard batteries.[254]

The 114th Pennsylvania was known collectively as Collis' Zouaves. These Philadelphians were named for the unit's former commander, a feisty Irish immigrant who migrated to America in 1853 and became a successful Philadelphia attorney, Colonel Charles Henry Tuckey Collis. He had been born in the busy port of Cork, nestled amid the green rolling hills of southern Ireland. Although diminutive, the handsome Irishman was pugnacious, and Collis bestowed this combativeness to his fine regiment. Consisting of enlisted members with an average age of twenty-four but also including a good many eighteen-year-olds, this Zouave Pennsylvania regiment had demonstrated its worth at Fredericksburg and Chancellorsville, where the command suffered a high percentage of loss. During its baptismal fire at Fredericksburg and after snatching the regimental colors from a dismayed flag-bearer, Colonel Collis had led a fierce counterattack to push the Rebels back, saving Captain Randolph's Rhode Island battery and two other batteries from capture. The Irish colonel won a Congressional Medal of Honor for valor.

The 114th Pennsylvania now once again supported the New England gunners of the Rhode Island Light Artillery in yet another, but much more important, dramatic showdown. These colorfully attired 114th Pennsylvania Zouaves were mostly city boys from Philadelphia—clerks, laborers, shoemakers, and carpenters, in contrast to the mostly yeomen farmers of Barksdale's Mississippi Brigade. Fancy Zouaves d' Afrique uniforms were modeled after those worn by French soldiers, who had fought the fierce North African Berber tribesmen of Algeria, which had been first occupied by a colony-hungry France in 1830.[255]

Ironically, Collis, when a captain, and his initial command of Zouaves, an independent company known as the Zouaves d'Afrique, had nearly met Barksdale's men at Ball's Bluff, but they had remained in a support role when the isolated Union task force was crushed. Unfortunately for Collis' Zouaves this afternoon, the thoroughly seasoned Mississippians were now far more lethal than in October 1861.[256] Ever-mindful of their distinctiveness compared to the other "Blue Legs" in regulation uniforms, these jaunty Pennsylvania Zouaves referred to themselves as "Red Boys," "Zoo Zoos" and the "Zoos."[257]

An awed private of another Union regiment described Collis' high-spirited Zouaves in a most revealing letter: "they are beauties I tell you— but when they 'Charge bayonets' with such a yell as Zouaves only can give, the rebels'll skedaddle even if the greybacks have five times as many men as the red breeches have." The Pennsylvania Zouaves' reputation for hard fighting had preceded them, because the Rebels said "that they didn't like to fight the Red Legs [because] they say we look like Devils and fight too hard [and] they say we try our best to kill and I think they are about right." However, Barksdale and his Mississippi Rebels were about to destroy this myth and erode the regiment's lofty reputation.[258]

No longer led by the dapper, 115-pound Colonel Collis, who was on leave, this Keystone State regiment of highly motivated Zouaves was now commanded by Cuban-born Lieutenant Colonel Frederic Fernandez Cavada. Cavada was a classic example of the forgotten Civil War among Latinos, or Hispanics, including Cubans who wore both blue and gray. Symbolizing the deep pre-English roots in America, more than 20,000 Hispanics fought on both sides. And the showdown at Gettysburg was no exception, with Latino Rebels serving mostly in Texas, Louisiana, and Florida regiments. Explaining motivations, Confederate Tejano Captain Joseph Rafael de la Garza, who died in battle in 1864, was "fighting for our country," in his words from a letter.

Educated at an excellent school in Philadelphia, Cavada was a romantic, liberty-loving poet, the product of a Cuban father and American mother. His slave-owning family had departed Cuba when he was young, migrating to Philadelphia. A fiery Cuban nationalist, Cavada hated the autocratic rule of Spain, which governed its wealth-producing Caribbean colony with an iron hand. Lieutenant Colonel Cavada now commanded the Zouave regiment despite suffering from recurring bouts of malaria. He had acquired the deadly tropical disease when surveying a railroad line through the tropical jungles of the Isthmus of Panama. The enlightened Cuban had also served as an army engineer and on the personal staff of Major General Birney, a Philadelphia attorney who had commanded his own Zouave regiment (Twenty-third Pennsylvania Volunteer Infantry) early in the war.

In his own personal crusade to destroy slavery in a struggle that was "the cause of all humanity," handsome Lieutenant Colonel Frederic Cavada, dark-haired and with black eyes, took command of the regiment at Chancellorsville after Colonel Collis became ill. Because of politics and anti-Latino and anti-Catholic sentiment, the easy-going Cuban faced unfair charges for his role at Fredericksburg. Knowing of Cavada's love of liberty, President Lincoln, remitted the court martial's unfair sentence, however. Lieutenant Colonel Cavada then took command of the Zouave regiment, eager to redeem his reputation and demonstrate the worth of his well-training fighting men.

Meanwhile, along with the 57th Pennsylvania, the 114th Pennsylvania began to advance west of the Emmitsburg Road in order to protect Bucklyn's guns. A 114th Pennsylvania soldier described how the Zouave command advanced to the west side of the road "with alacrity and passed through and to the front of the battery." However, these sturdy Pennsylvania blue-clads gained a more advanced position not on orders of General Graham. Instead, the Pennsylvanian's advance across the Emmitsburg Road was born of desperation. A desperate Captain George E. Randolph, chief of the Third Corps' artillery brigade and although wounded in the shoulder by a Mississippi skirmisher's bullet, had ridden up to the Pennsylvanians and implored: "You boys saved this battery once before at Fredericksburg, and if you will do it again, move forward!"

Positioned on the open ridge before the Pennsylvania Brigade, Bucklyn's Rhode Island cannoneers had suffered more damage from Alexander's artillery fire than the infantrymen. Private Ernest Simpson was one of the battery's early losses. He was a young, heartsick man who had lost the will to live because of a recent letter from his strict, God-fearing parents. They had refused to approve his marriage to a pretty girl of questionable reputation. Instead of remaining safely in the rear as usual as the battery's clerk, the tortured New England gunner overly-exposed himself at the front, where he was decapitated by a shell, to his comrade's horror but perhaps to his own relief.

Taking full responsibility for the spontaneous decision to advance the Pennsylvania Zouaves, as if taking a cue from Sickles' own decision to shift the entire Third Corps so far before the main line without Meade's consent or knowledge, Captain Randolph exercised independent thought and tactical flexibility. After having been unable to locate General Graham, Randolph acted on his own, displaying the kind of bold initiative that was now necessary for any hope of stopping the hard-charging Mississippi Brigade.

Without hesitation, therefore, he had ordered the Pennsylvanians forward out of a sense of desperation in an attempt to save his battery during the emergency, when the Mississippi Brigade was about to descend upon Bucklyn's guns. Sections of the rail fences along the Emmitsburg Road had been torn down earlier by the Yankees in preparation for just such an emergency. The removal of these obstacles facilitated the last-minute movement of the two Pennsylvania regiments across the Emmitsburg Road to protect the artillery; however, the partial dismantling of the fences on both sides of the road shortly worked likewise to the Mississippians' advantage. After knocking down more of the fence and advancing, the 114th Pennsylvania hurriedly reformed across the open stretch of high ground west of the road. Why no Federals utilized any rails for defensive purposes has remained a mystery.

Nearly 400 soldiers of the 114th Pennsylvania now presented the most colorful sight on any battlefield yet seen by the Mississippians. These men wore their distinctive brass belt buckles, marked: "114 REGT. Z.D' A. P.V" along with their fezes and fine red leggings. However, their appearance did nothing to awe the ill-clothed Mississippians, in their homespun garb. Instead, these colorful Zouave uniforms, described as "oriental," would only draw a greater concentration of Mississippi bullets like magnets this afternoon. As if hunting game in the shadowy woodlands back home, the Mississippi boys relished nothing more than the opportunity to thoroughly punish these gaudy Yankees in their circus-like uniforms. But the Zouave's fighting qualities could not be gauged alone by its outlandish uniforms. The 114th Pennsylvania, explained one soldier, was "as well-drilled and disciplined, as efficient and as brave a regiment as there was in the" army.[259]

At Chancellorsville, Graham's brigade had launched a counterattack that stemmed the tide after the Eleventh Corps' collapse after Stonewall Jackson's flank attack. However, through no fault of their own, they then had been driven back in confusion during the bitter fighting around the Chancellor House. More than 400 Zouaves of the 114th Pennsylvania went into battle and 180 men were cut down. Fortunately for Barksdale's Mississippi Rebels at this time, the Pennsylvania troops had not sufficient time to fully recover from the beating that they had suffered in Chancellorsville's haunted forests, and now numbered only 259 men.[260]

As one 57th Pennsylvania bluecoat described the last-minute tactical adjustments when "the 57th and the 114th were ordered across the road where we beheld the enemy, which proved to be Barksdale's Mississippi brigade, advancing through the fields toward us. Our regiment at once took advantage of the cover that the house, outbuildings and trees afforded and opened fire on the enemy who were within easy range, and did not reply to our fire . . ." Indeed, to the 57th Pennsylvania's right and beyond, or north of the Sherfy House, the 105th Pennsylvania, whose right was aligned along the east-west running Abraham Trostle Lane and anchoring the right flank of Graham's Keystone State brigade, also now advanced west of the road. Therefore, from left to right, the 114th, 57th, and 105th Pennsylvania Regiments were aligned in a lengthy formation stretching across the elevated area in the Sherfy House sector to meet Barksdale's troops, who were drawing ever-closer with ear-splitting Rebel Yells. While the 105th Pennsylvania held an advanced position on commanding high ground just to the right of the Sherfy House, the 57th Pennsylvania aligned before the house and the 114th Pennsylvania occupied the ground between the house and barn farther south. From the commanding heights of the western edge of the Emmitsburg Road Ridge, the Pennsylvania soldiers now gained a full and chilling view of the onrushing Mississippi formations, whose sprawling length in double lines were marked by a good many bobbing battle-flags of bright red.

After he saw the dense blue formations of determined Philadelphia troops rising over the immediate open eastern horizon as if they had sprung from the earth's bowels after they had advanced across the dusty road, Barksdale finally ordered his troops to unleash their first organized and concentrated volley of the day. The gray and butternut ranks exploded with an intense fire, and a sheet of flame ran down the line's length. Barksdale's primary target, Buckyln's Rhode Island Battery, was cut to pieces, losing the highest number of casualties (nearly 30) than any other Third Corps Battery. Bucklyn's horse was shot from under him. He was horrified to see that "My Battery is torn and shattered and my brave boys have gone never to return. Curse the Rebs." And forty artillery horses were felled, making the removal of the hard-pressed Rhode Island guns more difficult in the crisis situation.

A solid sheet of musketry also thoroughly punished the Pennsylvania infantrymen for their audacity in advancing across the road. Because the 114th and 57th Pennsylvania had pushed forward with fixed bayonets to cover the inevitable withdrawal of the Rhode Island guns, this new high ground perch just west of the road only made them more vulnerable. In the words of Captain Edward R. Bowen, a wool merchant in his mid-twenties from Philadelphia who eventually became the 114th Pennsylvania's commander, the men advanced "to the Emmitsburg Road, in the face of the murderous musketry fire of the advancing enemy . . . reaching the road we clambered over the fence and crossed it [and moved on, while] Sherfy's house and outbuildings intervening between us and the approaching enemy, the right of the regiment was advanced to the rear of the house. While advancing in this way our men were loading and firing as rapidly as possible, and several times pauses were made, notably as we stood on the Emmitsburg road, and corrected the alignment, which was broken by clambering over the fence. During all this time we were receiving a terrible musketry fire from the rapidly approaching enemy, and the men were falling by scores."

The commander of Company F and a former Philadelphia saloon keeper, Captain Francis Fix, who stood beside his brother, Lieutenant Augustus, "Gus," Fix, fell with a mortal wound, when a Mississippi bullet shattered his knee. All the while, the Pennsylvanians fired from good defensive positions across a slight, level ledge or plateau, which marked the open western edge of the Emmitsburg Road Ridge. Blasting away like well-trained veterans, Cavada's 114th Pennsylvania poured a hot "fire out between the house and barn," wrote Philadelphia-born diarist Sergeant Major Given, whose wife Anne Patton had sent him off to war with a kiss and the words, "Go and God be with you."

Beloved by the men for his kind, generous nature, Lieutenant Colonel Cavada, who commanded the 114th Pennsylvania with skill this afternoon, had been earlier warned about Barksdale's attack by Sergeant Major Given that "You [can] bet your life they are coming in full force." Cavada attempted to stabilize his hard-hit ranks, providing inspired leadership, while the torrent of Mississippi bullets cut down Yankees in groups and made the sulfurous air sing. The Mississippians' rolling volleys that were unleashed with a murderous accuracy caused severe damage among the finely uniformed Pennsylvania boys.

One such soldier falling to rise no more was a young Pennsylvania Quaker named Corporal Robert Kenderdine, an old Anglo-Saxon name. He had long dreaded just such a brutal "killing day" as this one in Adams County, Pennsylvania. Kenderdine had protected the beautiful regimental banner as one of the few surviving color guard members. Barksdale's men were now so close that Sergeant Henry H. Snyder, amid the deafening noise, was shocked when he saw cheering Mississippi Rebels with fixed bayonets emerging through the dense layers of smoke, taking deliberate aim, and shooting down Corporal Kenderdine like expert hunters picking off a squirrel. But the Mississippi marksman who cut down Corporal Kenderdine, who had cast aside his Quaker pacifism to fight for his country, was almost immediately felled with a well-placed shot. Here, on this killing ground along the treeless western edge of the Emmittsburg Road Ridge, large numbers of Lieutenant Colonel Cavada's men "were killed and wounded here in the oatfield and around Sherfy's house and barn."[261]

Meanwhile, the hard-pressed 114th Pennsylvania received some timely support when General Andrew Atchinson Humphreys, at Graham's frantic request and Sickles' immediate concurrence, ordered one of his favorite regiments, the 73rd New York Volunteer Infantry, known as the Second Fire Zouaves of the "Excelsior Brigade," south from its unengaged position on his division's left along the Emmitsburg Road.[262] Having enlisted at age nineteen and destined to fall wounded during this tempestuous afternoon in hell, Lieutenant Frank E. Moran, a New York City painter who now commanded Company H, 73rd New York, described how "we moved toward the orchard at double-quick through a shower of bullets and bursting shells."[263]

At this time, Moran, of Irish descent, wrote how, the "114th [Pennsylvania], stretched along the Emmetsburg [sic] road from the gate of the Sherfy house and past the barn, were hotly at work and sorely pressed [and] fearfully exposed on the crest which rises at that point, was gallantly disputing the ground with the Mississippians, who, [led] by Barksdale, came swarming up yelling like demons."[264] Meanwhile, after pushing south to the Sherfy House sector, the breathless New York soldiers, gasping for air in the intense heat, covered in sweat and dust, and coughing amid the drifting layers of smoke, aligned about thirty yards behind the 114th Pennsylvania. As fate would have it, the largest concentration of Zouaves on the Gettysburg battlefield now faced the Mississippians. After the 73rd New York troops formed "quickly in line, and the 'click, click' of cocking muskets" rang through the sulfurous air," alerting Barksdale's attackers of another sweeping volley soon headed their way.[265]

One of the most fiery Cuban nationalists in America, like his lieutenant colonel brother Frederic, Lieutenant Adolfo Cavada, a respected member of General Humphrey's staff, was concerned about his brother's welfare now that he was caught in the path of Barksdale's onslaught. He described how the "enemy's fire slackened then came the rebel cheer sounding like a continuous yelp, nearer and nearer it came" to the Peach Orchard salient that was now at the vortex of the swirling storm.[266] Meanwhile, Colonel Frederic Cavada ordered his men to stand firm and fire more rapidly.[267] Colonel Cavada was determined to redeem the good name of all freedom-loving Cubans in blue, because so many of his native countrymen fought for the South. He yet lamented that these Cubans in gray had sacrificed "the broad principle of humanity to a narrow and pitiful geographic necessity," and "I am proud of their scorn," because he now wore the blue.[268] Cavada's regiment, along with the 57th Pennsylvania to its right, now bore the brunt of Barksdale's attack, especially from Colonel Carter's 13th and Colonel Griffin's 18th Mississippi.[269]

Meanwhile, Barksdale had no idea that the 114th Pennsylvania Zouaves, aligned from the Sherfy House to just south of the Sherfy barn, were supported by the 73rd New York to their rear, and that his onrushing troops were about to plow into a double-line of veteran defenders.[270]

As ordered by Barksdale, his soldiers had actually launched their bayonet attack earlier than usual when first directed to double-quick over the open ground, but yet the firing from the ranks continued unabated by his veterans. By this time, these seasoned Mississippians were adept at the art of loading and firing on the run with a surprising degree of accuracy. Therefore, the 73rd New York was immediately greeted with a hot fire from Barksdale's men, who suddenly emerged through the drifting smoke to shoot down a good many more Zouaves, as if this kind of slaughter was nothing more than sport. With the 114th Pennsylvania positioned to their front, the New Yorkers were unable to return a concentrated volley in reply.

By this time, the Rebels could not be stopped by the salvos of musketry and artillery vomiting forth from the Peach Orchard and the Emmitsburg Road sector. Some enterprising 57th Pennsylvania snipers, no doubt young farm boys, had even scaled cherry trees on the Sherfy property along the open ridge. These sharpshooters in blue blasted away from their lofty perches, including from the narrow windows, flanked by handcrafted wooden shutters, of the two-story Sherfy house poised on the high ground just west of the Emmitsburg Road Ridge. This steady stream of punishment from above was described by one lucky Magnolia State survivor as simply "terrible." Meanwhile, hundreds of veteran Union defenders continued to fire from the advantage of the high ground, blasting away as if there was no tomorrow. Delighted to be defending home soil, Private Joseph S. Beaumont, Company F, 57th Pennsylvania, yelled encouragement to his fast-firing men, "Give it to them boys, we have them on our own ground!"

All the while, Barksdale's men continued to surge ahead with abandon, even though, as one of Colonel Humphreys' men, Private McNeily described, "at points of the defense the enemy's infantry was covered by stone fences and farm buildings [and] their deadliest fire was at such places." Even the Pennsylvania Federals felt a growing admiration at the rather remarkable sight of a single Confederate brigade charging without support on either side or even support troops in the rear. The 57th Pennsylvania defenders positioned before the Sherfy House were perplexed by the unusual spectacle of an isolated Confederate infantry assaulting a high ground defensive position for "there were then no rebels to the left of those [which] engaged us, and for a while we had the best of the fight owing to our sheltered position."[271]

With battle-flags flapping through the smoke, the Mississippi Rebels continued to charge toward the fire-spitting ridge around the Peach Orchard and the Sherfy House, while loading and firing as fast as they could on the run with the mechanical ease and drill-book precision of seasoned veterans. Making especially colorful targets along the high ground, the 114th Pennsylvania Zouaves continued to suffer heavily. They steadily fell in bunches to the Mississippians' fire, especially that unleashed by Colonel Carter's 13th Mississippi, which swept Cavada's front with a close-range volley. More good Pennsylvania fighting men, such as Sergeant Henry C. McCarty, Company K, who had won the Kearny Cross for past heroics, were fatally cut down in the hail of Mississippi bullets.[272]

The severe punishment delivered by the Mississippians' fire-spitting rifles was too much to endure at such close range, and hard-hit Federals began to break for the rear. Private John Saunders Henley, 17th Mississippi, described how he and his comrades continued "firing on them, and they ran in crowds."[273] But despite the escalating losses, most of these tough Pennsylvanians held firm, especially in defending the slightly sunken roadbed of the Emmitsburg Road and firing from behind the post-and-rail fences alongside it. A member of the Buena Vista Rifles, Henley described how a "Pennsylvania regiment was posted behind an embarkment, and they killed lots of our boys."[274]

Encouraging Company F's soldiers of the Benton Rifles onward, Lieutenant William R. Oursler was one of those "boys" of Private Henley's 17th Mississippi who was killed "near a Negro blacksmith shop near the Peach Orchard."[275] Ironically, Lieutenant Oursler, of German descent, received his death stroke on the land of a German farmer.[276] But even more ironic, the son of John and Mary Wentz, whose log farmhouse stood just north of the crossroads in the Peach Orchard, now served in one of Alexander's batteries, Captain Osmund B. Taylor's Virginia Artillery, that had pounded the Peach Orchard.[277]

Not even the remaining double line of sturdy post-and-rail fences, lining both sides of the Emmitsburg Road, slowed down the Mississippians' onslaught. Yelping their distinctive war-cry, Barksdale's veterans, sensing victory, simply barreled over the wooden fences without stopping or halting to realign, as if they had long drilled for this most difficult of maneuvers. Captain Harris Barksdale described how "the first heavy line is encountered; one volley from their deadly rifles, and reloading as they rush on. Onward, still Onward! Vaulting over a rail fence they encountered the second heavy line of the enemy, consisting chiefly of artillery and of gaudily-dressed Zouaves. We drove them before us." McLaws' staff officer, Captain Lamar, penned that when the Mississippians swarmed over the fence "the slaughter of the 'red-breeched zouaves' on the other side was terrible!" And Private Joseph Charles Lloyd, the Kemper Legion (Company C), 13th Mississippi, recorded the extent of the Mississippi Brigade's success at this point, for "scarcely a minute and we were at the barn and scaling the fences at the lane and right across and in among the enemy, literally running over him."[278]

The fleeing Pennsylvania Zouaves, jumbled-up and never so hard-hit, presented ideal targets. Private Henley described the slaughter: "You could not shoot without hitting two or three of them," with lead balls passing through stacked-up bodies like a knife cutting through butter.[279] To the 57th Pennsylvania's right, the 105th Pennsylvania troops, after having advanced up the slope to the west side of the road with the 114th Pennsylvania and the 57th Pennsylvania, also riddled the 18th Mississippi from the advantageous high ground.[280] Representing the third, or main, line, the lengthy, blue formations of veterans of the three Pennsylvania regiments blasted away with a rapid fire, but they "were now alone in battling Barksdale's men."[281] Rolling volleys cascaded down the open slope to rake the Mississippi Rebels, knocking down more attackers. A 114th Pennsylvania soldier described the Philadelphians' stubbornness on the Emmitsburg Road Ridge's western edge: "Standing on elevated ground, with open fields on all sides, the steady fire of the men, as the enemy's infantry pushed forward, was delivered with excellent effect."[282]

Just before pulling out in a hurry to escape Barksdale's onslaught, the guns of Bucklyn's battery, situated just south of the Sherfy House, continued to roar defiance into the Mississippians' faces. Surging ahead with his Winston County comrades, Private Judge E. Woodruff, Winstson Guards (Company A), 13th Mississippi, described how, "The Yankee battery was on top of the rise where there was a dwelling house and barn and orchard. In back of them were . . . other cannon firing on us. It seemed as if you could hold up your hat and catch it full of grapeshot."[283]

Entire swaths of 13th Mississippi attackers were cut down by artillery salvos. Manned by expert gunners, these fast-working New England cannon unleashed double loads of canister, the infantryman's ultimate nightmare, at close range into the cresting waves of shouting Mississippi soldiers. The 57th Pennsylvania's defenders not only possessed the advantage of occupying the dominant terrain just west of the Emmitsburg Road, but also the fast-firing "men of the 57th who were in the house kept up a steady fire from the west windows," blasting away with abandon from both upstairs and downstairs.

Playing a role in leading the 21st Mississippi, which struck the 350-man 68th Pennsylvania, around the dusty crossroads that suddenly had become strategic, Captain Harris Barksdale continued to encourage the attackers onward across the body-strewn Emmitsburg Road. Colonel Humphreys' veterans quickly formed a line with well-oiled precision to unleash a more concentrated volley, wreaking even greater havoc. Then, Humphreys' furious attack continued up the slope and past the Emmitsburg Road, with the Mississippians "literally running over" a good many stunned 68th Pennsylvania bluecoats, who hardly knew what had hit them.

In a letter, Adjutant Harman, 13th Mississippi who was charging toward Bucklyn's blazing Rhode Island guns, described when "the center of the Brigade struck the road at or near the 1st farm house on the Emmitsburg road to the north of Sherfy's Peach Orchard. I crossed the road just to the south of the house." Meanwhile, to the right, the fast-moving 21st Mississippi soldiers poured deeper into the Peach Orchard with wild shouts. Humphrey's troops gained the Peach Orchard in less time—not much longer than five minutes—than what even Barksdale believed possible, when he had earlier boasted of that distinct, but seemingly unrealistic, possibility to Longstreet. Meantime, after observing Barksdale's attack Longstreet later wrote, "With glorious bearing he sprang to his work, overriding obstacles and dangers. Without a pause to deliver a shot, he had the battery."

Meanwhile, on the Mississippi Brigade's left flank to the north, Barksdale's elated 18th Mississippi soldiers surged "forward until both parties met at or near the old barn," which now became the eye of the raging storm on the north. Here, wrote one Southerner, "within a few feet of each other these brave men, Confederates and Federals, maintained a desperate conflict." A disbelieving Federal colonel attempted to describe the "the carnage inflicted on us boys in Blue [but it] would be impossible to detail."[284] Another Union officer could hardly believe how Barksdale's rapidly-firing men, who seemingly never missed a shot, "liked to have killed them all before they could get away."[285]

As on no previous battlefield, the hard-hit "Red Legs"of the 114th Pennsylvania, considered one of Pennsylvania's "star regiments," fell in ever-greater numbers, while hundreds of Union troops were hurled rearward by Barksdale's onslaught. These finely-uniformed city Zouaves, with clerk the most common occupation but also including "rowdies of the city," from Philadelphia's close-knit, insular neighborhoods, found themselves in serious trouble. Quite simply, these city boys from the "City of Brotherly Love" were no match for the young country boys, backwoodsmen, small farmers, and hunters from across Mississippi.[286]

On the Mississippi Brigade's left flank and duplicating Humphreys' hard-hitting performance on the right, Colonel Griffin's 18th Mississippi packed a hard-hitting punch that sent the Yankees reeling. He described how, "We steadily advanced, driving the enemy before us."[287] After unleashing their last devastating pointblank volley, Barksdale's men closed in for the kill with bayonets. With slashing sabers and jabbing bayonets, the Mississippians literally tore apart the Pennsylvania formations.[288] To the south of the Griffin's 18th and Carter's 13th Mississippi, respectively from left to right, the hard-charging 17th Mississippi likewise inflicted considerable damage, "leaving the ground nearly covered with their dead," wrote Private Henley of the systematic devastation of the city boys.[289] As emphasized by Private Thurman Early Hendricks, a member of the Minutemen of Attala, which attacked on the 18th Mississippi's right flank, the 13th Mississippi once again reconfirmed its hard-won reputation as the "Bloody 13th" in the close combat, including hand-to-hand.[290]

From his perch atop Cemetery Ridge to the northeast, Captain Haskell described the dramatic sight of the devastation wrought by Barksdale's knock-out blow, writing how the Third Corps troops now "fight well, but it soon becomes apparent that they must be swept from the field, or perish there. It is fearful to see. . . . To move down and support them with other troops is out of the question. There is no alternative—the Third Corps must fight itself out of its position of destruction!"[291]

As on so many past battlefields, the brigade's crack regiment, the 21st Mississippi, achieved the most significant tactical gains of any of Barkdale's regiments, delivering the blow that collapsed the salient angle and crushed its stunned defenders. With rounding yells, a close-range fire, and jabbing bayonets, Humphreys' troops smashed through the apex of the Third Corps' protruding salient angle, and then continued on without stopping to rest or reload. Charging astride the Wheatfield Road which led directly to the sector's highest ground, the knoll of the Peach Orchard, Colonel Humphreys' regiment struck a decisive blow that overpowered and crushed the salient angle, thus beginning the process of unhinging both arms, one extending northeast along the Emmitsburg Road and the other southeast down the Wheatfield Road.

The 21st Mississippi's left ripped into the vulnerable and exposed left, or southern, flank of the 114th Pennsylvania—a flank that hung in mid-air—while its right struck the equally exposed right of the 68th Pennsylvania, situated just south of the intersection along the Emmitsburg Road. Because of the wide gap that extended between the left of Cavada's regiment and the 68th Pennsylvania's right, Colonel Humphrey's troops penetrated sufficiently deep into the Peach Orchard on the left to outflank both regiments.

The right of the 21st Mississippi, yet astride the Wheatfield Road after crossing the Emmitsburg Road, continued to maul the 68th Pennsylvania, while the 114th Pennsylvania suffered severely from a flank fire unleashed by the 21st Mississippi's left. In essence, the 21st Mississippi smashed simultaneously into the ends of two vulnerable flanks, and then penetrated the gap. A hard-fighting 114th Pennsylvania captain, Edward R. Bowen, was amazed by the lethal effectiveness of the Mississippians' slashing attack. He wrote with surprise how "the enemy had already advanced so quickly and in such force as to gain the road" hardly before the Pennsylvanians knew what had hit them. Sensing a dramatic victory with the smashing of the Peach Orchard angle, Colonel Humphreys encouraged his 21st Mississippi soldiers onward to exploit their significant gains without pausing. With fixed bayonets and firing on the run, these hardened veterans continued to charge thorough the choking smoky haze that made them look like ghostly devils from hell suddenly emerging to the hard-pressed boys in blue.

Colonel Andrew H. Tippin's 68th Pennsylvania had just attempted to advance in a belated attempt to close the dangerous gap and support the battered left of the 114th Pennsylvania. But by this time it was far too late for such an adroit maneuver. The 68th Pennsylvania was thoroughly punished under the sledgehammer-like blows of the 21st Mississippi's right. Bolstered by the 2nd New Hampshire Volunteer Infantry, Burling's brigade, Humphreys' Division, that had moved to its rear, after changing from front from facing south to west toward the 21st Mississippi, the 68th Pennsylvania attempted to confront the seemingly unstoppable momentum of Humphreys' onslaught as best it could. A calm Colonel Tippin ordered his troops to hold their fire until the rampaging Mississippians were close. A concentrated volley from the 68th Pennsylvania momentarily staggered the 21st Mississippi, knocking down a good many attackers. Feeling a sense of admiration, Private McNeily described how the Yankees "fought back bravely," standing firm for as long as they could.

Screaming orders above the guns' deafening roar, Humphreys hurriedly formed his troops along a fence that ran along the Wheatfield Road to reorganize his ranks, allow his panting men a breather, time to reload, and provide some protection amid the open field swept with a torrent of bullets. Here, the soot-smeared veterans from companies like the Hurricane Rifles, Sunflower Guards, and Vicksburg Confederates busily reloaded and returned a devastating fire upon the New Hampshire and Pennsylvania troops from the north. One New Hampshire soldier described the vicious combat as "close, stubborn and deadly work," which was the bloodiest in the regiment's history.

Meanwhile, in a most timely arrival, Colonel Holder and the 17th Mississippi's right added timely strength to the busily engaged 21st Mississippi along the fence-line now swept by 68th Pennsylvania bullets. With the 13th Mississippi and 18th Mississippi's right and the 17th Mississippi's left driving Cavada's Zouave regiment rearward, the 17th Mississippi's right turned to help exploit the gap between the 114th Pennsylvania and the 68th Pennsylvania, assisting the 21st Mississippi in timely fashion. Then, the two Mississippi regiments delivered a concentrated volley on Colonel Tippin's 68th Pennsylvania near the small log cabin, with a stone foundation (the John Wertz House) which stood on the east side of the Emmitsburg Road. This blistering fire cut down the color bearer, dropping the 68th Pennsylvania flag, the regiment's lieutenant colonel and major, and a good many fine men.

This well coordinated, combined one-two punch and blistering flank fire delivered by the 21st Mississippi and the 17th Mississippi's right mauled the obstinate 68th Pennsylvania, whose right flank had been turned. Under heavy pressure, Tippin had no alternative, and the 68th Pennsylvania was forced to retreat. However, this sudden withdrawal left the 350-man 2nd New Hampshire, the first unit facing south along the Wheatfield Road, under Colonel Edward L. Bailey, exposed on the right flank to the 21st Mississippi's onslaught. After having been dispatched to support Graham, the youthful-looking Bailey said he suddenly found "myself unsupported, and the enemy steadily advancing" with piercing, high-pitched yells that echoed over the Emmitsburg Road Ridge. After capturing more prisoners, including wounded Federals who took refuge in the Wentz House cellar, Colonel Humphreys ordered his troops to charge onward through the Peach Orchard and down the slope.

Surging east and parallel to the Wheatfield Road, the 21st Mississippi's attackers forced the outflanked 3rd Michigan Volunteer Infantry to retire and then next slammed into the 2nd New Hampshire's exposed right flank, thanks to the retreat of the Maine and Michigan regiments. Therefore, the 2nd New Hampshire was likewise forced to withdraw. After losing nearly 200 men and faced with encirclement by Humphreys' attackers, Bailey ordered his battered regiment rearward around 150 yards across the grassy, open ground of the eastern slope of the Emmitsburg Road Ridge to about the Peach Orchard's center to escape the 21st Mississippi's furious onslaught. After sending the Pennsylvanians under Colonel Tippin reeling along with Colonel Bailey's hard-hit New Englanders, Humphreys' 21st and the 17th Mississippi's right then focused their full attention to their next unfortunate victim, the 114th Pennsylvania and its vulnerable left flank hanging in mid-air to the northeast.

As greater carnage swirled around him and his devastated Zouaves, Captain Bowen described how the attacking 21st Mississippi's left and the now reunited 17th Mississippi turned to enfilade the 114th Pennsylvania from left to right, or south to north. All the while, the onrushing Mississippians busily loaded and fired with an amazing rapidity, "pouring a murderous fire on our flank, threw the left wing of the regiment on to the right in much confusion." Keystone State soldiers like Sergeant John R. Waterhouse, a steady Company F veteran at nearly age forty with a large Philadelphia family—wife Sarah and five children—went down when two bullets smashed into his right thigh, tearing flesh and breaking bone.

The fatal combination of "the enemy advancing so rapidly and my men falling in such numbers," wrote Captain Bowen, the regiment's acting major, explained how the 114th Pennsylvania was all but vanquished by the hard-charging Mississippians hardly before the fight had begun. Indeed, both the 21st Mississippi and the 17th Mississippi attackers, working together effectively with business-like efficiency as on past battlefields, continued to wreck havoc on the 114th Pennsylvania's vulnerable left flank that was even more exposed, after hurling back the 68th

Pennsylvania and the 2nd New Hampshire. Throngs of defeated survivors of the two battered regiments now headed east down the slope for Cemetery Ridge to escape Barksdale's onslaught.

Barksdale's regiments had not achieved their gains without paying a heavy price, however. James B. Booth, Company F, 21st Mississippi, described the escalating losses that decimated Humphreys' regiment, including President Davis' beloved nephew. Leading the young men of the Hurricane Rifles (Company E), darkly handsome, dignified Captain Isaac D. "Stamps was killed [mortally wounded] in three feet of me [when] we were just entering the peach orchard when he was stricken down." As a cruel fate would have it, Captain Stamps went down with a bullet through his bowels, while he was waving the ornate saber that Colonel Jefferson Davis had carried during the attack of the First Mississippi Rifles at Buena Vista. Stamps' haunting prophecy about receiving a death stroke had been fulfilled in tragic fashion. Private Henley, 17th Mississippi described with a mixture of pride and sadness, "We went through the Peach Orchard [but] lost many" of the regiment's best soldiers, both officers and enlisted men.

On the brigade's right, Humphreys' gains were growing. In the face of the 21st Mississippi's onslaught, the two out-flanked regiments, the 68th Pennsylvania and the 2nd New Hampshire, were simply swept aside. Most important after having hurled back the two Federal regiments, Humphreys' 21st Mississippi effectively flanked the Peach Orchard salient and Union regiments, starting with the 114th Pennsylvania, on the left, and the 3rd Maine Volunteer Infantry (the farthest south regiment), on the 68th Pennsylvania's left.

This gaping hole was fully exploited when Humphreys' men charged ahead to widen the fissure in the defensive line that grew with each passing minute, collapsing Sickles' determined bid to hold the salient's apex like a pierced hot air balloon. Thanks to the 21st Mississippi's hard-hitting style, the smashing of the line's apex was the beginning of the end for Sickles, his Third Corps, and the Peach Orchard salient, resulting in a classic case of falling dominoes. Private McNeily, 21st Mississippi, recorded how the steamrolling "21st struck and flanked the Peach Orchard angle," delivering a powerful blow that collapsed the salient as Barksdale and Humphreys had originally envisioned.

But the most extensive damage was inflicted by Humphreys' 21st Mississippi after it surged across the Emmitsburg Road and began charging southeast along the Wheatfield Road, which was lined with a lengthy row of Union artillery. To Humphreys' delight and making his tactical dreams come true, the Wheatfield Road now became a golden avenue of opportunity for Barksdale's most hard-hitting regiment. After overrunning the salient angle and continuing to advance southeast over open ground beyond the body-filled Peach Orchard, the 21st Mississippi's devastating blows continued to wreck havoc at every point. In the words of Colonel William R. Livermore, once "the apex of Sickles' line was broken, both wings collapsed." But this sudden collapse had required much hard fighting by both Barksdale and Humphreys in order to push aside the stubbornly defending Yankees.

All the while, the number of victims of the 21st Mississippi's assault soared. Continuing to wreck one Federal unit after another and despite the lack of contact with Kershaw's brigade to the right, Humphreys' regiment reaped more success by unhinging additional Federal regiments. It is also possible at this juncture that the Union troops could see Wofford's Brigade coming up behind the 21st Mississippi, thus enhancing their fear of being overwhelmed. Afterward, however, Wofford would veer to the right, plunging into the hell of the Wheatfield.

The significant gains achieved by the 21st Mississippi presented a host of new tactical opportunities not only for the 21st but also for the 17th Mississippi, on Humphreys' left. Working efficiently together as an experienced team, the 21st Mississippi and the 17th Mississippi sandwiched the 68th Pennsylvania, now in a new position near the Peach Orchard's center after it retired east, between two irresistible forces, with Colonel Carter's men turning the 68th Pennsylvania's right and Humphreys' troops turning its left. After the 68th Pennsylvania and the 2nd New Hampshire were driven back, departing in haste from the bullet-swept fenceline along the Wheatfield Road to escape the punishment, the 17th Mississippi, now slightly in the left-rear of the Union regiments along the Emmitsburg Road, had turned back to face northeastward to outflank the Pennsylvanians on their left.

After inflicting extensive damage on Cavada's Pennsylvania Zouaves, Colonel Holder's 17th Mississippi, now facing northeast and immediately to the right of the Emmitsburg Road, slammed into the left flank and rear of the 57th Pennsylvania around the two-story Sherfy house, and then headed toward the vulnerable left flank of the 105th Pennsylvania. Both Pennsylvania regiments took a severe beating under the close-range volleys unleashed by Barksdale's men, who proved to be experts in delivering lethal fires and at cutting even fine Union regiments to pieces.

Trying desperately to stem the howling wave of triumphant Rebels, Colonel Calvin A. Craig, who led the hard-fighting Wildcats of the 105th Pennsylvania, holding the right flank of Graham's brigade, described the nightmare scenario: "The regiments on my immediate left (114th and 57th Pennsylvania) cluster in groups behind the brick house and adjacent out-buildings" and then retired, "leaving my left flank entirely unprotected [and the Mississippians] taking advantage of this, advanced across the Emmitsburg road, in front of the house, and immediately opened fire upon our left flank." With bluecoats dropping around him like leaves on a windy day, Colonel Craig ordered his western Pennsylvania boys to fall back before it was too late to save themselves. One 57th Pennsylvanian explained the damage that the Mississippians inflicted on the fast-crumbling Union defensive line: "Although the angle at the peach orchard was . . . bravely defended by our troops there, they were at last compelled to yield ground, and by so doing the regiments along the Emmitsburg road were enfiladed and obliged to fall back also."[292] Fulfilling Barksdale's most ambitious expectations, Humphreys' 21st Mississippi had caved-in the salient angle, which doomed the defensive lines of blue that stretched both northeast along the Emmitsburg Road and southeast down the Wheatfield Road.[293]

In consequence, a fast-paced chain reaction resulted: Humphreys' left and the 17th Mississippi had smashed into the 114th Pennsylvania's left flank, and the 18th Mississippi hit the 57th Pennsylvania troops from the front, before the 21st Mississippi continued to attack southeast down the Wheatfield Road, after Humphreys' regiment was reunited. Both Colonel Carter's 13th Mississippi and Colonel Holder's 17th Mississippi had then poured through the gap to severely punish the left flanks of the bluecoat defenders around the Sherfy House and barn, first the 114th Pennsylvania, and then the 57th Pennsylvania and next the 105th Pennsylvania, the last of Graham's regiments on the line. Thus the surging Mississippians applied heavy pressure simultaneously from both front and flank in a deadly vise that closed ever-tighter on both sides of the boys in blue.[294] Meanwhile, on the brigade's left, Colonel Griffin's 18th Mississippi swarmed over the Sherfy farm with victory cheers, after shooting down and bayoneting every Yankee in sight. In the words of Major Gerald, his onrushing troops steadily pushed "the enemy before us until we reached the houses with the trees on the left, the trees proved to be a peach orchard. On the end of the orchard was a barn in which a part of the enemy had taken refuge."[295]

But the vicious fighting for the Emmitsburg Road was far from over, because of the double defensive line of veteran Federals in this sector: essentially a defense in-depth. After decimating and hurling the 114th Pennsylvania rearward, Major Michael Burns' 73rd New York, to Cavada's right-rear in support and positioned just east of the Sherfy House, prepared to receive the hard-hitting impact of the Mississippians pouring across the road and over the open crest. Hurried onward by one of Sickles' staff officers, the 73rd New York had been hastily dispatched south just to time to watch the shocking sight of Cavada's Zouave regiment overrun by the Rebel tide. Leading Company H, 73rd New York, Lieutenant Moran described the final flurry of resistance of Cavada's boys along the bullet-swept ridge-top: "At last the 114th, with a parting volley in the very faces of the Mississippians, made room for us, and our regiment poured a quick and well-directed volley at the enemy, who fell in scores among the wounded and dead of the 114th."[296]

With firm resolve, the New Yorkers met the surging tide of the 18th and 13th Mississippi that poured over the body-strewn crest of the Emmitsburg Ridge. However, unleashing their first fire of the day now that Cavada's Zouave regiment had been swept away, the New Yorkers' close-range volley knocked clumps of Mississippi boys to the ground. But the sheer momentum of Barksdale's attack could not be stopped. With a sense of awe, Moran wrote how Barksdale's soldiers "staggered, but closed up, and with the familiar 'Hi-yi! returned our fire and pressed forward with the savage courage of baited bulls."[297]

Lieutenant Moran described the hellish turmoil in this embattled sector east of the Emmitsburg Road: "The smoke grew thicker each minute and the sound of exploding shells was deafening. Officers and men were falling every minute and on every side . . . Every door, window and sash of the Sherfy house was shivered to atoms. The barn close by was riddled like a sieve from base to roof, and cannon shot at every instant spilt its boards and timbers into showers of kindling-wood. A shell burst under a load of rails beside it, and whipped them through the air like straws in a whirlwind."[298]

Like the 114th Pennsylvania's decimation in its front minutes before, so the 73rd New York was now cut to pieces by the hard-charging Rebels, the 17th Mississippi attacking on their exposed left flank and the 13th and 18th Mississippi striking in front. Lieutenant George Dennen, whose twin brother had been killed at Chancellorsville less than two months earlier, went down with a mortal wound, fulfilling his dark prophesy of impending doom. Suffering the recent fate of other hard-hit Union regiments, the New York regiment's left flank was turned, and the mauled New Yorkers retired back above, or north of, the Abraham Trostle Lane from where they had been dispatched to reinforce Graham's troops.[299] However, the stubbornness of the 73rd New York soldiers played a key role in buying time for the shattered remains of Graham's brigade to withdraw.[300]

Meanwhile, in the embattled Wheatfield Road sector east of the Emmitsburg Road, Humphreys led his 21st Mississippi eastward and deeper into the heart of the shattered Peach Orchard salient in a sweeping attack. After having already retired around 150 yards further, Colonel Bailey hurriedly aligned his surviving 2nd New Hampshire troops under the brow of a slight rise near the Peach Orchard's mid-section with Humphreys' screaming Rebels on their heels. Colonel Bailey described the unnerving situation, with "the enemy, distant but 20 yards," before the Second New Hampshire boys could unleash a volley.[301]

Indeed, nothing could stop the 21st Mississippi once unleashed with the bayonet, especially in the skilled art of flanking, which was Humphreys' expertise. Knowing that his New Hampshire regiment now faced certain annihilation, despite being aligned with the battered 63rd Pennsylvania, which likewise had fallen back to realign at this ad hoc second defensive position, Colonel Bailey described the pounding delivered by Humphreys' attackers that once again outflanked the 2nd New Hampshire: "The enemy continued advancing until they reached the brow of the hill, when their left swept toward the 63rd Pennsylvania in such overwhelming numbers as to cause it to give way . . . I gave the order to retire" after losing nearly 200 men.[302]

Humphreys' destructive task was made only slightly easier by the redeployment of the 141st Pennsylvania that had been ordered from supporting Captain Judson A. Clark's New Jersey battery along the Wheatfield Road to the Sherfy House's rear and behind the 68th Pennsylvania. Here, the hard-hit 141st Pennsylvania remained in position on its own, while the 68th Pennsylvania "engaged with the enemy in front of the barn, near the brick house [but when] I took this position the 68th withdrew and I was thus left alone," wrote Colonel Henry J. Madill.[303]

Despite the smashing of the southwestern end of Sickles' defensive line along the Emmitsburg Road Ridge, the bitter fighting had only begun on this bloody afternoon. By this time, the Peach Orchard, wreathed in billowing clouds of smoke and deafening noise, was the vortex of the

Mississippians' raging storm. After the broken fragments of the 57th Pennsylvania—which lost more than half its strength today, including Colonel Sides—and the 114th Pennsylvania were hurled east across the Emmitsburg Road to leave ghastly piles of dead and wounded comrades behind, the contest for possession of the Sherfy barn, house, and out-buildings was yet to be decided. Meanwhile, many 114th Pennsylvania survivors fled north up the Emmitsburg Road, while other Philadelphians retreated east through the open grain fields beyond the road.

At this crucial moment, Barksdale now realized that he could not leave the occupied strongholds on the Sherfy farm along the Emmitsburg Road in the rear of his three regiments. After all, Barksdale's great goal was to advance all the way to Cemetery Ridge to tear through the left-center of Meade's line. Consequently, all of these remaining Pennsylvania defend-ers, tenacious in defending home soil, had to be roused out of their ad hoc fortified positions just west of the road with the bayonet.

One 57th Pennsylvania soldier, who viewed the 114th Pennsylvania's collapse to his regiment's left, described how "when we found the [17th Mississippi] coming up the road in our rear, Captain Alanson H. Nelson, who was soon to command the regiment [after Colonel Sides fell wounded], tried to notify those in the house, and order them to fall back, but amid the noise and confusion it was impossible to make them under-stand the situation, and they kept on firing with abandon from the win-dows after the rest of the men fell back, and they were summoned to surrender by the rebels who came up the stairs in their rear." Thirty-five-year-old Captain Nelson, whose father had been killed during the bitter nightmare that was Florida's Second Seminole War, saw from the porch of the Sherfy House that "the enemy was in the yard in large force, not fifty feet away." Several of Griffin's 18th Mississippi soldiers, instead of shooting the surprised captain, yelled for the shocked father of more than a half-dozen children to surrender. Not worried about them becoming orphans, Captain Nelson decided to "never be taken prisoner as long as I could fight or run."

Therefore he bolted in a desperate attempt to dash through the Sherfy yard to escape: "I saw at a glance that they were in a bunch, and but few of them could shoot without endangering themselves. So I thought I could run quartering past them, and possibly escape. I took the chance, and made a dive past them, then firing began. Either their aim was poor, or else I outran their shots, for they never touched me [but] as each would whizz past me it increased my efforts. There was some kind of a yard fence around the buildings, how high I do not know; what I do know is, that I did not touch it." Not unlike the earlier sparing of Jim Duke and his friend when they tore down the picket fence as directed by Longstreet, some Mississippi Rebels may have yet recalled chivalry, even amid the slaughter, refusing to kill the bold Pennsylvania captain from Crawford County. Nelson escaped, unlike Colonel Sides and a high percentage of the 57th Pennsylvania's officers who were cut down by Barksdale's sharp-shooting men. The 57th Pennsylvania suffered a devastating 57.4 percent loss on bloody July 2.

A cruel fate also awaited many Yankees, including the regiment's second in command, Major William B. Neeper, who were now surrounded by Barksdale's attackers. Of the 59 57th Pennsylvania soldiers captured by the Mississippi Rebels, 44 were fated to die in Southern prisons, principally in the squalor of Andersonville. In addition, the revered regimental colors were nearly captured by the swarming Mississippians, after two 57th Pennsylvania color bearers were shot down.[304]

Overpowered by the raging tide, the 114th Pennsylvania was cut to pieces, losing nearly 50 percent of its strength during the nightmarish combat.[305] As planned by Barksdale, the Mississippians' rapid, sweeping attack—based on the concept of dashing forward over the open fields of fire at a sprint rather than advancing slowly in a parade ground-like manner (like "Pickett's Charge")—had paid off immensely. In fact, the Mississippi Brigade's charge, both in front and on the left flank of Cavada's regiment, was so swift that a good many Zouave prisoners were knocked to the ground and literally run over.[306]

Indeed, more 114th Pennsylvania soldiers were captured or missing than killed or wounded.[307] Historians have estimated that only around 250 Yankees were captured by the Mississippi Brigade at the Peach Orchard, but in fact the total was far higher.[308] This veteran Zouave regiment's decimation was complete, after having suffered from the blistering flank fires from Holder's 17th Mississippi while simultaneously hit in front by Carter's 13th Mississippi. Humphrey's scorching flank fire pouring from the northeast and into the left flank of Yankee units in and around the Emmitsburg Road also played a key role in assisting the advance of Barksdale's other three regiments. Around 100 Zouaves were killed and wounded (13 killed or mortally wounded and another 86 wounded) in the tempest that swirled around the Sherfy House and barn, until the bodies of Cavada's men in colorful uniforms dotted the green fields, pastures, and yards of the Sherfy farm like spring flowers on a rain-drenched morning.

The decimation of Cavada's Pennsylvania Zouaves was thorough with the loss of nearly 170 men. Captain Bowen, soon destined to command the battered fragments of this once magnificent Zouave regiment, described the 114th Pennsylvania's rout: "Already they were on our left and in our rear, the regiments on our left having been swept away. It seemed as though we were surrounded and could not escape capture, and many of the regiment [were] taken prisoners at this point. Only one avenue of escape was open to us, and that was up the Emmitsburg road."[309]

Meanwhile, the 73rd New York Fire Zouaves fought gamely, trading volleys with the Mississippians at close range. But the New Yorkers suffered the same dismal fate as the 114th Pennsylvania, caught in a vise of close-range frontal fire, while outflanked on the left and raked by a vicious enfilade fire. Lieutenant Moran described the cruel and systematic decimation of a fine command: "Our little regiment was melting away fast in the deadly cross-fire . . . and closed at last in semi-circle around its riddled flag."[310] This terrible punishment was too much for any troops to endure, and the survivors of the reeling 73rd New York retired northeast through the open fields east of the Emmitsburg Road, "leaving their dead and dying" behind in the dust, blood, and gore, wrote Lieutenant Moran, a plucky Irishman who had no idea that he faced large numbers of Irish in Barksdale's ranks, especially in Humphreys' regiment.[311]

At this juncture, Humphreys' 21st Mississippi in the Wheatfield Road sector now embarked "on one of the most memorable freelance odysseys of the entire battle," in the words of historian Noah Andre Trudeau.[312] Indeed, the 21st Mississippi, employing discipline and a hard-hitting style, now served as the tip of Barksdale's penetrating spear, and what Humphrey continued to skillfully orchestrate was a virtuoso tactical performance second to none during the three days of fighting at Gettysburg. By overwhelming the salient angle, Humphreys' regiment now gained the most advantageous of positions "on the left flank [of a] delectable row of Yankee cannon" neatly aligned along the defensive line spanning southeast down the Wheatfield Road: a row of dominos just waiting to be toppled over by the 21st Mississippi.[313]

After tearing through the apex of the Peach Orchard salient angle that unhinged the entire Third Corps' defensive line and hurling the 63rd and the 68th Pennsylvania and the 2nd New Hampshire rearward,

Colonel Humphreys and the 21st Mississippi were now fighting on their own hook and maximizing flexibility by focusing on the best targets of opportunity. The Second Day of Gettysburg's most magnificent solo offensive effort by any Confederate regiment began with the presentation to Colonel Humphreys of an ample number of highly-lucrative targets: both the exposed right flank of additional Union infantry regiments and a lengthy row of Yankee batteries aligned along the Wheatfield Road.

Demonstrating an exceptionally high level of initiative and tactical flexibility in so quickly adapting to the confusing battlefield situation obscured by deafening noise, drifting clouds of sulfurous smoke, and chaos swirling around him, Colonel Humphreys, in his mid-fifties, now needed no orders from superiors to achieve additional gains on his own. Indeed, there was no time for the issuing of new orders or ad hoc debates about the most appropriate tactics. Therefore, like Barksdale to the north, the versatile Humphreys now relied upon sound judgments and snap tactical decisions made on the fly. Meanwhile Barksdale likewise wasted no time. At the head of his three regiments, he now prepared to charge northeast along the Emmitsburg Road on his own in the hope of smashing one exposed Union regimental left flank after another.[314] Barksdale prepared his three regiments, separated from Humphrey's free-wheeling unit, which was now fighting on its own hook to the south, onward to inflict more extensive damage and reap greater gains.[315]

The only attempt to mount a Union counterattack came when General Graham rose to the challenge in splendid fashion. He ordered the stabilized 68th Pennsylvania, known as Philadelphia's Scott Legion, after it had been pushed rearward down the eastern side of the Emmitsburg Road Ridge, to stop the hard-charging 17th Mississippi. Colonel Holder's regiment now advanced northeast below the Emmitsburg Road and toward the Sherfy House, "coming down on our right flank," wrote one Pennsylvanian, and the 68th was quickly repulsed with almost effortless ease.[316]

With all bluecoat infantry pushed aside by Humphreys in the Wheatfield Road sector, the right flank of Union artillery lay vulnerable as never before. At this time, the 21st Mississippi now possessed the best opportunity to capture additional artillery pieces, both Third Corps and Artillery Reserve guns, aligned along the Wheatfield Road. Therefore, on their own, Humphreys and his men embarked on one of the most devastating of all Confederate attacks at Gettysburg and a special mission in which the main priority was "to do a little battery busting," but on a scale unsurpassed during the three days of fighting at Gettysburg.[317]

Retiring northeast below the Emmitsburg Road with his battered 73rd New York, Lieutenant Moran surveyed the slaughter along the southern arm of the Peach Orchard defensive line. He described the unbelievable sight of the damage inflicted by the 21st Mississippi: "A glance to the left revealed the shattered line was retreating in separated streams" toward Cemetery Ridge.[318] Colonel Humphreys' success also relieved pressure on the hard-hit left of Kershaw's South Carolina brigade to the right to increase the chances for greater gains in this sector below the Wheatfield Road.[319]

Meanwhile, Barksdale's blows along the Emmitsburg Road were equally devastating, matching Colonel Humphrey's ever-growing list of achievements along the Wheatfield Road. After taking the worst beating in the regiment's history, the surviving 114th Pennsylvania Zouaves, followed not long thereafter by the battered 73rd New York, headed northeastward either up or parallel the road. And a good many Yankees fled from the Mississippians in panic and headed through the open grain fields to the east. Other Keystone State soldiers loaded and fired in stubborn defiance, while they retreated northeast in the open fields. Sergeant Edward T. Marion, age twenty-four and fated to be killed in 1864, was seriously wounded in both buttocks: perhaps a wound that caused more embarrassment than pain. But this wound partly revealed that the Mississippi Rebels were firing sufficiently low to hit targets instead of firing too high like inexperienced troops.

In desperation, meanwhile, Captain Bowen ordered the regimental colors and the "Stars and Stripes" of the 114th Pennsylvania farther rearward to prevent their capture. The battered Pennsylvanians retired northeast in an effort to seek safety among other Union regiments. With the 21st Mississippi charging southeastward with "Rebel Yells," only the Emmitsburg Road northeastward and the open fields to the east offered escape routes from Barksdale's attackers."[320]

Atop Cemetery Ridge and looking on in horror at the Third Corps' systematic destruction, meanwhile, Captain Haskell, the former attorney, was shocked by the sight of the surging tide of Mississippians overrunning the Peach Orchard, where the neat rows of fruit trees had long lost their white blossoms and were now consumed in swirling smoke: "The Third Corps is being overpowered—here and there its lines begin to break—the men begin to pour back to the rear in confusion—the enemy are close upon them."[321] All the while and especially in the Wheatfield

Road sector, fast-thinking Union artillerymen began to prepare to get their guns out of the 21st Mississippi's path.[322]

After Barksdale's men swarmed over the Emmittsburg Road with their red regimental banners waving amid the drifting wreathes of smoke, a good many routed Federals, of both the 114th Pennsylvania and the 57th Pennsylvania, had fled into the large Sherfy barn now full of bullet holes, to seek shelter from the tide. In the 21st Mississippi's ranks, Private McNeily described the tactical situation at this time along the Emmitsburg Road Ridge: "Our left regiment, the 18th, breasted a hot fire from a large brick barn—converted into a fortress by a Zouave regiment of Graham's brigade . . . The 13th and 17th swept the line between these two salient. All met with stiff resistance."[323]

The general's nephew whose diminutive size belied his outsized fighting spirit, Captain Harris Barksdale, described the extent of the Mississippi Brigade's success. He wrote how after "the turnpike reached, and a half mile has been gained, six Napoleon guns are here taken, and at least 300 prisoners." Meanwhile, without resting or losing momentum, the Mississippi Rebels continued to hotly press the reeling Yankees at every point, punishing those Third Corps units caught in their path.[324]

With the "blue-bellies" on the run as far as the eye could see and fleeing in three directions, including toward Cemetery Ridge, Barksdale now fully understood the tactical necessity of capturing the large Sherfy barn, which had become a defensive bastion held by quite a few determined 114th Pennsylvania Zouaves and 57th Pennsylvania boys, despite the cost in time that it would take in reducing it. The Mississippi Rebels now employed finely-tuned skills from hunting in Mississippi's magnolia, oak, and pine forests and cypress swamps since boyhood and most recently sharpened in the nightmarish urban combat that had swirled through Fredericksburg's streets last December.[325]

Clearly, to Barksdale's clear tactical reasoning and at all costs, the twin strongholds—the house and barn—on the Sherfy farm had to be reduced as soon as possible. Before Barksdale's three regiments could yet resume the attack northeast up and parallel to the Emmitsburg Road, the threat posed by a large number of Philadelphians defending the immense barn, nearly twice the size of the house, had to be reduced as soon as possible before additional gains could be reaped by continuing the assault. Such a concentration of Federals simply could not be left in the Mississippi Brigade's rear to serve either as a rallying point for defeated

bluecoats or a staging area for resurgent Yankees to strike at the Mississippians' rear once Barksdale continued the advance northeast.

Consequently, the Yazoo County-born Major George Bruce Gerald
prepared to take action. He was soon to command the 18th Mississippi,
which advanced on the brigade's left, because Colonel Griffin and Lieutenant Colonel William Henry Luse were shortly cut down and later captured. The resourceful Major Gerald embarked upon the task of reducing
the dual strongholds that stood close to each other and well within mu-
tual-supporting distance. On Griffin's orders by way of Barksdale, Major
Gerald, age twenty-eight, gathered a band of reliable 18th Mississippi
soldiers and led them in an assault on the barn. To inspire his men, the
major dashed ahead with a waving saber in the attack upon the stronghold, lit up by Pennsylvania rifle-fire in response.[326]

These 18th Mississippi boys were more than willing to follow their
young major to hell and back if necessary. Gerald described his plan, "I
called to the men that the barn must be captured and to follow me and I
would open the door."[327] A tough, hard-nosed fighter throughout his life,
Major Gerard was destined to kill two opponents in a classic gunfight in
the streets of Waco, Texas near the turn of the century, nearly two
decades before his cremated ashes were spread in the Gulf of Mexico.[328]
The Pennsylvania Yankees who made their defiant last stand in the Sherfy
barn—one of the forgotten struggles of the battle of Gettysburg—had no
idea that they were about to meet one of the 18th Mississippi's toughest
leaders in a bloody showdown.[329]

As Major Gerald described the attack on the blazing Sherfy barn,
which stood atop the ridge beside the Emmitsburg Road like a giant red
beacon now ablaze with Pennsylvania gunfire: "They followed me with
a rush" to eliminate the Yankee threat. Gerald was the first to reach the
barn, somehow surviving the hail of bullets that kicked up spouts of dust
around him. He unhinged and began to force open the large barn door.
Major Gerald then swung the door wide open, allowing his 18th Mississippi soldiers, with fixed bayonets and fierce yells, to storm into the midst
of the Pennsylvania defenders inside the imposing three-story structure.
In terms of width, height, and overall size, this was no ordinary barn,
looking more like a giant warehouse than a typical Mississippi barn to
Gerald's Deep South soldiers.

Flashing musketry instantly erupted from inside the enclosure, dropping the first handful of 18th Mississippi Rebels who charged in. Gerald
never forgot how the embattled Sherfy "barn was filled with smoke so

dense that it was very nearly impossible to distinguish a man's body in it, such a continuous fire had the enemy within kept up." A factor not considered when the 114th Pennsylvania regiment was organized in the summer of 1861, when everyone believed that the war would be glorious and brief, was that the bright red colors of the Zouave uniforms now made excellent targets for Gerald's men even amid the smoky haze of the Sherfy barn.[330]

Young men unleashed fire at point-blank range in the confined setting which looked more like night than day. But now the Mississippian's experience in nasty urban fighting from the slick, wintry streets of Fredericksburg came to the fore against the Zouaves in early July. Major Gerald's men used bayonets with finesse and deadly skill, jabbing and thrusting at the dark outlines of opponents in the smoky near-blackness. Doing what had to be done to gain possession of the barn as quickly as possible, Gerald's veterans worked in business-like fashion, plunging and slashing with their sharp implements of steel. Other Mississippians swung muskets like clubs, cracking skulls and bashing the heads of fiercely resisting Pennsylvanians. Cavada's Zouaves and the 57th Pennsylvania boys proved difficult to overcome when cornered. Amid the choking haze of sulfurous smoke and dust filling the Sherfy barn, young men from Mississippi's small farms and Philadelphia's cobblestone streets came to deadly grips. Soldiers fought each other like primeval animals trapped in a life-or-death struggle, grappling with each other in mortal combat. Mississippi and Pennsylvania veterans fought each other without pity or remorse, rolling in the dirt and blood, swinging fists and cursing in the confused, point-blank fighting in the dusty semi-darkness.[331]

The wild melee inside the Sherfy barn's chaotic confines was brief but vicious. Major Gerald recorded how: "within less than two minutes we had killed, wounded or captured every man in the barn." The Pennsylvanian's tenacity in defending the Sherfy barn stemmed from coming to grips with their hated invader, defending home soil, and the belief that God was on their side: ironically, young Americans frantically fighting each other, despite from comparable classes and thinking very much alike in fundamental ways, while possessing more similarities than differences. In the end, Major Gerald and his men captured the Sherfy barn and additional prisoners, but at a stiff price. Dozens of dazed, powder-grimed Yankee prisoners were quickly hustled out of the hellish barn of farmer Sherfy and rearward by Gerald's victors. Feeling a sense of elation, Adjutant Harman, one of Colonel Carter's trusty 13th Mississippi officers, described in a letter the intoxicating sight: "a large number of Zouaves supposed to be as many as a Reg't or more surrendered to us in a body at the farm house." Although it was certainly not the complete regiment, the sight of captured Pennsylvania Yankees was exhilarating, fueling the Mississippi Rebel's hope of winning decisive victory before the sun went down on July 2.[332]

Meanwhile, Barksdale led the 17th and 13th Mississippi east of the Emmitsburg Road on a wide two hundred yard front, after overrunning the open ridge-top, to eliminate threats just east of the road. Likewise Colonel Humphreys continued to lead his 21st Mississippi onward to smash into its next victim in the Wheatfield Road sector. Colonel Henry J. Madill's 141st Pennsylvania, having been only recently positioned behind Cavada's regiment, stood below the crest of the Emmitsburg Ridge Road, after retiring northeast from the Wheatfield Road and its ill-fated assignment to support batteries against the 21st Mississippi's slashing attack. Positioned near the road, the regiment was now all alone after the 68th Pennsylvania had been hurled rearward. One of Madill's soldiers described with disbelief how with a wild "yell as though all Pandemonium had broken loose," the 21st Mississippi charged toward Madill's isolated regiment, after the colonel watched in horror as the remains of the 3rd Maine and 3rd Michigan retired rearward in a hurry. Organized in the summer of 1862 and having suffered around 60 percent losses at Chancellorsville after launching a bayonet attack, the 141st Pennsylvania, including soldiers who had only recently recovered from Chancellorsville wounds, gamely stood ready with regimental and national flags flying to receive Humphreys' attack.

These men had recently garrisoned the defenses of Washington, D.C., where they had grown soft. They had served less than a year, and were simply no match for Humphreys' hardened veterans, who were about to inflict the highest percentage loss suffered by any regiment of Graham's brigade. Unfortunately, for the 141st Pennsylvania, now on the Wheatfield Road's north side, they stood squarely in the path of the 21st Mississippi, rolling down the open slope parallel to the Wheatfield Road. With terrific force, they tore into Madill's exposed left flank east of the Wentz House. The 141st Pennsylvania never stood a chance, especially when men from the 17th Mississippi also came up on their right. But Humphreys' soldiers inflicted the most damage, shooting down nearly 30 men, finely-uniformed officers and color-bearers with the first volley.

In only a few minutes, more than 180 north Pennsylvania boys, including the entire color company, were cut down by the blazing 21st Mississippi rifles. Clearly, despite attacking on his own, Humphreys continued to reap dramatic gains along the southern arm of the Peach Orchard salient and on Sickles' rapidly collapsing left wing.[333]

In Colonel Madill's words that described the swift elimination of another fine Union regiment dropping by the wayside from the 21st Mississippi's combat prowess: "The enemy, after the falling back of the Sixth-eighth, advanced to the barn. I [was] overpowered by the large numbers of the enemy. I was compelled to retire."[334]

The price paid by Colonel Madill's brave soldiers, barely 200 men of a very small regiment for attempting "alone" to exchange volleys with the Mississippians was frightfully high. Firing from higher ground and down the open eastern slope of the Emmitsburg Ridge Road to sweep the Wheatfield Road sector unmercifully with a hail of lead, Humphreys' tried veterans aimed low to make every shot count, avoiding the rookie's sin of overshooting. Therefore, in short order, the 141st Pennsylvania was decimated by the Mississippians' rolling volleys and more than 150 men were cut down and all but three officers, with the unit losing more men in percentage terms (nearly 74%) than any other Third Corps regiment.[335]

One of the finest 141st Pennsylvania officers hit and left behind to the 21st Mississippi's mercy was Major Israel P. Spalding, age thirty-eight. Mississippi bullets tore into one thigh and shattered his ankle, leaving the major mortally wounded on the ground. The capable major would never see his wife Ruth, who he had married in December 1852, daughter, and two sons again.[336] In his final letter to his family not long before he was mowed down by the Mississippi bullets: "The enemy are now in my native state and I shall not fail in my duty to the flag we follow or disgrace the uniform I wear." Major Spalding backed up his words with his life, courageously fighting to the very end.[337]

Finally, after more bitter fighting that seemed like an eternity to the sweat-stained combatants, the last close-quarter fighting around the Sherfy farm sputtered to a bloody end, after the stubborn 141st Pennsylvania had been routed and hurled rearward down the Wheatfield Road. Saddened by the loss of so many good men, Colonel Madill carried the colors rearward himself through the drifting smoke, after his color guard had been slaughtered. Often overlooked, the tenacious defensive stand made by the Federals at the Sherfy House and barn was one of the forgotten stories of the Peach Orchard's defense that cost the Mississippians a good many fine men and officers, who could not be replaced this afternoon.

Among those Zouaves captured by the Mississippians was the 114th Pennsylvania's commander, Lieutenant Colonel Frederic Cavada, who was left behind at one of the Sherfy outbuildings. Lieutenant Colonel Cavada, the well-liked Hispanic officer, would survive Libby Prison's hell—along with the equally unlucky General Graham who was also about to be captured this afternoon—in Richmond. Once exchanged, Cavada served as the United States Consul in Trinidad, Cuba, from late 1864 to 1869, when he resigned to become a leading Cuban Rebel commander in the nationalist struggle against Spain. However, Cavada's legendary luck finally ran out when he was captured by the Spanish. Despite signed petitions from Generals Grant, Birney, Meade, and Sickles to save the respected Cuban, Cavada was executed by a Spanish firing squad on a July day in 1871, eight years after the battle of Gettysburg. In his beloved city known as the "Pearl of the South," he defiantly threw his hat into the air and shouted, "Goodbye Cuba, forever!" just before a hail of Spanish bullets ended his life, after having escaped so many Mississippi bullets at Gettysburg.

Scores of other Pennsylvania soldiers were captured by the Mississippians after the collapse of the Emmitsburg Road defensive line. Shocked by the extent of Barksdale's sparkling success in smashing through the Peach Orchard salient, Colonel Cavada's brother, who now served on General Humphreys' staff, Adolfo F. Cavada, never forgot the Mississippians' "diabolical cheer and yells coming on like devils incarnate." Frederic was de-horsed by a swarm of Mississippi bullets, but was unhurt. After Cavada's capture, the reliable Captain Bowen commanded what little remained of the 114th Pennsylvania, which had been severely manhandled.[338] As a sad fate would have it, both Cavada brothers finally died not in Gettysburg's tempest, but for the great republican dream of Cuban independence.[339]

The rounding up of Yankee prisoners took time, delaying the resumption of Barksdale's' attack northeast up the Emmitsburg Road. Another forgotten factor also caused delay. After capturing the Sherfy House and barn on a ridge now covered with dead and wounded soldiers and a large number of slaughtered artillery horses, the most opportunistic threadbare Mississippi boys reaped the harvest of the spoils of war, taking shoes, articles of clothing (the color blue made no difference), and gear from the

Yankee dead. One Rebel officer exchanged a handkerchief for a sword belt from a wounded 73rd New York captain, who was escorted rearward as a prisoner and back to the Sherfy House area, where the growing mass of captives were collected. Other Rebel soldiers, famished and hungry, hunted for pieces of hardtack to gobble down. One of Barksdale's men, Private John M. Hawthorne, Company G, 18th Mississippi, picked up and kept a photo of the brother of the mortally wounded Corporal Robert Kenderdine, who had served courageously on the 114th Pennsylvania's color guard. The photo would be returned to the Quaker family after the war's end.[340] Meanwhile, after systematically wiping out the Pennsylvania defenders of the Sherfy House and barn, Major Gerald and his 18th Mississippi victors rejoined the brigade, taking their flank position on Barksdale's left next to the road. "We left the barn," in Gerald's words, and prepared for resuming the attack northeast and toward additional Yankees and cannon.[341]

But one last horrific coda remained for the Peach Orchard sector and the Sherfy farm. After Barksdale's men swept through, the Sherfy barn was accidently set on fire by exploding shells. Unable to move, some wounded Pennsylvanians went up in the flames before they could escape or be rescued. Captain Edward R. Bowen, now commanding the Zouave regiment, described the sad plight of some injured 114th Pennsylvania soldiers: "Some of the wounded sought refuge in the barn, and being too badly wounded were not able to escape from it when it was burned and perished in the flames; their identification was impossible, but their remains were recognized as members of the regiment by fragments of their distinctive uniform," such as white leggings, baggy red pants, the fezs, etc.[342]

After Graham's brigade had been mauled and swept aside, Barksdale's considerable hard-hitting power was now turned on the Second Division, Third Corps, under General Andrew Atchinson Humphreys, a tough old army regular and Seminole War veteran, who promised to put up a stiff fight. Here, northeast of the Peach Orchard carnage stood two of General Humphreys' brigades along the Emmitsburg Road, now crowded with the broken fragments of Graham's vanquished Pennsylvania brigade. Meanwhile, the 21st Mississippi continued to attack on its own, sweeping through the Wheatfield Road sector with a vengeance, firing on the move, and inflicting even more damage: the methodical, destructive work more often accomplished by a brigade rather than a single regiment battling on its own hook.

But ironically, the accidental division of force—usually a fundamental sin in the art of war—into two separate wings in the midst of battle actually continued to work to the Mississippi Brigade's advantage. Indeed, in two different directions, the Mississippi Brigade's separate wings now advanced in two freewheeling offensive efforts that packed a lethal punch. Lucrative tactical opportunities beckoned to Barksdale on the left wing because the Emmitsburg Road led to the flanks of General Humphreys' regiments, while the Wheatfield Road led the right wing (the 21st Mississippi) southeast to the vulnerable right flanks of Federal artillery poised farther to the south.

While Barksdale surged northeast up the Emmitsburg Road beyond the Sherfy House and toward the east-west running Abraham Trostle Lane, perpendicular to the Emmitsburg Road, with three regiments, Colonel Humphreys continued to push southeast with his crack regiment down the gently sloping ground on both sides of the Wheatfield Road. In addition, the topography also served to enhance the momentum of Barksdale's assault up the Emmitsburg Road, because the attackers surged across open ground—an expanse of broad fields—while steamrolling along the shallow, low ridge-top free of trees and underbrush. The Emmitsburg Road Ridge was high at the Peach Orchard, but the ridge gradually leveled out and dipped slightly, and then rose again along the dusty road that led to the highest point along the open ridge at a commanding knoll upon which sat the Daniel F. Klingel House before descending toward Gettysburg. The ground around the Sherfy House was just slightly higher than the Peach Orchard, while the Klingel House knoll was higher than both the Peach Orchard and Sherfy House knolls.

The 13th, 17th, and 18th Mississippi charged northeast up, and parallel to, the Emmitsburg Road, smashing into what was left of Sickles' already defeated units, which were knocked down like ten-pins by the rejuvenated flank attack. The first encounter was with the remnants of the retiring 73rd New York in the rear, which had been dispatched to the assistance of Graham's men. By this time, the "Excelsior Brigade" regiment was in bad shape. The regiment had been hurled north and parallel to the road from its initial defensive position behind the 114th Pennsylvania. After having been first struck by Barksdale from the west, the seemingly ill-fated 73rd New York was now hit from the southwest by the same howling Mississippians. Limping with a wound in the right ankle, Lieutenant Moran described his regiment's dilemma: "Our line was now in considerable disorder. . . . For a few minutes we were in a perfect tornado of bullets and shells from both friends and foes, the open field affording no shelter. At last the enemy came hot and hard upon us. As the centre of the 13th Mississippi passed over me, the men, firing and shrieking like the Indians . . . ."[343]

Clearly, the Emmitsburg Road offered a ready avenue for the rampaging Mississippians to roll-up the left flanks of Union regiments deployed along the road. Consequently, the 105th Pennsylvania, which had been positioned to the 57th Pennsylvania's right along the road and with its right on Trostle Lane, was the last regiment of Graham's brigade, holding the lonely right flank. The 105th Pennsylvania was likewise severely punished by the resurgent tide of Barksdale's 13th, 17th, and 18th Mississippi. Indeed, after Barksdale's troops had mauled the 114th and the 57th Pennsylvania regiments and the 73rd New York, the 105th Pennsylvania's left flank, to the right of these routed troops at the brigade line's northern end, was fully exposed. In horror, Colonel Craig realized the extent of the danger for "a few minutes later the 114th [Pennsylvania] fell to the rear and the 57th very soon followed, leaving my left flank entirely unprotected," as the Mississippi Rebels continued surging northeast up the Emmitsburg Road beyond the Sherfy House and toward the colonel's vulnerable left flank from the southwest.

This golden tactical opportunity was fully exploited by Barksdale, who just kept up the momentum and the relentless pressure. Loading and firing as fast as possible, the Magnolia State soldiers continued to pour a murderous enfilade fire into the Pennsylvanians' exposed left flank. Watching helplessly as his fine regiment was destroyed around him, Colonel Craig described how "the enemy, taking advantage of this, advanced across the Emmitsburg road, in front of the [Sherfy] house, and immediately opened fire upon our left flank." Loading and firing on the run, the Mississippi woodsmen, farmers and bear hunters raked the vulnerable left flank of the Pennsylvania "Wildcats" with a vengeance.

One good officer falling to the Mississippians' blistering fire was Schuylkill County's Lieutenant Isaac A. Dunsten, Company C, 105th Pennsylvania. He went down mortally wounded, when Mississippi bullets shattered both thighs. Despite taking heavy losses these surviving Pennsylvanians gamely held their ground, facing south and standing firm to blast away at the Mississippians, who continued to scream like banshees and surge northeast as if nothing could stop them. Sensing victory in the thick, sulfurous air, Barksdale's soldiers continued to sweep onward like an avalanche, with bayonets flashing and red battle-flags bobbing up and down through the palls of drifting smoke. The charging 18th, 13th, and 17th Mississippi, from left to right, steadily applied pressure to the vulnerable flanks, including groups of rallied Pennsylvania men from some of Graham's defeated units. Quickly exploiting another opportunity, Barksdale likewise directed troops to strike the 57th Pennsylvania's rear. Hit from the left flank and rear, the 57th Pennsylvania was hurled back, because, in Sergeant Ellis Strouss' words, the howling "Confederates were swarming in our rear."

Before Barksdale's onslaught, each and every new ad hoc blue line of resistance was quickly overwhelmed, crumpling under the relentless pressure and murderous fires. With many good officers cut down and acting on their own, Mississippi men in the enlisted ranks often took over, encouraging their comrades onward into the swirling smoke. Here, the battered survivors, mostly Scots-Irish boys, of the notoriously tough Wildcat Regiment discovered to their dismay that the Mississippi Rebels in ragged, dirty butternut jean uniforms were the real wildcats at Gettysburg. Colonel Craig attempted to save what little remained of his badly mauled 105th Pennsylvania, "being so small and both flanks being entirely unprotected, I ordered the regiment to retire" to the rear to escape.[344]

After having been smashed by the hard-hitting team of Barksdale-Humphreys, the rout of Graham's once proud brigade of more than 1,500 veteran Pennsylvania troops, who lost 740 men, was thorough. All that remained of the Federal unit were scattered knots of rallied Pennsylvanians, yet stubborn and defiant, turning to fire at their tormentors, while they retreated to escape. With the loss of leading officers, battered Union regiments were left to largely fend for themselves, forced to make the best out of a bad situation in the face of Barksdale's sweeping onslaught that now had a life of its own.

Private McNeily, of the Hurricane Rifles, 21st Mississippi, described the extent of the damage when the Union "retreat became a rout in which our men took a heavy toll for the losses inflicted on them."[345] Indeed, the collapse of Graham's brigade and other regiments of Birney's First Division in attempting to defend the Peach Orchard now "meant real trouble for [General] Humphreys, who faced an aggressive enemy flushed with victory on his right and rear, with all the signs in his front indicating that a serious attack [from Wilcox's Alabamians] was coming there next."[346] Therefore, General Humphreys desperately sought to protect his heavily pressured left as best he could, after he discovered to his horror that there was "nobody [now left] but myself—Birney's troops cleared out."[347]

Knowing the importance of keeping up the momentum and initiative, the elated Mississippi troops continued to surge up the Emmitsburg Road with Rebel Yells. With Barksdale leading the way as usual, the 13th, 17th and 18th Mississippi, from right to left, tore savagely into those reinforcing units that supported Graham's mauled brigade, consisting of Colonel William R. Brewster's Second Brigade, Second Division, Third Corps. Urged onward by Barksdale, the Magnolia State brigade's fast-moving left wing charged Colonel Brewster's famed brigade. Bestowed with the proud name "Excelsior," the Latin motto of the State of New York, the Second Brigade, Humphreys' Second Division, Third Corps, of more than 1,800 tough New Yorkers was positioned just beyond, or north of, Trostle Lane and east of the Emmitsburg Road to pose a threat to Barksdale's right flank. Commanded by the relatively inexperienced Brewster, these New Yorkers were part of a dual defensive line that had been positioned to the right-rear of the 105th Pennsylvania on the road's east side and directly in the path of Barksdale's regiments attacking below the road.

Raised by Sickles and Graham, the ambitious engineer of the Brooklyn Navy Yard who had recruited many workers from the dry docks of the naval facility, the famous "Excelsior" Brigade was a premier combat unit. The brigade consisted of the 70th, 71st, 72nd, 73rd (whose battered remains had rejoined the brigade), 74th Volunteer Infantry, which included a good many dockworkers of Graham's old regiment whom he had commanded since the Peninsula Campaign, and the 120th New York Volunteer Infantry, which had been organized by Sickles at the war's beginning. These New York regiments were composed of a good many Irish, Germans, and soldiers of old New York Dutch descent like Sickles, whose ancestors were the Van Sickelns from Holland. So many Irish served in the 74th New York that its chaplain was Father Joseph O'Hagen. He was a devout and respected Jesuit in blue, who fortified the enlisted men's resolve for meeting Mississippi Rebels this afternoon.

Without losing momentum, Barksdale's attackers tore into the left flank of Colonel Brewster's New York brigade around 6:30 PM. They once again delivered a punishing blow, despite Humphreys, who one Pennsylvania fifer referred to a "Goggle-eyes," having ordered Brewer's brigade to turn left from facing west to the southwest to meet Barksdale's threat. To their destructive delight, the Mississippi woodsmen, frontiersmen, and yeomen farmers made the most of another chance to vanquish yet another respected unit of highly touted Zouaves in one afternoon, after the 114th Pennsylvania and 73rd New York. With tattered battle-flags waving in the swirling clouds of dust and smoke, the Magnolia Staters slammed hard into the New York brigade's left flank. Musketry erupting from Empire State formations dropped additional Mississippi boys, but Barksdale's attack never faltered or lost steam. More falling comrades only fueled the determination of Barksdale's soldiers to charge onward and inflict more damage this afternoon.

Swathes of New Yorkers went down when struck from three sides by the blistering musketry erupting from the swarming Mississippians, firing on the run and making their shots count. Taking their worst punishment to date in a hard-fought sector that had become a hornet's nest, the New York troops began to waver under the pounding. Two entire regiments, facing southwest, the 71st and 72nd New York, were quickly pushed aside. Thoroughly punished, larger numbers of the foremost New Yorkers on the left fell back northeast up and parallel to the Emmitsburg Road. While a good many New York soldiers fled in panic with cries of "Run boys, we're whipped," others withdrew more stubbornly through the pelting hail of Mississippi bullets. By a narrow margin, the "Excelsior Brigade" troops fought their way out of Barksdale's tightening trap to narrowly escape their tormenters, who were determined to bag even more Zouaves to add to the day's already impressive total of nearly 1,000 prisoners. Throughout this bloody afternoon, Barksdale's attackers seemed to harbor a special grudge toward the colorfully uniformed Zouaves, inflicting terrible damage on the most splendid-looking troops at Gettysburg. After all, the Zouaves had long boasted of vanquishing large numbers of Rebels across the South. And Barksdale's men were now determined to set the record straight.

Indeed, the Mississippi hellions were proving to be a nightmare-come-true for the hard-hit Zouaves. Colonel Brewer's old regiment, the 73rd New York lost 162 men out of 350. This was a bad day for the "Second Fire Zouaves," after their fateful second bloody meeting with Barksdale's boys. Eliminating the threat of Barksdale's right flank, the mauling and hurling back of the "Excelsior Brigade" opened the way for Barksdale and his rampaging Mississippians to achieve even greater gains.

But the "Excelsior Brigade's" defeat was not just the destructive work of Barksdale's men. To the left of the Mississippians. General Wilcox's Alabama brigade of General Richard H. Anderson's Division had finally advanced, sending destructive volleys into the right of Brewster's brigade from the northwest, while the Mississippians blasted away from the southwest. Therefore, Humphreys' two brigades fought at right angles to each other, with Brewster facing southwest and most of Carr's brigade, on Brewster's right along the Emmitsburg Road, facing west. In a futile effort to hold the south-facing line, a desperate Brewster had bought some precious time when he wisely formed the 120th New York Volunteer Infantry, which had been placed in reserve, at a right angle to his wavering line along the Emmitsburg Road. Behind a low stone wall that provided some protection, the New Yorkers of the 383-man regiment under Lieutenant Colonel Cornelous D. Westbrook, who fell wounded, made a determined stand amid the killing fields. Here, while the regiment was "shot apart," they bought time for other brigade members to escape.

But Barksdale was not to be denied this afternoon, especially when the 120th New York was left isolated and alone, after the other "Excelsior Brigade" regiments had fled before the Mississippians' attack. A close-range New York volley halted the Rebels, who quickly realigned and then returned a volley "when within a few yards of us," wrote an astounded Charles Santvoord. But Colonel Westbrook's defiant regiment, with its front struck by Barksdale and the right pressured by Wilcox, never had a chance All "Excelsior Brigade" troops, including even the stubborn 120th New York boys, finally retired at around 7:00 PM. The 120th New York left more than 200 fallen comrades behind after they were pushed rearward up the road toward Gettysburg.[348]

Private John Saunders Henley, of the 17th Mississippi, described Barksdale's slashing attack northeastward that knocked back hundreds of Union troops, "who jumped out of the Emmitsburg road in front of the charge [and these] were several regiments of troops from New York. They ran three or four deep."[349] Clearly, the combined effect of high-pitched Rebel Yells, sharpened bayonets, and expert marksmanship were not only lethal but also terrifying to a good many boys in blue. But these fears were well warranted, because the "Excelsior Brigade" lost 778 men, a more than a 42% loss. One of General Humphreys' aide-de-camps never forgot how the Mississippians' charge was distinguished by a "roar and a cheer" from the elated attackers, who were "coming on like devils incarnate" and destroying everything before them.[350]

But the price of reaping one victory after another proved terribly high for Barksdale's left wing attackers. When a captured Lieutenant Moran, "Excelsior Brigade," was escorted back to the Sherfy House sector, he was appalled by the scene of slaughter. He saw the farm "strewn with killed and wounded [Mississippians], mixed with a number of our own men. Many of the wounded, friend and foe, had sought refuge in Sherfy's barn, which was riddled with shot and shell. Around it, as well as on the slope in its front, up which the Mississippi Brigade had advanced in the face of an incessant fire of musketry and artillery, the dead encumbered the ground."[351] These dead and dying young men and boys included some of the Mississippi Brigade's best and brightest, lying mangled and broken in the gory fields.

William Barksdale, pictured here in 1859 when he served as a U.S. Congressman. During the Civil War he broke the mold of a "political general" by proving himself a brilliant combat leader. He was mortally wounded while leading his Mississippi Brigade toward Cemetery Ridge at Gettysburg, in an attack that nearly won the battle for the Confederacy.

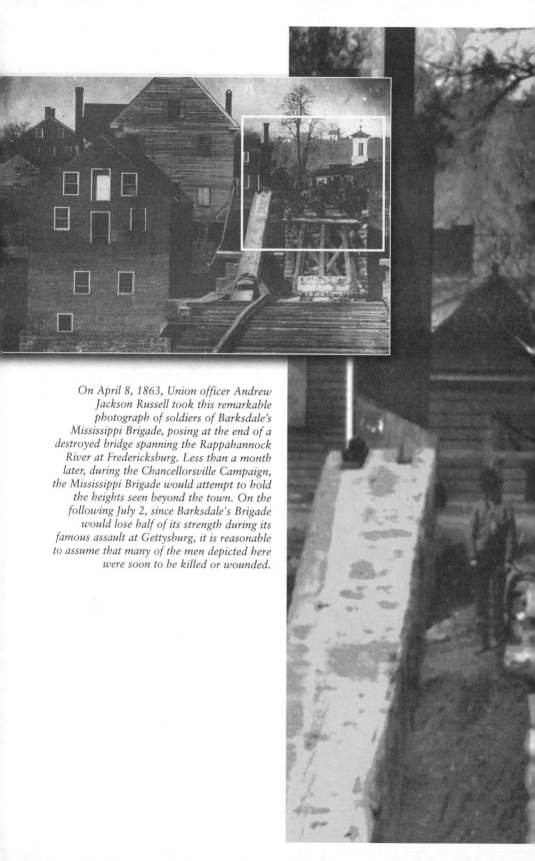

On April 8, 1863, Union officer Andrew Jackson Russell took this remarkable photograph of soldiers of Barksdale's Mississippi Brigade, posing at the end of a destroyed bridge spanning the Rappahannock River at Fredericksburg. Less than a month later, during the Chancellorsville Campaign, the Mississippi Brigade would attempt to hold the heights seen beyond the town. On the following July 2, since Barksdale's Brigade would lose half of its strength during its famous assault at Gettysburg, it is reasonable to assume that many of the men depicted here were soon to be killed or wounded.

*Sergeant John C. Lowe,
Company E, 13th
Mississippi Infantry
Regiment, Army of
Northern Virginia,
C.S.A.*

*John's brother, Private
James M. Lowe,
Company E, 13th
Mississippi Infantry
Regiment, Army of
Northern Virginia,
C.S.A.*

Right: *Colonel Erasmus R. Burt led the 18th Mississippi Infantry with distinction before being mortally wounded at the Battle of Ball's Bluff, Virginia, on October 21, 1861. Burt left behind a widow and eight orphans back home in Jackson, Mississippi, as well as a company in the 18th Mississippi that continued to be known as Burt's Rifles.*

Below: *This famous photo of the Sunken Road at Fredericksburg shows casualties and equipment of the 18th Mississippi after Sedgwick's Sixth Corps finally overran the position during the Chancellorsville Campaign, May 3, 1863.*

A postwar photo of Generals Carr, Sickles & Graham on the Gettysburg battlefield, on the spot at the Trostle Farm where General Sickles lost his leg, and near the Peach Orchard where Graham was wounded and captured by Barksdale's men.

An 1863 photograph of the Peach Orchard, now leveled, with Little Round Top in the background.

Colonel Benjamin Grubb Humphreys, a brilliant tactican and the hard-hitting commander of the 21st Mississippi. He was Barksdale's top lieutenant and most aggressive regimental commander, especially during the supreme challenge at Gettysburg. After Barksdale fell he took command of the brigade, and after the war was elected governor of Mississippi.

Private Billy Blake, 18th Mississippi Infantry. He was seriously wounded in the attack on the Peach Orchard and subsequently had his leg amputated at the hip in a Union field hospital.

Every Union commander in this picture was wounded at Gettysburg. Seated is Winfield Scott Hancock; leaning against the tree is Francis Barlow, and to his left are David Birney and John Gibbon.

The Trostle House after the battle, with the men having been buried but not the horses. Originally Sickles' headquarters on July 2, it was here that Humphreys' 21st Mississippi overran Bigelow's Union battery. Photograph by Timothy O'Sullivan

The grim killing field of the Peach Orchard.
Farmer Joseph Sherfy's Orchard became hell on earth for hundreds of young
men and boys, North and South, on the afternoon of July 2, 1863.

Statue honoring heroic Union artillerymen, who attempted in vain to stem the tide of Barksdale's Mississippi Brigade that swept over the Peach Orchard.

Below: *The monument that honors the memory and sacrifice of Barksdale's Brigade at the point where the Mississippians were unleashed and launched their sweeping attack on the Peach Orchard. The statue captures the fighting spirit of Barksdale and his men as well as the savage nature of the struggle for possession of the Peach Orchard.*

These photos of the modern battlefield in the vicinity of the Peach Orchard help to convey a sense of the open terrain upon which Barksdale's men fought. In the photo below can be seen Little Round Top, some 1,000 yards away, along with a sense of the natural strength of the Federals' true main line at Gettysburg.

Private John Byers, 17th Mississippi, was a farmer before the war, and this photo was taken in Richmond, Virginia, in the summer of 1862. Private Byers was wounded and captured during Barksdale's Charge on July 2, 1863. He was later exchanged but then killed in battle in 1864.

Private John I. Neely, Company F (Tallahatchie Rifles), 21st Mississippi, died of disease in 1862.

Captain Isaac D. Stamps, the respected commander of Company E (Hurricane Rifles), 21st Mississippi Confederate Infantry, Wilkinson County, Mississippi. Leading his troops by example and in the forefront as usual, the beloved captain of so much promise was killed during Barksdale's assault on the Peach Orchard. Stamps was one of the typical inspirational company commanders of the Mississippi Brigade, whose efforts played a role in the overrunning of the Peach Orchard, fueling the attack onward to Cemetery Ridge, and bringing the Confederacy closer to decisive victory than ever before.

The wool jean uniform coat of the irrepressible Colonel Benjamin Grubb Humphreys. The popular colonel's uniform was presented to him by the society of patriotic women of Woodville, Mississippi, and symbolizes the sacrifices of men and women on the home front during the war. Courtesy of The Museum of the Confederacy.

George Gordon Meade, who was given command of the Army of the Potomac only five days before Gettysburg. It was his task to defeat Robert E. Lee and his Army of Northern Virginia, which had not yet tasted defeat in the Civil War.

Lafayette McLaws, whose division included Barksdale's Brigade. A solid, sturdy fighter, he was sometimes accused of being slow.

James Longstreet, commander of the First Corps of the Army of Northern Virginia. The part he played at Gettysburg has been controversial for 150 years; however, the Rebels never came closer to winning the battle than when his men went into action. And he had said from the start he didn't wish to go into the fight without Pickett's Division, or as he put it, "with one boot off."

Joseph Kershaw, whose South Carolina Brigade attacked at Gettysburg just before Barksdale's Mississippians. Churned up in the Wheatfield, he helped draw off so many Union reinforcements that Barksdale was nearly able to fight his way to Cemetery Ridge.

A painting of Brigadier General William Barksdale, CSA, by artist Jaime Cooper. A newspaper editor, U.S. Congressman, and finally one of Robert E. Lee's most successful battlefield commanders, the humble-born Barksdale had proved himself throughout his life to be a natural leader of men. At age 42 he fell at the foot of Cemetery Ridge at Gettysburg, after nearly achieving a breakthrough that might have decided the war.
(Jaime Cooper's original historical oil paintings and prints [www.jacooper.com] are available from Pictors Studio, www.pictorsstudio.com.)

— 6 —

"We want those guns!"

BY SMASHING THROUGH the apex of the Peach Orchard defensive line, crushing the salient angle and pushing all foremost Union regiments aside, Colonel Humphreys' 21st Mississippi was now in a most advantageous position to capture more artillery pieces than any other regiment—Union or Confederate—during the three days fighting at Gettysburg. After having struck "the critical blow" in collapsing the Peach Orchard salient and gaining the vulnerable right flank of Federal batteries positioned along the southern arm of the angle, the 21st Mississippi was poised to enfilade the lengthy row of Union batteries that stretched along the Wheatfield Road. Best of all, the Wheatfield Road led southeast all the way to an undefended Cemetery Ridge and the gaping hole in Meade's left-center.[352]

From Cemetery Ridge, as described in a letter, Captain Haskell ascertained the peril for the life of not only the Army of the Potomac but also the Union by this time, while also revealing the extent of the great opportunity gained by Barksdale's three regiments along the Emmitsburg Road: "With [Sickles'] Corps out of the way, the enemy [were now] in a position to advance upon the line of the Second Corps, not in a line parallel with its front, but they would come obliquely from the left."[353]

Indeed, that was Colonel B.G. Humphreys' intent. Despite commanding only a single regiment, Barksdale's top lieutenant continued to outdo what was thought possible by a small unit in the midst of a major offensive. The 21st Mississippi was most responsible for punching a hole in the Peach Orchard's salient angle and unhinging the Third Corps' defensive line, while also helping to pave the way for the success of Barksdale's other three regiments northeast of the orchard and providing timely support for McLaw's troops south of the Wheatfield Road.[354] After smashing through the salient angle, one Mississippian explained how "the 21st regiment made a slight detour to the right to take in ten more Napoleon guns, which were now firing into the flank of the [South Carolina] brigade," even before Barksdale had turned his three regiments northeast to attack beyond the Sherfy House.[355]

Leading his 21st Mississippi with well-honed tactical skill, Colonel Humphreys explained the challenge that had early forced him to make the necessary tactical adjustments. While the three regiments under "Barksdale continued 'to swing to the left' until I was forced to abandon it—being on his extreme right, and made a direct charge with my Regiment against the guns in the Peach Orchard."[356] A tactically astute officer who had briefly attended West Point, Humphreys knew that he could not turn left to follow Barksdale up the Emmitsburg Road and leave Union troops and guns in the Mississippi Brigade's rear. Therefore, he knew that he had to sweep the enemy before him.

Humphreys' accomplishments were already more spectacular than what had been achieved by Barksdale's three regiments. After overrunning the salient angle, the 21st Mississippi had smashed through the south-facing Colonel Andrew H. Tippin's 68th Pennsylvania. With its right flank turned by Humphreys, three-fourths of the Pennsylvania regiment's officers were quickly killed or wounded by the Mississippians' deadly fire. The 68th Pennsylvania's Private Alfred J. Craighead wrote, "It was a terrible afternoon in that orchard." Colonel Humphreys wrote of the success: "Their infantry supports fled and the guns were captured" by his 21st Mississippi boys, who were "whooping with delight as they swarmed over" the artillery. One attacker, Private McNeily, described "several guns and caissons whose teams were shot down and captured at the Peach Orchard line."

Not even the inspiring presence of General Graham, who busily attempted to rally his troops, was enough to beat back the 21st Mississippi's onslaught, after Humphrey's men burst through the apex of the Peach Orchard. A sharp-eyed Mississippi marksmen targeted Graham and hit him with a well-placed shot.[357] But the irrepressible New York City-born general, a former sailor in the prewar Navy who had first gone to sea at age seventeen, was down but not out. After being carried rearward by his men, the fiery Graham, age thirty-nine, demanded his horse. Knowing that the day's greatest crisis was at hand, Graham then gamely rode back to the vortex of the Mississippi storm, ignoring his painful wound. With his troops fleeing around him after the 21st Mississippi hurled back the 68th Pennsylvania, 2nd New Hampshire, and other mauled regiments, General Graham exhibited gallantry in attempting to patch together a last-minute defense against the charging 21st Mississippi. Private McNeily admired Graham for his heroics, writing, "General Graham with becoming courage rode out of the orchard behind his men. His horse was wounded and pitched the General over his head, leaving him in a dazed state of mind."[358]

But getting thrown to the ground with sufficient force to have broken his neck was not the worst of Graham's woes. At the same time that his horse was hit, General Graham also took a Mississippi bullet that tore through both shoulders.[359] Graham lay "dazed" in a bloody clump, while charging 21st Mississippi soldiers descended upon him like a pack of wolves. The half-stunned general was captured by Humphreys' Rebels. Some Mississippi boys pulled the blood-splattered general from under the weight of his dead horse. This unnamed 21st Mississippi soldier coveted the honor of capturing rather than killing a Yankee general. Private McNeily described how General Graham "was passed over and captured by the 21st Mississippi and sent to the rear" as a prize. Humphrey's men had gained yet another trophy in overrunning the Peach Orchard.

Colonel Humphreys described the tactical situation and his extensive gains, after the "21st Miss regiment pushed on through the Peach Orchard, only to see the Federals fleeing to the right and left—Barksdale and his other three regiments pursued the infantry to the left with the 21st Miss to the right after the artillery—four pieces of which Genl Graham had retired to a stone fence in the valley and turned them on Kershaw to my right. Seeing it hazardous to leave these guns on my right to rejoin Barksdale, I wheeled to the right and charged Genl Graham" and many of his soldiers, who were outflanked along the southern arm of Sickles' collapsed salient. Lieutenant Owen, Washington Artillery, wrote how "among the prisoners was Brig.-Gen. Graham, who asked us the name of the general officer who led the charge today." After being given a courier's horse to ride, an amazed Graham lamented with regret that "our generals don't do that sort of thing."[360] In a steamrolling attack that had only begun to wreak havoc and achieve spectacular gains, the "21st Mississippi quickly snatched [General Graham] up along with hundreds of other prisoners, and sent him rapidly to the rear. Several cannon were also captured."[361]

But Colonel Humphreys and his 21st Mississippi had more work to do this afternoon, with hundreds of Yankees fleeing east to escape and gain Cemetery Ridge. Through the thick palls of drifting smoke, the Mississippi Delta colonel marveled at a spectacle to the southeast and farther down the Wheatfield Road that took his breath away: one Union artillery piece after another facing south and fully exposed to a flank attack. While Union artillery yet faced south toward Kershaw's South Carolinians, Humphreys' troops continued to surge toward the right flank of the blazing Union guns, which were ripe for the taking.[362]

But by this time, the bluecoat gunners were attempting to get out as fast as they could to evade the 21st Mississippi's onslaught.[363] In addition, along the embattled Wheatfield Road, the bluecoat cannoneers of Captain A. Judson Clark's Battery B, First New Jersey Light Artillery, were vulnerable, after Thompson's four Pennsylvania light artillery guns from Pittsburgh, and the 15th New York Battery, under Captain Patrick Hart, now out of ammunition, retired before Humphreys' attackers. Therefore, after expending its canister at Kershaw's South Carolina soldiers to the southeast, the stubborn New Jersey field pieces stood alone with their right flank exposed before the surging 21st Mississippi. The Confederates, with Humphreys imploring everyone onward, continued attacking without a pause to exploit their already significant gains, screaming like banshees and rushing onward. Determined to win it all today, Humphreys' sweat-stained soldiers charged southeast down the open slope parallel to the Wheatfield Road, rolling onward to exploit their breakthrough The unnerving sight of howling Mississippi Rebels pouring onward was too much for many Yankees, including the cannoneers of Captain Clark's Garden State battery, now without infantry support after Madill's 141st Pennsylvania had been swept away.

All the while, Colonel Humphreys' attackers continued to load and fire on the run, cutting down more New Jersey artillerymen, who now knew that they should have been long gone. A sheet of bullets whistled through the busy New Jersey gunners, while they frantically attempted to get their field pieces off the field in time. All the while, the stream of Mississippi projectiles ricocheted off the bronze and iron barrels of the New Jersey cannon, making a sharp pinging sound like summer hail hitting a tin roof. Bullets splintered the spokes, wheels and carriages of field pieces, and tore into wooden limbers, which contained ever-dwindling supplies of artillery ammunition.

Humphreys' veterans made every shot count, taking time to aim and hit their mark. As on so many past battlefields, the fast-firing Mississippi

Rebels knocked bluecoat leaders out of action. With these exposed Garden State guns isolated, without infantry support, additional sharp-eyed Mississippi Rebels turned their muskets on the battery's horses, which were whinnying, rearing and wild with fear and pain. With the New Jersey cannon being withdrawn as rapidly as possible by the dwindling band of surviving gunners, it was now horses and not men that had to be shot down if the guns were to be captured. Riddled with bullets, battery horses dropped in piles, still in their leather traces and harnesses.

After a stream of minie balls cut down the lead horse of one frightened team, the howling Mississippians closed in for the kill. Now the blue-clad gunners were forced to cut the traces and attempt to pull aside the heavy bodies of dead horses before it was too late. With Humphreys' wild-looking men, long-haired and bearded, descending upon them with gleaming bayonets, frantic cannoneers worked frantically to complete the task. All the while, a hail of bullets passed through the crippled New Jersey battery to make the air sing around the Garden State gunners. The eerie chorus of "Rebel Yells" rose higher, until they became deafening to the terrified New Jersey artillerymen. In a deadly race, 21st Mississippi Rebels rushed Captain Clark's guns, before the fast-working artillerymen re-hitched teams and pulled out. On and on through the choking smoke, Rebels sprinted toward the exposed guns with bayonets to finish the job not completed by .577 caliber Enfield rifle bullets.

One breathless 21st Mississippi soldier reached the New Jersey battery of Parrott rifles, and yelled at the bluecoat gunners above the din, "Halt, you Yankee sons of bitches; we want those guns!" Showing that plenty of fighting spirit yet remained among the New Jersey cannoneers, Corporal Samuel Ennis, a spunky Irishman, screamed back in defiance, "Go to hell! We want to use them yet awhile." All six horses of one team and four horses of another team of the decimated New Jersey battery were cut down.

Now dead and dying Federal gunners and horses, writhing in pain and sounding almost human, were piled around the Garden State battery that was dying along the slightly sunken Wheatfield Road that ran along open ground. Some precious time for the New Jersey guns was won by the unleashing of a last-minute volley from a retiring group of soldiers of the battered 68th Pennsylvania, which had briefly rallied along the Wheatfield Road before heading east toward Cemetery Ridge. Fortunately for the survivors of Captain Clark's battery, the bravado of Corporal Ennis' defiant boast was backed up by the sudden Pennsylvania volley which cut down the foremost 21st Mississippi attackers, who had nearly reached the New Jersey artillerymen. Also thwarting Humphreys' bid to capture the New Jersey guns was a hot fire from the 7th New Jersey Volunteer Infantry, which fought a delaying action that bought time for the escape of Clark's guns.

Despite the heavy losses, the exposed New Jersey guns, including one affectionately known as "Old Betsey," were withdrawn rearward by the surviving New Jersey cannoneers, who left behind only a single caisson and a red-stained pile of dead horses and fallen comrades. Indeed, 20 gunners, and more than 20 horses were cut down mostly by 21st Mississippi musketry—but also Kershaw's skirmishers and Alexander's artillery. In total, Captain Clark's New Jersey guns fired 1,300 rounds on bloody July 2, but now were hastening to leave the field.

Although raked from the right flank by the onrushing 21st Mississippi from the west, the hard-pressed Union artillerymen of other "long arm" units along the Wheatfield Road Line fought with equally desperate valor. After sweeping over the body-strewn position of Captain Clark's New Jersey battery with a cheer, Humphreys' men then swarmed toward Captain James Thompson's Pennsylvania battery of four three-inch ordnance rifles. These guns had stood to the right, or northwest, of Captain Clark's battery, defending the northern arm of the salient angle, until pushed rearward by Barksdale's assault. Once again, the Mississippi marksmen butchered the battery's horses with well-paced shots, killing the horses of two teams. At the last minute and after all of its horses had been killed, one Pennsylvania artillery piece was laboriously pushed rearward by hand by desperate gunners and some helpful infantrymen, before the raging tide of Mississippi Rebels unleashing "Rebel, mongrel cries" in one Yankee officer's words. But with Humphreys' attackers so close and bluecoat infantry support having been swept aside, the endangered Pennsylvania cannon was abandoned by the frustrated artillerymen.

Yet another three-inch gun of Captain Thompson's battery was especially vulnerable before the onrushing 21st Mississippi attackers, who fairly lusted for this opportunity to capture as many artillery pieces as possible this afternoon. Private Casper R. Carlisle, of Captain Thompson's Battery, won the Congressional Medal of Honor for rushing back to save one remaining cannon—freeing it from a grisly pile of dead horses and pulling it rearward with Thompson's assistance after most of the Keystone State battery's horses had been shot down and every driver was hit by bullets. But by the narrowest of margins, meanwhile, the other

Pennsylvania field pieces were withdrawn east toward Cemetery Ridge. While Humphreys' soldiers blasted away, Private Carlisle and Captain Thompson cut the dead animals from the tangled leather traces to free the lone gun left behind. They then hooked up the surviving horses to get the cannon off the field in time, with the Mississippi Rebels close behind. In desperation, a mounted Colonel McGilvery ordered the last two remaining batteries along the Wheatfield Road—Captain Charles A. Phillips' Company E, 5th Massachusetts Light Artillery, and Captain John Bigelow's 9th Massachusetts Battery—to retire before the 21st Mississippi's onslaught.[364]

At the intersection of the Emmitsburg and Wheatfield Roads, the Peach Orchard knoll dominated the surrounding area on all sides. East of the Peach Orchard stood the Abraham Trostle House nestled down in the picturesque valley of Plum Run, just before the ground ascended to Cemetery Ridge, while southeast of the 21st Mississippi loomed the heavily-forested, towering hill, the highest in all Adams County, known as Big Round Top. Slightly to the right of Humphreys' attackers and just to the left, or north, of Big Round Top was clearly seen the rocky face of the treeless western slope of Little Round Top, which was a bloody bone of contention and a key objective of Hood's division this afternoon.

After having shattered one Yankee regiment after another, the dynamic team of Barksdale and Humphreys sensed the golden opportunity that lay before them: the ever-widening breach in Meade's left center. Therefore, neither commander of their respective wings wasted time by halting or reorganizing their sweat-stained troops under the blazing July sun, before hurling their troops onward. While Humphreys and his 21st Mississippi on the right wing continued to surge southeast, Barksdale steadily led his three regiments of the left wing northeast and parallel to the Emmitsburg Road in pursuit of his routed opponents. Because of the lateness of the echelon assault to the north, Barksdale was only partly assisted in striking the left flanks of General Humphreys' units, while they faced General Anderson's Division, especially Wilcox's Alabama brigade, attacking through the open fields before the Emmitsburg Road Ridge from the west. Most important, the gap between the hard-hit units of General Humphreys' Division and the Second Corps, to the northeast, and the Fifth Corps units, to the southeast, defending the Wheatfield, grew ever-larger, while the lethal team of Barksdale and Humphreys continued their relentless attack to achieve additional gains without stopping to waste precious time.[365]

Looking to the south, Captain Frank Moran of the 73rd New York Volunteer Infantry, which had been belatedly dispatched from Colonel William R. Brewster's Brigade to reinforce the collapsing Peach Orchard sector and had been hurled rearward by Barksdale's attack, never forgot the sight of the 21st Mississippi's systematic smashing of all resistance and the extent of the havoc caused by Colonel Humphreys' attackers among the row of Third Corps artillery amid "the leaden hurricane that swept it from two sides . . . the shattered line was retreating in separated streams, artillerists heroically clinging to their still smoking guns, and brave little infantry squads assisting them with their endangered cannon over the soft ground. The positions of these batteries showed broken carriages, caissons and wheels, while scores of slain horses and men lay across each other in mangled and ghastly heaps."[366]

Much hard fighting and bloody work yet remained to be completed by the Mississippi Brigade, however, if decisive victory was to be won today. Undefended Cemetery Ridge lay to the east beyond the waters of Plum Run, located at the foot of the commanding ridge that promised decisive Confederate victory if only reached in time. One frustrated Union soldier admitted with some astonishment how "nothing we could do seemed to confuse or halt Barksdale's veterans [who] just came on and on."[367]

However, the Mississippians' dual attacks of widely-separated wings promised to shortly run into difficulties because of the loss of so many good men and the great distance yet required to reach Cemetery Ridge's strategic crest. In addition, aside from the brief, but important few minutes when Barksdale and Wilcox's Alabamians had cooperated to crush the remnants of Sickles' Second Division, the Mississippi Brigade had no other infantry supports in sight. But incredibly, and for the moment, assistance was not really needed by Colonel Humphreys and his hard-charging regiment, which continued to systematically rip the heart out of Federal resistance in the Wheatfield Road sector. Describing the extent of the 21st Mississippi's amazing success, Lieutenant Owen of the Washington Artillery wrote how, "on swept the line, breaking out with a yell when they came face to face with the foe, but, on the whole silently. The guns in the peach-orchard were pounced upon, and half of them taken in a trice; the rest limbered up and made off in a hurry. Hundreds of prisoners were taken, and . . . it was thought that we would drive the enemy to and beyond the heights."[368]

Staggered by the sight, one of Sickles' staff officers, Jesse Bowman

Young also described the sledge-hammer blows delivered by the 21st Mississippi: "The batteries at the Peach Orchard stood their ground until their horses were all disabled or killed, and then the men that were left saved their guns by 'firing with fixed prolonge' as they withdrew to the rear, loading and firing as they retreated."[369]

However, Humphreys' remarkable success in smashing the Peach Orchard salient and then barreling farther southeast to roll up the southern arm of the salient was expensive. Gory clumps of dead and wounded soldiers of his regiment were left behind, littering the ground like fallen leaves. Leading the attackers of the Volunteer Southrons (Company A), 21st Mississippi, from Vicksburg, Lieutenant Walter W. Wolcott, a former sergeant, was one inspirational officer fatally cut down. The young Warren County lieutenant was among the ever-increasing number of casualties among the Mississippi Brigade's officer corps.[370]

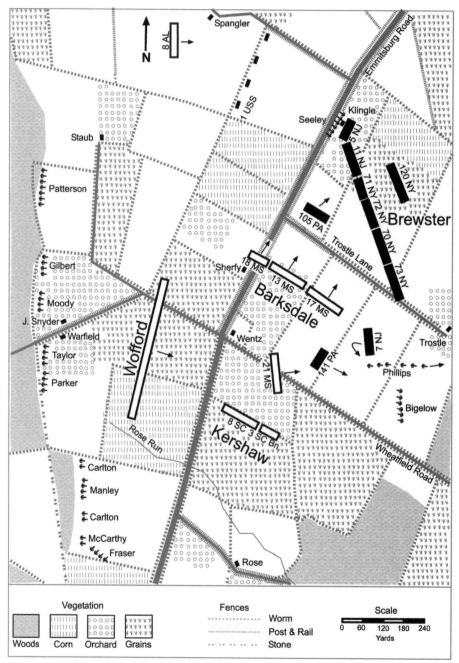

Map courtesy of Bradley M. Gottfried

$\backsim$ 7 $\backsim$

"The guiding spirit of the battle"

MEANWHILE, BARKSDALE CONTINUED to lead the 13th, 17th, and 18th Mississippi northeast up the Emmitsburg Road, smashing resistance in the open fields to its east. After hurling aside the New Yorkers of the Second Brigade of Humphreys' Division, Third Corps, the attacking soldiers surged onward to threaten additional units on the exposed left flank of General Joseph B. Carr's First Brigade, Second Division. Union General Humphreys described Barksdale's gains: "My infantry now engaged the enemy's, but my left was in air . . . and being the only troops on the field, the enemy's whole attention was directed to my division, which was forced back." Humphreys realized that he had "never been under a hotter fire of musketry and artillery combined [and] for the moment I thought the day was lost."

To the onrushing Mississippians, this fight was turning into a turkey-shoot, with the yelping Rebels loading and firing on the run as rapidly as possible. Crossing the east-west running Abraham Trostle Lane that led over the fields descending down to Trostle's house and barn in Plum Run's valley, they continued to charge onward with wild shouts. Despite the heavy losses and his men's exertions, Barksdale still refused to halt the troops to either reload or rest with so many Federals on the run, and the left of Carr's brigade giving way under the relentless pressure. No time, not a minute, could be wasted, if decisive victory was to be gained before the sun went down. During his sweeping attack along the Emmitsburg Road, Barksdale not only continued to inflict punishment on the vulnerable left flanks of additional Federal units aligned parallel to the road, but also on steadily retiring, but stubborn, Union regiments which had already been hurled out of the Peach Orchard.

With his regiment cut to pieces after losing nearly half of its numbers in tangling with the Mississippians today, Captain Edward R. Bowen, now commanding what little was left of the 114th Pennsylvania, continued to withdraw before Barksdale's onslaught: "All this time we were being hotly followed by the enemy, and very close they were to us, our main endeavor being to get our colors safely off . . . what remained of the regiment, amounting altogether to not much more than a color guard, faced to the enemy and fired . . . the masses of the enemy were almost on them. We left the Emmitsburg road covered with our dead and wounded." As the final insult, at least one Mississippi officer now led his elated troops northeast with a captured Zouave fez on his head: a trophy that inspired his jubilant troops in their steamrolling attack.[371]

With many Magnolia State officers already shot down, surviving leaders rose to the fore during the swirling combat. A 27-year-old farmer from Early Grove in north-central Mississippi was one such resilient leader. Lieutenant James, or "Jim," Ramsuer was hit when a lead ball tore through the fleshy part of his cheek and mouth, barely missing bone and teeth. Nevertheless, he continued to lead his shouting Mississippi Rangers (Company B), 17th Mississippi, while splashed with red from the ghastly wound. The sight of a charging Confederate officer covered in blood no doubt unnerved some young men in blue. Rebel Private William Meshack Abernathy never forgot the inspiring sight of Ramsuer who, "with a shot square through his mouth, unable to speak, a sword in his right hand, his left hand shattered, holding the brim of his hat with his thumb and forefinger, was waving the boys forward."[372] Like so many other inspirational Mississippi officers, Ramsuer finally went down when hit by yet another bullet. But he was one of the lucky ones, surviving his wounds.[373]

Likewise many of the best fighting men from Barksdale's enlisted ranks also had been cut down. One of the youngest Mississippi Brigade soldiers who fell to rise no more was teenage Private Ross Franklin, the fun-loving prankster of Company B, 17th Mississippi. Originally from the port of Mobile, Private Franklin had enlisted with high hopes of winning glory at only age fifteen.[374]

But such a high sacrifice in lives was necessary because of the tenacious fighting required for overcoming so many battle-hardened Federals, who had never battled so stubbornly because they were now defending home soil. However, the Mississippi Brigade's attack had already achieved a measure of success beyond expectations. Indeed, Barksdale delivered a devastating knock-out blow to the formidable Third Corps, capturing not only the Peach Orchard salient angle but also the defensive line northeast of it along the Emmitsburg Road. Then, to the south, Humphreys rolled up Union infantry and artillery units like an old carpet along the Wheatfield Road. Graham's brigade had been cut to pieces, losing 740 of 1,516 soldiers. Most important, the decimation and rout of Graham's brigade exposed the right flank of the Union defenders along the Wheatfield Road, while assisting in Wofford's and Kershaw's success in sweeping across the Wheatfield. These hard-won Confederate gains in the bloody Wheatfield sector, however, ensured that the Mississippi Brigade continued to fight on its own hook. In the words of Private McNeily, "not from the time we charged until [nightfall] did our brigade get in touch with the other division brigades."[375]

Serving on Sickles' staff, Pennsylvanian Jesse Bowman Young described the collapse of the Third Corps: "Sickles was flanked and driven [and his units] without exception . . . were flanked, crowded back, and at last forced in more or less confusion toward the rear."[376] After smashing through Graham's brigade, Barksdale then caught Carr's and Brewster's brigades on the left flank to inflict more damage. On this short afternoon, the Mississippi Rebels captured nearly 1,000 prisoners, which was more than two-thirds of Barksdale's total strength. Barksdale's onslaught was already one of the most devastating infantry assaults of the war.

One Union officer described the Mississippi Brigade's attack, saying that neither musketry nor "cannon seemed to confuse or halt Barksdale's veterans. We [had] five regiments fronting Barksdale's small Brigade and these were supported by two additional Pennsylvania regiments stationed just behind the five . . . but nothing daunted Barksdale and his men and nothing seemed to be in their way [as they] came on, and on, and on, and when they came in gun shot of us, the carnage . . . inflicted on us boys in Blue would be impossible to detail. Before we could get to the rear, the ten guns were captured, the 80 horses killed and they drove the five regiments from the field, ran over the two lines of reserves as the five regiments in front and carried everything before them with cyclonic force."[377]

The 21st Mississippi had already been severely punished for its success, however. Anchoring the regiment's left, the 40-man Jeff Davis Guards, or Company D, 21st Mississippi, was especially decimated, losing 9 killed, and 18 wounded. Already the 21st Mississippi, wrote one soldier, had "lost many of her best & bravest sons." Nevertheless and as if he commanded a full brigade instead of a single regiment fighting almost alone, Colonel Humphreys continued to lead his soldiers down and parallel to the Wheatfield Road.[378]

Meanwhile, with Barksdale's left resting on the Emmitsburg Road, the 18th, 13th, and 17th Mississippi, from left to right, steadily surged northeastward. With flashing saber and still mounted, Barksdale led his soldiers deeper into General Humphreys' Division. Continuing to drive Brewster's remaining New Yorkers of the "Excelsior Brigade" up the Emmitsburg Road toward Gettysburg, the Mississippi Rebels pressured the withdrawing 71st and 72nd New York Volunteer Infantry troops, which had been the first to break.

The elated 18th Mississippi soldiers continued to unleash their pent-up rage against the remaining "Excelsior Brigade" troops, seeking a full measure of revenge for the capture of the 18th's banner by the 71st New York during the second battle of Fredericksburg. And the homespun Mississippians obtained their long-sought revenge with considerable relish. In the words of the Excelsior Brigade's Colonel Brewster, "the troops on our left being obliged to fall back, the enemy advanced upon us in great force, pouring into us a most terrific fire of artillery and musketry, both upon our front and left flank . . . the troops on our left being, for want of support, forced still farther back, left us exposed to an enfilading fire, before which we were obliged to fall back . . . but with terrible loss of both officers and men."

Describing the bitter contest in the Emmitsburg Road sector, Private Abernathy of the 17th Mississippi wrote how "we drove [Graham's brigade] back and on to the New York Excelsior Brigade, and here another desperate struggle resulted. Here was a battery of artillery, and around this battery, a terrific struggle ensued. Twice we took it, and then on a final charge we ran up over it." Attacking in the surging ranks of the Kemper Legion (Company C), 13th Mississippi, Private Joseph Charles Lloyd recalled how "after a divergence to the left we ran over and capture[d] a battery." This was just south of the Daniel F. Klingel House, a log cabin situated atop a knoll, immediately on the east side of the Emmitsburg Road north of where the Abraham Trostle Lane met the Emmitsburg Road.

Twenty-five-year-old Private John Alemeth Byers, a Water Valley, Yalobusha County farm boy of Company H, 17th Mississippi, fell along with quite a few comrades. Private Byers, one of the Panola Vindicators, was eventually captured on the field. He was fated to be killed in battle in 1864.

With the capture of this battery, Company K, 4th United States Artillery, along the Emmitsburg Road, an excited Private Abernathy "sprang on one of the guns and was shot off of it, but we held the battery, and then came another effort to retake it, but without avail." The lithe private jumped atop the captured gun despite having just seen the first Rebel to do so get promptly shot off the piece. At the point of the bayonet, Barksdale's men captured three guns positioned along the Emmitsburg Road. Adjutant Harman, 13th Mississippi, was elated "after crossing the Emmitsburg road [when] the Brigade continued to advance and a short distance beyond were the captured canon [sic], but I cannot say to what battery or batteries they belonged." Immediately, veteran Mississippians manned the captured Napoleon 12-pounders, turning them on the Federals, who now felt the sting of their own shot and shell.

Barksdale and his three regiments continued northeastward. With full force, they hit the southernmost Federal unit—the 11th New Jersey, on their right just south of the Klingel House—of Carr's First Brigade, which was the second to last (after the 12th New Hampshire) of the regiments of Humphreys' Division still positioned along the Emmitsburg Road. Barksdale's men mauled the left flank of Carr's brigade with a fire so deadly that one Yankee officer feared that "it seemed as if but a few minutes could elapse before the entire line would be shot down." All the while, the Mississippians continued to deliver punishing blows at the "several new lines of battle which appeared to be reinforcements of fresh troops," wrote Adjutant Harman, 13th Mississippi.

The 11th New Jersey, organized near Trenton, was hurled back. Veterans of Fredericksburg and Chancellorsville, the New Jersey boys were brushed aside like Graham's Pennsylvanians and the New York regiments. Upon earlier having taken position on high ground along the Emmitsburg Road near the orchard of the Klingel farm, regimental commander Colonel Robert McAllister, 11th New Jersey, wisely positioned his troops to "fire by rank, rear rank first, so as to be enabled to hold in check the enemy after the first fire [but] our own men around the house and garden seemed to remain as though no enemy were near them . . . the rebels took possession of the house and garden and I ordered 'Fire!' at which time I fell, severely wounded by a Minie ball in my left leg and a piece of shell in my right foot, when I was carried to the rear." Meanwhile, McAllister's regiment was vanquished by the Mississippi Rebels, who continued attacking up the slope toward the top of the knoll, where the Klingel House stood. Not only was Colonel McAllister cut down but also the major who had just taken command of the heavily pressured regiment. Likewise, the regiment's senior captain was hit by the scorching fire. Clearly, the Mississippi Rebels were especially efficient at targeting officers, especially when exposed on high ground. In total, Barksdale's men shot down 153 of the 275 11th New Jersey men, who now lay sprawled across the open fields lining the Emmitsburg Road around the Klingel House.

In this emergency situation, Adjutant John Schoonover quickly took command of the 11th New Jersey, but he could only watch its further decimation in horror. Schoonover described how "the fire of the enemy was at this time perfectly terrific . . . men were falling on every side [and] more than half of our number had been killed and wounded." Attempting to rally his reeling troops, Adjutant Schoonover himself shortly fell with two wounds.[379]

After the regiments of the Excelsior Brigade and the 11th New Jersey had been swept aside, Barksdale's three regiments continued to charge across the open fields to the right of the Emmitsburg Road, keeping up the momentum. The exposed left flank of another regiment of Carr's First Brigade was their next target. Just north of the Klingel House, immediately to the road's east, stood the 12th New Hampshire Volunteer Infantry. These 224 "granite-hard veterans" presented a formidable challenge to the Mississippians, who were by now winded and had already suffered heavy losses. Indeed, the New Englanders were reliable veterans of imposing size, both in height and muscular bulk. Most significant, these rawboned soldiers had already earned respect from their opponents. Consisting of American-born "mountaineers" of mainly Scots-Irish stock, this hardy New Hampshire regiment also included sturdy fighting men from Wales, Canada, Scotland, and Germany.[380]

At Chancellorsville, the 12th New Hampshire troops had demonstrated their stubbornness by holding Confederate attackers at bay with a determination to fight "until the last man falls."[381] Firing from behind the cover of trees and logs, they had nearly fulfilled their promise, losing more men (72 in fatalities alone) than any regiment on either side during the battle.[382]

With his lieutenant colonel cut down at Chancellorsville, Captain John F. Langley now commanded the 12th New Hampshire, just north of the modest, two-story Klingel House. In a spirited repeat performance of Chancellorsville, the regiment was standing firm before the belated advance of Cadmus Wilcox's Alabama Brigade from the west, when all of a sudden they were hit on the left flank by Barksdale's three regiments. Humphreys' Division was now caught in an ever-tightening "Confederate vise," between Barksdale from the left flank and Wilcox from the front. Therefore, immediate orders were issued for the New Hampshire boys to fall back to Cemetery Ridge before the regiment was crushed.[383]

Just northeast of the Klingel House the 16th Massachusetts, consisting of Middlesex County men under Colonel Waldo Merriam, who fell wounded, then Colonel Port D. Tripp's 11th Massachusetts, farther up the road, were Barksdale's next victims. As in earlier routing Graham's brigade from Philadelphia, the mostly lower and middle-class farm lads from Mississippi now vanquished more city boys in the 11th Massachusetts, men from Boston, after pushing aside the mostly farmers of the 16th Massachusetts. One Union officer described how the onrushing Mississippians killed a good many Massachusetts men, including those of the "Boston Volunteers," before "they could get away" from the onslaught on their flank while hit by the Alabamians in front.[384] Indeed, the 11th Massachusetts, which had first fought in the Peninsula Campaign, lost 129 out of 286 men in the bloody Emmitsburg Road sector, including nearly 40 soldiers either killed or mortally wounded.[385]

After smashing the famed Excelsior Brigade and, with Wilcox's assistance, rolling up the bulk of Carr's First Brigade, including the 12th New Hampshire and the two Massachusetts regiments, Barksdale and his men, advancing immediately east of the Emmitsburg Road, still faced northeastward. After smashing through Carr's brigade, Barksdale's troops then struck the left flank of the 5th New Jersey Volunteer Infantry of Colonel George C. Burling's Third Brigade. But Barksdale, after the last blue troops were swept away and having gained the top of the Klingel House knoll, now realized that he could not possibly achieve decisive victory by continuing to attack up, or parallel to, the Emmitsburg Road as originally envisioned. He had already gained the highest ground along the Emmitsburg Road Ridge at Klingel's open knoll, and now the ground sloped down toward Gettysburg to the northeast. Barksdale realized that smashing one Union regiment after another was only bringing him closer to the Union center, with the Army of the Potomac's primary concentration of forces, and not Meade's left flank.[386]

Almost as if he had never been the cerebral, ever-opinionated editor of the leading newspaper in Columbus, a well-known attorney, and a respected politician in what now seemed like another lifetime, Barksdale's natural leadership and tactical instincts rose to the fore. He fully realized that he was not moving toward Meade's exposed left flank but only smashing through the Third Corps' right, not yet gaining eliminating any possibility of inflicting a decisive blow. The Army of the Potomac's real left flank, because of the Third Corps' absence, was now located to the left of the Second Corps far to the east on Cemetery Ridge, where Sickles' Corps should have been positioned had not the New Yorker advanced to the Peach Orchard.[387]

By this time after sweeping so many Yankee units off the Emmitsburg Road Ridge like a giant broom and overwhelming the highest point (the Klingel knoll) at its northern end, Barksdale realized that the Peach Orchard position had been only an advanced salient, or bulge, in Meade's line, and that the main Federal position lay to the east on Cemetery Ridge. Demonstrating flexibility in this key situation, Barksdale thus made adroit tactical adjustments to adapt to the situation on the fly. With maneuvering his lengthy formation now relatively easy amid the wide, open fields that descended toward the low ground of Plum Run to the east, he quickly shifted his three regiments from a northeast direction to face straight east toward Cemetery Ridge.

After the Third Corps had been mauled and hurled rearward, Cemetery Ridge now lay undefended in a wide area south of the Second Corps' left, behind the Trostle House and barn to the east. Indeed, the gap was even larger now than before, as the Second Corps' leftmost division, Caldwell's, had been dispatched into the inferno of the Wheatfield. The key strategic high ground, which was to have been the Third Corps' well-supported defensive position before Sickles advanced to the Peach Orchard, was now undefended as what little remained of Sickles' Corps now streamed rearward.[388] Therefore, Barksdale was determined to exploit the more than 500-yard gap between the Second Corps and the Fifth Corps on Little Round Top. The golden tactical opportunity that offered the most decisive results of the day lay directly before Barksdale, and he was determined to exploit this opportunity to the fullest.[389]

Here, on the high ground amid the little smoke-wreathed orchard just north of the log Klingel House, Barksdale sensed the chance to drive a wedge completely through the Army of the Potomac's left-center. He therefore galloped before the lengthy butternut-hued formations of his three regiments, which were now facing toward his ultimate objective, which, if gained, would cut Meade's Army in half. And now a colorful carpet of crop lands—entirely devoid of Union defensive lines—lay along the eastern slope of the Emmitsburg Road Ridge toward Cemetery Ridge, promising a relatively easy march to gain the high ground on Plum Run's east side and win the war's most decisive victory.[390]

Barksdale would now follow the shattered Third Corps units fleeing east—instead of northeast—toward Cemetery Ridge. Before moving onward with his 18th, 13th, and 17th Mississippi, Barksdale hurled a lengthy skirmish line down the sloping ground and through the open fields of the Trostle Farm, before launching his audacious bid to bring about the victory. Knowing that more hard fighting lay ahead in advancing farther east and hopefully all the way to Cemetery Ridge, wrote Adjutant Harman in a letter, "Gen'l Barksdale sent back twice for reinforcements," but to no avail.

From this high point atop the Emmitsburg Road Ridge, which was now strewn with the bodies of blue and gray, just north of the Klingel House, Barksdale led his troops off the high ground and through the rows of fruit trees of the Klingel Orchard just north of the house. With confidence for success despite having suffered heavy losses, the Mississippi regiments advanced east with high hopes and red battle-flags flapping in the smoke-laden air. On the left flank, Major Gerald, 18th Mississippi, never forgot the dramatic moment when Barksdale's attack continued down the eastern slope of the Emmitsburg Road Ridge, when the three regiments "moved through the orchard and towards the heights" of Cemetery Ridge. Beyond the right of his three Mississippi regiments, Barksdale could see the large red Trostle barn to the southeast. Barksdale now surged east like his hard-charging top lieutenant, B.G. Humphreys, who continued to push onward astride the Wheatfield Road.

Once again, high-pierced "Rebel Yells" erupted from the throats of seasoned troops of Barksdale's three regiments, resounding over a picturesque, open landscape—a farmer's paradise but a soldier's hell—turned red. Mounted out in front and leading the way, Barksdale pointed his sword toward his final ambition, Cemetery Ridge, which loomed on the eastern horizon about a half mile away. As in earlier targeting the Sherfy House as a focal point of the attack to gain the Emmitsburg Road Ridge, so Barksdale now utilized another prominent man-made feature upon which to guide his attack—the red Trostle barn, on his right-front. He now led his lengthy line of troops over the sloping ground northwest of the imposing red barn and the farmer's white-painted house, located about 600 away. As repeatedly demonstrated on past battlefields, the

Mississippi Rebels continued to prove to be as unstoppable as their white-haired commander. Miraculously, in leading the way, he had not yet been hit by a bullet or fragment of shell.

Throughout this sweltering afternoon and despite the swirling smoke of battle and rising dust that mixed together to obscure the field, Barksdale continued to demonstrate tactical flexibility, skill, and resourcefulness. He had adjusted repeatedly to meet a host of new challenges in an ever-changing battlefield situation. Without specific orders or directions from Lee, Longstreet, or McLaws, and without immediate support to the rear or on his flanks, Barksdale continued to advance on his own in independent command of three regiments: a situation that allowed maximum tactical flexibility. Indeed, far from Barksdale, Longstreet and McLaws were yet focused on developments not north but south of the Wheatfield Road.

Across the colorful stretch of pastoral expanse, the Trostle House could not be clearly seen by Barksdale and his top lieutenants from the eastern slope of Emmitsburg Road Ridge, because the large red barn stood before the much smaller house, which was situated on slightly lower ground closer to Plum Run. However, like no other man-made feature in this sector, the Trostle barn, built of red brick and resting on a sturdy rock foundation, dominated the rolling landscape to Barksdale's southeast. Nothing now lay before Barksdale but a wide stretch of open ground that dipped gradually down into the shallow valley of Plum Run, which flowed slowly just in the rear of the Trostle house.

With a sense of renewed confidence, the Mississippians headed steadily toward the lengthy, open stretch of Cemetery Ridge, where decisive victory now lay for the taking. Meade's aide-de-camp, his son Colonel George Meade, Jr., recalled how during this crucial time, "affairs seem critical in the extreme [as] the Confederates appear determined to carry everything before them. Will nothing stop these people?" The hard-fighting Mississippians were indeed proving that they were, in the words of one Southerner, "irrepressible" on this bloody afternoon.[391] Like Meade's son, Captain Haskell asked after the Third Corps had been smashed and pushed aside, "What is there between" Cemetery Ridge "and these yelling masses of the enemy?"[392]

But despite vanquishing every Yankee regiment he had encountered along the Emmitsburg Road, there was still plenty of enemy fire to cope with. Although droves of Third Corps men were fleeing pell-mell from the field, others, singly or in groups, stopped at intervals to fire back at their pursuers. General Humphreys claimed to have personally halted his men 20 times to return volleys. Union regiments such as the spunky 12th New Hampshire continued to fight back with spirit, even as they withdrew, keeping up a harassing fire and dropping more Mississippi soldiers from the ranks.[393]

Tall in the saddle, General Barksdale continued to serve as an inspirational force to his troops. Private Abernathy of the 17th Mississippi recalled how the onrushing men were inspired by Barksdale's exhilarating "order 'Forward with Bayonets' and over the wheat fields." With reloaded muskets, the rejuvenated Mississippians continued to surge down the slope with high-pierced war cries that echoed over the broad expanse of Trostle's fields. By this time the fighting that had swirled so savagely had "kindled in [Barksdale] an incandescence." Indeed, the general's fighting blood was up. He was invigorated by the sweet taste of victory in the sulfurous air. The series of dramatic successes reaped by Barksdale likewise inspired his troops with the unshakable conviction that they could continue to do the impossible this afternoon. Like a man possessed, Barksdale continued to serve as the primary driving force for his attackers. Clearly, and like his top lieutenant Humphreys to the south, Barksdale was having his finest day. But Barksdale was not basking in his success because he wanted to achieve much more; or as Longstreet put it, he "moved bravely on, the guiding spirit of the battle."[394]

With discipline and in firm ranks that displayed years of training and discipline, the Mississippi Rebels moved relentlessly onward down the slope. Most important, "though in 'rough uniform and with bright bayonets,' these veterans, now covered with dust and blackened with the smoke of battle, with ranks depleted by shot and shell, and faint from exhaustion, responded with cheers to the clarion call of the intrepid Barksdale. . . . Mounted and with sword held aloft 'at an angle of forty-five degrees,' he exclaimed: 'Brave Mississippians, one more charge and the day is ours'!"[395]

Exchanges of musketry continued to erupt across the open fields of farmer Trostle, but no fresh, organized formation of blue now stood east of the Emmitsburg Road before Barksdale's fast-moving ranks. During their flight east toward Cemetery Ridge, however, the most resilient survivors of the broken Third Corps units still turned to offer resistance. These Federals blasted away from behind fences and few rocks too heavy to have been cleared even by the industrious German farmers. Here, stubborn pockets of defiant Yankees made brief defensive stands around their brightly colored flags, unleashing a continual harassing fire.

However, this persistent, pesky fire continued to drop Mississippi Rebels, increasing the butternut attackers' ire and fueling their burning desire to reach Cemetery Ridge as soon as possible. Earlier, when Sergeant Joshua A. Bosworth, 141st Pennsylvania, fell wounded, he received initial compassion from onrushing Mississippians instead of a swift bayonet thrust. He asked a passing Mississippi Rebel for water. With compassion, the powder-stained Rebel handed his canteen to the injured Yankee. Meanwhile, the ragged Mississippian busily reloaded his rifled musket, but suddenly had second thoughts about assisting an enemy, who might mend and kill him or one of his comrades, perhaps even a relative, one day in the future. He consequently yelled to the injured Pennsylvanian that he "hated our men . . ." And as if to prove his point and to reveal how much the war had changed since its early days, this veteran, whose sense of Southern "patriotism" overcame his fast-fleeting compassion after having seen so many friends, or perhaps a relative, killed, had a change of heart. After rushing forward a short distance, the Rebel stopped, turned and then fired at the wounded Federal, who had just drank from the Mississippian's canteen.[396] For this Johnny Reb, it was too late for chivalry or other niceties of a brother's war.

A lucky survivor of the Mississippians' onslaught, one dazed Union prisoner offered a rare compliment to the Mississippi Brigade's combat prowess. As Private Joseph Charles Lloyd, 13th Mississippi, described the encounter after "we ran over a battery of seven guns [and] the major commanding them [stated] 'Why, you were the grandest men the world ever saw [and] you made the grandest charge of the war.' 'Your line was perfect and you held it, too, long [and] I was giving you all the canister my guns could carry but you never halted, but charged right on over us'."[397]

With drums beating and red battle-flags waving in the late afternoon sunlight, a mounted Barksdale continued to lead his lines forward down the gently sloping ground toward Plum Run, situated about three-quarters of the way from the Emmitsburg Road Ridge to Cemetery Ridge. The three veteran regiments, including Barksdale's old 13th Mississippi in the center, moved relentlessly onward, easing ever-closer to Cemetery Ridge and the fulfillment of Confederate ambitions.[398]

Barksdale believed that if any troops in Lee's army could deliver the decisive stroke to win the war, it was his Mississippi troops. He had complete confidence in his own 13th Mississippi soldiers, who now advanced with disciplined step in companies like the Spartan's Band, Alamucha Infantry, Winston Guards, Secessionists, Newton Legion, Minute Men of Attala, Lauderdale Zouaves, Pettus Guards, Kemper Legion, and Wayne Rifles. The McElroy boys were just the kind of tough Celtic soldiers who he needed to win it all this late afternoon. Barksdale knew the McElroy band, of Lauderdale County's Company E, quite well. These men never forgot how Miss Sophronia McElroy presented the company's battle-flag to Captain Peter Henry Bozeman, who led the Alamucha Infantry of Company E. Unlike the half dozen McElroy soldiers of the yeomen class, Captain Bozeman owned ten slaves. Included in the ranks of the McElroy clan were two father-son teams, John R. McElroy, Sr. and his son John R., and Isaac R. McElroy, Sr., and his son, Isaac R.

The highest-ranking McElroy was Kennon, now the regiment's lieutenant colonel, who was second in command of the 13th Mississippi. He had organized the Lauderdale Zouaves as part of the Zouave craze at the war's beginning. Because of demonstrated leadership ability in leading the attack at Malvern Hill, Kennon McElroy took command of the 13th Mississippi when Colonel James W. Carter was wounded in that attack. McElroy won Barksdale's praise for gallantry at Antietam, where he was wounded but remained in command of the 13th Mississippi On this bloody afternoon at Gettysburg, four of the McElroy boys were destined to be either wounded or captured in the Mississippi Brigade's bid to win it all.[399]

A natural fighter in the warrior tradition of his forefathers, Kennon McElroy was now enacting an impressive repeat performance. After Colonel Carter was killed in leading the 13th Mississippi's onslaught in the struggle along the Emmitsburg Road Ridge, the capable Lt. Colonel McElroy, who had been promoted for gallantry to second in command, once again led the 13th Mississippi during its greatest challenge. McElroy survived the holocaust at Gettysburg, but not the war that destroyed so much of his clan of self-sacrificing Scots-Irish warriors.[400]

On this day General Barksdale now rode a magnificent horse, a high-spirited bay, which had been secured by the cunning of a horse-savvy Mississippi picket. He had "whistled" the animal, while the horse drank from the Rappahannock's waters, across the river at Fredericksburg.[401] In his diary, Private William H. Hill, of the 13th Mississippi, recorded how a magnificent thoroughbred "horse, belonging to the Yankee army, swam the river this morning to our lines."[402] The pickets had then presented Barksdale with the splendid animal. Knowing exactly where concepts of chivalry needed to end, the pragmatic Barksdale refused to return this "very fine horse," evidently a high-ranking Union's officer's mount, despite repeated requests sent across the lines for the animal's return.[403] Whatever Federal officer, especially if now poised in Meade's defensive line along the Cemetery Ridge, had lost his most prized horse, he could not have possibly imagined that a Mississippi general was now riding it and leading Lee's most successful attack on July 2.[404]

Meanwhile, back on Cemetery Ridge with the Second Corps, Captain Haskell described the golden opportunity presented to Barksdale's onrushing brigade at this time: "The last of the Third Corps retired from the field, for the enemy is flushed with his success. . . . The Third Corps is out of the way. Now we are in for it. . . . To see the fight, while it went on in the valley below us, was terrible—what must it be now, when we are in it, and it is all around us, in all its fury?"[405] All the while, due to the collapse of Sickles' Corps, a wide gap now lay open between the Second Corps on Cemetery Ridge and the Fifth Corps on the army's far flank.[406] "The way was open for Barksdale's Confederate Brigade," in the words of Union artillery officer Bigelow, "to enter, unopposed, our lines between Little Round Top and the left of the Second Corps."[407]

To exploit the gains won by the Mississippi Brigade in overrunning the Peach Orchard and clearing the Emmitsburg Road of defenders, Colonel Alexander, the tall, lanky, and capable acting commander of Longstreet's artillery, flew into action. Like a well-trained West Pointer (Class of 1857) with keen tactical insights about the importance of providing both close and timely artillery support for the advancing Mississippi Brigade at the height of its success, he rushed his six batteries on the double to the Peach Orchard and the Emmitsburg Road Ridge. Believing the remarkable success had been bestowed by "Providence," Colonel Alexander "rode along my guns, telling the men to limber to the front as rapidly as possible" to exploit Barksdale's hard-won gains. Sweat-stained and covered with black powder, the experienced cannoneers in gray were eager for the opportunity to play their part in exploiting the gains reaped by the Mississippians.[408]

Consequently, these experienced gunners of Alexander's reserve artillery battalion, of Longstreet's Corps, were "in great spirits, cheering & straining every nerve to get forward in the least possible time [and the more than twenty guns of] all six batteries [the Ashland Virginia Artillery, the Bedford Virginia Artillery, the Brooks South Carolina Artillery, Madison Light Artillery, Captain Parker's Virginia Battery and Captain Taylor's Virginia Battery] were going for the Peach Orchard at the same time and all the batteries were soon in action again."[409]

Indeed, now believing that not only the battle but also the war had been all but won by Barksdale's dramatic breakthrough, Alexander's "battalion of artillery followed fast on the heels of Barksdale's charging Mississippians and seventeen Confederate guns were planted on the high ground abandoned by the Federal troops," advancing some 600 yards east on the double. Wrote an impressed Colonel Alexander: "I can recall no more splendid sight, on a small scale—and certainly no more inspiring moment during the war—than that of the charge of these six batteries. An artillerist's heaven is to follow the routed enemy and throw shells and canister into his disorganized and fleeing masses. . . . there is no excitement on earth like it. It is far prettier than shooting at a compact, narrow line of battle, or at another battery. Now we saw our heaven just in front, and were already breathing the very air of victory."[410]

Winning the Confederate guns "general race and scramble to get there first," the Louisiana battery, under the command of Captain Moody, a hot-tempered duelist who was obsessive about matters of honor, was "the first battery that reached the high ground of the Peach Orchard," wrote a thankful Colonel Humphreys.[411] The first Louisiana guns quickly unlimbered across the commanding perch near the Wheatfield Road and among the rows of peach trees. Moody then began firing with rapidity from just east of the Emmitsburg Road north of farmer Sherfy's orchard.

But it was not easy getting so much artillery into ideal firing positions on the high ground north of the Peach Orchard along the Emmitsburg Road. Dead horses and wounded soldiers, blue and gray, and sections of wooden fences obstructed the unlimbering and placement of Alexander's artillery. A 114th Pennsylvania soldier was surprised by the gray cannoneers' display of humanity amid a scene of slaughter, when a seasoned "battery of the enemy came thundering down, and when the officer commanding it saw our dead and wounded on the road, he halted his battery to avoid running over them and his men carefully lifted our men to one side, and carried the wounded into a cellar of the house, supplied them with water, and said they would return and take care of them when they had caught the rest of us."[412]

Alexander, who stayed in the Peach Orchard through the night, never forgot the carnage of the area, writing, "What with deep dust & blood,

& filth of all kinds, the trampled & wrecked Peach Orchard was a very unattractive place."[413]

Once unlimbered, Alexander's guns turned on the fleeing Yankees now spread out in the open fields to the east leading to Plum Run. Erupting from the high ground of the Peach Orchard and the Emmitsburg Road Ridge, these fiery blasts raked the retreating Federals from behind, adding insult to injury and adding to the shock value of Barksdale's hard-hitting assault. By this time, Mississippi spirits could not have been higher, because they had finally received tangible support to follow up their success, even as the once-stubborn bluecoat infantry fled before them. Or as artillery chief Alexander put it after seeing the Union line collapse, "Now we would have our revenge, and make them sorry they had staid so long."

By not advancing farther east, however, the Rebel artillery actually provided relatively little close-range support for Barksdale's attackers, who surged ahead on their own. Captain Haskell described the severe limitations of Lee's "long arm" units, which many Federals held in disdain: "The Rebels had about as much artillery as we did; but we never have thought much of this arm in the hands of our adversaries . . . they have courage enough, but not the skill to handle it well. They generally fire far too high, and the ammunition is usually of a very inferior quality."[414] These severe limitations of Confederate artillery also played a role in sabotaging the best efforts of Barksdale and his troops this afternoon.

Meanwhile, Alexander and his cannoneers were jubilant with the extent of Barksdale's success in overrunning the Peach Orchard. Colonel Alexander explained the tactical situation and elation after most of Sickles' Third Corps had been swept aside by the Mississippi Brigade's "unsurpassed" offensive effort: "When I saw their line broken & in retreat, I thought the battle was ours. . . . All the rest would only be fun, pursuing the fugitives & making targets of them."[415]

Excited about the seemingly endless possibilities of the Mississippi Brigade's remarkable success, an elated Alexander shouted to his elated artillerymen, "We would 'finish the whole war this afternoon'."[416] But first, this requirement called for the capture of the strategic crest of Cemetery Ridge. Alexander himself realized as much once he had advanced and unlimbered his six batteries: "And when I got to take in all the topography I was very much disappointed. It was not the enemy's main line we had broken. That loomed up near 1,000 yards beyond us, a ridge giving good cover behind it and endless fine positions for batteries." For a moment the Georgian had felt that the Mississippi Brigade's success had already had been a decisive one, but now he realized that Barksdale still had one more major obstacle ahead.[417]

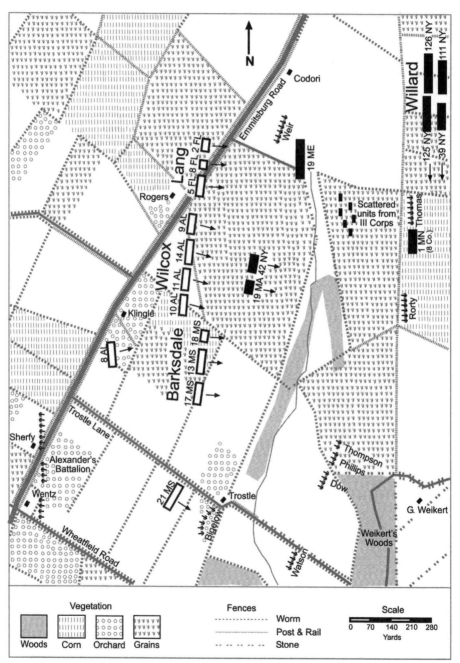

Map courtesy of Bradley M. Gottfried

— 8 —

"On to Cemetery Ridge!"

OVERRUNNING CEMETERY RIDGE on Meade's left-center was now a classic case of now or never, because it would be too late for Confederate fortunes on July 3 if the capable Meade was allowed time to redeploy troops, reinforce weak spots, and align additional batteries to create an impregnable defensive position across the height. Therefore, with Barksdale gaining additional ground during his relentless push, this was the critical moment of the battle of Gettysburg.[418]

Indeed, if Barksdale failed to gain the strategic crest of Cemetery Ridge, then the basic formula was already in place to guarantee decisive Union success on July 3, as emphasized by Captain Haskell: "The enemy must advance to the attack up an ascent, and must therefore move slower, and be, before coming upon us, longer under our fire, as well as more exhausted. These, and some other things, rendered our position admirable for a defensive battle."[419]

Consequently, what the surviving Mississippi Brigade soldiers and their hard-hitting commanders now possessed was a narrow window that was the best opportunity to achieve victory during the three days of Gettysburg.[420] Indeed, Lee's greatest desire at Gettysburg was "to end the war in a single afternoon," and Barksdale was now in hot pursuit of that greatest of Confederate goals, chasing down a dream that lay invitingly atop Cemetery Ridge.[421] This golden moment would never come again for either Lee and the Army of Northern Virginia, and Barksdale realized as much.[422] Before it was too late and before the precious moment faded away forever, the Mississippi Brigade must keep up its attack to exploit its extensive gains, before Meade rushed reinforcements into place to fill the gap.[423] The wide gap that existed between the Second Corps' left on

Cemetery Ridge and the right of the Fifth Corps on Little Round Top
was the passage through which the Mississippi Brigade must push to gain
Cemetery Ridge's crest and win a decisive success.[424]

Thanks to what the Mississippians had already achieved by this time,
an increasing number of Federals believed that the day was lost. Sickles'
Third Corps had been overrun not only in the Peach Orchard and along
the Emmitsburg Road Ridge, but also in the Wheatfield and the Devil's
Den, from northwest to southeast. More than any other brigade of Longstreet's Corps, however, the Mississippi Brigade had succeeded in "ripping Sickles' Third Corps to shreds . . ." Before his disbelieving eyes,
Haskell was shocked by the sight of thousands of defeated Union troops
continuing "to pour back to the rear in confusion, the enemy are close
upon them—and among them organization is lost to a great degree, guns
and caissons are abandoned and in the hands of the enemy; the Third
Corps [was] literally swept from the field . . . [425]

Longstreet, who had never wanted to launch the tactical offensive
this afternoon, was not only more pessimistic but outright defeatist. He
ordered no troops to follow-up behind Barksdale. Historian Noah Andre
Trudeau said it best: "Even as Alexander was setting his guns into place
[in the Peach Orchard], James Longstreet was making one of the hardest
decisions of his life. Carefully evaluating the ebb and flow of the combat
[unfortunately except in the Mississippi Brigade's sector he] concluded
that a victory was not possible [and he] now began to bring [the fighting]
to an end."[426] Indeed, Longstreet had belatedly and only "directed [his]
attacks with a heavy heart," summarized historian Stephen W. Sears.[427]
But worst of all, Longstreet took no personal supervision to ensure that
support troops, especially Wofford's Georgia brigade, followed directly
behind Barksdale in timely fashion to exploit tactical gains.[428] As usual
the consummate delegator, Lee also failed to closely supervise and man-
age the offensive effort, especially in supporting Barksdale's dramatic
breakthrough. Even before Barksdale was unleashed, Lee possessed no
strategic reserve to follow-up on Barksdale's success, or any other that
might be achieved that day.[429]

Meanwhile, not aware of his reluctant, if not defeatist, corps commander's having given up hope for success, Barksdale and Humphreys
continued to wage their own war which brought out the best in both of
them, encouraging their men toward Cemetery Ridge looming on the
horizon. Before Barksdale and his three fast-moving regiments, the way
east was obstacle free, with the land open, dipping down gradually from

the Emmitsburg Road Ridge to the low ground of a wooded, brush-covered depression along the upper reaches of Plum Run.

Yet making his own decisions without a single word from Longstreet or McLaws, who remained focused on the sector below the Wheatfield Road, Barksdale was determined to keep his attack moving. Consequently, when regimental commanders Holder, 17th Mississippi, and Griffin, 18th Mississippi, dashed up to Barksdale and requested a few minutes to halt and realign ranks along the open, descending slope east of the Klingel House before descending all the way into Plum Run's valley, Barksdale recoiled at the thought. He immediately rejected the notion without a moment's deliberation. Instead he emphasized that now was the time to continue moving at a brisk pace and to keep up the pressure, because the enemy was "on the run." Most of all, and much like Lee himself since July 1, in Longstreet's estimation, not only was Barksdale's "fighting blood up," but also his well-honed aggressive instincts.[430] Barksdale's battle sense and tactical judgment were correct because time was now indeed of the essence. Most of all, Barksdale understood the urgency of continuing the attack at all costs without any delay. In the past, too many Confederate victories had slipped away at almost the last minute, despite the magnificent fighting of the men in the ranks, from the lack of aggressiveness and killer instinct of top commanders, and Gettysburg was no exception.

Barksdale was determined that no opportunity or time would be wasted this afternoon, because he possessed the long-awaited chance to bring about decisive victory before the day's end. Yet mounted, General Barksdale merely barked to his two lieutenants, Holder and Griffin, that there would be no halt or rest for the troops, regardless of their condition or escalating losses. In a booming voice, Barksdale yelled his orders that equated to the correct tactical formula for decisive success: "Crowd them—we have them on the run [and] move on your regiments" toward Cemetery Ridge. Both soon to be cut down, Colonels Holder and Griffin returned to their respective regiments and led them onward down the slope toward Plum Run without a break.

Despite that McLaws' reserve brigade, Wofford's battle-hardened Georgians, had failed to provide support, and despite having suffered high losses, the Mississippians were not waiting for reinforcements from the rear or on either flank. Kershaw's South Carolina brigade on Barksdale's right was fighting on a battle of its own, in cooperation with other units. And instead of being supported by Wofford, as McLaws appeared to originally intend, the Mississippians had instead lent him a hand. When Wofford finally advanced, his left barely skirting the Peach Orchard's southern edge, it had already been swept clean of Federal units—except for the piles of dead and wounded—by Barksdale's troops, after some of the hardest fighting yet witnessed at Gettysburg.

And neither was the Mississippi Brigade now benefiting from the support of Wilcox's Alabama brigade to its left, after Barksdale turned his three regiments east to advance down the Emmitsburg Road Ridge. Because of orders to advance in echelon, these Alabama Rebels were also not advancing simultaneously with Barksdale's onrushing troops, or even within close supporting distance. The extent of the Mississippians' rapid advance and swift success had taken them far ahead of the troops that should have supported them. Private Bailey George McClelen, 10th Alabama Infantry, Wilcox's Brigade, wrote that although the Mississippi Brigade attacked to the Alabama brigade's right, "yet a considerable interval [lay] between us."

At this critical juncture, consequently, the attacking Mississippi Brigade continued to advance on its own in two separate wings and fight its own private war largely on its own hook. Both rampaging wings of Mississippi Rebels rolled down the long, gradually sloping ground that plunged ever-deeper toward Plum Run's shallow valley and the lowest point at the creek bottom.[431] Looking to the north, one of Wofford's Georgia boys was astounded by the grisly sight of the havoc caused by the 21st Mississippi's attack through the Peach Orchard and beyond: "The Yankee dead lay thick around their guns and dead and wounded horses literally cumbered the ground. "[432]

The Mississippi Brigade's self-imposed mission of winning the war before sunset was now to begin in earnest, especially for Colonel Humphreys' hard-hitting regiment. After sweeping over the Peach Orchard, the 21st Mississippi had out-flanked the foremost of General Caldwell's rightmost units on the north, playing a key role in forcing them to retire from the Wheatfield, after swiftly gaining their exposed right and rear. One infantry unit early smashed by the 21st Mississippi was the 7th New Jersey, which had moved into the Peach Orchard sector from Colonel Burling's Third Brigade, Humphreys' Division, north of Trostle Lane to protect the batteries. This regiment had supported Captain Clark's New Jersey battery in the rear north of the Wheatfield Road. Fighting a delaying action in a desperate, but failed, attempt to save the Federal batteries along the Wheatfield Road from the charging 21st Mississippi, the

7th New Jersey consisted of 275 men from the southern and northern-most counties of the Garden State.

This fine regiment contained a large number of ethnic soldiers from Switzerland, Prussia, and Austria, which contrasted sharply with Mississippi Brigade's demographics, which contained few such "Aryan" warriors. Such widespread ethnicity was appropriately symbolic because the 7th New Jersey was commanded by twenty-four-year Colonel Louis Raymond Francine. The promising son of a French immigrant, the colonel possessed knowledge of the ways of war gained from not only an American military school but also from France's most prestigious military academy, the L'Ecole Polytechnique in Paris. Francine and his 7th New Jersey had fought well at Chancellorsville, but the 21st Mississippi presented the regiment with its most formidable challenge to date.

While facing Kershaw's South Carolinians in front, the New Jersey boys were hit hard on the right flank by Humphreys' attackers. Colonel Francine was cut down with a mortal wound, along with the regiment's lieutenant colonel and adjutant. So punishing was Humphreys' onslaught that the Garden State regiment was nearly "overwhelmed and captured" by the Mississippians, who were destroying anything and everything caught in their path. To escape annihilation and after suffering 34 percent casualties, the battered 7th New Jersey retreated with the yelling Rebels close behind in pursuit.

After pushing aside all Peach Orchard infantry defenders and hurling back the support troops protecting the Wheatfield Road artillery, a new threat suddenly appeared as the 21st Mississippi continued to attack east roughly parallel to the Wheatfield Road. Astride the narrow, dirt road, Colonel Humphreys' regiment surged onward down the gentle slope that led to Plum Run. At this time, Captain George B. Winslow's First New York Light Artillery, Battery D, presented the next challenge to Humphreys. On high ground facing south toward the bloody Wheatfield to punish the South Carolinians, these New York guns, manned by seasoned artillerymen who won distinction at Chancellorsville, were aligned just south of the Wheatfield Road and along the Wheatfield's northern edge. Commanding his battery of 12-pounder Napoleon guns with a good combat record that extended back to the Seven Days, Captain Winslow described his early no-win situation: "The enemy's advance [Kershaw's South Carolina troops] being within 25 yards of my left, and covered by woods and rocks, I ordered my left section limbered [but] Before this was accomplished, the enemy had advanced under cover of the woods upon my right, and was cutting down my men and horses. Having no supports in rear, and being exposed to a heavy fire of musketry in front and upon both flanks, I deemed it necessary to withdraw in order to save my guns." With the 21st Mississippi on the move toward Winslow's right flank and unleashing a descending flank fire, the desperate artillery captain was not able to get all of his guns out in time.

But first he posed a serious threat to the bulk of Barksdale's Brigade, which had by now come on a line with him to the north, with the 17th Mississippi closest to the danger. As Private John Saunders Henley, Company A, 17th Mississippi, explained the tactical situation: "We had driven the Yankees about a mile from their first line [but] our ranks had grown so thin that orders had been given to close to the left, which left a space of at least 400 yards between the right of our division and Hood's left [and now Captain Winslow's New York battery which] could have destroyed our whole brigade." This was because the New York guns were now on Barksdale's flank, and with an enfilade fire could have devastated the brigade. Therefore, Colonel Holder, 17th Mississippi, "quickly saw the dilemma."

The colonel "rushed to" the right and reached Humphreys on the Mississippi Brigade's far flank. Holder informed Colonel Humphreys that Barksdale's regiment, the 13th Mississippi in the line's center, was about to be enfiladed by a right flank fire if Captain Winslow's battery was not eliminated as soon as possible. Out of desperation, the colonel then requested of Humphreys, "If you will give me Company A of the 17th (under Capt. Jack Pulliam) I will take that battery before it can fire a gun." Captain Andrew Jackson ("Jack") Pulliam, commanding the Chickasaw County boys of the Buena Vista Guards, was a most resourceful officer. He was up for the challenge. While Captain Winslow and his New York artillerymen were occupied with the troublesome South Carolina troops in the Wheatfield sector, Colonel Humphreys now devised yet another one of his patented flank attacks from the west.

Clearly, the threat of the barking New York guns, which could turn to enfilade the right flank of Barksdale's three regiments, now facing east, to the north, had to be quickly eliminated, if the victorious Mississippi Brigade was to exploit its already extensive gains. Humphreys quickly formulated a tactical plan, while Captain Winslow's Empire State battery now stood "off to the right some three hundred yards [which meant that they could] enfilade [Barksdale's] column," wrote one correctly concerned Confederate officer. Therefore, the powder-stained soldiers of the 21st

Mississippi prepared to launch yet another strike to capture additional Federal artillery.

Leading the charge, Humphreys once again continued to play his key role in bringing the Army of Northern Virginia ever-closer to decisive victory. Indeed, "in a flash 'Right well, charge!' rang above the roar of battle, and with the rattle of muskets, the clang of bayonets, and the shouts of victory Winslow's Battery fell a prize to the sons of Mississippi."

As Private Henley, age twenty-three, described the sweeping attack that captured the New York cannon after his Company A, occupying the 17th Mississippi's right flank, detached itself from Holder's regiment and moved south to link with the 21st Mississippi: "The order was given to take my company and Co. A of the 21st. The two companies wheeled into line under a terrible infantry fire and Col. Holder ordered us to take that battery before they could load the guns. The command was obeyed; not a cannon was fired, and not a man or horse was left to tell the tale. We left some of our company dead in the famous charge in which we captured and spiked the enemy's guns. Col. Holder was critically wounded and rode off holding his protruding entrails in one hand and guiding his horse with the other. Joe Pulliam, of my company, was shot in the charge and lay all night in his own blood [while] my brother [Private Eldridge Newton Henley] was left on another part of the field. We went into the charge with 41 men, and left 22 killed and wounded outside of our lines." Ironically, the capture of some of Captain Winslow's New York Battery's guns has been incorrectly attributed to Kershaw's South Carolina brigade instead of to Colonel Humphreys.

After capturing the guns of Winslow's Battery, Colonel Humphreys and his attackers "just then discovered another battery of five guns wheeling into position about 175 or 200 yards up the opposite slope, I at once ordered a charge," as the colonel wrote of his desperate bid to eliminate another serious threat. Once again, the Mississippians charged southeast with shouts and flashing bayonets in an attempt to capture the next battery, which was caught unlimbering on the open slopes before the Trostle House.

Continuing to perform more like a brigade than a single regiment this afternoon, the 21st Mississippi continued to attack eastward astride the Wheatfield Road. As historian Edwin Coddington wrote, "These men were making it their business to seek out batteries, dash in, brush aside their infantry supports, and catch them on the flanks." Despite being separated from the right of Barksdale's three regiments just to the north and without support on either side, Colonel Humphrey's regiment spearheaded the Mississippi Brigade's most hard-hitting offensive effort.

Humphreys was at his best, demonstrating that he was a masterful and flexible tactician on a fast-paced battlefield shrouded in smoke and confusion, while leading his elite regiment as shock troops. Again and again in advancing independently as Barksdale's hard-hitting right wing, the 21st Mississippi was instinctively drawn like a magnet to any Union battery in sight and within striking distance. In a southeast direction, Humphreys and his troops continued to surge ahead without supports, or counting costs, or stopping to fire a volley in textbook fashion, pushing aside all infantry support to strike the vulnerable batteries on their flank. Repeatedly, the Mississippi Rebels charged among any exposed Union guns and subdued Yankee artillerymen in fierce hand-to-hand combat. During some of the best fighting on July 2, Colonel Humphreys' single regiment continued to push toward the great goal of reaching Cemetery Ridge. By the end of the day the 21st Mississippi was destined to capture "in all 15 guns."[433]

And now yet another Union cannon was quickly gobbled-up by the 21st Mississippi. Captain Charles Phillips and his gunners of Company E, 5th Massachusetts Light Artillery, had frantically labored to get their field pieces, positioned along the Wheatfield Road, out of the path of Humphreys' onslaught under Colonel McGilvery's frantic orders, before it was too late. After Hart's 15th New York Battery retired, Phillips' right was exposed to the 21st Mississippi. However, one field piece remained behind, and the desperate New England artillerymen of McGilvery's Reserve Artillery, under a long-range fire from Kershaw's skirmishers to the south, hurriedly brought out a five-horse limber team. But the extra horsepower was quickly eliminated, with the 21st Mississippi Rebels, attacking southeastward, firing on the run, cutting down all five horses and determined officers like Lieutenant Henry D. Scott, who was knocked unconscious when a bullet smashed into his cheek, to ensure the capture of the Massachusetts field piece.[434]

After reaping one success after another, Humphreys and his victorious 21st Mississippi soldiers could now hardly believe the sight that was now before them to the east. "No other guns, or a solitary soldier could be seen before us—the Federal army was in twain," wrote the elated colonel of the sight. A gaping hole had been torn in Meade's left-center and the war's end seemed in view as never before.[435] At long last, it seemed to Humphreys that the moment of decisive victory had come. Like his top lieutenant to the south, Barksdale also possessed an open avenue leading to victory. Private Joseph Charles Lloyd, 13th Mississippi, never forgot the sight that indicated a resounding success: "We cleared the whole of our front from the enemy as far as I could see to the bushes around Plum Run."[436] He also explained how Barksdale's three regiments had swept everything before them "until no enemy was seen in our front."[437]

Colonel Humphreys and his triumphant 21st Mississippi men also now realized that above all else, their hard-won gains had to be exploited to the fullest, if decisive victory was to be won this afternoon. Consequently, he ordered his boys to turn the captured artillery pieces upon fresh lines of Union troops that were pushing toward Barksdale from the northeast. Now this extra firepower from the larger caliber, rifled, and more accurate Union guns could yet inflict damage on any rallied or counterattacking Federal troops opposing Barksdale's three regiments to the north. However, Humphreys' best efforts were thwarted. "I endeavored to turn my captured batteries on these lines," he wrote, "but the Federals had carried off rammers and friction wires." Consequently, it was now entirely up to the battle-hardened Mississippi infantrymen who would have to win it all for the Confederacy on their own with bayonets, musket-butts, and well-placed shots.[438] And with Longstreet and McLaws yet focused on the sector below the Wheatfield Road and Barksdale attacking to the north, Humphreys continued to make his tactical decisions on his own and while on the move without hesitation.[439]

But boding ill for Humphreys' fortunes, Sickles was now busily organizing resistance around the Trostle House, the New York City general's Third Corps headquarters located around a quarter mile north of the Wheatfield. Situated about three-quarters of a mile from where Barksdale had first launched his assault, this vital sector just west of Plum Run shortly became the vortex of the storm because of its key location: just below, or south, of the house, Trostle's dirt lane that ran parallel to the Wheatfield Road some 900 feet to the south. From the farmer's house, Trostle's lane continued east across the north-south running Plum Run and on to Cemetery Ridge.

With the Mississippians tasting decisive victory as never before, having collapsed his remaining units on the Emmitsburg Road, Sickles was knocked out-of-action by "a freak wounding" to further increase Barksdale's and Humphreys' chances of success. While astride his horse on the open, slight knoll just before the Trostle barn, Sickles was hit by a glancing blow from a cannon ball fired from one of Alexander's guns. The projectile struck the bellicose New Yorker in the right leg, near the knee. Humphreys described how "Sickles lost his leg by a shot from Moody's battery—over our heads." But the fire of the Madison Light Artillery also caused losses among the onrushing 21st Mississippi troops, revealing that Humphreys' men had advanced farther and faster than anticipated by the Louisiana artillerymen blazing away from the Peach Orchard. With regret, Humphreys explained how Captain "Moody also killed some of my men by premature explosions" of shells.[440]

Meanwhile, fearing that he would fall into the Mississippians' hands, Sickles "repeatedly urged us not to allow him to be taken," in the words of the Third Corps artillery commander, Randolph.[441] Clearly, by this time and in an understatement, the Trostle House sector had "become too hot for a corps headquarters."[442] Meanwhile, before it was too late, Federal batteries of Lieutenant Colonel Freeman McGilvery's reserve artillery were in the process of assembling on the western slope of Cemetery Ridge—the future Plum Run Line about 200 yards east of the creek and along the gradual slope just before Cemetery Ridge's crest—in a last-ditch effort to stop the Mississippians' onslaught.

At the Peach Orchard, Alexander described how Union "batteries in abundance were showing up & troops too seemed to be marching & fighting everywhere. There was plenty to shoot at. One could take his choice & here my guns stood & fired until it was too dark to see anything more."[443] It wasn't prudent for Alexander to advance his guns any further in the uncertain situation; therefore, in the bid to capture Cemetery Ridge's crest, an ever-decreasing number of Mississippi infantrymen had to eliminate resurgent Union batteries on their own. Fortunately for Barksdale, Humphreys' battle-hardened soldiers were the right men for the crucial job.

But for now, this was fundamentally a race between the Mississippi Rebels and Meade's sizeable and powerful reserve artillery to see which would arrive first to gain permanent possession of Cemetery Ridge at Meade's most vulnerable sector. All the while, the Mississippi Rebels of both wings continued surging east toward Cemetery Ridge, going for broke in the late afternoon light. However, the Mississippi Brigade, depleted from escalating losses but not in regard to fighting spirit, continued to attack on its own.

Performing well below what was required to reap a decisive success, neither Lee nor Longstreet ordered any Southern units forward to follow behind the Mississippians to exploit their already significant gains. A frustrated Adjutant Harman described in a letter how "Gen'l Barksdale sent back twice for reinforcements but as Picket's [sic] division was not up and as the whole of McLaws' and Hood's divisions were actively engaged the asked for reinforcements were never sent."[444]

With the Army of the Potomac on the ropes as never before on the most decisive day at Gettysburg, therefore, Barksdale remained in front and somehow yet untouched by bullets, encouraging his boys onward through the yellow fields of grain like a thoroughbred hunting hound chasing after a fox. After achieving their greatest success to date, the howling Mississippi Rebels surged onward, following their red battle-flags in the relentless push toward Cemetery Ridge. Pennsylvania-born Jesse Bowman Young, who served on Sickles' staff, described how the "sun was now dropping behind Seminary Ridge. Customarily mellow over these woods and farmlands, the waning rays were unable in many places to penetrate the alien screen of smoke and dust. The entire Union line, from north to south, was in retreat." Indeed, a large, wide gap continued to exist along Cemetery Ridge, which was devoid of Union infantry regiments and rows of artillery, to the Trostle House's rear and just north of Little Round Top to the Second Corps' left.

One Federal wrote of the extent of the ever-growing disaster: "The evening, and our prospects, grew dark together. The 3rd Corps had been driven back, broken and shattered, its commander wounded and carried from the field and every man felt that the situation was grave." Indeed, both wings of the Mississippi Brigade continued to surge nearer to the low-lying ground of Plum Run. Meanwhile, with battle-flags flying and Humphreys pointing the way, the 21st Mississippi charged through the near ripe grain fields southeastward and parallel to the Wheatfield Road.[445]

To Colonel Humphreys' north, meanwhile, Barksdale and his three regiments overran additional Union guns, adding to their already impressive tally. Lieutenant John G. Turnbull's Battery F and K, 3rd United States Artillery, had escaped from Barksdale's flank attack up, and parallel to, the Emmitsburg Road, thanks to General Humphreys' urgent orders to retreat. The battery retired nearly 400 yards through the open fields leading down the slope but never reached Plum Run. After some 45 artillery horses were shot down along the open slope, the battery of six Napoleon 12-pounders were trapped when Barksdale's troops descended upon them with a yell. Another half dozen bronze cannon were captured by the 18th, 13th, and 17th Mississippi.[446]

At this moment, the golden opportunity for success had never been brighter for both onrushing wings of the Mississippi Brigade. Quite simply, not only "the crisis of the engagement had arrived," in the words of Colonel McGilvery, but also the most critical moment in the Army of the Potomac's life, which by this time seemed close to its end.[447] In the 17th Mississippi's ranks, an elated Private Abernathy never forgot the dramatic sight as they advanced "on and on until no enemy could be seen in our front."[448]

Here, on the open slope amid the fields before reaching the dense underbrush along Plum Run, Barksdale's troops halted near where Turnbull's artillery pieces were captured, when they encountered a slight tributary of Plum Run that flowed east down the slope directly east of the Klingel House and just before entering the run. Hot, thirsty, and out of water, exhausted Mississippians halted to drink the cold, spring-fed waters, and fill canteens out of absolute necessity on one of the year's hottest afternoons. Quite possibly, the Civil War might have been lost to the Confederacy at this little, unnamed creek because of precious time lost. Here, Barksdale also might have attempted to organize crews to man the captured guns and to allow his worn men time to catch their breath before continuing onward down the slope toward Plum Run.[449]

Clearly, Basksdale was now on the verge of reaping an unprecedented success. However, additional good soldiers, both officers and enlisted men, had been culled from the Mississippi Brigade's ranks. The losses continued to steadily pile up, and there were no replacements to bolster the thinned ranks. Some of the Mississippi Brigade's finest officers had been cut down, including Colonel Carter who commanded the 13th Mississippi. Colonel Holder, the former Mississippi state legislator who represented Pontotoc County and commanded the 17th Mississippi, also suffered a severe wound. Carter was "wounded in the stomach. His entrails were shot out, and he held them in [while] my crippled brother got him on his horse, and led the horse back to the hospital," lamented Private Henley of the horror.[450] Despite doubting that he would ever see his farm and family again, Colonel Holder survived his wounds and lived another two decades. However, in the end, the colonel's injuries suffered at Gettysburg eventually led to his death.[451]

During such a lengthy assault over such a wide stretch of open ground, the Mississippi Brigade's enlisted ranks had also suffered severely. Private John Alemeth Byers, a planter's son of the Panola Vindicators (Company H), 17th Mississippi, was cut down. Byers, whose black servant was named Gilbert, fell to an exploding shell, taking multiple wounds in the neck, head, and shoulder. A handsome, blond-haired, blue-eyed youth who had long made the farm girls of Panola County swoon, Private Byers, age twenty-seven, survived the serious wounds, only to be killed at Cedar Creek in the Shenandoah Valley in October 1864.[452]

And David H. Williams, Pettus Guards, 13th Mississippi, went down with a fractured skull. As he wrote: "I was shot down in twenty feet of the cannon and reported dead."[453] The Mississippi Brigade was well on its way to losing half of its men on this afternoon: the inevitable price for smashing through the Third Corps, capturing rows of field pieces, and pushing aside one Union regiment after another.[454] But what continued to loom before them was the best opportunity of the battle: a broad, open stretch of ground for more than "1,500 yards, between [Little] Round Top and the left of the 2nd Corps, the lines were open [and] there were no reserves," penned one Union officer of the crisis.[455]

While the Mississippians continued to advance, a desperate General Hunt attempted to patch together an ad hoc defensive line of artillery just below Cemetery Ridge's crest to stop Barksdale's rampage. Such a new defensive line was urgently needed while what was left of Humphreys' division, under pressure from Barksdale and his three regiments, continued to stream rearward north of the Trostle farm, while the shattered remains of Graham's brigade continued to fall back across the Trostle farm to the south.

With so many Federal gunners and artillery horses shot down, meanwhile, the battered remains of several Union batteries retired east and also northeast over the open fields below the Trostle House to escape Humphreys' attackers, who seemingly could not be stopped by either artillery or infantry. Some guns, like Lieutenant Turnbull's battery to the north where natural growth along the creek was heavier than around the Trostle House, had been unable to retire across Plum Run. Lined with trees and thick underbrush that hampered the Union flight, this creek was not wide but was relatively deep at spots, where silent, clear pools of water formed.

Heavily-whiskered Lieutenant Colonel Freeman McGilvery, a thirty-seven-year-old Maine seaman who had sailed around the world for two decades, was about to rise to the occasion while commanding the First

Volunteer Brigade, Artillery Reserve. Carrying a heavy burden, the Scots-Irishman's greatest challenge was now to make sure that the charging Mississippians would not deliver a death-blow to the reeling Army of the Potomac.

Fortunately for the Union, Lieutenant Colonel McGilvery knew how to inspire his artillerymen to greater exertions during this crisis. He possessed "a tolerable appreciation of the value of discipline in situations" of importance. Most important, McGilvery retained "the coolness and rapidity of thought and action . . . at critical moments." As the 6th Maine Battery's commanding officer, he had won distinction at the battle of Cedar Mountain on August 9, 1862 in Culpeper County, Virginia. During the battery's baptismal fire, McGilvery and his Maine cannoneers, in one general's opinion, had "saved the division from being destroyed or taken prisoners." At Second Manassas, despite being without infantry support, the battery earned distinction as the last Union artillery unit to depart the field. Such a distinguished record of battlefield performances paved the way for McGilvery gaining command of the First Volunteer Brigade, Reserve Artillery, Army of the Potomac in mid-May 1863. Barely a month later, the capable McGilvery won his coveted lieutenant colonel's rank.

McGilvery, like the army's artillery chief, General Hunt, was now in the process of having his finest day on July 2. He commanded a large part of the army's mighty reserve artillery, the crucial last ace in Meade's ever-weakening hand. Fortunately, Hunt already had made this "powerful" reserve even more formidable by having recently ordered that each battery should carry an additional twenty rounds that exceeded regulation limitations. Most significant, Meade had recently allowed Hunt the all-important command independence that had been denied to him by Hooker, and the energetic Hunt made the most of the opportunity.

In frantic haste, McGilvery attempted to make a last-ditch defensive stand at the Trostle farm to buy precious time for the creation of the Plum Run Line. Here a line of Massachusetts, Pennsylvania, and New York guns were turned west in a final desperate bid to slow the Mississippians' attack. However, Humphreys allowed no time for McGilvery to orchestrate his defensive stand. With charging Rebels closing in on both his right (Barksdale) and left flank (Humphreys), McGilvery wisely ordered his surviving guns rearward to an excellent high ground position that eventually became the hastily patched together line on Cemetery Ridge's west slope.

While McGilvery's other batteries along the Wheatfield Road hurriedly pulled out before Humphreys' charge, six 12-pounders of the lone 9th Massachusetts Battery were threatened below, or south of, the Wheatfield Road by Kershaw's South Carolinians and Wofford's Georgians pressuring his left and Humphreys' Mississippians rapidly descending on his right. By this time, the 9th Massachusetts Battery "alone remained after the 3d Corps had been driven from its position—both infantry and artillery," wrote Captain John Bigelow of the crisis situation. Before the Massachusetts guns were overwhelmed, Lieutenant Colonel McGilvery shouted to Bigelow, "All of Sickles' men had withdrawn and I was alone on the field, without supports . . . limber up and get out" before it was too late.

Bigelow's Massachusetts gunners were positioned along the Wheatfield Road, roughly halfway between the Peach Orchard and the Wheatfield. Here, the 9th Massachusetts gunners had punished Kershaw's South Carolina soldiers, especially those troops on the enfiladed left flank, and the Georgians under General Paul J. Semmes. Unfortunately for Humphreys and his 21st Mississippi, one Georgia soldier described the fateful decision that ensured the Mississippi Brigade's continued lack of support, "We were going toward a Peach Orchard, but were ordered to right oblique." Therefore, Semmes' Georgia brigade had attacked the Wheatfield beyond supporting distance of Humphreys, coming under Bigelow's scorching enfilade fire that ensured that a good many young men and boys would never see the Peach State again. Very likely, General Semmes was mortally wounded on the embattled Rose Farm by the fire from Bigelow's New England gunners, before they withdrew from the Wheatfield Road sector to escape the 21st Mississippi's onslaught.

Acting in concert together to thwart Confederate ambitions this afternoon, Generals Meade and Hunt already had made most excellent use of their artillery reserve, thanks not only to its superior strength but also to the advantage of interior lines. They had initially ordered McGilvery's artillery reserve of four batteries to bolster the left center of Sickles' line along the Wheatfield Road southeast of the Peach Orchard, filling the wide gap between the Peach Orchard and the Wheatfield. But after the 21st Mississippi smashed and then swept through the salient angle with a tornado's force, McGilvery had ordered his batteries to retire to the relative safety of Cemetery Ridge. As fate would have it, Captain Bigelow's 9th Massachusetts Battery was the last unit along the Wheatfield Road to receive orders to retire.

Young Captain Bigelow described his quandary, for his battery's exposed "position at that moment was indeed critical [because] If [we] stopped firing, Kershaw's sharpshooters would quickly empty every saddle; while only two hundred yards on [the] right, extending to [our] right and rear, as far as one could see, was Barksdale's Confederate brigade, flushed with the victory which their stubborn fighting had won at the Peach Orchard, and preparing to cut [us] off." To Bigelow who knew that limbering up his guns to withdraw would allow Humphreys' men the opportunity to rush and capture his artillery, therefore the only remaining solution had been to connect "the trail of guns to limbers, with a rope or prolonge, in order to keep alignment correct, with a slow, sullen fire [to allow] the recoil to withdraw guns, keeping the sharpshooters back with canister, and ricocheting solid shot through the ranks of Barksdale's men. Thus, one thousand yards in advance of our own lines, without infantry support or a single friendly shot from any of our batteries, with the enemy advancing on our front and flank," the Massachusetts guns retired northeast over the open ground toward the white-washed Trostle House.

Sergeant Baker recalled how "as we commenced retiring, Barksdale's brigade emerged from the Peach Orchard about 400 yards on our right, and halted to reform their lines," before resuming the attack toward the Trostle House defensive position. In a bad fix, Captain Bigelow described how there were "no friendly supports, of any kind, [that] were in sight; but Johnnie Rebs in great numbers. Bullets were coming into our midst from many directions and a Confederate battery added to our difficulties." While directing his "long arm" unit for the 400 yards northeast across bullet-swept open fields and a scattering of rocks and boulders toward the Trostle House and down through the fields along the open eastern slope of the Emmitsburg Road Ridge, Captain Bigelow's six smoothbore, bronze 12-pounder Napoleons fired both west toward Barksdale's attackers and south toward Kershaw's South Carolinians, inflicting damage on both.

An aristocratic, blue-blood raised in the Boston suburb of Brighton, John Bigelow was only twenty-three, but he looked and acted older than his years. At age sixteen, he had entered Harvard in the autumn of 1857, but then left the classroom as a senior in April 1861 to serve his country. He was the first member of his class at Harvard College to wear the blue. At Malvern Hill, Bigelow had first viewed the potential of Union artillery, and was cited for gallantry. Despite taking a wound, he had ignored the pain and continued to personally serve a gun to inspire his artillerymen.

Bigelow was then given command of the 9th Massachusetts Light Artillery before the Pennsylvania Campaign. He restored the discipline of a unit demoralized by garrison duty at the nation's capital and too long near the notorious sin binds, bordellos—both black (such as "Misses Seal & Brown" on Marble Alley) and white (such as the one operated by Ann Benton on Tin Can Alley)—and the free-flowing whiskey houses of Washington, D.C. More than anyone else, Captain Bigelow had honed the 9th Massachusetts Battery into a disciplined and highly motivated outfit. Bigelow was just the kind of dynamic officer who would stand firm during a crisis situation, despite the fact that the 9th Massachusetts received its baptism fire on July 2. This fine New England battery had only recently joined the army to become part of McGilvery's Artillery Reserve during its push north to Pennsylvania.

Bigelow's privileged upbringing and splendid Harvard education masked a toughness that matched the hardy working class boys who manned his guns. Consequently, the young captain was the right man for facing the day's most serious crisis. Indeed, in many ways, "the outcome of the battle [now] hinged on the actions of a handful of cannoneers" from the Bay State. Less than one hundred Massachusetts men now stood between Humphreys' Mississippi Rebels and their lofty objective of penetrating the main battle line of the Army of the Potomac.

Captain Bigelow never forgot the sight of the onslaught of the victorious Mississippians, who "had come through and were forming a line 200 yards distant, extending back, parallel with the Emmitsburg Road." Indeed, Colonel Humphreys had spied Bigelow's Massachusetts guns retiring northeast and unlimbering before the home of Abraham and Catherine Trostle just south of east-west running Trostle Lane. As usual, Humphreys wanted to possess these guns as soon as possible, but this meant pushing northeast across open ground to Plum Run and closer to Barksdale, who now approached Plum Run's environs from the east.

Humphreys now acted on well-honed instincts. Most of all, he knew the necessity of not only keeping his troops on the move but, more important, to immediately exploit any existing opportunity as quickly as possible. The astute Mississippi Delta colonel reasoned correctly that the best way to assist Barksdale was to achieve additional gains to the south. Humphreys now saw Bigelow's New England battery alone and isolated amid a "natural amphitheater" without infantry support and thus vulnerable: a golden opportunity that needed to be exploited without hesitation. Therefore the 21st Mississippi's commander dispatched no courier north to Barksdale to request reinforcements or instructions about when and where he should strike. Humphreys knew what he had to do.

As throughout this afternoon, Humphreys wasted no time, with the great goal of Cemetery Ridge yet looming just before his eyes, a tantalizing incentive to keep his troops pushing onward to reap the ultimate gain before the sun went down. In Humphreys' own words: "I discovered that a federal battery to my right had rallied and was annoying Kershaw to our right and rear, and would soon turn on Barksdale's brigade as enfilade fire. I immediately wheeled the 21st to the right and headed directly against the battery." One Mississippi soldier analyzed the tactical wisdom of Humphreys' bold decision to attack without hesitation, consultation, or orders: "He, guided by soldierly genius, [planned to catch] Bigelow's gunners unprepared, where had he waited two minutes he would have had their shrapnel and canister pouring into his flank."

Humphreys later described his decision to eliminate the final Massachusetts Battery under Bigelow, after the withdrawal of Captain Phillips' 5th Massachusetts Light Artillery: "When we broke Sickles' line, Barksdale inclined to the left and Kershaw to the right, and when Barksdale emerged from the Peach Orchard, his right flank was on your right flank 200 yards off. I saw at once our peril in leaving you [Bigelow] to enfilade our line. I promptly wheeled the 21st Mississippi Volunteers to the right, and charged down on you [which] afforded infinite relief to Kershaw's Brigade, with whose sharp-shooters on your left front you were engaged." However, the onrushing 21st Mississippi yet took fire from Massachusetts, Pennsylvania, and Michigan troops of Colonel William S. Tilton's brigade, Fifth Corps, from the Trostle's Woods. Before those woods just south of the Trostle House, Corporal James J. Donnelly picked off a 21st Mississippi color bearer with a well-placed shot from his carbine.

With the high-pitched "Rebel Yells" of Humphreys' men growing more audible on the other side of the grassy rise, or swell, that sheltered the 9th Massachusetts gunners, amid the slight depression, southwest of the Trostle House and about a hundred yards distant, the four Massachusetts guns on the center (guns no. 1 and 2) and right (guns no. 5 and 6) fired solid shot low along the open ground. Bigelow and his gunners could not see the 21st Mississippi but knew its general location from the piercing war-cries. Meanwhile, guns no. 3 and 4 fired at Kershaw's skirmishers to the south. The cannonballs from the four guns bounced over the swell, or "bowl rim," before them to strike the onrushing 21st Mississippi boys on the swell's other side. This unconventional tactic was the deadly game of "bowling solid shot towards Barksdale's men," recalled Bigelow. Hurled mostly in a southwest direction, the ricocheting 12-pounder shot bounded along the ground and then bounced up to hit Humphreys' soldiers, surging northeastward across open ground, in the legs, angles, and thighs. The iron balls crushed bone and ended the lives and promising futures of young men and boys who never saw home again, knocking over Mississippians like ten-pens in a nightmarish bowling alley.

All of Captain Bigelow's cannon were now poised to meet the Mississippians at the northern edge of a small field or pasture just below, or south, of the two-story Trostle House just on the lane's north side. The row of six field pieces stood unlimbered almost directly opposite the white colored house and the large red barn just to the west. The Trostle barn, like the Sherfy barn captured earlier by the 18th Mississippi, was located on commanding ground, looming above the farmer's house to the west. Behind Bigelow's guns, a lengthy stone wall ran southward from higher to lower ground in the marshy area along Plum Run that flowed in that direction to enter a wide, grassy meadow of grazing land for livestock. Here, in an angle formed by and surrounded by stone walls, amid the rock-strewn corner of a small pasture adjacent to the Trostle barn and house, these hardy New Englanders bravely made their last stand in this fence corner, before the fierce onslaught of the 21st Mississippi attackers.

Bigelow's Massachusetts artillerymen had first planned to retire to Cemetery Ridge until Lieutenant Colonel McGilvery suddenly dashed up on a blood-streaked horse hit by four bullet holes. He yelled, "Captain Bigelow, there is not an infantryman back of you along the whole line from which Sickles moved out; you must remain where you are and hold your position at all hazards, and sacrifice your battery, if need be, until at least I can find some batteries to put in position and cover you. The enemy are coming down on you now." Before riding off to gather his hard-hit artillery units in the hope of creating a defensive stand east of the Trostle House on the excellent defensive ground of Cemetery Ridge, McGilvery shouted a final command to the Massachusetts gunners that revealed their precarious situation: "Give them grape and canister!"

Indeed, revealing the golden opportunity yet open to the Mississippi Brigade, McGilvery rode back to Cemetery Ridge in a desperate attempt to form his new defensive line on high ground. McGilvery realized quite correctly that above all else "the crisis of the engagement had now arrived." Only drastic action could save the day during the most serious crisis ever faced by the Army of the Potomac. Therefore, McGilvery concluded that it was now necessary above all else "to sacrifice his Batteries, if necessary, in an effort to stay the enemy's advance into the opening in the Lines."

Here, at the German farmer's house a mile and a half south of Gettysburg, Bigelow's 9th Massachusetts Light Artillery made one of the most important last stands at Gettysburg, after all other Union artillery pieces of the Peach Orchard and Wheatfield Road line had been either captured or escaped rearward. Consequently, Bigelow was directed to "hold his position at the Trostle farm, whatever the cost" to buy precious time, or the Mississippi Rebels would overrun Cemetery Ridge's crest, where no Union infantry or artillery yet stood. Here the New Englanders made their last-ditch stand at the point where the two stone walls met just south of the dusty Trostle Lane and the Trostle house. The New England guns were formed in a tight defensive quarter circle with the stone walls to their rear. Bigelow realized that "the sacrifice of the command was asked in order to save the line."[456]

From his vantage point atop the high ground of Cemetery Ridge to the north, Captain Haskell contemplated the unthinkable: the realization that Meade's Army was now facing decisive defeat. In his letter, Haskell asked the key question upon which the battle's outcome and the Union's fate now hung by the narrowest of margins, thanks to Barksdale's slashing attack: with "That Corps [Sickles] gone, what is there between the Second Corps, and these yelling masses of the enemy?"[457] The answer to Haskell's question upon which the fate of two American republics now hinged was: only a mere handful of feisty New England gunners of Bigelow's 9th Massachusetts Light Artillery.

With its left-center pierced by swarming Mississippians, the hard-hit Army of the Potomac, hovering on the verge of decisive defeat, now faced its supreme moment of crisis and its darkest hour to date, setting the stage for the most important artillery action of the war. Here, the Massachusetts cannon stood firm on its own, after the other mauled Union batteries had retired from the Emmitsburg and Wheatfield Road and toward Cemetery Ridge and safety. These retreating Yankee artillerymen were possessed by a single impulse: to get as far away from the Mississippi Brigade's relentless attackers as possible. Therefore, the lone Massachusetts battery was in the most important and tightest of spots. As penned Captain Bigelow of his great dilemma, our "retreat under fire was cut off by the stone wall [and our] flanks were exposed and a swell of the ground in front [would allow] Barksdale's advancing line to approach within fifty yards."

Indeed, Bigelow most of all now realized that "the task seemed superhuman, for the knoll allowed the enemy to approach as it were under cover within 50 yards of my front, while I was very much cramped for room and my ammunition was greatly reduced" by this time. In addition, the stubborn New England gunners were faint from exertion and the heat, and in overall bad shape after fighting for two hours and suffering heavy casualties. Hence, wrote one cannoneer, in this most disadvantageous and vital of situations, "we were left in a critical position," as he knew that no Union troops stood atop Cemetery Ridge's strategic crest to his rear.

Given a directive from their superior who had "literally ordered their destruction," the stoic, young Massachusetts gunners knew that they had to somehow buy precious time, so that the formation of a new defensive line on high ground to the rear could be cobbled together in time. The sprawling gap left in Meade's line by the Third Corps' rout had widened into a great chasm in a defensive line that already stretched for three miles. North of the isolated 9th Massachusetts guns, the Second Corps' left marked the north end of the gaping hole in the Union lines, while the Fifth Corps' right on Little Round Top marked the gap's south end. All the while, hundreds of yards north of the Trostle house, the remains of the battered units of Humphreys' division continued to retire toward the Second Corps' left on Cemetery Ridge. Mauled Federal units retired through this gap, but did not yet rally, and no fresh or strong blue lines of troops were now aligned against the onrushing Mississippi tide.

When Lieutenant Colonel McGilvery rode back to Cemetery Ridge, he was stunned to find no infantry support for his cannon because the Third Corps "had left the field." Indeed, he had expected Birney's division to rally on Cemetery Ridge, to which he could pull back his guns and continue the fight in support of the infantry [but] Riding up the ridge and looking to his rear, he could see no organized body of troops for many hundreds of yards" along Cemetery Ridge.[458] Consequently, the strategic crest behind the Trostle farm was "fearfully unprotected." The 9th Massachusetts Battery's last stand at the Trostle farm was in essence now "the pivotal point in the action of the second day" at Gettysburg, because neither Union artillery nor blue soldiers stood in line to the rear to defend Cemetery Ridge's strategic crest on Meade's left-center, which lay there for Barksdale's taking.

Captain Bigelow realized the full extent of the crisis. He described the now undeniable reality that set the stage for one of the most dramatic clashes of the war, because by this time "the way was open for Barksdale's Confederate Brigade . . . to enter, unopposed, our lines between Little Round Top and the left of the Second Corps." Indeed, "the infantry of Graham's, and the three regiments of [Burling's] Brigade, in falling back, retreated across the fields north of Trostle's, leaving a wide gap between the left of Brewster's Brigade of Humphrey's Division and the troops down by the Wheatfield—a gap which the 9th Mass. Battery was to hold" at all costs. Whatever Bigelow and his cannoneers might accomplish in slowing down the hard-charging Mississippi Rebels was now absolutely "critical in determining the outcome of the fighting on the second day of the battle."

Not long after enlistment, the 9th Massachusetts battery's officers had hired a Frenchman who was a "master of the broadsword" for personal lessons. Hence, the Massachusetts officers were trained for the kind of close-quarter combat that was about to swirl over the Trostle farm. Some of these mostly Protestant New England gunners had clashed with the Italians, mostly Catholics, especially Captain Achille De Vecchi. But these Massachusetts artillerymen, thanks to Captain Bigelow's efforts, were now united, and ready for their greatest challenge to date. Bigelow was determined to hold firm, because such a "long stretch of our lines was open from the Round Tops to the left of the Second Corps."[459]

Assisting Captain Bigelow in this crucial situation was First Lieutenant Christopher Erickson, age twenty-eight, who commanded one section of guns. Born in Norway, Erickson had migrated to the United States in 1854 at age nineteen, and was married with small children. The former cabinet and furniture maker had gained early experience in a prewar state militia artillery unit. Erickson was now Captain Bigelow's trusty "right arm." He was popular with the New Englanders, having led the battery with skill before Bigelow took command. Most important for the dramatic showdown with Colonel Humphreys, he had drilled the Massachusetts gunners with a zeal only matched by his burning religious faith. Erickson was the model Christian warrior, who carried the Holy Bible into battle. At this moment, the mounted Erickson was considered "the personification of a Centaur."

One proud Massachusetts cannoneer wrote that "we have got the best Battery," thanks in part due to Erickson's tireless efforts. He had been wounded at the battery's first position along the Wheatfield Road by a small piece of shrapnel from a shell fired from one of Alexander's guns. Nevertheless, he gamely remained in action with the battery. Captain Bigelow had ordered Erickson, pierced in the chest, rearward. But this modern-day Viking in blue soon returned and then boldly "sent word to me that he would again take charge of his section." Bigelow was delighted by the news.

The 9th Massachusetts Light Artillery was destined to earn the distinction as "the battery that save[d] the Union army" and "save[d] the day" by slowing the Mississippi Brigade's onslaught. "We were all calm and many realized that perhaps it was the last time we should be all together," wrote Sergeant Baker. In preparation for meeting the fast-approaching storm from Mississippi, Captain Bigelow wisely barked out orders to hurriedly take ammunition from limbers and stack shell and canister piles beside the guns. Indeed, no time could be wasted by the New England artillerymen in loading and firing, when 21st Mississippi attackers were in close range. Then, the young captain screamed above the high-pitched chorus of "Rebel Yells," for his gunners to "double shot with canister and lay the contents of your limber chests by your guns for quick work."[460]

Without either artillery or infantry support on either side or behind, it was up to these New Englanders to somehow "hold that line at all hazards until the Union line could be reformed in his rear." Indeed, neither the Plum Run Line nor the Cemetery Ridge Line, which would be later formed after the Plum Run Line, east of the Trostle House had yet taken shape, while the battered Third Corps units continued to fall back. Cemetery Ridge's crest beyond the Trostle farm remained entirely devoid of Union troops.

Meanwhile, the Massachusetts guns made their last stand inside the confining angle of farmer Trostle's white stone walls and without a quick means to escape the 21st Mississippi's onslaught. Nevertheless, amid the fence corner, the New England boys stood firm, while Humphreys' Rebels descended upon them from the southwest with wild yells. Lieutenant Richard S. Milton's two-gun section on the left roared defiance south at the pesky South Carolina skirmishers and sharpshooters. Meanwhile, the remaining pair of sections under Lieutenants Erickson and Whitaker on the center and right awaited for the moment when Colonel Humphreys' soldiers charged over the top the open, grass-covered rise that formed a crest line about 50–60 yards distant and southwest of the Trostle House, before they unleashed their fire at close range. With the Mississippi attackers now closing in after Humphreys shifted his ranks to strike more directly from the west and with Kershaw's South Carolina sharpshooters blasting away from the belt of woods to the south, a desperate Captain Bigelow shouted out a new directive. He ordered the four guns of Erickson's and Whitaker's sections to be crammed with double-loads of canister. Then Bigelow directed his men to cut "the fuses of your case shot and shell so that they would explode near the muzzle of your guns." Bigelow's timely order ensured that the maximum punishment would be inflicted upon Humphreys' attackers.

Now the highly-disciplined Massachusetts gunners stood firm amid the bright green, luxurious pasture of farmer Trostle, waiting for the Mississippi Rebels to come pouring over the rise. Doing their duty for God and country, the steady New Englanders remained surprisingly calm while standing in position around their assigned bronze field pieces. All the while, the high-pitched chorus of "Rebel Yells" grew louder from the grass-covered rise's other side. It seemed as if Hades itself had unleashed these unearthly hellions, who were rapidly descending upon the band of gunners like demons from the underworld. Standing tall beside their quarter circle of Napoleon 12-pounders, the New Englanders felt it their righteous duty to destroy as many of these Deep South soldiers, who were equally determined to destroy the 9th Massachusetts Battery, as possible.

Bigelow, the articulate, polished Harvard man, recalled how "hardly were the four guns double-shotted before the enemy appeared above a swell of the ground about fifty yards on my right and front." Captain Bigelow finally ordered, "Fire!" when the rising row of Mississippi heads and chests of a brownish-hued mass first became visible beyond the crest. Arranged close together within the angle's confines, the four Massachusetts cannon on the battery's center and right fired as one. Lethal blasts sprayed hundreds of canister balls into Humphreys' ranks, cutting down clumps of Mississippi boys, who were literally blown apart at such close range. One Mississippi attacker was hit by five pieces of canister which exploded from a bronze barrel. Captain Bigelow never forgot the awful destructiveness of that first salvo that unleashed a sheet of flame from his 12-pounders, "waiting till they were breast high, my battery was discharged at them every gun loaded [and] with double shotted canister and solid shot, after which through the smoke [we] caught a glimpse of the enemy, they were torn and broken but still advancing."

Bigelow described how 21st Mississippi attackers "opened a fearful musketry fire, men and horses were falling like hail." On the opposite, or south, side of the road from the Trostle house, the six 12-pounder Napoleons were quickly reloaded by the expert New England gunners. Ensuring a most concentrated fire, this compact arrangement of guns formed a mini-salient, with the stone wall situated behind the Massachusetts guns, which faced south and west to defy lofty Mississippi ambitions. The most formidable side of this innovative New England artillery defensive array faced west and northwest toward the attacking 21st Mississippi soldiers, who descended upon the battery's center and right sections with high-pitched Rebel Yells. Meanwhile, in this symbolic standoff between New England and the Deep South, the remaining Massachusetts guns, faced southwest at an angle to the others.

South of the Trostle Lane, Humphrey's right poured over the swell, while his left continued to charge down the open, sloping ground leading across the fields to the valley of Plum Run and straight toward the concentrated firepower of the blazing 9th Massachusetts guns from the west. A most inspiring sight, the broad expanse of the open slope of Cemetery Ridge could be seen beyond the Trostle House by the attackers. Contrary to Captain Bigelow's belief that he was being attacked by a brigade, the number of men still standing in the 21st Mississippi was probably less than 300 by now. With only a relative handful of Kershaw's South Carolina sharpshooters providing assistance with a light harassing fire from the south, it was once again up to the 21st Mississippi to eliminate yet another Union battery which lay in its path, before the guns could escape to Cemetery Ridge.

Despite facing a row of angry cannon and racing across Trostle's open fields, the swiftly-advancing 21st Mississippi had been most fortunate in having benefited from the grassy swell which had screened the attack until only about 50–60 yards from the 9th Massachusetts guns. As Sergeant Baker explained the tactical disadvantage which had allowed the Mississippians to close in without paying a higher price while surging across open fields: "The situation was not one an artillery officer would have chosen, as the ground on our front and right was much higher, and we could not see more than fifty or sixty yards in those directions; neither was there room enough to work six guns at usual intervals; and the ground was broken by boulders, with heavy stone walls in our rear and left, with a gateway about in the rear of the second piece from the right."

With its immediate retreat farther east toward Cemetery Ridge blocked by the stone wall that spanned for considerable length southward behind Bigelow's guns to the east, and its forward field of fire limited by the swell, the unsupported 9th Massachusetts guns were badly boxed in. Between the Trostle house and barn, only a small gate in the stone wall offered a limited means of withdrawal, a narrow escape hatch entirely unsuitable for a battery's retreat with an onrushing opponent so close. With all six cannons crammed close together in a narrow corner of the angle, and without an adequate avenue of retreat, it was now do or die for Captain Bigelow's boys. The stone wall, the narrow gateway, and rocks and boulders ensured that there could be no easy retreat or escape from the Mississippians' sharpened bayonets, and increased anger at losing so many comrades.

The punishment delivered upon the 21st Mississippi along the swell's crest was most severe, and a good many more of Humphreys' boys went down to rise no more. Sergeant Baker described how "as soon as the enemy appeared over the ridge, they were received with a vigorous fire, some of which was with double canister." Incredibly, when the thick palls of sulfurous smoke finally cleared away, the New Englanders were presented with an unbelievable sight that took their collective breath away: despite the slaughter and clumps of fallen soldiers, piled in dead and wounded in bloody clumps and writhing on the ground in pain all across the swell, the 21st Mississippi's survivors continued to attack. With red flags waving through the drifting smoke, the Mississippi Rebels rolled onward as if nothing in the world could stop them. Captain Bigelow never forgot the unnerving sight: "They were too near the prize to be stopped, and pressed on and received our fire."

But now trying to slow the onrushing Mississippians was like attempting to stop a flood. To escape the worst fires and damage from the double loads of canister and to adapt to yet another tactical challenge literally on the run, Humphreys shifted his regiment toward the left, easing toward the Trostle House and the New England battery's vulnerable right flank. All the while, the sharpshooting Mississippians continued to hurriedly load and shoot, laying down a scorching fire. They systematically shot down the battery's horses by the dozen, and swept the gunners, caissons, limbers, and cannon with a deadly hail of lead. As ordered by Bigelow, desperate Union artillerymen cut fuses so that shells would explode almost before leaving the bronze muzzles of the 12-pounders. The battery's red and white battle-flag, decorated with the Massachusetts coat of arms, that had been presented by the patriotic ladies of West Roxbury in Boston's southwest corner, was riddled with bullets. A precious unit emblem of Bigelow's gunners, this colorful banner provided a tempting, irresistible target to the onrushing Mississippi Rebels.

Seemingly always in the right spot to inflict the most damage this afternoon, the 21st Mississippi soldiers gained the vulnerable right flank, Lieutenant Alexander H. Whitaker's section, of the fire-spitting Massachusetts cannon. Captain Bigelow was horrified to suddenly see that the Mississippians' rapidly advancing line now "extended far beyond our right flank, and the 21st Miss swung without opposition and came in from that direction, pouring in a heavy fire all the while." On the run, the Mississippi soldiers raked the Bay State cannoneers with a deadly fire from the north.

A perfect target while shouting orders before his fast-working cannoneers, Bigelow described how, "I sat on my horse calling the men [as] six sharpshooters on our left [were] taking deliberate aim at" him and his bugler. Captain Bigelow fell when hit in the side with two minie balls. As he described, "I stopped two, and my horse two more of their bullets." Also mounted and a most conspicuous target was the handsome Norwegian, Lieutenant Erickson. He now battled against the onrushing Mississippi tide like an ancient Norse warrior. Strong and vigorous in his late twenties, he had been earlier jolted in the saddle with a chest wound from a shell fragment. But the lieutenant had somehow remained in the saddle, while a froth of blood from his pierced lung dripped from his mouth and onto his officer's uniform of blue. Private Bugler R.L. Willis, from North Bridgewater, Massachusetts, never forgot how "I saw Lieut. Erickson, as he passed near me, reeling in his saddle; he was frothing at the mouth; asked me for some water, drank nearly a canteenful," while the cheering Mississippians drew ever closer.

Despite being mortally wounded, the fearless Norwegian continued to encourage the hard-working gunners of his section in the center of the defiant array of fire-belching Massachusetts guns. But soon a Mississippi marksman took careful aim, after Erickson rode to the endangered gun, no. 5, on the far right, which was now the special target of the 21st Mississippi's onrushing left. He slowly pulled the trigger, and a bullet struck the Norwegian, whose Holy Bible in his pocket could no longer protect him, square in the head. Bugler Willis described the death of Lieutenant Erickson, the spiritual leader of the 9th Massachusetts Battery, who finally met his Maker far from his native Norway, when he "saw the right gun some distance to the rear and in danger of capture, rode up to it and was shot through the head; fell dead, his horse going into the enemy's line." Private John K. Norwood wrote how Private Ralph C. "Blaisdell and I were trying to limber up the gun when Lieutenant Erickson rode up and asked if he could help us. Just then a bullet crashed through his head . . . "

Appalled by the horror, Captain Bigelow recalled how his top lieutenant was simply "riddled with bullets; fell dead, his horse passing into the midst" of Humphreys' attackers. Other fine leaders of the hard-hit Massachusetts battery were hit amid the tempest. Shot in the knee while remaining in the saddle, Boston-born Lieutenant Alexander H. Whitaker, "a good French scholar" who had been involved in the commercial Mediterranean trade, was another victim. He was a highly respected officer, only age twenty-two. He now filled the leadership gap left by Lieutenant Erickson's death. Whitaker was so young at the war's beginning that his initial efforts to enlist were rebuffed. Mississippi bullets continued to zip around Whitaker, while he gamely inspired the Massachusetts gunners to stand firm, before falling with a mortal wound.

One Massachusetts sergeant was killed and another five were wounded, John Fenton mortally, among the ever-dwindling band of New Englanders. Captain Bigelow described how "Sergeant after Sergt. was struck down, horses were plunging and laying about all around" in the confusing chaos of the hellish angle of the low stone wall, which was becoming a slaughter pen. Now freed from its unfortunate owner who was no more, Lieutenant Erickson's terrified horse bolted forward, galloping wildly into the Mississippians' surging ranks. No doubt one of Barksdale's men became the proud owner of the Norwegian's fine horse. Besides officers, quite a few enlisted men of the Massachusetts Battery were fatally cut down, such as Privates James Gillson and Charles Nutting. And Private Austin Packard dropped mortally wounded in the hand-to-hand combat. One lucky survivor of Mississippi lead, musket-butts, and bayonets this afternoon was Sergeant Augustus Hesse, of Weymouth. He described in a letter how by the time "the blood run all over me [and] I was Sweting [sic] . . . and Smoke blacked my face . . ."[461]

But as important as the systematic elimination of the top 9th Massachusetts Battery officers was the shooting down of artillery horses, so that the guns could not withdraw. Many Mississippi veterans continued to target frightened artillery horses huddled around the caissons and limbers, sending a hail of bullets into the harnessed animals. The vulnerable array of guns, cannoneers, and horses exposed on open ground and in a low spot in the fence corner made ideal compact targets. Each recoil of the 9th Massachusetts field pieces had gradually pushed the 12-pounders deeper into the cramped angle of the stone wall: presenting an even more compact mass of desperate men and defenseless horses to expert marksmen.

Trapped not only in a fence corner but also in a twisted tangle of leather harnesses and traces, the panicked horses pitched and reared, whinnying in terror. But the animals could not escape the stream of minie balls. The bodies of dozens of bullet-riddled horses piled up on the south side of the Trostle House, dropping dead in harness in jumbled clumps. Here, on the grass-covered ground in Trostle's yard just northeast and to the rear of the blazing Massachusetts artillery pieces situated on Trostle Lane's other side, the mass of dead horses piled together looked eerily almost as if were only resting or asleep. Meanwhile, the perfect flow of Mississippi bullets made the air sing, splintering limbers, wheels and caissons, sending sharp wooden splinters flying. Nevertheless, blue-coated cannoneers continued to load the guns with double-charges of canister as rapidly as possible.

One New England private, Eleazer Cole, a thirty-two year-old machinist from the cobblestone streets of North Bridgewater, recalled that when the 21st Mississippi's left began to close in on the battery's vulnerable right "at every discharge they were mowed down in swathes." But yet Colonel Humphreys and his screaming men continued onward through the deadly blasts of double canister. In the words of one Mississippi Rebel: "We suffered awfully; but were bound to silence [those] damn brass guns." The tide finally turned when larger numbers of Mississippians surged beyond the battery's right flank, racing across Trostle Lane to reach the higher ground around the house and barn. From the more elevated terrain that offered a commanding perch that gradually rose higher to the knoll just before the barn, the 21st Mississippians raked the right flank and rear of the hapless Massachusetts battery now caught in a deadly enfilade fire.[462]

The 9th Massachusetts gunners could not escape the hard-charging Mississippians, who were determined not to be denied this afternoon. A journalist of the *Cincinnati Gazette*, Whitelaw Reid, witnessed the 21st Mississippi's fierce attack, describing how "with depressed guns [firing] double charges of grape and canister, he smites and shatters, but cannot break the advancing line. His grape and canister are exhausted, and still, closing grandly up over their slain, on they come. He falls back on spherical case, and pours this in at the shortest range. On, still onward, comes the artillery-defying line, and still [Bigelow] holds his position.[463]

Rapidly loading and firing their rifles on the run, the Mississippi Confederates shot down additional New England gunners with a lethal swiftness. Faithfully standing beside the battery's third gun, Private Arthur Murphy of Charlestown was about to pull the lanyard when killed. Then, Private Henry Fen, of North Bridgewater, stepped forward to fire the canister-loaded cannon, but he was also soon hit by a fatal bullet. Next Private John Crosson, of Boston, attempted to jerk the lanyard, when a Mississippi bullet killed him on the spot. With three good men cut down in seconds, Smith survived the torrent of .577 caliber bullets long enough to fire the cannon one last time as the swarming attackers closed in.

Captain Bigelow knew that the demise—a necessary sacrifice to save an army—of his once fine battery was as imminent as it was now inevitable, but he had to hold on because "not an infantryman" in blue stood behind him on Cemetery Ridge. While the blasts of double-shot canister had mowed down the Rebels in front, Humphreys' onrushing "lines extended far beyond our right flank," wrote Bigelow of the cresting Mississippi tide. He watched in horror when "the 21st Miss. swung without opposition and came in from that direction, pouring in a heavy fire all the while" to more thoroughly decimate his battery. Therefore, "owing to large stone boulders interfering with my left section, I ordered Lieut. [Richard S.] Milton to take it out and to the rear." But most artillery horses, yet strapped to harnesses, were shot down by this time. Therefore, "one piece was drawn off by hand, but the right and centre sections remained until overwhelmed by the enemy, who came in on their unprotected flanks." However, "ninety-two rounds of canister were expended, mostly at close quarters," making the 21st Mississippi pay a high price. While Lieutenant Milton's two-gun section, partly drawn by wounded horses, headed rearward as best they could, the guns of Lieutenants Erickson's and Whitaker's sections continued to fire as if there was no tomorrow. Indeed, there was no tomorrow for the Army of the Potomac or the Union, if the Mississippi Rebels gained Cemetery Ridge to split Meade's Army in two.

Before the charging Mississippians reached their prize, one of Milton's guns overturned at the Trostle gateway, blocking the only avenue of escape. While bullets whizzed around them, New England gunners worked frantically to remove the artillery piece before it was too late.

The 9th Massachusetts Battery's loss of personnel and the overall reduction of firepower, after two of the six-gun battery pulled away east toward Cemetery Ridge, gave the 21st Mississippi an added impetus to overwhelm the remaining four guns. Soon, in another wild sprint that had become a deadly race to reach the remaining Union artillery pieces before they could unleash one final lethal load, the first long-haired Mississippi Rebels, covered in sweat and smeared with powder, descended upon the four Massachusetts guns with victory cheers. Then, all hell suddenly exploded in their faces. Fiery eruptions of the last remaining double-loads of canister crammed into cannon barrels practically blew the foremost attackers out of southeast Adams County. Sergeant Baker described how members of Humphreys' regiment "received our fire not six feet from the muzzles of our guns." One Federal described how Bigelow's cannoneers "blew them from the muzzles and filled the air with the shattered fragments of human bodies [but] still they came on with demoniacal screams . . ."

Nevertheless, not even this terrible punishment at point-blank range failed to stop the hard-charging 21st Mississippi Rebels. Even while firing his cannon one last time, Private Brett was amazed by his comrades' stubborn tenacity. He wrote in a letter how "not a man ran [and] 4 or 5 fell within 15 feet of me [and thirty-three-year-old Private Henry Finn] was one of the number. He was shot throug[h] the head just below the ear [and] the blood flew all about" us. But without infantry support of any kind and with the New England battery's flanks hanging in the air, Humphreys' soldiers rushed around both flanks of the 9th Massachusetts Battery to gain its rear.

Unleashing their high-pitched war cries, the Mississippians swarmed among the bronze guns, thrusting with bayonets, clubbing with Enfield rifles, swinging sabers, and firing muskets point-blank at the feisty New Englanders. As he described in a letter, Private Brett never forgot how the Mississippi soldiers "fought like tigers." During the savage combat, defiant Massachusetts cannoneers fought back with sponge-staffs, handspikes, and shovels, swinging rammers and fists amid the choking cloud of dust and smoke.

An Italian in blue who ironically had migrated to America with high hopes in part to escape the horrors of nonsensical European wars, Private John Ligal smashed one Mississippian's head with his rammer. And one bluecoat artillerymen cut down another one of Humphreys' soldiers with a vicious swing of a handspike that caught the unfortunate man full-square. Another Massachusetts cannoneer who fell before the Mississippians' wrath was a former battery cook. He possessed the well-deserved nickname of "Burnt Chowder" for his utter lack of culinary expertise, and perhaps some comrades felt relief at the final end of his disastrous cooking career.

Sergeant Baker was proud of the fact that his boys fought so tenaciously. He described how "our cannoneers were driven at the point of the bayonet, and were shot down from the limbers," which now served as elevated firing positions for Mississippi Rebels. Despite the Mississippians rushing through the guns with ear-piercing war cries, bayoneting, and clubbing down New England artillerymen left and right, some Yankee gunners gamely worked their field pieces until the last moment. Sergeant Baker described the terrifying sight when the Mississippians "came in on our flank . . . standing on the limbers shooting horses, and men still serving their guns." The popular Private Aldoph Lipman, a Russian immigrant from West Roxbury whose family yet lived in the port city of Riga, was shot in the head and killed. In total, six of seven 9th Massachusetts Battery sergeants were cut down, along with three of four officers. Kind-hearted Sergeant Charles E. Dodge, who had been a lumberman in Virginia and lived peacefully among Southerners at the war's beginning, died in his gun's spirited defense.

After killing off the last obstinate Massachusetts gunners with bayonets and musket-butts, the Mississippi victors celebrated their sparkling success in overrunning yet another defensive position and capturing additional artillery pieces. Bigelow saw triumphant Mississippians clamoring atop his caissons, limbers, and guns, "yelling like demons" in the ecstasy of victory.

One Yankee of the 118th Pennsylvania Volunteer Infantry, Tilton's brigade, witnessed the sight of the 21st Mississippi's flowing silk battle-flag and the daring color-bearer, when he "advanced through the gate of the Trostle House" in triumph. Here, the powder-streaked Rebel "stood gallantly and courageously waving his colors in the midst of the thickest of the melee" around the four captured Massachusetts guns. Meanwhile, Mississippians continued to stand atop captured limbers and caissons, picking out targets and then snapping off shots at fleeing New Englanders from their elevated perches.

Only two of Bigelow's Massachusetts cannon escaped the pent-up fury of the 21st Mississippi's onslaught. A shocked Bigelow could hardly believe his eyes when he saw some of the powder-streaked Mississippi Rebels, after "swarming in on our right flank, standing on the limber chests and firing at the gunners, who were still serving their pieces; the horses were all down." In a tribute to his personal bravery in orchestrating one of the most magnificent last stands during the three days at Gettysburg, Captain Bigelow himself had narrowly escaped almost certain death. Chivalric 21st Mississippi officers somehow restrained their veterans, amid the choking haze of drifting smoke, from unleashing a close-range bullet to end the life of the already wounded battery commander, who had just seen his finest day.

Meanwhile, the last flurry of hand-to-hand fighting continued between the New Englanders and Mississippians just south of the Trostle House. One young artilleryman in blue was clubbed down with a musket while attempting to spike his gun at the last second. Other New England gunners were shot down at point-blank range, after refusing to surrender in a nightmarish struggle amid the body-strewn fence corner. Bigelow's cannoneers gave as good as they received, however. One Massachusetts artilleryman not only knocked down a Rebel, but also attempted to drag off his stunned prisoner. This bold Yankee could only be thwarted from capturing the dazed, bloodied 21st Mississippi soldier when one of Humphreys' infantrymen, who had no time to reload, picked up a cannoneer's hand spike and cut him down with one vicious swipe.

Private Brett made the mistake of attempting to reclaim his hat that had fallen off when hurrying one of the Massachusetts cannon rearward. No doubt saving his life, a comrade dashed forward to retrieve the hat of "Uncle David" Brett, before the flashing bayonets of the Mississippians, who must have marveled at the sight of yet another display of Massachusetts audacity under fire. Therefore, nearby Deep South warriors held their fire, while watching in disbelief as one New England cannoneer saved his comrade, regardless of his own safety. Both Yankees then escaped, slipping away in the smoky haze. Around the four New England cannon, 28 Massachusetts artillerymen were cut down. The slaughter caused Private Brett to lament in a letter that "we . . . lost so many officers and men it does not sem [sic] like the same Battery. The dead were so thick . . . you had to pick your way so as not to step on them . . ." Forty-five dead battery horses were also heaped in piles just below, or south, of the Trostle barn and house.

Private Brett wrote in a letter how the Mississippians "took 4 Guns after they shot the horses." But, proudly continued the private, "we fought with our guns untill [sic] the rebs could put their hands on the guns." Nevertheless, the 9th Massachusetts Light Artillery had been virtually destroyed by the 21st Mississippi in a vicious "dock brawl" with men battling hand-to-hand. Bigelow's battery suffered one of the highest losses of any Union battery in the war. Later, Bigelow wrote to Humphreys of the "gallantry and bravery of the men who so fearlessly faced my guns, double-loaded with canister, though of course it was my exposed flanks and lack of infantry support that caused the destruction of my command." Bigelow also described how his fine battery, "surrounded, men and horses were shot down and finally overcome, but not until the purpose of sacrifice had been accomplished." Nevertheless, the 21st Mississippi captured four of the six 9th Massachusetts Light Artillery guns in another remarkable tactical success during one of the most devastating charges of the war. Lucky to have survived the slaughter, Private Brett wrote how "the bullets flew thick as hailstones [and] it was a wonder we were not all killed."[464]

Charles Wellington Reed, a twenty-two-year-old bugler, won a Congressional Medal of Honor for his heroics. He rescued Captain Bigelow, who was hit by two bullets, after he fell from his horse in the battery's rear. A music lover and an independent illustrator of middle-class status, Reed saved his captain at the last minute, despite having recently despised Bigelow as "a regular aristocrat worse than any regular that ever breathed." Reed and Irishman Private John H. Kelly, the captain's orderly, came to Bigelow's rescue with Humphrey's onrushing men only few yards behind him. Bugler Reed had disobeyed orders by remaining in the fight. Ironically, Reed's proven penchant for defiance of authority proved an unexpected blessing for Captain Bigelow instead of the usual source of irritation.

Now de-horsed, a bleeding Captain Bigelow was quickly helped onto his orderly's mount, while Mississippi bullets zipped by. Both Bigelow and Bugler Reed narrowly eased out of harm's way, despite the foremost Mississippi Rebels attempting to pull them off their horses. Only the last-minute intervention by a sympathetic 21st Mississippi officer prevented his men from shooting down the pair at close range. Bugler Reed described one of the most amazing episodes of the battle of Gettysburg: "We tried to get away [but] some of the Confederates saw us [and] several of them tried to take us prisoners. They did not fire at once, but tried to pull us from the horses' backs, but were unsuccessful, as the horses kicked and I was able to do some execution with my saber we were still struggling when an officer told them not to murder us in cold blood."

With multiple wounds and half-stunned by the surreal carnage, Bigelow later described his personal ordeal and close call around the Trostle house after "my horse, when I fell from him, was wounded at the same time, leaped the wall and went back into our lines. Recovering [I saw the] men on my limber chests, shooting my cannoneers, still hard at work, when I gave the order to cease firing and fall back. I was taken over the wall. One of my officers, Whitaker, though mortally wounded, rode up and gave me some whisky. I was then lifted on to my orderly's horse, and slowly taken back."

Despite two wounds, Bigelow had orchestrated the withdrawal of his two remaining guns and the survivors east to escape the Mississippi attackers. The two surviving teams, limbers and guns of Lieutenant Milton's section had gone over the stone wall to the rear and that ran southward from near the Trostle House, after the top stones were pushed off the wall, about half-way between his first defensive position and the Trostle House, by the desperate gunners. Only when Captain Bigelow gave the final word to withdraw east toward Cemetery Ridge had the Massachusetts artillerymen finally given up the fight, after holding their ground as long as possible.

After having forsaken rear area duties to man the guns during the day's supreme crisis, Sergeant Nelson Lowell, of the Puritan-founded town of Malden on the Mystic River, described the withdrawal's final confused minutes with shouting Mississippians swarming around them: "Near the gateway the other horse was shot, and limber overturned; ammunition gone. I immediately joined the next serviceable gun, which was Gunner Wm. Tucker's, who was almost alone . . . Next, the left section was limbered up and were trying to get out to escape [and then] the right gun of the hard-pressed section was partly overturned, and I, with some others, righted it, and prevented the drivers from cutting traces and leaving; the other gun was over the wall and making good time to the rear. I had mounted old Tom to escape, when a Reb presented his musket in my face; 'Surrender, you damned Yankee.' Pictures of Libby and Andersonville flashed through my mind, as I reached round for my revolver, resolving to fight for it. Before my revolver was drawn, my horse fell, shot dead, and I was under him. I lay still, hoping to save myself."

Young Lieutenant Whitaker was able to escape, dripping blood. He died of his wound on July 23 in Baltimore before reaching his family in Boston. Later, an embittered Captain Bigelow lamented how the capable lieutenant had "died from bad treatment at the hands of army surgeons." Meanwhile, the last remaining New England gunners escaped the 21st Mississippi, after close brushes with death. Private Norwood, who took a serious wound, had "his horse shot away by a cannon ball; he freed himself, 'cut the dead animal loose,' and then coolly mounted another, which in turn was soon shot, as were all the others attached to his piece." For masterfully conducting the most important defensive stand made by Union artillery on July 2, the 9th Massachusetts Battery was cut to pieces.

One Federal lieutenant compared the piles of bodies and horses to "a scene of slaughter that surpassed anything recorded of Lodi bridge or Marango [sic] ridge." Nevertheless, in its first battle, the 9th Massachusetts had played a key role in saving the day. Ironically, had Captain Bigelow's artillerymen been "old soldiers, [then perhaps they] never could have held together for so long a time, so far in advance of our lines, in an open field, without supports, and suffering such fearful losses."[465]

After overrunning the battery, the 21st Mississippi's color bearer stood atop one captured gun and waved the bullet-tattered banner in triumph as Humphreys' men cheered yet another remarkable success. An additional group of artillery pieces were captured by a single regiment that continued to out-perform expectations. An elated Colonel Humphreys never forgot the sight when Lieutenant George Kempton stood "astride of a gun waving his sword and exclaiming, 'Colonel, I claim this gun for Company I[,]' [while] Lt. W.P. McNeily was astride of another, claiming it for Company E."[466]

— 9 —

"It seemed as if nothing could live an instant"

EVEN WHILE HIS ecstatic boys were celebrating around the captured Massachusetts artillery pieces, Colonel Humphreys busily surveyed the field through the drifting smoke, hunting for additional targets of opportunity in the sudden sultry calm. And he soon found one before attempting to shift his troops north and up the west side of Plum Run to link with Barksdale and his three regiments, which continued to fight their own war. In the words of the ever-opportunistic colonel from the Mississippi Delta: "Just then another battery was seen in position three hundred yards off, beyond the ravine. The order was given to charge it."[467]

With bullet-tattered battle-flags flying in the fading light of this hellish afternoon with no cooling breeze, the 21st Mississippi once again surged forward, embarking upon another formidable challenge in their desperate effort to gain the great prize of Cemetery Ridge's crest. Relying without hesitation on the aggressive instincts of a natural fighter with a keen eye for exploiting tactical weaknesses before the arrival of reinforcements in blue, Humphreys led his troops across Plum Run and then up the grassy western slope of Cemetery Ridge to exploit the tactical advantage won by additional hard fighting. Most of all, Humphreys and his 21st Mississippi were going for broke on the bloodiest afternoon of the war, while the golden vision of securing the strategic crest of Cemetery Ridge stood before them like a marvelous gift bestowed by a Confederate God.[468]

Confident after reaping so much significant success, including smashing through one Union regiment after another and capturing clumps of artillery pieces, Barksdale, leading the brigade's northern wing, and Colonel Humphreys, leading the brigade's southern wing, encouraged

211

their elated soldiers ever-eastward in a desperate bid to drive an even deeper wedge into Meade's left-center and split the Army of the Potomac in half. All the while, battered Third Corps units continued to head rearward, after having taken a brutal mauling. It now seemed as if nothing in the world could stop the rampaging Mississippians, who continued east on the double with cheers that split the air. All the while, they pushed deeper into the gap before Cemetery Ridge, hoping to win the race through the wide open breach. With no blue formations defending Cemetery Ridge at this point, one Yankee wrote how "our fate was hanging in the balance," and the Army of the Potomac hovered closer to extinction than ever before.

However, much precious time had ticked away, and victory had been most costly for the Mississippi Brigade that had left a bloody path behind them in two separate sectors. Ironically, its success in smashing so many Yankee units and gobbling up one battery after another was about to play a role in Barksdale's and Humphreys' undoing. East of Plum Run at what would become the so-called Plum Run Line some 1,200 feet northeast of the Trostle house, Generals Meade and Hunt and Lieutenant Colonel McGilvery were hurriedly attempting to patch together a desperate defense at the last minute. This final Union line of unsupported artillery pieces situated just before Cemetery Ridge's crest was being pieced together from McGilvery's battered Reserve Artillery units which had been hurled back by Barksdale from the Emmitsburg Road sector, as well as any other guns he could find.

On the spot, McGilvery frantically rushed any available "long arm" unit into his last-ditch line, while hoping that beaten Third Corps formations might rally or that reinforcements from some other sector of the line would arrive. As Captain Bigelow described the critical situation just east of the Trostle House in a postwar letter to Colonel Humphreys: "My command suffered but you were delayed long enough to get the 6th Maine and part of the 5th Massachusetts Batteries in position [and] for half an hour or more they filled the long gap on the rising ground, front of the wood, opening on you when I stopped firing." However, because these Union guns were yet without infantry protection or support, the Mississippi Brigade yet possessed the golden opportunity to win the battle, the day, and the war.

By any measure, this was Humphreys' finest day in which "Old Ben, 'the old stem-winder,' went in the fight with elegant impudence and out of it . . . with sublime magnanimity [and he] rode at the head of the old

21st with the same nonchalance that he offered 'to go the gal's security'," wrote one Mississippian of the unforgettable moment when decisive victory appeared well within the Magnolia State soldier's grasp.

However, the precious time won by self-sacrificing units such as the 9th Massachusetts Light Battery was crucial in buying time for the final creation of the Plum Run Line on the western slope of Cemetery Ridge. Four veteran Union batteries of McGilvery's First Volunteer Brigade, Reserve Artillery, consisting of six Ordnance Rifles of Captain Charles A. Phillips' 5th Massachusetts, and the six Ordnance Rifles of Captain James Thompson's 1st Pennsylvania Light Artillery [Batteries C and F combined], Lieutenant Edwin B. Dow's 6th Maine Light Artillery, and Battery I, 5th United States Artillery batteries, which had been withdrawn by hand from the Peach Orchard sector before the surging 21st Mississippi troops, were shortly aligned along the Plum Run Line. Sparkling in the sunlight along open ground just below the tree-line, these guns stood, from south to north, along the rise situated on open ground just before Cemetery Ridge's crest. Unfortunately for the Mississippi Brigade, the Army of the Potomac now immensely benefitted from the availability of a powerful artillery reserve, unlike Lee's Army, which had made the fatal error of abolishing its artillery reserve corps just before invading the North.

Battery I, 5th United States Artillery anchored the ad hoc line's left, closest to Trostle Lane to the south on lower ground. Soon the energetic McGilvery had perhaps as many as fifteen guns of four batteries aligned along the ridge's western slope. These batteries stood along commanding high ground overlooking the pastoral settings of the brushy bottoms of Plum Run and the Trostle House from left to right or south to north. Without infantry support, this elevated position was now the only Federal defensive line remaining before the onrushing Mississippi Brigade. Fortunately, Porter Alexander's fast-working Rebel guns now came to the Mississippians' assistance, taking on the Union cannon they could now see on the high ground position.

Like Captain Bigelow's heroic band at the Trostle farm, the lengthy row of Union cannon was vulnerable, standing alone without infantry support, which had yet to arrive. By this time Captain Bigelow, wounded in the hand and side, was still retiring up the open slope before McGilvery's new line of artillery. Bluecoat gunners yelled for the slow-moving Bigelow, with both himself and horse wounded, to hurry in order to get past the 6th Maine cannon, because the howling Mississippi Rebels were close behind. Bigelow yelled, "I could not, and told them to fire away, which they did." Luckily, Bugler Reed again came to the rescue. He guided Bigelow out of harm's way and safely between two cannon. Bigelow had accomplished his vital mission: "to sacrifice his battery to give the others time to form a new line" to defend the most vulnerable point of Cemetery Ridge

Indeed, with the Mississippians having crossed Plum Run to surge up the slope, McGilvery screamed "Fire!" and the row of artillery roared as one, firing straight ahead at targets framed against the background of the dark-hued thickets along the creek. Near the left flank, Lieutenant Dow, commanding the four 6th Maine guns that were turned northwest to fire on Barksdale's three regiments, described how "a battle line of the enemy coming through the woods distant . . . with a design to drive through and take position of the road to Taneytown, directly in my rear. I immediately opened upon them with spherical case and canister . . . " Barksdale's men could see the line of guns aligned across the open slope that dominated the immediate horizon. One bluecoat remembered how the point-blank fire of "our batteries plowed lanes through the living masses in front of them," blowing holes in the gray and butternut swarm and inflicting terrible damage. With the weight of cartridge-boxes, bouncing off their hips, now lighter from expending so many rounds, Barksdale's troops just kept coming with the Rebel Yell, heading up the open slope toward Cemetery Ridge, determined to smash through any new line of blue formed before them.[469] And now McGilvery's isolated, unsupported guns along the slope were "the only line of defense for this portion of Cemetery Ridge."[470]

Meanwhile, several hundred yards to the south, the 21st Mississippi was yet intent on turning the exposed left flank of this last line of cannon, securing the high ground, gaining the Taneytown Road, and planting their tattered red battle-flags on Cemetery Ridge. Therefore, wrote Humphreys, "on the brave regiment moved, yelling and firing." Such a success, still well within reach, meant splitting the mighty Army of the Potomac in two, and perhaps ending its existence. Waving his saber and shouting encouragement, Humphreys continued to inspire his surviving Mississippi men onward.

Union commanders also saw the crisis, however. General Winfield Scott Hancock had already sent his leftmost Second Corps division, Caldwell's, into the Wheatfield, where it had been utterly wrecked. Now he was flinging units forward to meet the oncoming brigades of Richard Anderson's Division, A.P. Hill's Third Corps, who were advancing off to the left of the Mississippians. The 19th Maine was dispatched to confront David Lang's small Florida Brigade. Alexander Webb's Brigade confronted the charging Rebel brigade of Rans Wright. The 19th Massachusetts and 42nd New York, also of Gibbon's Division, were sent forward to intercept Wilcox's Alabamians, but could only do so for a few minutes. They fell back while Wilcox kept coming on. In desperation, Hancock seized upon the 1st Minnesota and flung it at the Alabama Brigade. The Minnesotans were practically wiped out, losing 80 percent of their number, but their courageous effort managed to halt Wilcox.

But to Hancock's left was still the yawning gap on Cemetery Ridge toward which Barksdale was advancing. He may have expected the retiring Third Corps to take position on the ridge, but for the moment they were too shattered to rally. Hancock now commanded what was left of the Third Corps after Sickles' fall, and was horrified by the realization that "there was nothing left of [Humphreys' Second] division." He looked around and found one more unused brigade of his own corps, the Third Brigade of Alexander Hays' Division, under Colonel George Lamb Willard. He immediately ordered it to the left to face Barksdale's oncoming Mississippians.

Willard's brigade had been the last Second Corps unit to reach the field, but the command was in overall good shape after a cozy stint in the capital's defenses. Known derisively within the corps as the "Harpers Ferry Brigade," for having surrendered there practically without a fight the previous September, it had something to prove to its Second Corps comrades. And now as the day's light was fading away, Willard's brigade was called upon to face its supreme challenge. It now advanced toward Barksdale's three regiments, moving all the way from Cemetery Ridge's northern end to meet their old antagonists from the Antietam Campaign. As if knowing of the slaughter to come, a New York chaplain had already said words of faith before the New Yorkers moved out to confront the Mississippians.

But even worse for the irrepressible Barksdale, fresh units of the Twelfth Corps were also arriving in the sector to help plug the gap at the last moment. They had been pulled from Culp's Hill on the Federal far right, where Ewell's Corps had remained silent, and dispatched to Meade's left to help deal with the crisis. The Mississippians had already mauled some of the Army of the Potomac's best regiments, but more were now arriving.[471] That the situation of Meade's collapsed left-center "had become exceedingly critical" was evident when Willard's men found so many broken Third Corps troops, including General Birney, streaming rearward.[472] Indeed, a badly-shaken Birney, whose troops had been mauled by the Confederates' onslaught, had declared to Hancock how "the 3d Corps had gone to pieces and fallen to the rear."[473] However, Barksdale's three regiments had taken quite a beating themselves in having achieved so much for so long. Private John Saunders Henley, 17th Mississippi, described how, "we had driven the Yankees about a mile from their first line; our ranks had grown so thin."[474]

Hancock described the crucial situation and what he accomplished in the face of the day's greatest challenge: "I established Willard's brigade at the point through which General Birney's division had retired, and fronting the approach of the enemy, who were pressing vigorously on. There were no other troops on its right or left." Willard's vital mission was now to plug the wide breach in Meade's left-center that now lay before the onslaught of Barksdale's three regiments. The brigade deployed with the 125th and 126th New York, left to right, in its front line, supported respectively by the 39th and 111th New York. Here Lieutenant Colonel Levin Crandell, leading the 125th New York, described in his diary the punishment inflicted by Colonel Alexander's guns, which provided timely assistance to the Mississippians: "We deployed under a heavy fire of shot & shell." A soldier in the regiment described how there were "shells screaming and cannon balls tearing in the air . . . now bursting above and around us."[475]

Having heretofore escaped the initial carnage of Gettysburg, Willard's brigade had already won a key advantage without so much as firing a shot, holding elevated terrain before Cemetery Ridge's crest, while Barksdale's three regiments surged up the slope east of Plum Run.

Colonel Willard was a promising officer well qualified to smash the most vivid dreams of Barksdale and his Mississippi Rebels. He was a dark-haired, no-nonsense martinet from New York City who had made a career in the regular army despite his family's objections. A veteran of the Mexican War, he had been part of General Winfield Scott's successful attack on Chapultepec Castle in September 1847. At age thirty-five and a West Pointer, Willard was one of the finest junior officers in the Second Corps, a rising star of promise. Fortunately, for the Army of the Potomac at this time, Willard represented a classic case of a commander and his troops united by a shared bond, lusting for validation, redemption, and vindication.

With the New York City colonel leading the way, the 125th and 126th New York, over 800 men, pushed down the slope with fixed bayonets, rolling like a blue tidal wave off the high ground of Cemetery Ridge. For the first time all day, Barksdale's men were forced back. The New Yorkers advanced toward the brushy, elderberry thickets and rocks clogging the low ground of Plum Run. Known simply as "the swale," the bottoms now contained hundreds of Mississippi Rebels still full of fight. After taking punishment from Colonel McGilvery's artillery fire, including canister, pouring off the high ground, the Mississippians had prudently retired back to the cover along Plum Run to regroup, reload muskets, and take good defensive positions in preparation for meeting Willard's attackers rolling down Cemetery Ridge's western slope.

Yet to be issued their distinctive diamond emblems of the Second Corps to sew on their hats, the New Yorkers had much to prove, and the Mississippi Rebels were about receive the brunt of their pent-up emotions. In fact, Willard's soldiers had been ordered by Hancock to "knock the Hell out of the Rebs" from Mississippi, their old foes from Harpers Ferry. For the first time all day, and recently fortified by the words of Chaplain Ezra Simons, only Willard's troops took the initiative to strike back, because, wrote one Yankee, "there were no other troops on [our] right or left" at this time.[476]

General Alexander Hays, their division commander, wrote with pride how the "Harpers Ferry boys have turned out trumps, and when we do get a chance look out for blood."[477] Unfortunately, for the breathless Mississippians, now exhausted, low on ammunition, and with many leading regimental and company officers cut down, they could not have encountered more highly-motivated soldiers than these New Yorkers, who were determined to set the record straight once and for all.[478] In the words of one of these revenge-seeking Union soldiers, the so-called Harpers Ferry brigade "panted to remove that stigma," which called now for Mississippi blood and the thwarting of Barksdale's soaring ambitions to win it all.[479] And the youthful-looking Willard, who had suffered a severe setback to his ambitions because of the Harpers Ferry episode, was about to rise to the occasion when so much was at stake. All in all, Willard and his much-maligned New York boys were a "good match" for meeting Barksdale's three now seriously-depleted regiments.[480] Meanwhile, Hancock sent the 400 men of the 111th New York forward to extend Willard's right, while keeping the 39th New York in reserve on the brigade's left, facing southwest.[481]

Mounted before his lengthy formations of bluecoats eager to meet their old tormentors from September 15, 1862, Colonel Willard waved his saber and shouted, "Charge!" The New Yorkers poured down the open slopes like an avalanche, charging on the double with fixed bayonets in the fading sunlight. The sheer momentum of their downhill attack increased as they neared the Mississippians, now positioned in good cover amid the low, brush-clogged valley of Plum Run. Because of the heavy growth along the creek, Willard had no idea that three entire Mississippi regiments—albeit bloodied and the worse for wear—were in position amid the underbrush, rocks, and timber waiting his arrival. When the New Yorkers were near, Barksdale screamed for his line to unleash their first volley, which swept through the New York ranks. Willard now realized he had stirred up a hornet's nest. One Union officer described how "the rebels fired on the brigade as it advanced, which fire was returned by a portion of the brigade as it advanced without halting. Many fell in the charge."

Soon to take a New York bullet in the arm, Private Joseph Charles Lloyd of the 13th Mississippi never forgot the sight: "They had come out from the top of the hill and were fresh" unlike the exhausted, powder-smeared Mississippi soldiers, who had been fighting for over an hour. Nevertheless, Barksdale's veterans unleashed sheets of rolling volleys upon this new threat in a desperate effort to protect the brigade's flanks, which both hung in mid-air to the north and south. The explosion of fire burst out of the brushy bottoms, raking Willard's bluecoats with a murderous musketry that left a good many widows and orphans across New York. Indeed, the Mississippians' Enfield rifles continued to prove to be deadly widow-makers this afternoon. Bunches of Willard's Yankees went down, screaming and crying out in pain, as a torrent of Mississippi bullets tore savagely through the brigade.

On the right flank, Private Abernathy, 17th Mississippi, long remembered the inspiring sight of Lieutenant Colonel "Fiser on his little Blaze face bay horse [when he] rode along the lines calling the troops to halt and form." All the while, the Mississippians busily loaded and fired from behind good cover—compared to the open fields that they had been charging across—among the trees, rocks, and brush along Plum Run. Along with the clouds of thick battle-smoke, the clumps of bushes and dense new growth of willows on Plum Run's bottoms hid the Mississippi Rebels, who found easy targets when Willard's brigade halted to realign its ranks. An officer in the 111th New York described a solid "line of riflemen giving us minie balls with such rapidity that it seemed as if nothing could live an instant exposed to their fire."

Low on ammunition, the Mississippians gathered rounds from the cartridge-boxes of the dead and wounded. Known as "Old Barks" to the boys who would follow him to hell and back if necessary, Barksdale rode back and forth and waved his saber, urging his troops to fire faster at the New York troops. Holding the low, brushy ground along Plum Run yet promised potential future gains, if Barksdale's offensive effort could be resumed. Realizing that no infantry support was forthcoming, the Mississippi Brigade's soldiers were fully prepared to self-sacrifice themselves for the chance to yet win the day.

All the while, the opposing lines continued to frantically exchange fire while the New Yorkers applied heavy pressure to Barksdale's exposed left flank on the north. In this sector, Colonel Clinton MacDougall's 111th New York, on the brigade's right, struck the 18th Mississippi, which anchored Barksdale's left. Demonstrating their worth, the Empire State troops, surged down the slope with fixed bayonets while screaming, "Remember Harpers Ferry."[482]

Nevertheless, while the 18th Mississippi was hard-hit, the 13th Mississippi and the 17th Mississippi remained firm in firing positions amid the body-strewn, underbrush-choked, and smoke-drenched swale. Here, they stood up against Willard's surging blue tide. Loading and firing as rapidly as possible, Barksdale's veterans shot down New York officers and color bearers, raking the lengthy Federal lines with a murderous fire. However, by this time the Mississippi Brigade had been decimated also, and "all the field officers of the brigade were either killed or wounded," save Colonel Humphreys. And the determination of large numbers of fresh troops, with cartridge-boxes full of forty rounds, to redeem themselves against "Barksdale their nemesis at Harpers Ferry" could not be overcome by an ever-dwindling band of worn soldiers low on ammunition, isolated, and without support. A cruel fate had seemingly intervened at the last moment to cheat Barksdale out of decisive victory.

Indeed, Lieutenant Haskell revealed the key tactical advantage now enjoyed by Meade's army to turn the tide: "On account of the convexity of our line, every part of the line could be reinforced by troops having to move a shorter distance than if the line were straight; further, for the same reason, the line of the enemy must be concave, and consequently longer, and with an equal force, thinner and so weaker than ours." Indeed, "any fool could see that Gettysburg had become Fredericksburg in reverse!" Longstreet's views now proved correct, especially in regard to Barksdale's offensive effort: "Even if we carried the heights in front of us and drove Meade out, we should be so badly crippled that we could not reap the fruits of victory."[483]

Nevertheless, the vicious, close-range fighting continued unabated along Plum Run for about half an hour, with the Mississippi Rebels standing firm, exchanging punishment with 1,200 fresh New York soldiers. At close range, the exchanges of musketry grew even more intense, rolling back and forth, with gunfire raging along the length of Plum Run. Clouds of choking smoke blanketed the bottoms and combined with the dropping sun to cast an eerie atmosphere and distorted reddish light, obscuring vision to create more confusion. Hiding the carnage and horrors from the eye of survivors, drifting layers of smoke shrouded the ever-increasing number of bodies of dead and wounded Mississippi boys, who began to stack up like cordwood before a hard winter.

In the riddled ranks of the Mississippi Rangers, Captain Andrew Jackson Pulliam's Company B, 17th Mississippi, two British-born Rebels were cut down. Hit for the third time along Plum Run, Private Abernathy explained how "Billie Gast, another native of England, stepped up to a little bush, knelt, and placing his gun between the branches of a bush, took deliberate aim, and fired kneeling. Just as he did so, a bullet struck him square in the forehead and with a gasp he settled back dead on his knees."

⌁— 10 —⌁

Death in the Gloaming

BY THIS TIME and in part because no support had been sent his way, Barksdale was "almost frantic with rage," while attempting to prepare his hard-hit troops for yet another offensive effort to smash through yet another Yankee line. Above all, he knew that he had to get the attack beyond Plum Run rolling once again. One 126th New York captain never forgot the sight of Barksdale during the general's last moments of life: "Gen. Barksdale was trying to hold his men, cheering them and swearing, directly in front of the left of the 126th near the right of the 125th who both saw and heard him as they emerged from the bushes."[484] Private Joseph Charles Lloyd, 13th Mississippi, recalled the sight of the mounted Barksdale encouraging the boys onward, yelling "Forward through the bushes."[485]

Incredibly, Barksdale surged forward in yet another attack with only a portion of his troops beyond Plum Run, "leading his command in a desperate charge on our left centre," in the words of Yankee Robert A. Cassidy. Large numbers of Mississippi Rebels charged up the ascending slope of Cemetery Ridge with cheers.[486] The resurgent Mississippians lashed back at their New York attackers, threatening to turn the right flank of Willard's brigade and pushing on toward McGilvery's Reserve Artillery and Cemetery Ridge.

In the 17th Mississippi's ranks on Barksdale's right, Private Abernathy described the counterattack of his Mississippi Rangers, how "Jim Crump sprang over him, called for a 'forward charge with bayonet' and the line went forward leaving a ghastly row" of dead and wounded, while "Arch Lee had run up with the flag of the old 17th. On it had been embroidered the names of the battles in which it had fought. Manassas,

221

Leesburg, Yorktown, Williamsburg, Seven Pines, Gaines Mill, Savage Station, Fraser's Farm, Malvern Hill, Sharpsburg, Fredericksburg, and then the cry for another forward movement." All the while, the savage, close-range fighting swirled to new furies among the brush-covered and second-growth timber amid the bloody swale of Plum Run. Like the open fields over which the Mississippi Brigade had charged all afternoon, the swale, once a pristine and picturesque creation of nature, had been transformed into a gory, killing ground, where large numbers of Mississippi boys fell.

By this time, scores of Barksdale's men had fallen during this lethal duel of musketry. Outflanked on the left by attackers of the 111th and 126th New York, the first hard-hit 18th Mississippi soldiers, without ammunition or luck, sullenly began to retire to the west.[487] However, in the smoky confusion, most surviving Mississippians remained in place in defensive positions, reloading and firing as long as rounds in cartridge boxes remained, while Barksdale continued to urge his troops—at least those who followed him, mostly 13th Mississippi soldiers—up the open slope on Plum Run's east side in a last-ditch effort to gain Cemetery Ridge. After having fought all afternoon and being depleted of ammunition, however, additional Mississippi Rebels on the left were forced to withdraw. This was even as more counterattacking 126th New York soldiers who continued to attempt to turn Barksdale's left flank were killed by the Mississippians' accurate fire.

While additional Mississippi soldiers retired to consolidate new defensive positions on Plum Run's west side, the New York brigade surged ahead upon seeing many of Barksdale's hard-hit Rebels redeploying. As Lt. Colonel Crandell, 125th New York, recorded in his diary, when the New York brigade charged and "entered the bushes we went firing as we advanced [and] with a yell we sprang forward [and] we drove them at the point of the bayonet with an impetuousty that drives irresistibly onward. The ground we charged over was covered with killed & wounded but we had done what all the regiments had failed to do at the point of the bayonet." Believing that victory had been won, the New Yorkers charged across the creek to exploit what they believed was their greatest battlefield success to date; in fact, by halting Barksdale's Brigade, something no other Union formation had been able to do that day.

Instead they ran into a wall of fire. The Mississippi Rebels had quickly reformed on the west side of Plum Run, and they now delivered a punishing volley with what little ammunition remained in their cartridge-boxes. Falling wounded, Colonel MacDougall, commanding the 111th New York, paid a high price for turning Barksdale's left flank, writing how "so severe was the fire to which we were subject that my loss in that charge was 185 men killed and wounded in less than 20 minutes, out of 390 taken into the fight." And Lt. Colonel Levin Crandell lamented in his diary how his 125th New York "lost 135 men out of a little less than 400."[488]

The high losses resulted from the swirl of confused fighting at close-range amid the underbrush and thickets along Plum Run's bottoms, where the dense summer foliage and layers of smoke, stagnant in the breezeless July heat and humidity, hovered low on the ground. In the confusion of the close-range, back-and-forth combat, some prone Mississippians, lying in the underbrush, turned to fire into the backs and flanks of the New Yorkers, who charged over the creek. Fighting beside his comrades of The Kemper Legion, 13th Mississippi, Private Joseph Charles Lloyd was shocked to look around and "see the enemy bursting through the bushes." While some Mississippians, especially on the left, had been either outflanked or surrounded and then forced to surrender, most of Plum Run's defenders remained fighting. However, the shooting down of New Yorkers while they were taking prisoners incensed Willard's men, who incorrectly believed that Barksdale's men were giving in. But most Mississippi Rebels had no thought of surrender, especially with Cemetery Ridge so near and yet within reach.[489]

However, Longstreet, who had been stubbornly against Lee's concept of taking the offensive all day, and had lost control of his troops and the fast-paced tactical developments, had mentally disengaged from the offensive effort, unlike Barksdale and his men who were going for broke.[490] Tragically, hundreds of Mississippi Brigade soldiers had already been cut down in part because of the lack of unity in tactical thinking between the offensive-minded Lee and the defensive-minded Longstreet, whose dispute about how best to reap victory at Gettysburg now came back to haunt the best efforts of Barksdale, Humphreys, and their hard-fighting men.[491]

After the war, Longstreet, as if feeling guilty for his failure to adequately support Barksdale's all-out offensive effort and early pulling the plug on the assault that in part led to the Mississippi Brigade's repulse, wrote to McLaws to explain how "this attack went further than I intended that it should, and [would result] in the loss of your gallant Brigadier Barksdale. It was my intention not to pursue this attack if it was likely to prove the enemy's position too strong for my two divisions. I suppose that Barksdale was probably under the impression that the entire Corps was up."

Considering Longstreet's words, it is here worth considering whether "Pickett's Charge" could indeed have gone down in history as the climactic, victorious blow struck for Southern arms—if it had been launched in the twilight of Day 2 at Gettysburg rather than on Day 3. At the moment late on July 2 when Barksdale's men were grappling with a severely depleted Union line on the slope of Cemetery Ridge, one can only imagine the effect of 4,500 fresh Virginia troops coming up behind them in support. No force at Meade's disposal would have been remotely able to prevent a clear breakthrough by Pickett's eager, unbloodied brigades led by Armistead, Kemper, and Garnett. Further, they would have had a nearly unmolested approach march, able to release their full fury right at the very foot of a haphazard Union defense line.

Pickett's division had begun arriving near the battlefield around 2:00 that day, and perhaps by 5:00 it was fully assembled. Like A.P. Hill's division after its long march to Antietam, it could have gone straight into battle; more so if it had begun its march a few hours earlier and thus could get some needed rest. However, Lee apparently never considered the option, sending perhaps the most fateful order he ever issued: "Tell General Pickett I shall not want him" on July 2.[492] Pickett was thus kept in reserve, saved "for another day," while it was on the very afternoon of his division's arrival that the Army of Northern Virginia was within a hairs' breadth of winning the most important battle of the war.

Given all the mistakes made at Gettysburg, small and large by both sides, the "what if's" of the battle are too numerous to count and tend to only lead to as much frustration as fascination. However, one must recognize that the often-castigated Longstreet may have been correct in the first place after he learned that he was to launch an offensive on July 2, and mused to John Bell Hood, "[Lee] wishes me to attack; I do not wish to do so without Pickett. I never like to go into battle with one boot off." There can be little doubt that if Pickett's fresh division had been available to throw into the fray in support of Barksdale, the battle would have been won by the South. Among the cascading effects of a clean breakthrough of the Union left-center by Longstreet would have been increased contributions by Ewell's and A.P. Hill's corps, who would have faced a severed Army of the Potomac on the verge of panic that evening, rather than virtually unassailable heights.

As it stands, Longstreet later described the attack of his First Corps troops on Day 2 as "an unequal battle," but this situation was far more valid in the Mississippians' case than for any other Confederate command that afternoon. Without exaggeration, "Old Pete" maintained that "in this attack Hood's and McLaws' Divisions did the best fighting ever done on any field" during the four years of war. And no brigade of either division fought harder and longer to achieve more significant gains than Barksdale's Mississippi Brigade.

As the climax of Longstreet's offensive on the second day of Gettysburg unfolded, the Mississippi Brigade continued to apply pressure on its own, after Barksdale had ordered, "Forward through the bushes!" At the head of his troops to the 18th Mississippi's right, Barksdale encouraged his men onward, especially his own 13th Mississippi in the center, and at least part of the 17th Mississippi to its right, threatening to break yet another Yankee line. If possible, Barksdale was now the one leader yet capable of snatching victory from the jaws of defeat. Consequently, he "was frantic in his efforts" to push the attack all the way to Cemetery Ridge.

But one especially enterprising Union colonel, George Childs Burling, who now led his rallied mostly New Jersey brigade, Humphreys' Division, prepared to personally checkmate Barksdale's desperate bid to win it all. This opportunistic Union colonel, born on a farm in Burlington County, New Jersey, knew that drastic action needed be taken to somehow reverse the surging high tide of Confederate fortunes. By this time, any lingering romantic concepts about chivalry in this first of all modern wars no longer existed in such a key situation, when so much was at stake. Upon first sighting the foremost leader of the Mississippians' charge, Burling targeted this dynamic, mounted officer for immediate elimination.

Before his troops, the Mississippi general was relatively easy to pinpoint by the foremost New Jersey soldiers, who had rallied along with other Third Corps troops, including "Excelsior Brigade" men. Besides riding up the open ground east of Plum Run at the head of his attackers, Barksdale also stood out because of his distinctive long flowing locks of gray hair that streamed down to his shoulders. At the top of his voice, the forty-two-year-old general was in "our midst," recalled Private Lloyd of the 13th Mississippi, yelling, "Forward!" Feeling that decisive victory was within his grasp, General Barksdale shouted, "They are whipped. We will drive them beyond the Susquehanna."

Barksdale's mounted presence before his onrushing troops was awe-inspiring to the boys in blue. But the astute New Jersey colonel, who knew what it took to win decisive victory this afternoon, was not admiring his counterpart in gray. Instead of allowing chivalry to muddle his tactical thinking, Burling wanted to kill the Mississippi leader, who was encouraging his troops in his desperate bid to win the war before sunset. Colonel Burling called for an entire company of his best New Jersey marksmen, perhaps as many as 50 fighting men. He ordered them to level their Springfield .58 caliber muskets and unleash a concentrated volley at the mounted Barksdale.

However, eager to gain recognition, several other Union leaders took credit for directing a concentrated fire upon Barksdale. The 11th New Jersey, which had already taken a severe beating from the blazing Mississippi muskets in the struggle along the Emmitsburg Road, had rallied by this time. Brig. General Joseph Carr gave Company H, 11th New Jersey—which had suffered more than 50 percent casualties, mostly at the Mississippi Brigade's hands—a special mission. Above the roaring guns, Carr shouted to every Company H veteran to "bring down the officer on the white horse!" Another account has it that Captain Ira W. Cory of Company H ordered all his men to fire at Barksdale. But in fact, Cory and his men only killed an unlucky Mississippi staff officer, mounted on a gray horse and wearing a Zouave fez in triumph. The finely uniformed officer of Barksdale's staff went down with five bullets in his body.

Another account gave credit for targeting of Barksdale to the 126th New York, on Willard's right, when an entire company fired their rifles at him. And a 126th New York captain wrote that his troops and those of the 125th New York "both fired at him and he fell hit by several bullets." Another New York soldier later told Henry Stevens Willey of the 16th Vermont that "during the hottest of the battle [General Barksdale] came out and tried to rally his men and that he had a star on his collar [and that] he had a splendid chance so he fired on the General and saw him fall." And Colonel Norman J. Hall wrote, "The rebel Barksdale was mortally wounded and two colors left on the ground within 20 yards of the line of the Seventh Michigan Volunteers."[493] Under the circumstances, the honor of having made the decision to kill Barksdale in a desperate effort to take the steam out of the Mississippians' attack was eagerly sought by quite a few victors years after the war.[494] However, another Union soldier, who saw the general close-up after he fell, believed that Barksdale was cut down not by musketry but by a canister round from one of McGilvery's guns.[495]

Clearly, by this time, Barksdale was living very much on borrowed time and tempting fate in leading the attack across Plum Run. As a mounted brigadier general with three stars on his jacket's collar, long conspicuous in riding before his troops, it was nothing short of a miracle that Barksdale had escaped harm so far after leading the attack over such a long distance. Willard's New Yorkers in particular wanted revenge for the Harpers Ferry disaster by killing the Mississippi general most responsible for orchestrating their supreme humiliation.[496]

Regardless of which troops fired the deadly volley and which commander deserved recognition for issuing the final order that toppled Barksdale from the saddle "in a field, no trees about," in Private John Saunders Henley's words, the assigned veterans in blue took steady aim on the daring brigade commander. At least one, perhaps more, Union officer roared "Fire!" above the crashing musketry. A well-aimed volley exploded from the leveled row of guns, rippling down the blue line, as a sheet of yellow flame leaped toward "Old Barks."

In a split second, projectiles ripped through Barksdale's uniform, splattering gray wool with bright red in the thin, fading July light. Minie balls smashed through his left leg about halfway between the knee and ankle, and another bullet ripped through Barksdale's other leg. But the general's stocky 240-pound frame absorbed the shock, and he bore up to the pain. So many minie balls streamed around Barksdale that even the blade of his beautiful saber was broken when he was holding it high over head to encourage his troops onward. In disbelief, Captain Harris Barksdale described the awful sight when his uncle was hit. He wrote how "Gen. Barksdale was wounded, and he reeled but did not halt. He moves on with his band of heros. Onward! and the fourth line is met and vanquished—can nothing stop these desperate Mississippians?"

During the final, but brief, penetration of the New York line in this sector, a piece of canister from the roaring Union field piece positioned on the high ground of the Plum Run Line tore through the general's left breast, knocking Barksdale off his horse. Because he was so far ahead of his troops and due to the thick smoke of battle and Plum Run's dense thickets, few, if any, of his soldiers saw Barksdale's fall, unlike the boys in blue. Yankee Private William M. Boggs never forgot that as "our attention was directed to a general officer leading the first line to the attack and we distinctly saw him fall." And one Federal officer described how the Mississippi Brigade had "carried everything before it with cyclonic force. I saw brave General Barksdale fall from his horse leading his men and when he fell I could not help shedding a tear at seeing so brave and valorous a soldier killed [as by this time the Mississippians] had us badly whipped." Serving as one of Longstreet's couriers, young William Young-blood formerly of Colonel Oates' 15th Alabama Infantry, recalled how General Barksdale was putting "spurs to his horse [and] dashed a little ways along his line, giving the order to charge at double-quick, when I distinctly heard a shot struck him and saw him fall from his horse." Youngblood paid a high compliment in declaring that "no troops were ever commanded by a braver man than General Barksdale."[497]

The inspirational sight of Barksdale leading the way, which had emboldened Magnolia State attackers all afternoon, was no more. As could be expected, Barksdale's fall took much of the steam out of the Mississippians' final offensive effort. One Yankee described how, "His fall—at the very moment when the presence of a commanding officer is most required to encourage men to renewed exertion and sacrifice—was "a severe blow, causing his attackers to fall back.[498]

Even now, however, Barksdale was down but not out. Wearing a fine cotton or linen shirt of white, now splattered in red, with Masonic emblem stubs under his gray coat, he remained conscious. He yet breathed life, but it was severely labored. As could be expected, the wound to his left lung made the general's breathing difficult. All that Barksdale could now do was hope and pray that his injuries and multiple wounds were not mortal. However, like the once-seemingly unstoppable momentum that had propelled his assault eastward, Barksdale was already slowly dying, after making aa supreme offensive effort unmatched by any of Lee's lieutenants on this day. Adjutant Harman, 13th Mississippi, described in a letter how Barksdale "was mortally wounded about the time the Brigade fell back. Jack Boyd was with him at the time he was shot and he and one or two of our boys tried to bring the Gen'l. off the field, but being a very large man and mortally wounded he begged them to leave him where he was which they finally did."

Private Boyd attempted to comfort the still-conscious general, whose thoughts remained focused on the battle's outcome. Barksdale now issued his last directive: order Alexander's artillery up to support his boys in their final desperate bid to gain Cemetery Ridge's crest. Then, with the counterattacking bluecoats only fifty yards away, Boyd left Barksdale, whose lung wound emitted "a sputtering sound," where he had fallen. Boyd now rode away on his new mission to secure "long-arm" assistance for the hard-fighting Mississippians before it was too late. A short time later, wounded in the arm, Private Lloyd of the 13th Mississippi found the general splattered in blood. He described the horror of discovering "Old Barks" when, "I hear a weak hail to my right, and, turning to it, find General Barksdale, and what a disappointment when I hold my canteen to his mouth for a drink of water and found a ball had gone through and let it all out. I took his last message to his brigade and left him, with the promise to send litter bearers."[499]

Barksdale's mortal wound meant much more than just the fall of one of Lee's brigadier generals. In many ways, his fall symbolized the zenith of not only the Mississippi Brigade's attack but also the real "High Water Mark" of the Confederacy at Gettysburg. In leading the charge that brought the Confederacy closer to decisive success than ever before, Barksdale's fall just east of Plum Run marked the zenith of the Army of Northern Virginia's most devastating attack and two hours of perhaps the best fighting of the war.

By this time, Barksdale's units of both wings had been cut to pieces, after capturing one position after another, smashing through numerous Union commands, and battling for most of the bloodiest afternoon in the Army of Northern Virginia's history. While leading the 13th Mississippi, Colonel Carter had been killed when four minie balls tore through his body, while his trusty "right arm," Lieutenant Colonel Kennon McElroy, the former captain of the Lauderdale Zouaves, was hit in the shoulder. And the third in command of the 13th Mississippi, Major Bradley, was shot in the ankle, knocking him out of action.[500]

Meanwhile, the survivors of the 13th, 17th, and 18th Mississippi were now caught up in a simultaneous scenario of fighting, withdrawing, or surrendering in the noisy confusion, as the onslaught of Willard's fresh regiments finally turned Barksdale's left flank, swarming into the under-brush-filled swale in greater numbers. Lieutenant Richard Bassett of the 126th New York described the carnage: "While we were crossing the ravine, I noticed [the colors] faltered, and finally fell; directly they were raised again and went on [but then] my dear brother [Color Sergeant Erasmus E. Bassett and] the boys were falling all around me . . ." After cutting down more bluecoat attackers, Mississippi Rebels fought hand-to-hand amid the blinding layers of sulfurous smoke that choked the low ground along the blood-stained stream.

Meanwhile, even more Mississippi boys fell during a brutal struggle of attrition along Plum Run. One half-dazed survivor, Captain Harris

Barksdale, described the undeniable reality presented by the counterattacking Federals: "Will nothing stop them,—Yea, *death* will do it and had already done it!—Look up and down the lines! Where are the fourteen hundred men that left the woods, now a mile in the rear? From that point to this they strew the ground while it drinks their blood, and not five hundred have gone this far . . . they are scattered over the ground, like a picket line, vainly endeavoring to move forward."[501]

However, following Barksdale's final orders to hurry forward Alexander's artillery and evidently not seeing his fall, die-hard Mississippians in the line's center continued to charge recklessly onward beyond Plum Run in a last-ditch attempt to capture Lieutenant Colonel McGilvery's booming cannon to the east. With Willard's brigade applying the most pressure on the flanks, the attackers now surged only from the brigade's center, some 13th and 17th Mississippi soldiers, who were not aware of Barksdale's fall. However, the Plum Run Line guns easily wiped out the foremost attackers. In the words of one Mississippi Rebel, "Thinned by the storm which swept down with such terrific fury from the ridge, the advance line staggered and began to waver."[502]

Private Nimrod Newton Nash, along with a few Company I comrades of the 17th Mississippi—and a few soldiers of other companies—in the brigade's center, charged up the open slope toward Cemetery Ridge, targeting one of McGilvery's batteries in the fading light. But the attack of the determined Minute Men of Attala and an unknown number of other 17th Mississippi soldiers was quickly cut to pieces in the open field by blasts of canister. In a letter that described the short-lived final assault up the open western slope of Cemetery Ridge, Sergeant Frank M. Ross, 17th Mississippi, penned in a letter how Private Nash "fell while nobly defending his country in a charge on one of the enemies batteries near sunset."[503] Meanwhile, the tough New Yorkers of Willard's brigade continued to gain even more of the tactical advantage. Corporal Harrison Clark grabbed the regimental colors of the 125th New York, when the color bearer was shot down. He then led his men toward the row of flame erupting from the blazing Mississippi rifles, earning the Congressional Medal of Honor for his heroics.[504]

Along the blood-stained bottoms of Plum Run, a number of surviving Mississippians, in the words of Captain Harris Barksdale, were unnerved by the shocking sight of "General Barksdale's horse seen galloping over the field. Their general has fallen, and they fall, sullenly backward, contesting every inch of ground. It was known to the men that their beloved general had fallen, wounded or dead, within the lines of the enemy. Their grief was intense, and those brave men wept like children."[505]

Meanwhile, flurries of fighting continued to rage in the smoke-laced thickets and dense stands of willows, when larger numbers of cheering New Yorkers charged through Plum Run's environs with bayonets at the ready, firing on the run, and mopping up the last clumps of resistance. Angry over taking high losses, the past Harpers Ferry humiliation, and the belief that a number of Mississippians who had surrendered had turned to shoot down their comrades from behind, some 126th New York soldiers became vengeful. Evidently, in consequence, a few wounded Mississippians were shown no mercy, being shot or bayoneted by enraged New Yorkers, who delivered the coup-de-grâce to some defenseless men who lay not far from Barksdale.[506]

Even worse, the wounded Barksdale also may have received rough treatment at the hands of some New Yorkers, whose own fighting blood was up after having lost so many good men. He was left alive, and remained defiant. Even with mortal wounds, Barksdale cursed the Yankee victors, and refused medical treatment from the boys in blue.[507] At least one officer, Captain Charles A. Richardson, 126th New York, believed that Barksdale was harshly treated. The general suffered immensely from the wounds in the chest and "in the leg [that] produced a fracture which caused considerable pain . . . ."[508]

Colonel Willard's counterattack ended the final offensive effort of Barksdale's left wing, stopping the day's most serious threat.[509] However, Willard himself would not survive to savor his triumph. While leading his men in pursuit of the Mississippians, as they sullenly fell back to the main Confederate line, he was hit full in the face by a fragment of shell and died instantly. Barksdale's only support in his last-ditch attack, Alexander's artillery, still firing away from the Peach Orchard, had claimed a measure of retribution for the fall of their champion.

At the Peach Orchard, Captain Charles Squires, Washington Artillery, witnessed the return of Lt. Colonel John Calvin Fiser, 17th Mississippi, "just out of the fight. He had received two wounds in the leg and a bullet had passed through his cheek [but] he did not fail even under these distressing circumstances to call to me that he had captured the guns he promised me."[510] Not only faith in achieving victory but also the striking good looks of this fine officer were never quite the same after taking this nasty wound. But at least Fiser, the young merchant and promising officer from Panola, had survived the worst horrors of Gettysburg.[511]

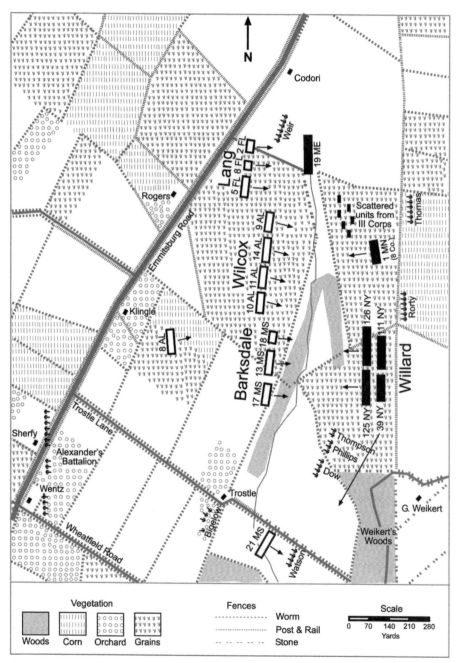

Map courtesy of Bradley M. Gottfried

∽— 11 —∽

"Great God! Have we got the universe to whip?"

DESPITE BARKSDALE'S FALL and without support of any kind to the north in the Plum Run sector, after the gradual, piecemeal withdraw of the 13th, 17th, and 18th Mississippi from their slugfest, Colonel Humphrey's indefatigable regiment was still on the move in a desperate bid to gain Cemetery Ridge. After surging across Plum Run, the 21st Mississippi continued to advance on its "battery busting" mission, after capturing the four guns of Bigelow's 9th Massachusetts Light Artillery. Attacking through the wide-open avenue between the Second Corps' left and the Union concentration before Little Round Top, Humphreys' Rebels surged steadily upward. Just ahead lay the fulfillment of the most optimistic Confederate dreams at Gettysburg, the Taneytown Road and Cemetery Ridge, whose capture might spell decisive Southern success, especially if reinforcements were yet hurried forward to Humphreys' support.

Intrigued at the sight of another tactical opportunity, Humphreys and his 21st Mississippi soldiers had already seen the five guns of Battery I, Fifth United States Artillery galloping over the open ground just below the crest of Cemetery Ridge, and then unlimbering in a great hurry to anchor McGilvery's left. Barely 150 paces beyond the elevated position of the battery lay Cemetery Ridge's crest. Therefore, on the 21st Mississippi's attack toward the mainly barren crest of Cemetery Ridge now "hung the hopes of a struggling Southern nation and people, for if "the last line was carried, the last battery was captured, the enemy's line was cut in twain," wrote General John Bell Hood of the enticing possibility. The Union battery was commanded by Lieutenant Malbone Francis Watson, the son of a respected New York Supreme Court judge. Only two years out of West Point, Watson now faced Humphreys, who had attended the academy forty years before. Much depended upon this up-coming meeting between these two gifted officers, who now wore uni-forms of different colors. Ironically, after replacing Captain Ames' Battery G, New York Light Artillery, in the Peach Orchard, Watson's battery had hastily departed after making only token resistance before pulling out to escape the hard-charging 21st Mississippi. Now Watson would have to face them again, with much more at stake.

Cheering wildly and with their red battle-flags streaming overhead, the 21st Mississippi poured up the open, grassy slope as if nothing could stop them, toward the exposed far left, or extreme southern, end Mc-Gilvery's line. Captain A.P. Martin described the glaring vulnerability of yet another cluster of Union guns that hoped to do what had yet to be accomplished: somehow stop Humphreys and his rampaging troops. In-deed, Watson's "battery was without support of any kind [as] the enemy approached nearly in front at a distance of about 350 yards and the bat-tery immediately opened fire on them with shell."

As the 21st Mississippi drew closer, Captain Martin described how Watson's five guns unleashed loads of "canister, some twenty rounds" into the onrushing line. Despite the swaths torn through the ranks, the 21st Mississippi absorbed its losses and kept going. Clearly, Watson's roaring cannon were no insignificant challenge for Humphreys' veterans, threatening to stop the most successful Confederate assault of the day. This experienced United States battery had seen service during the Seven Days and all of the Army of the Potomac's campaigns since, and the ex-pert artillerymen worked swiftly and efficiently to cut down more attack-ers with business-like efficiency.

But Humphreys' men gave as good as they got. While shooting down Watson's cannoneers and artillery horses while on the run, Humphreys' troops continued to pour up the western slope of Cemetery Ridge. After reloading, and with the Mississippians descending upon them, Watson's cannon unleashed a stream of fire one final time, cutting down another handful of Humphreys' attackers, who were in a desperate race to reach the guns before they were all downed. Lieutenant Watson and his sea-soned gunners, from New York City and Luzerne County, Pennsylvania, were tough army regulars, whose discipline and fast-loading capabilities were renowned. They now proved that their lofty reputation was well-deserved.

But regular army discipline now ensured the destruction of this com-pany of the Fifth United States Artillery at the hands of these young, self-reliant fighting men from the southwest frontier. The Fifth Corps battery, manned by nearly 80 well-trained gunners, simply did not stand a chance without infantry support and when fully exposed before the sharp-shooting Mississippians. With methodical skill, fast-firing Rebels blasted away to slaughter more than twenty gunners and half of the exposed battery horses, dropping them with seemingly each shot, while they closed in for the kill.

The mounted Lieutenant Watson was a most conspicuous target. In frantic haste, the 21st Mississippi boys fired again and again at the battery commander in the smoky haze. Indeed, so many "men and horses were shot down or disabled" by the 21st Mississippi that the field pieces could no longer be worked. So furious was the fire of Humphreys' soldiers that it was almost as if they had known that their beloved General Barksdale had been cut down to the northwest by canister fired from one of these Union cannon. One bluecoat artillery officer was killed and another went down wounded, while eighteen enlisted men fell to the terrible fire.

Finally the hard-charging 21st Mississippi swarmed up the slope and poured over Watson's artillery pieces like a gray and butternut flood. A handful of dazed Yankee gunners were captured, including England-born Sergeant George Davis. As in recently sweeping over Captain Bigelow's Massachusetts cannon in the now-quiet, body-strewn valley below, Humphreys' men captured the five 3-inch guns of Battery I, Fifth United States Artillery. All the guns that anchored the left of McGilvery's Plum Run Line were taken with a thorough, lethal swiftness, representing yet another significant success by the 21st Mississippi. Lieutenant Watson was knocked out of action, hit by a bullet in the knee, resulting in the usual gory procedure of his leg's amputation. Thanks to the combined effect of Barksdale's battering ram to the north, and the near turning of the right flank of Willard's brigade, the 21st Mississippi's sledge hammer-like blows, and Humphreys' determined attempt to roll up McGivery's line of artillery pieces from the south, the Yankees were now "down to a dozen operable guns, then six, and the end seemed close at hand" for the Army of the Potomac's battered left-center.

McGilvery's ad hoc line of artillery was unraveling quickly, one of his batteries overrun, and another, Captain Thompson's, out of ammunition and pulled rearward before it was too late. The First New York Battery, Company B, likewise had retired, leaving only a handful of guns—only half a dozen out of the original fifteen of the Plum Run Line.

Lieutenant Dow believed that the end was near for the Army of the Potomac for "it was evidently their intention, after capturing Company I, Fifth Regulars, to have charged right through our lines to the Taneytown Road, isolating our left wing and dividing our army." Indeed, Humphreys and his 21st Mississippi soldiers now possessed the opportunity to make that day's greatest ambition come true: splitting the Army of the Potomac in two and reaping decisive victory on northern soil. Private McNeily, 21st Mississippi, described the breathtaking opportunity gained by some of the hardest fighting of the war: "Taking his bearings after capturing Lieutenant Watson's battery, Colonel Humphreys found himself the center of a remarkable situation. Looking to his left, some half a mile distant, he saw the other regiments of the brigade engaged with Willard. Behind him, at about the same distance, were Alexander's guns making trouble for the enemy in two directions. To our right, toward Round Top, half a mile off, was a disorganized mass of apparently some thousands of the enemy, fleeing before Hood with Wofford and other brigades of McLaw's division . . . but the view on our front was the most singular. Looking almost to Mead's [sic] bent back right, not an enemy appeared in sight. The 21st Mississippi had fought its way into the enemy's rear, and was planted squarely between his left and center."

Now the 21st Mississippi, continuing to serve as the sharp head of the point of Barksdale's spear, had once again outflanked another Union defensive position, thanks to hard fighting, tactical flexibility, and Humphreys' inspired leadership. The capture of the five 3-inch guns of Watson's battery, just after the capture of the four Massachusetts guns of Bigelow's battery, marked the most significant Confederate success east of Plum Run and the day's deepest and most significant penetration. The gains won by the 21st Mississippi unhinged McGilvery's Plum Run Line from the left flank, and opened the way to gaining the strategic crest of Cemetery Ridge. Even more, if Humphreys turned his soldiers north, they could yet strike the exposed left flank of Willard's Brigade, relieving pressure from Barksdale's other three regiments and to perhaps rally them to resume a united offensive in the drive to capture Cemetery Ridge. Or Humphreys could lead his victorious troops south down the ridge to outflank Union commands on his right. Incredibly, the Mississippi Rebels were on the verge of a remarkable breakthrough.

Humphreys himself never forgot the moment when he surveyed the extent of his improbable success from the commanding elevation of the slope just west of the undefended crest of Cemetery Ridge: "From the position I occupied, no enemy could be seen or heard in my front. Not a gun was being fired at me. The federal army was cut in twain." One bullet-shredded Confederate banner that now marked the most successful penetration and the most significant gains achieved by the Army of Northern Virginia during the three days at Gettysburg was carried by the Wilkinson County soldiers of Company D, 21st Mississippi. A proud emblem of the Jeff Davis Guards, this banner, made of sturdy wool fabric instead of silk, had been donated by the good ladies of Woodville in the state's southwest corner. This flag now flew in triumph to mark the apex of the Confederate offensive on the second day of Gettysburg.

Amid the wreckage of what once had been an excellent United States artillery unit, Humphreys' exhausted soldiers caught their breath on the high perch overlooking Plum Run. With his fighting blood up and his tactical instincts sharpened to a razor's edge, the colonel ordered soldiers with past artillery experience to quickly turn the field pieces south to widen the gap torn into Meade's left-center. A handful of volunteers in dirty gray and butternut began to turn the captured cannon around. Humphreys explained the tactical situation that promised greater gains at this time: "Eight hundred yards, to my right a confused mass was retreating, driven by McLaws, and Hood. I attempted to turn the guns just captured on them but no rammers or friction wires could be found. Eight hundred yards to my left, the enemy's line was kept busy by Barksdale." Meanwhile, Humphreys hurriedly reformed his ranks to continue the assault eastward to gain Cemetery Ridge's crest.

But the hard-won tactical advantage gained by the 21st Mississippi's combat prowess was now fleeting. Daylight was fast fading away—it was past 7:30—along with opportunities to reap additional gains when time was now of the essence. It was a harbinger of the Confederacy's own final sunset, while Humphreys' men busily reloaded their muskets for more hard fighting that lay ahead.

Indeed, Captain John B. Fassitt, General Birney's aide-de-camp, was stunned when suddenly told by a dejected young lieutenant of Watson's captured battery that all of his guns had been captured by Mississippi Rebels. Even more, the frantic artillery officer warned that if the victorious 21st Mississippi soldiers were "able to serve my guns, those troops you have just been forming on the ridge won't stay there a minute." Indeed, the 21st Mississippi was in a perfect position to wreak havoc on their exposed left flank, and Captain Fassitt realized as much.

Fortunately, Fassitt "knew of the Garibaldi Guards being detached" in the second line, or reserve, on the left of Willard's Brigade, and that they were now available for an attempt to save the day. These men of the 39th New York had been held in reserve to protect Willard's left flank, making them readily accessible for just such an emergency as presented by the 21st Mississippi's success. Acting without orders, a desperate Fassitt galloped frantically up on a frothing horse to the only available Union troops in reserve in the vicinity of Humphreys' latest conquest. The 39th New York's commander, Colonel Hugo Hildebrandt, initially refused Fassitt's shouted orders to advance against the 21st Mississippi because Fassitt was only a staff officer of Birney's Division, Third Corps, while the New Yorkers were part of Hancock's Second Corps. Therefore, the fast-thinking young staff officer repeated the orders in Hancock's name, instead of Birney's. Now satisfied, and probably seeing the 21st Mississippi's red banner flying over the five captured artillery pieces of Watson's battery down the open slope, Hildebrandt ordered his 39th New York, the southernmost of Willard's regiments, to the left on the double to meet the day's most urgent threat.

Fortunately for the Union, these New Yorkers were ably led by Major Hildebrandt, a hard-nosed Prussian commander. Led by Captain Fassitt, the Third Corps staff officer, on horseback, the hardy New Yorkers surged forward by the left flank with fixed bayonets and cheers that indicated high morale. Most of all, they were determined to recapture Watson's lost battery now in possession of a depleted band of Magnolia Rebels, who were entirely on their own.[512]

By this time, many of the 21st Mississippi's finest soldiers, both officers and enlisted men, lay strewn across the bloody fields along the path of Humphreys' onslaught. Attrition and the lack of ammunition combined with sheer exhaustion to effectively diminish any real chance of successfully resisting the New Yorkers, who were fresh, well-led, and confident.[513] Already five Gibson cousins of the 21st Mississippi had been hit, including one mortally wounded. Lieutenant Tuing Gibson and Private Gadi Gibson, who suffered wounds in the neck and groin, of the Sunflower Guards (Company I), were casualties by this time.[514] Most important, the sunset of not only July 2 but also of the Confederacy was fast-approaching on the western horizon, and this ultimate demise was heralded in dramatic fashion by Willard's attackers.

Here, on the high ground just below Cemetery Ridge's crest, the remains of the 21st Mississippi were about to meet hundreds of highly motivated New Yorkers. The 39th New York was a heavily ethnic unit, consisting of what the yeomen farmers from Mississippi referred to derisively as "foreigners." Hence, this fine Excelsior State unit was known throughout the army as the "Garibaldi Guard." These hardy New York bluecoats consisted of Germans, Italians, Hungarians, Frenchmen, Spanish, Swiss, and Portuguese, including fighting men who had gained solid military experience in European armies. General George B. McClellan, when once describing his army's regiments, said the most "remarkable of all was the Garibaldi Regiment [for] the men were from all known and unknown lands, from all possible and impossible armies: Zouaves from Algiers, men of the 'Foreign Legion,' Zephyrs, Cossacks, Garibaldians of the deepest dye, English deserters, Sepoys, Turcos, Croats, Swiss, Beer-Drinkers from Bavaria, stout men from North Germany . . . such a mixture was probably never before seen under any flag."[515]

These high-spirited 39th New York attackers wore red shirts inspired by Garibaldi's liberation campaigns in Italy. And the regiment's ranks included more than a hundred seamen—an anomaly amid Pennsylvania's pastoral farmlands—from around the world, and also non-English speaking soldiers from Russia, Greece, France, Austria, Slovakia, Poland, Belgium, Scandinavia, French Canada, Spain, Holland, and Alsace-Lorraine. After their recent exchange from capture at Harpers Ferry, like the rest of Willard's brigade, the 39th New York's soldiers were especially eager for the long-awaited opportunity to redeem themselves this afternoon.[516] Consequently, the bloodied survivors, low on ammunition and manpower, but not courage, of Barksdale's best regiment faced even greater odds with the arrival of so many fresh troops with full cartridge-boxes.[517]

Watching helplessly as the blue formations rushed toward his exhausted ranks, a frustrated Colonel Humphreys felt a flush of anger at the lack of support of any kind for his deep penetration, knowing that he must continue to fight on his own against the odds.[518] Humphreys now "mingled vain and bitter regrets over the weakness of his force." Indeed, where were the promised reinforcements? Where was Wofford's brigade? Where was Pickett? Where was A.P. Hill's Corps? Or Ewell's divisions? What had gone wrong? Was not the army hurrying support forward at such a critical moment?

After fighting so long and hard, Barksdale's top lieutenant viewed the sickening sight of the beginning of the end of Confederate dreams as "soon a long solid line of infantry was seen advancing down the road towards us." Nevertheless, the defiant Colonel Humphreys was determined not to relinquish an inch of his hard-earned perch. Here, atop the open, high ground that overlooked Plum Run, Humphreys prepared for more hard fighting. By this time, some of McGilvery's guns were turned south on Humphrey's troops, who now took the punishment from canister delivered at relatively close range. Quite likely it was a frustrated Mississippi Rebel who famously swore that the Yankee commanders shouted, "Universe, forward! By Kingdom into line! Nations guide right!" and the onrush of Union reinforcements caused another soldier to declare "Great God! Have we got the Universe to whip?" Indeed, Colonel Humphreys and his surviving band of soldiers, drenched with sweat and streaked with black powder from biting open so many paper cartridges, continued to face the fire of yet another new Union battery and the advance of another veteran infantry command, as well as other Federal reinforcements now arriving on the scene.[519]

In a letter, Captain Josiah C. Fuller, 32nd Massachusetts, Fifth Corps, which advanced north to meet Humphreys' threat, recorded how "the rebs tried to . . . get possession of a road [Taneytown] and thus have a full play on our trains," but it was not to be. Captain Fuller also proudly penned with a sense of triumph how "Genl. Barksdale (Reb) is dead."

However, after capturing Watson's battery and in a final bid to redeem the day, Colonel Humphreys continued to lead his troops farther east up the open slope and ever-closer to Cemetery Ridge's crest. Humphreys' men surged onward while it "thrilled the heart of a soldier to catch sight of his red battle-flag," especially one now pointed toward the strategic crest of Meade's main line. At this time the 21st Mississippi pushed on in one final offensive effort. Later, to embellish their war records, Union veterans swore that the Mississippians had been immediately and easily pushed rearward by the 39th New York's counterattack, almost as if to deny Humphreys his final achievement in reaching so close to decisive victory.[520] However, Humphreys' final bid to exploit his dramatic breakthrough continued unabated in a renewed surge up the slope.[521]

However, suddenly the 39th New York's attack hit the 21st Mississippi's left flank, raking it with a great rolling sheet of flame that erupted from rows of leveled New York muskets. Here, in a forgotten showdown just below Cemetery Ridge's crest, the 21st Mississippi and the 39th New York clashed in the last flurry of bitter fighting which swirled savagely beyond Captain Watson's five captured guns positioned on the slope. One Yankee described how the Mississippians simply "were not willing to give up the battery and position without a struggle, and the fight was a fierce one." Desperate Mississippi boys thrust bayonets and swung musket-butts at the swarming Federals, but these fresh troops, with full ammunition could not be stopped by those with cartridge-boxes either empty or nearly so.

Fighting on foot and before his men as usual, Humphreys somehow was not touched amid the hail of bullets, while continuing to lead a charmed existence, unlike the unfortunate Barksdale along bloody Plum Run to the northwest. Amid the hand-to-hand combat, Captain Fassitt, the only mounted officer leading the New Yorkers into the fray, lost control of his horse when a 21st Mississippi Rebel grabbed the bridle in an attempt to capture him. Another Mississippian stuck his musket into the captain's face to deliver the coup-de-grâce. But just before the soldier pulled the trigger, Captain Fassett knocked the gun away with his saber. Nevertheless, the bullet, most likely a .577 caliber Enfield round, tore through the captain's kepi's visor. It was a close call. A Garibaldi Guardsman promptly ran his bayonet through the Mississippi Confederate.

Meanwhile, amid the swirling hand-to-hand combat, Captain Fassitt aimed his pistol with a steady hand at the bridle-holding Johnny Reb, shooting him down, and thence winning the Congressional Medal of Honor for his key role in saving the day. There were simply too many fresh Garibaldi Guards to fight off, and the tide finally turned against the 21st Mississippi for the first time all day. One New Yorker described how after more bitter fighting, literally under the shadow of Cemetery Ridge's crest, "the Mississippians were driven off from the guns, the Battery became ours as well as the just honor of the day." Indeed, without support, ammunition, reinforcements, or a prayer this late afternoon, Colonel Humphreys had no choice but to prepare to retire west and back down the slope leading to the low ground of Plum Run.[522] In Humphreys' words: "I saw my safety was in a hurried retreat."[523]

Once and for all, the threat of the howling tide of victorious Mississippi Rebels pouring through the gap in Meade's left-center had finally receded. Lieutenant Dow, commanding the four smoothbore Napoleons of the 6th Maine Battery just north of Watson's battery, was awed by the ferocity of the 21st Mississippi's desperate bid to "charge right through our lines to the Taneytown road, isolating our left wing and dividing our army."[524] In the end, the Mississippians' bloody repulse on both wings was the turning point in the savage fighting on July 2, "ending that threat to the Union center," in the words of Noah Andre Trudeau, in what was the true location of the "High Water Mark" of the Confederacy.[525]

All the while, large numbers of further Federal reinforcements were on the way, converging on Humphreys, who now faced more than the 39th New York. General Henry H. Lockwood's Maryland and New York brigade, General Thomas H. Ruger's First Division, Twelfth Corps, suddenly appeared before Humphreys. Indeed, thanks to the advantage of interior lines and timely leadership decisions, as General Oliver O. Howard described, thousands of "troops came from all parts of the army to assist Sickles" and his beaten Third Corps. They would have been too late, however, if Barksdale's Brigade had been properly supported.

With heartbreak, the hard-fighting Colonel Humphreys wrote of the no-win situation and the moment that he dreaded most of all, when he realized that all his efforts had been in vain: "I discovered a long Federal line marching from the direction of Cemetery hill directly against me— Looking again to my right and rear I saw Wofford retiring, towards the Peach Orchard—To my left the 3 other regiments that were with [Barksdale], were also retiring—I could see no other reinforcements coming, and determined to retire to the stone wall where I captured Graham and 4 guns and there make a stand—once safely behind the stone fence I could control the ground on which I left the 5 guns—The enemy did not urge his claim to them—and as I know the Federal Army was cut in twain, and hoping for reinforcements to hold what we had gained, and thus secure a triumph over the separate wings I felt the jubilation of the victor."[526]

After tenaciously battling the 39th New York and now thwarted by Lockwood's fresh brigade in front, Humphreys' exhausted Mississippians, including a good many blood-stained walking wounded, slowly retired down the slope and back across Plum Run and its shallow valley of broken dreams. Here, on the ascending ground just near the Trostle house and before the prized 9th Massachusetts Battery guns, which none of Humphreys' men wanted to relinquish, the 21st Mississippi's survivors made yet another defensive stand with what few rounds remained in their cartridge boxes. Humphreys was yet determined to preserve the precious ground gained and retain Captain Bigelow's bronze cannon.

But as the night closed in on the isolated but still defiant 21st Mississippi survivors, one of Barksdale's staff officers, a captain, finally reached Humphreys with new orders from Longstreet. Because Barksdale had fallen in the Plum Run sector to the north, Humphreys now commanded what was left of the decimated Mississippi Brigade, which had withdrawn back to the Peach Orchard. Not ready to concede defeat, Colonel Humphreys described how "greatly to my mortification I was ordered to fall back to the Peach Orchard. I demurred and protested but the order was final." Consequently, the 21st Mississippi now retired all the way back to the Emmitsburg Road. Longstreet described how "when Humphreys, who succeeded to Barksdale's brigade, was called back to the new line he thought there was some mistake in the orders, and only withdrew so far as a captured battery. And when the order was repeated, retired under protest." Quite simply, the Mississippians had been the last troops willing to retire after achieving the greatest gains of any of Lee's regiments on July 2, after some of the bloodiest fighting of the war.

Colonel Humphreys described the bitter end: "I spiked one of the guns, and unmolested by pursuit I formed on the left of Wofford at the Peach Orchard from which we had driven Sickles Corps." Humphreys now took command of what little was left of the battered Mississippi Brigade.

All in all, no single Confederate regiment during the three days at Gettysburg achieved more significant gains when more was at stake than the 21st Mississippi. Even though only a single regiment, which fought independently as Barksdale's freewheeling right wing, Humphreys' 21st Mississippi had unhinged the Peach Orchard defensive line by first overwhelming the apex of the salient angle and overrunning Union regiments and artillery. Then, Humphreys captured guns from Winslow's, Bigelow's, and Watson's batteries, as well as undetermined guns. Most of these afterward had to be relinquished. In sum, the 21st Mississippi's remarkable success "by a single regiment was an unexcelled, it ever equaled, achievement" of the Civil War. In John Bell Hood's words: "Thus it was that the 21st Mississippi Regiment bore the stars and bars to the very farthest point reached in the enemy's line on the bloody field of Gettysburg."

Private McNeily described the 21st Mississippi's sweeping onslaught that resulted in the capture of the guns of Bigelow's and Watson's batteries as "one of the most thrilling battle episodes of the war . . . while these two batteries were wholly unsupported by infantry, they were captured by a regiment which entering the battle with three hundred men, numbered then but little more than two hundred." General McLaws declared with pride that the 21st Mississippi was the "'flower of Southern chivalry,' with one of its companies [having] four men pledged to remain always privates, who were worth $400,000." But perhaps Union General

Hunt bestowed the best tribute to what the 21st Mississippi had accomplished in establishing the true "High Tide" of the Confederacy by writing with admiration how he believed that "Colonel Humphreys' 21st Mississippi the only regiment which succeeded in crossing Plum Run" on the bloody July 2nd.[527] Barely escaping alive after having two horses shot from under him and with nine bullets "through his cloak," Colonel Humphreys had orchestrated one of the most brilliant offensive performances of the Civil War.[528]

On this single afternoon in hell, Lee "had staked everything—his splendid army, the fate of Richmond, and perhaps even the Confederacy itself—on destroying the Federal army."[529] And that best chance for winning the war's most decisive battle had come and gone, slipping away forever before the sunrise of July 3, after the Mississippi Brigade's attack had been thwarted.[530] The great opportunity to win it all would never come again for either the Army of Northern Virginia or the Confederacy, after Lee and his generals had their worst day. Perhaps Porter Alexander said it best, although in a private note to his father which never saw light in his official writings: "Never, never, never did Gen. Lee himself bollox a fight as he did this."[531]

Indeed, in the words of historian Stephen W. Sears about why the Army of Northern Virginia had failed in the battle: "George G. Meade, unexpectedly and against the odds, thoroughly outgeneraled Robert E. Lee at Gettysburg."[532] But while the army's commander and his top lieutenants had been badly outgeneraled on July 2, the Mississippi Brigade had not been outfought by any unit on either side. And no one had outgeneraled Barksdale on his finest day. But in the end, no amount of heroics, successes, or gains reaped by Barksdale and his men, not even their "dash and fanatical desperation," could compensate for the glaring leadership failures at the highest levels in the art of war.[533] Nevertheless, and against the odds, and despite the handicaps and obstacles to success set in place by their own leadership, Barksdale and Humphreys and their crack troops had come tantalizingly close to achieving decisive results.

— 12 —

When Glory Was Out of Date

ONCE AGAIN, CONFEDERATE valor had been in vain, only resulting in unprecedented slaughter. During the three days of fighting at Gettysburg, Lee lost 22,625 men, including 4,536 dead on the field. Meade's losses were about the same. The desperate attempt to win it all on northern soil was the most costly of all of Lee's campaigns.[534] The small town of Gettysburg was transformed into a sea of misery and suffering for more than 20,000 wounded from both sides, after the bloodiest battle in North American history.[535]

One Gettysburg civilian, appalled by the war's horrors and the long trenches of mass graves, wrote how Lee's Confederates had "boasted that in coming into [Pennsylvania] they had got back into the Union—many who thus boasted occupied those trenches. Their boasting had met a fearful verification." In the words of Private McNeily, 21st Mississippi, General Lee "had tempted fate in former campaigns and won victories with even greater inferiority of numbers than at Gettysburg," but the odds, like a cruel trick played by the Gods of war, had finally caught up with him in Pennsylvania.

During the long, weary retreat back through the rain and mud to Virginia, Private McNeily described how the surviving Mississippians were struck with a dual body-blow by the realization of two major setbacks in both the eastern and western theaters. He wrote, "We moved back into Virginia, our depression added to by the doleful news of the capture of Vicksburg. Such was the ill-starred ending of the campaign on which we had entered with utmost confidence and highest hopes."[536]

Like the stoic captain faithfully going down with his ship to disappear forever into oblivion, Barksdale's painful ordeal finally came to a merciful end within 24 hours of his brigade's all-out effort to win the war. Because of the confused fighting in the smoke-filled thickets and the blinding fog of battle, Barksdale had been left behind during the bloody repulse at Plum Run, after his three decimated regiments were finally driven back. Private Joseph Charles Lloyd, 13th Mississippi, shot in an arm that was soon amputated, had slipped rearward to escape from the piles of bodies along the red stained waters of Plum Run, and never forgot the sight of "General Barksdale lying upon the ground alone, weak and helpless, but uncomplaining and resigned to his fate."[537]

One captured Mississippian informed a Yankee officer, Lieutenant George G. Benedict of the 12th Vermont Volunteer Infantry, First Corps, that his revered commander now lay badly wounded in the underbrush. He emphasized how Barksdale needed immediate medical attention before it was too late. The compassionate commander in blue, who might have seen Barksdale's heroics while leading the attack, detailed three privates to search for the former United States Congressman in gray.

Private David Parker, 14th Vermont, one of the search party, described Barksdale's anguished ordeal to the Mississippian's brother, Ethelbert C. Barksdale: "We searched among the dead and wounded until about 11[:00] at night when we found him. He was suffering from bleeding inwardly and suffering very much. I immediately sat on the ground, took his head in my lap and gave him coffee that I had in my canteen from a spoon, as he could swallow but a small amount at a time. His mind was clear. He stated who he was and first told us that we could not carry him into our lines without a stretcher and (needed) more help as he weighed 240 pounds. Two men went for help. He commenced by telling me that he was dying; that he was leaving a good and loving wife and two sons [and said] 'Oh my wife, it will be hard for her. Tell her that my last words were words of love to her. But my boys! Oh, it seems that I cannot leave them. Their loss they will not fully comprehend. They need a father. Many times have I thought and planned for their future, and, oh, I loved them, so to leave them is the hardest struggle I ever knew. But tell them all that I died like a brave man, that I led my men fearlessly in the fight . . . tell them all, all my friends, wife and children. I do not regret giving my life in a cause that I believe to be right, but one thing I do regret is that I could not have lived to have done more for the cause. Oh, that I might again lead my men, but tell them that I die content that my last day's work was well done. I feel that I am most gone. May God ever watch over and take care of my dear wife and, oh, my boys, may God be a father to them. Tell them to be good men and brave, always defend the right.' He became unconscious talking of his family. We carried him on the hill to the left of Cemetery Hill. He breathed his last about daylight or a little before."[538]

Henry Stevens Willey of the 16th Vermont described the sad sight of the blood-stained General Barksdale, in intense pain, as he was taken rearward: "Another stretcher crew came along near me [and] Its occupant was saying, 'O God, boys, how much further is it to the hospital?' The answer was 'Only a little way, General.' Next day I learned that the Confederate General Barksdale was desperately wounded . . . ."[539]

At the busy Second Corps hospital located at the whitewashed Jacob Hummelbaugh House, Barksdale described his role during the attack, including the last-ditch offensive effort that had surged east of Plum Run, to Private Parker, who had assisted in carrying the semi-conscious general to the field infirmary. Barksdale stated: "I was wounded by a rifle ball in my left limb above the knee but I led my men. Next I was wounded by having my left foot off or nearly off near the ankle by a cannon ball. Though I was weak from loss of blood still I rode my horse and led my men in the fierest [sic] of the charge that we broke the lines and drove our enemy and at the moment of success I was pierced by a ball through the brest [sic] knocked senseless from my horse and left by soldiers for dead."[540]

Ohioan Lieutenant Homer H. Baldwin, Battery C, 5th United States Artillery, was another victor who encountered the mortally wounded Barksdale. He described how Barksdale "of Mis. was wounded in front of our battery. I gave him brandy and water then I got a surgeon and fixed him up as comfortably as possible." Numerous accounts revealed Barksdale's last words as filled with high-spirited defiance, despite enduring the agony of mortal wounds. Private William Henry Hill, 13th Mississippi, recorded in his diary of Barksdale's dying words to tell his family that he fought to the last and bravely "died at his post." And Captain Lamar, McLaws' aide-de-camp, stated that the general's final words were "I am killed. Tell my wife and children I died fighting at my post"—the ultimate honor and dignity to a man like Barksdale.[541] Displaying his characteristic spunkiness, Barksdale was also reported to have spoken his final words to a Union surgeon: "Tell my wife I am shot, but we fought like hell." Indeed, perhaps this last statement best summarized the Mississippi Brigade's never-say-die qualities on July 2.[542] In the end, Barksdale felt a certain serenity and peace because he had sacrificed himself and done all that was humanly possible to save the life of his "splendid republic," as he described the Confederacy, in leading one of the most devastating assaults of the Civil War.[543]

Indeed, even when within the Federal lines and at his captor's mercy, the dying Barksdale lost none of his feisty fighting spirit. Assistant Surgeon Alfred T. Hamilton, 148th Pennsylvania Volunteer Infantry, described the dying Mississippian's optimism for eventual victory at Gettysburg on July 3, when "Old Barks" declared to his captors, even though "He was shot through the left breast; & the left leg was broken by two missiles. He asked whether I considered his wounds necessarily mortal. I told him I did. He stated that he desired peace, but only on terms that would recognize the Confederacy [and] he asked about our strength and was answered that heavy reinforcements are coming. He said that Lee would show us a trick before morning, that before we knew it Ewell would be thundering in our rear."[544]

A kind-hearted Union soldier, musician Robert A. Cassidy, 148th Pennsylvania Volunteer Infantry, served as a medical assistant in the Second Corps hospital, and he became Barksdale's guardian angel. In a sad May 6, 1865 letter to his widow, Narcissa Saunders Barksdale, who would have otherwise never known the exact details of her husband's last moments in a life that had held such bountiful promise and potential: "Gen. Barksdale—leading his command in a desperate charge on our left centre—fell mortally wounded within less than a hundred yards of our lines. As soon as the . . . firing ceased, the General was conveyed, as tenderly as circumstances would permit, from the field. Here I found him just after dark, while moving around in company with [Surgeon Hamilton] I came upon the General accidently. Kneeling at his side, I asked him if he desired any assistance. He informed me that he was very thirsty, and I endeavored to give him water from the canteen but was unable to do so in consequence of his recumbent position, and the pain from his wounds was so great as not to admit of his being raised upright [so] taking my spoon from my haversack filled it several times and the General drank the water with feverish avidity [then Assistant Surgeon Hamilton] informed him in kind but confident terms that [his wounds] were mortal, and that the best that could be done was to render him as comfortable as possible; and to this end began to administer morphine as a means of assuaging the pain."[545]

Musician Cassidy saw what he thought were only two severe wounds: "one in the left breast, produced I should think by a grape-shot, as it was too large to have been made by a musket-ball (unless two closely impacted), and one through the left leg, about mid-way between the ankle and knee. The first was sufficient in itself to have produced death, as the lung was cut and at every inhalation the blood was forced copiously—with a sputtering noise—from the wound. This fact rendered respiration difficult and exceedingly painful. The wound through the leg seemed to have produced a fracture which caused considerable pain, and was evidently the work of a minie-ball."[546]

Covered with blood and broken in body, but not in spirit, Barksdale was most fortunate to have been taken to a makeshift Second Corps field hospital, where the fair-minded Union surgeon, Hamilton, who dedicated his efforts to cases of greatest need rather than the color of uniform, provided the kind gift and blessing of morphine to a severely-suffering Mississippi general instead of nearby wounded Yankees, including soldiers from his home state.

Continuing his kind May 6, 1865 letter to Barksdale's wife, Cassidy described the tragic end of the man who almost won the battle of Gettysburg for the Army of Northern Virginia: "Noticing that his strength was failing rapidly, I . . . continued to administer water; dissolved morphine and diluted liquor alternately until I saw that he was very near the edge of the dark river. I reminded him that he had but a few moments to live and that he would soon stand in the presence of the final judge. I am not certain that he made any direct reply although incoherent utterances escaped him frequently until the last."[547]

Lapsing in and out of consciousness, the forty-two-year-old Barksdale finally breathed his last on the night of July 2, far from his Columbus, Mississippi, home and family and his Magnolia State men, who had fought with their hearts and died in unprecedented numbers. Here, beside the dusty Taneytown Road, Barksdale died among the Yankees whom he had fought so tenaciously.

Even though Barksdale was treated with kindness by the Federals when alive, such was not the case after he died. He was hurriedly stripped of valuables "by despicable vultures who make robbing the dead a business," penned musician Cassidy. One Pennsylvania private cut off some of the gold braid on Barksdale's coat sleeve for a trophy. In his letter, Cassidy described how other "trophy hunters cut from his fatigue-jacket the insignia of rank, and all the buttons but one."[548]

Therefore, at 8:00 AM on July 3 and as if knowing that Lee had thought so highly of Barksdale, who had been destined for a major gen-

eral's rank had he survived the slaughter at Gettysburg, General Meade
was able to boast with a heightened sense of confidence, if not relief, by
telegram to General Henry W. Halleck, "General Barksdale's (Mississippi) dead body is within our lines." And General Abner Doubleday
bragged "among the circumstances worthy of mention which occurred
on the third day was the death of the rebel General Barksdale [whose]
dying speech and last message for his family, together with the valuables
about his person, were intrusted by him to Lieutenant-Colonel [C.E.] Liv-
ingston." Commanding the Fifth Corps, General George Sykes wrote on
July 5 how "I have the honor to send herewith a sword and flag captured
from the enemy [and] I believe the sword to have been taken from the
body of rebel General Barksdale on the field of battle."

By way of tribute to one of the South's most hard-fighting generals,
a good many Federals, officers of all ranks and enlisted men, made special
note of Barksdale's demise, almost as if his death itself had somehow
symbolized Southern defeat at Gettysburg and heralded the Confederacy's own demise, which was in fact the case. General Hancock specifically noted in his battle report that "Brigadier-General Barksdale, of the
rebel service, was left on the field, mortally wounded." And Captain
Josiah C. Fuller, 32nd Massachusetts Volunteer Infantry, scribbled with
some relief in a July 4, 1863 letter how, "We gave the rebs a severe drub-
bing [and] Genl. Barksdale (Reb) is dead."[549]

Without the men of his brigade realizing as much, the Mississippi
general was buried in the yard of the Jacob Hummelbaugh House under
a small carved piece of wood that stood atop the shallow grave, which
paid a brief, final tribute to the man who had come so close to winning
it all for the Confederacy on a single afternoon:

> Brigadier General Barksdale of Mississippi McLaw's
> division, Longstreet's Corps Died on the morning of
> 3rd July, 1863 Eight years a representative in United
> States Congress. Shot through the left breast, and
> left leg broken below the knee.[550]

Saddened by the most severe loss ever suffered by the Mississippi
Brigade (more than 800 officers and men), Private Dinkins lamented how
"we drop a tear to the memory of heroic General William Barksdale,
brave, patriotic and kind. He was a statesman, and a hero. We saw him
in battle, on the march, and in camp. He felt a personal interest in every

man in his brigade; he was proud of his men, and never doubted them. He believed they would follow him, nor was he mistaken. He fell with his face to the foe."[551]

Barksdale remained as inspirational in death as in life, as the Mississippi Brigade's survivors learned on August 23, 1863 of his supposed dying words, which were "published to us this evening on dress parade, the first order from our new Brig. Gen. Humphreys. In it appears the last words of our late Gen. Barksdale who fell at Gettysburg, Pa. 'The Rebels are invincible. Although repulsed today will be victorious to-morrow'."[552]

Hearing of his friend's death, President Davis described Barksdale to the beleaguered people of the Southern nation as a "Hero who fell at the head of a Brigade of Heroes." On a dreary, dank January in 1867, more than three and a half years after he was killed north of the Mason-Dixon Line, Barksdale's body was retrieved from a temporary resting place in South Carolina and brought back to his beloved Mississippi by Captain Harris Barksdale, who had served faithfully beside his uncle's side during the terrible storm of Gettysburg. Here, at the Greenwood Cemetery in the state capital of Jackson, Barksdale at long last found a permanent home in Mississippi soil in the Barksdale family's burial plot. Today, only the most modest of stone headstones now mark the forgotten grave of the never-say-die general, who almost won it all for the Confederacy at Gettysburg. Most appropriate, the Mississippi general's headstone was no different than that of a humble Mississippi Brigade private, as Barksdale would have most desired in true egalitarian fashion.

As for the other losses in Barksdale's Brigade, they were severe. In his diary, Private Moore, 17th Mississippi, summarized the Mississippi Brigade's dramatic achievements that had brought the Confederacy close to decisive victory: "Had a desperate encounter with the enemy this evening for 2 hours. Drove them before us for 1 mile but were forced to fall back for lack of support. Captured several batteries & stand of colors. Our loss was heavy, in the [17th Mississippi] 223 killed & wounded, in our Co., 29. Several of them were my dear friends. Every man acted the hero. Miss. has lost many of her best & bravest sons. How thankful should all be to God who have escaped. OH! the horrors of war."[553]

In terms of overall percentage, the 17th Mississippi lost more heavily than any other Mississippi Brigade regiment, losing 210 soldiers with 30 killed, 172 wounded, and 8 missing out of about 450 men. But these were only officially listed losses and incomplete totals. Private William Meshack Abernathy was more correct when he wrote of the awful truth of the terrible toll on Colonel Holder's regiment: "Nearly two-thirds of the regiment had been killed or wounded, but they held the field . . . three sets of brothers, two each, had been mortally wounded—the Ouslers, the Blackburns and the Kankades . . . " Indeed, the 17th Mississippi actually lost at least 64 killed, 108 wounded, and 99 missing, a total of 271. The 64 17th Mississippi men killed on the field was the highest number, with the 13th Mississippi second with 39 killed, followed by the 21st Mississippi with 22 killed, and 18th Mississippi with 20. Of the more than 550 listed as wounded in the brigade, another 63 soldiers died of their wounds. The brigade suffered 178 missing or captured, among whom were doubtless additional wounded. When the brigade joined the army's general retreat from Gettysburg they were forced to leave 224 seriously wounded behind, 50 of whom later died of their injuries.

Afterward, no one was more embittered by the attack's repulse and missed opportunities than Colonel Humphreys, who had accomplished as much as anyone in attempting to secure decisive victory. In an angry letter, he described the lack of support at the most critical moment on July 2: "I did not know, until Wilcox himself told me two days after the charge that he was engaged at all that day. I know that Wilcox was not in advance of Barksdale or myself—nor in our rear on that occasion . . . Wofford's Brigade was not driven back . . . Wofford must have gone back by orders from some superior authority."[554]

An embittered Private McNeily analyzed how "the exigencies of battle forced Longstreet to lead Wofford to the support of Kershaw and Semmes; thus depriving Barksdale's penetration through the enemy's line of the driving power that would have reached its vitals." Indeed, despite a host of disadvantages and handicaps, the Mississippi Brigade's achievements were some of the most remarkable of the entire conflict.[555]

Hardly before the firing had ceased on that bloody July 2, the trusty adjutant of the 17th Mississippi, Lieutenant John Ansley, informed Private James W. Duke that his brother Private Archibald Y. Duke was yet alive on the field of slaughter, but badly wounded. Jim described the personal torment of his anxious search in the haunted darkness: "I hunted until I found him [and] His first words to me were, 'Thank God! My prayers are answered. I have asked [God] to take me in place of you, as I am prepared and you are not. That is the first time that I ever weakened.

I promised him there that I would live a better life in the future."[556] Suffering a fate like so many of his comrades with comparable wounds, young Archy Duke survived his leg's amputation, but then gangrene took his life.[557]

In the tortured days after the unprecedented bloodletting at Gettysburg, scores of Mississippi soldiers died in field hospitals, houses, barns, stables, and in fence corners and under trees that offered too little shade in the scorching heat.[558] Private Edgar Gideon Baker was one such unfortunate young man, who paid the ultimate price. In a neat hand, Chaplain Owen Burton Owen, 17th Mississippi, penned a sad note to the father, Luman Baker, about the loss of his son, thirty-year-old Private Edgar. Baker was a proud member of the Hurricane Rifles, 21st Mississippi. The young man had been an adventurous soul early smitten with wanderlust that had caused him to depart his native homeland in search for a better future far away from the family's Greene County, New York, farm. Chaplain Owen wrote: "Your son Edgar G. Baker, Company E, 21st Mississippi Regt., . . . was wounded through the lungs on the 2nd of July, and died July 11th . . . I was with him much, after he was wounded, and conversed freely with him in regard to the future and I believe he is gone to rest. One of the evidences of his having been converted to my mind was this, that he desired to live that he might glorify God by going good, and another was his sorrow for having done wrong. He spoke of having probably ridiculed his sisters on account of their religion, and very sorry that he ever did it. . . . The death of your son will be sad news to you and your family, but I trust our Blessed Redeemer will give you all grace for this sad bereavement . . . ."[559]

Only days before he filled a shallow grave at Gettysburg, Private Nimrod Newton Nash, of Company I, 13th Mississippi, penned his last letter to his beloved wife Mollie. The sensitive, introspective private offered a final hope and prayer that went unanswered for him and so many of his comrades: "Give my love to all, and may the good Lord bring this unholy war to a speedy end, and may we all be permitted to return to loved [ones] at home is the daily prayer of your devoted Newton."[560]

Epilogue

NEVER AGAIN WOULD the Confederacy come closer to achieving nationhood than on the afternoon of July 2, 1863 with Barksdale's Charge.
Despite smashing through Meade's left-center, nearly splitting the Army
of the Potomac in two and reaching the strategic objective of Cemetery
Ridge, Barksdale's effort was fated to be forgotten in the years following
the war. In its stead, "Pickett's Charge" rose up like a great phoenix to
take its place as the battle's decisive turning point. Generations of American writers, journalists, and myth-makers created endless layers of ro-
manticism and glorification, combined with a powerful "Lost Cause"
mystique, to transform the third day of the battle, when Pickett took part,
into the single most decisive moment of Gettysburg.

This perspective, of course, does not stand up to scrutiny. The second
day of Gettysburg, July 2, was when the Army of the Potomac was truly
on the ropes. Barksdale's men persisted longer and advanced farther than
other Confederate brigades on that fateful day; however other units on
the Confederate right had helped to open the way for its success. To Barksdale's right the gallant brigades of Hood's Division and the rest of Mc-
Laws' men had battled mightily all afternoon, drawing Union reinforcements upon them.

To Barksdale's left, three brigades of Richard Anderson's Division
had advanced, having an easier approach to the Emmitsburg Road than
did Barksdale, but once nearing Cemetery Ridge they had been repelled
with severe loss. Either due to A.P. Hill's negligence, or Anderson's, none
of the Third Corps brigades were in the slightest supported by other
troops, so when Hancock's men, supported by batteries of Hunt's Re-

serve Artillery, beat them back there was no other recourse than retreat.
Of Anderson's remaining two brigades, Carnot Posey's stopped short of
the Emmitsburg Road. Another, under William Mahone, sat stubbornly
idle through the entire battle, despite repeated entreaties for it to advance. Longstreet had the sense to call back his men when he saw that
the odds were too heavily against them in that twilight. He wrote afterward: "While Meade's lines were growing my men were dropping; we
had no others to call to their aid, and the weight against us was too
heavy to carry." He added, more bitterly, "No other part of our army
had engaged!"[561]

Although the 21st Mississippi's B.G. Humphreys, for one, protested
the order to give up his gains, Longstreet at least kept control of his men.
A.P. Hill had no such thought, so his three brigades that entered the battle
suffered as many prisoners taken—once Federal reinforcements began to
pile in—as Longstreet's eight brigades put together.

Rans Wright of Anderson's Division afterward claimed to have conquered Cemetery Ridge, if only for a few minutes. However, his description of the terrain, including a rocky gorge, bear no resemblance to the
reality of the gentle slope in his sector. Historian Edwin Coddington has
said, "General Wright . . . maintained that his men after penetrating the
Second Corps line finally seized the top of Cemetery Ridge. His state-
ments, however, both in his report and in a letter to his wife written five
days after the battle are literally beyond belief, and none of the Union
accounts in any way supported his claim of having broken through the
main line."[562]

After darkness had fallen and Longstreet's offensive had died down,
Ewell's Second Corps finally launched attacks against the Union right.
Three brigades stormed Culp's Hill, which had been denuded of Union
troops—dispatched to resist Longstreet—so that the Confederates were
able to claim some unoccupied works. They were pushed out the following morning once Slocum's Corps returned to its position after the alarm.

Jubal Early launched two brigades directly against Cemetery Hill,
just south of Gettysburg, and they had excellent initial success, overrunning advanced lines of the woebegone Federal Eleventh Corps, and seiz-
ing two full batteries on the summit. But then the division to their right,
Robert Rodes', declined to attack. The Third Corps division on Rodes'
right also failed to move. Early had been prepared to throw his third
brigade, under John Gordon, into support of his assault, but after seeing
that his men were fighting alone against a growing concentration of

Union reinforcements, he simply withdrew them down the hill.

And so ended the second day of Gettysburg, even as the Mississippi Brigade's dead and wounded, including Barksdale himself, still littered a path, under the moonlight, from Seminary Ridge to Cemetery Ridge—a full mile of carnage—marking the true "High Water Mark" of the Confederacy.

The next day, July 3, much to Longstreet's chagrin, Robert E. Lee resolved to attack again. The plan resulted from the curious premise that what could not be achieved by eleven fresh Confederate brigades on Day 2 could now be achieved by only three fresh ones—Pickett's—accompanied by six brigades from Hill's Corps that had been severely damaged on the battle's first day. And this time, instead of achieving surprise, or a semblance of one, the entire Army of the Potomac would be waiting for them on their ridge, as George Pickett, Johnson Pettigrew, and Isaac Trimble crossed nearly a mile of open ground to meet them.

Seldom in the annals of military history has there been a more spectacular display of gallantry than when "Pickett's Charge" attempted to retrieve the fortunes of the Army of Northern Virginia. In a veritable amphitheater, with both sides looking on, they crossed the open field under bright sunlight in the face of intense fire—first artillery, then musketry. The left flank of the assault line was crushed almost immediately; enfilade fire from infantry and artillery on the right funneled the attackers toward the center. But Pickett's men refused to stop and actually pierced the Union center on Cemetery Ridge. But by then the few survivors were all alone and veritably swallowed by the Union response rushing in on them from all sides. They could only fall to Union fire, try to flee, or be taken prisoner, as there were no other Confederate formations to support their breakthrough.

Pickett's men did exeedingly well, though in a last sort of forlorn hope for victory. In truth they never stood a chance. Longstreet had hardly been able to bring himself to sanction the assault, while Lee afterward claimed a curious variation of honor by arriving on the scene afterward, telling the broken debris of the Virginia division that it was "all my fault." Yes, it may have been.

The climax of the battle had come the day before, which was the day that Pickett's Division should have gone in had it been arranged to arrive at the battle earlier. If it had been able to reinforce Barksdale's Brigade when it had created an open avenue to Cemetery Ridge, was fighting on the verge of the very crest, and when one more Rebel push would have toppled the entire Potomac Army, that's when gallants like Armistead, Kemper and Garnett would have gone down in history as victors rather than tragic footnotes, as casualties.

Naturally Union writers afterward much preferred to write about Pickett's Charge, which they crushed, rather than Barksdale's Charge, which made them retreat, sometimes in panic, for a mile and then barely hang on by a thread. Confederate writers were mysteriously also drawn to the valor of the Virginians rather than being forced to dwell on the lost opportunities and disappointments of Gettysburg's tumultuous second day.

Ironically, after the war, even Mississippi Confederate veterans, who had embraced the "Lost Cause" mythology, contributed to the obscurity of Barksdale's Charge by focusing on the efforts of Mississippi regiments in "Pickett's Charge." One orator at the dedication of a monument in Carroll County, Mississippi, to former Magnolia State soldiers in 1905, went so far as to declare that "Pickett's Virginians were made up largely of Mississippians [General Joseph R. Davis' brigade], a fact which the historians and poets seem often to overlook."[563] Incredibly, in the postwar period, Mississippians even entered the heated postwar controversy about "Pickett's Charge" by emphasizing in no uncertain terms how Davis' troops "went farthest up those fatal heights and broke the enemy's line of defense at the only point it carried in the charge."[564] Clearly, even in Mississippi of all places, the romantic lore, enduring legend, and universal appeal of "Pickett's Charge" obscured the importance of Barksdale's Charge in almost winning the most important battle of the war.

In the words of one fortunate survivor of the battle, Private McNeily of the 21st Mississippi, in regard to the Mississippi Brigade's unparalleled performance, Barksdale's success was achieved despite the disadvantages "of its wholly isolated attack upon the enemy's key point, it went far beyond all . . . its course was kept free from the fatal chain of error, miscalculation, and inopportunity that makes Gettysburg the worst wrought out of all Lee's battles. In no other was the 'team work' so poor. From all the counts in the indictment of ineptitude and error, Barksdale's brigade is free—it neither failed nor faltered, boggled or wobbled. It alone did all that was required of it, and more."[565]

From the west, even General Hood, although not from Mississippi, and who attempted in vain to capture Little Round Top on that bloody July 2, grew disenchanted with the excessive promotion of the Virginians' exploits at Gettysburg at the Mississippians' expense. After the war Hood deeply lamented how "no shaft marks the spot where [Barksdale fell because] Federal authorities refused to allow the point they reached to be designated by appropriate stones, but that gallant charge is written upon the hearts of his countrymen, and will be told in song and story as long as gallant deeds and heroism are virtues."[566]

Most revealing, no one in the Army of the Potomac was more keenly aware of how July 2 was actually the most crucial day at Gettysburg, and how close his army had come to defeat, than General Meade himself. In his official report, Meade concluded how Sickles' unauthorized advance to the Peach Orchard was "an error which nearly proved fatal in the battle."[567] Captain John Bigelow concluded that the Mississippi Brigade was presented with the "great opportunity for entering the lines of the Army of the Potomac, offered to them." The Peach Orchard salient's dramatic collapse just "barely escaped bringing disaster to the Army," said the artilleryman. "The way was open for Barksdale's Confederate Brigade . . . to enter, unopposed, our lines between Little Round Top and the left of the Second Corps."[569] Among Longstreet's various reflections on the battle was a singular explanation of why his attack on July 2 had failed. In regard to the splendid effort of his brigades, Longstreet "attributed their failure chiefly to Hood's wound and Barksdale's death."[570] Indeed, the fall of Barksdale explained in part why the most successful charge at Gettysburg was ultimately repulsed.[571]

On July 4, 1863, Lee's army began to retreat from Pennsylvania, and on that same day the mighty Confederate fortress on the Mississippi River, Vicksburg, surrendered. With a battle nearly won by Mississippi troops in the east ending in failure, simultaneous with the fall of the strategic citadel in Mississippi itself, the Confederacy's prospects had begun to look dim. However, there would still be nearly two more years of fighting. The Northern army had been crippled as much by Gettysburg as the Southern one, needing time to recover, and after which both sides would continue to grapple until the irrefutable logic of demographic and industrial arithmetic finally drove Dixie fully down.

On the 4th of July, 1863, while comrades, friends, neighbors, and relatives lay dead in the killing fields around the Peach Orchard, the Emmitsburg Road, Plum Run, and just below Cemetery Ridge's crest, where Barksdale and his men had once vividly envisioned red battle-flags flying in triumph, Lee's bone-weary survivors, traumatized and numbed by Gettysburg's surreal horrors, trudged south through a pelting rain that seemingly mocked the Confederates' lost opportunities. With thoughts yet consumed by the misery of defeat and the searing pain of having lost so many comrades, the surviving Mississippi boys marched through the clinging mud and toward a tragic one-way destination and a sorrowful fate that could no longer be denied. Up ahead lay what was now inevitable: the ultimate death of the Confederacy's experiment in nationhood.

Meanwhile, on hundreds of middle-class farms across Mississippi, the neat rows of corn, with ears covered in thick, tasseled tops, was high and luxuriant in the fields. The long-awaited harvest, now drawing near, promised to be a good one. But many of the young men and boys who had once plowed the farms of the Magnolia State now lay in final resting places in the equally fertile soil of Adams County, Pennsylvania. Their General, William Barksdale, was also now in the ground. But the weary survivors of one of the most devastating charges of the Civil War managed to keep on going, while maintaining hope in the future, because they embraced a single consolation among the encroaching clouds of despair: that they had almost won it all at Gettysburg and brought Lee's army, the hard-pressed Confederacy, and the Southern people closer to decisive victory than ever before. It could still not be known for certain that, despite Barksdale's and the Mississippi Brigade's best efforts on July 2, 1863, they would never be marching on Washington, D.C., as so vividly envisioned and almost realized at the zenith of Barksdale's Charge.

Notes

1. Jeffry D. Wert, *A Glorious Army, Robert E. Lee's Triumph, 1862–1863* (New York: Simon and Schuster, 2011), pp. xi, 12, 277–295.
2. Robert Stiles, *Four Years Under Marse Robert* (Marietta, GA: R. Bemis Publishing Company, 1995), p. 26; Bradley M. Gottfried, *Brigades of Gettysburg, The Union and Confederate Brigades at the Battle of Gettysburg* (New York: Skyhorse Publishing, 2012), p. 410; Clint Johnson, Civil War Blunders, Winston-Salem: John F. Blair Publishers, 1997), pp. 40–45; Ezekiel Armstrong Diary, Mississippi Department Archives and History, Jackson, MS.
3. Stiles, *Four Years Under Marse Robert*, pp. 64–65.
4. Joseph A. Miller Diary, Fredericksburg and Spotsylvania National Military Parks, Fredericksburg, VA; Compiled Military Service Records of Confederate Soldiers Who Served from the State of Mississippi, National Archives, Washington, D.C.
5. Pinkney M. Lewis to family, May 13. 1864 icollector.com live auction, item no. 3098.
6. Stiles, *Four Years Under Marse Robert*, pp. 98, 129; CMSR, NA; John K. Bettersworth, *YourMississippi* (Austin: Steck-Vaughn Company, 1975), pp. 2–14.
7. Bettersworth, *Your Mississippi*, pp. 206–217; Stephen W. Sears, *Gettysburg* (New York: Houghton Mifflin Company, 2004), pp. 2, 15; Carl Sandburg, *Abraham Lincoln, The War Years, 1861–1864* (3 vols: New York: Dell Publishing Company, 1960), vol. 2, pp. 287–288.
8. William C. Nelson Collection, Special Collections, University of Mississippi, Jackson, Mississippi.
9. Ibid.
10. CMSR, NA; William C. Davis, *The Man And His Hour: A Biography* (New York: HarperCollins, Publishers, 1992), pp.154–159; Mark Mayo Boatner, *The Civil War Dictionary* (New York: David McKay Company, 1959) pp. 43–44; Humphreys, General Barksdale Biographical Sketch, UNL; Byron Farwell, *Ball's Bluff: A Small Battle and Its Long Shadow* (McLean: EPM Publications, Inc.,

261

1990), pp. 32–33; Harold A. Cross, *They Sleep Beneath the Mockingbird: Mississippi Burial Sites and Biographies of Confederate Generals, Journal of Confederate History Series*, Vol. XII (Murfreesboro, TN: Southern Heritage Press, 1994), pp. 11–15; *Stiles, Four Years Under Marse Robert,* p. 129; Dinkins, *1861–1865, By An Old Johnnie*, p. 86; Grady McWhiney and Perry D. Jamieson, *Attack and Die: Civil War Military Tactics and the Southern Heritage* (Tuscaloosa: University of Alabama Press, 1990), pp. xiii; Glenn Tucker, *High Tide At Gettysburg* (Dayton, Ohio: Morningside Bookshop, 1983), p. 275; Bobby Roberts and Carl Moneyhon, *Portraits of Conflict: A Photographic History of Mississippi in the Civil War* (Fayetteville: The University of Arkansas Press, 1993), p. 20.

11. William C. Davis, *Jefferson Davis: The Man and His Hour, A Biography* (New York: HarperPerennial, 1992), p. 159.

12. Ibid; CMSR, NA; Farwell, *Ball's Bluff*, pp. 32–33, 130; Boatner, *The Civil War Dictionary*, pp. 43–44; Cross, *They Sleep Beneath the Mockingbird*, pp. 11–15, 20–21; Stiles, *Four Years Under Marse Robert*, p. 95; Humphreys, *General Barksdale Biographical Sketch*, UNL; *Campfires and Battlefields: A Pictorial Narrative of the Civil War* (New York: The Civil War Press, 1967), p. 259; Clifford Dowdey, *Death of a Nation, The Story of Lee And His Men at Gettysburg* (New York: Knopf Publishers, 1958), pp. 217–218; Bell Irvin Wiley, *Embattled Confederates: An Illustrated History of Southerners at War* (New York: Harper & Row, 1964), p. 7; Tucker, *HighTide at Gettysburg*, p. 275; Douglas Southall Freeman, *Lee's Lieutenants: Cedar Mountain to Chancellorsville* (3 vols., New York: Charles Scribner's Sons, 1971), vol. 2, p. 332; Gottfried, *Brigades of Gettysburg*, p. 410; Roberts and Moneyhon, *Portraits of Conflict*, p. 46.

13. Moore, *A Life for the Confederacy*, p. 114; McNeily, *Barksdale's Mississippi Brigade at Gettysburg*, p. 236.

14. Mississippians in the Confederate Army, website, internet

15. Joseph A. Miller Diary, Fredericksburg and Spotsylvania National Military Park, Fredericksburg, VA.

16. CMSR, NA; Humphreys, *General Barksdale Biographical Sketch*, UNL; Gottfried, *Brigades of Gettysburg*, p. 410.

17. Ezekiel Pickens Miller Diary, Fredericksburg and Spotsylvania National Military Park, Fredericksburg, VA; CMSR, NA; Gottfried, *Brigades at Gettysburg*, p. 410; Wert, *A Glorious Army*, pp. xi, 277–295.

18. John F. Henley, "Drove the Enemy Back," Fredericksburg and Spotsylvania National Military Park, Fredericksburg, VA.

19. Ibid; CMSR, NA.

20. CMSR, NA.

21. Ibid; Ezekiel Pickens Miller and Joseph A. Miller Diaries, Fredericksburg and Spotsylvania National Military Park, Fredericksburg, VA.

22. Joseph A. Miller Diary, FSNMP.

23. Ibid.

24. CMSR, NA.

25. Ibid; Joseph A. Miller Diary, FSNMP.

26. Joseph A. Miller Diary, FSNMP.

27. CMSR, NA; Frank Allen Dennis, editor, *Kemper County Rebel: The Civil War Diary of Robert Masten Holmes, C.S.A.* (Jackson, MS: University and College Press of Mississippi, 1973), pp. xi, 3–5; Robert K. Krick, *Lee's Colonels: A Biographical Register of the Field Officers of the Army of Northern Virginia* (Dayton, Ohio: Morningside Bookshop, 1992), p. 85; Shelby Foote, *The Civil War, A Narrative: Fredericksburg to Meridian*, vol. 2 (3 vols., New York: Random House, 1963), p. 26; Bettersworth, *Your Mississippi*, pp. 214.

28. Thurman Early Hendricks Memoir, Mississippi Department of Archives and History, Jackson, MS; CMSR, NA.

29. Ibid; CMSR, NA; John F. Henley undated newspaper articles from the *Aberdeen Examiner*, Mississippi, Fredericksburg and Spotsylvania National Military Park.

30. Wilbur Sturtevant Nye, *Here Come The Rebels!* (Dayton: Morningside Bookshop: 1988), p. 21; McWhiney, *Cracker Culture*, p. xxxii; Mississippians in the Confederate Army, website.

31. Nye, *Here Come The Rebels!*, p. 21.

32. Ibid.

33. Ibid.

34. Henley, "On the Way to Gettysburg," FSNAMP.

35. Joseph A. Miller Diary, Fredericksburg and Spotsylvania National Military Park, Fredericksburg, VA; Ezekiel Armstrong, Mississippi Department Archives and History, Jackson, MS; Robert E. May, *John A. Quitman, Old South Crusader* (Baton Rouge, LA: Louisiana State University Press, 1985), pp. 84–95; Farwell, *Ball's Bluff*, p. 89; Krick, *Lee's Colonels*, pp. 34, 195; CMSR, NA; Moore, *A Life For The Confederacy*, p. 16; McNeily, "Barksdale's Mississippi Brigade at Gettysburg," *PMHS*, p. 260; Roberts and Moneyhon, *Portraitsof Conflict*, pp. 52, 68; Holder, Bowles, Limerick, Stuart and Related Families, Rootsweb, internet; Bettersworth, *Our Mississippi*, pp. 5, 10, 12; John F. Henley, "Drove the Enemy Back," "One the Way to Gettysburg," and "The Career of a Soldier," Fredericksburg and Spotsylvania National Military Park, Fredericksburg, VA; Bettersworth, *Your Mississippi*, pp. 2, 174, 176, 181.

36. Moore, *A Life For The Confederacy*, pp. 54, 66–67, 82.

37. Joseph A. Miller Diary, FSNMP.

38. Ezekiel Armstrong Diary, Mississippi Department of Archives and History, Jackson, MS.

39. Joseph A. Miller Diary, FSNMP.

40. Compiled and edited Charles Kelly Barrow and J. H. Segars and Robert B. Rosenburg, "Forgotten Confederates: An Anthology About Black Southerners," *Journal of Confederate History Series*, Volume XIV (1995), pp. 23, 117.

41. CMSR, NA; Ronald S. Coddington, *African American Faces of the Civil War: An Album* (Baltimore: The John Hopkins University Press, 2012), p. 51.

42. William Meshack Abernathy Manuscript, "'Our Mess: Southern Army Gallantry and Privations, 1861–1865," Mississippi Department of Archives and

History, Jackson, MS; CMSR, NA; Tim Newark, *Highlander, The History of the Legendary Highland Soldier* (New York: Skyhorse Press, 2009), p. 18.

43. CMSR, NA; Abernathy Manuscript, MDAH; Bettersworth, *Your Mississippi*, p. 184.

44. CMSR, NA; Davis, *Jefferson Davis*, pp. 154–159.

45. William C. Nelson to Maria, January 15, 1862; UM; Hawley, "Barksdale's Mississippi Brigade at Fredericksburg," *CWH*, p. 17.

46. William C. Nelson to James H. Nelson, October 17, 1862, UM.

47. Ezekiel Armstrong Diary, MDAH; CMSR, NA.

48. Abernathy Manuscript, MDAH.

49. CMSR; Krick, *Lee's Colonels*, pp. 77, 169; Farwell, *Ball's Bluff*, pp. 96, 134–135.

50. Dinkins, *Personal Experiences and Experiences in the Confederate Army*, p. 86.

51. Dinkins, *Personal Recollections and Experiences in the Confederate Army*, pp. vii, 17, 24–25, 27, 27–28, 73–74, 77–78.

52. Ibid., pp. 37, 49, 87-88; McNeily, "Barksdale's Mississippi Brigade at Gettysburg," *PMHS*, p. 261; CMSR; George Alphonso Gibbs, "war is . . . a dirty, bloody mess,' With a Mississippi Private in a Little Known Part Of the Battle of First Bull Run and at Ball's Bluff," *Civil War Times Illustrated*, Vol. 4, No. 1 (April 1965), pp. 42–43; Bettersworth, *Your Mississippi*, pp. 3, 13–14.

53. Dinkins, *1861–1865, By an old Johnnie*, pp. 3–4, 17, 25.

54. J.E.B. Trammell, Jackson, Mississippi, Family Papers; CMSR, NA; J.E.B. Trammell email to author, September 18, 2012; "Narrative of Berkeley Green," June 27, 1863, J.E.B. Trammel Family Papers..

55. J.E.B, Trammell Family Papers.

56. "Narrative of Berkeley Green," June 27, 1863, J.E. B. Trammell Family Papers.

57. J.E.B. Trammell Family Papers.

58. Ibid.

59. "Narrative of Berkeley Green," June 27, 1863, J.E.B. Trammell Family Papers.

60. Ibid.

61. Ibid.

62. Ibid.

63. Oscar Ewing Stuart letter to Annie E. Stuart, December 17, 1862, J.E.B. Trammell Family Papers.

64. "Narrative of Berkeley Green," June 27, 1863, J.E.B. Trammell Family Papers.

65. John A. Barksdale to Oscar J. E. Stuart, June 29, 1863, J.E.B. Trammell Family Papers; CMSR, NA.

66. J.E.B. Trammell Family Papers; CMSR, NA

67. Ibid., pp. 39, 41, 71; William Miller Owen, *In Camp And Battle With The Washington Artillery* (Dayton: Morningside, 1972) pp. 215, 231; Biographical Files of Mississippi Soldiers, Mississippi Department of History and Archives, Jackson, Mississippi; CMSR, NA.

68. Perry Lee Rainwater, editor, "The Autobiography of Benjamin Grubb Humphreys," *MississippiValley Historical Review* (September 1934), vol. 20, pp. 244–245.

69. Wert, *A Glorious Army*, p. 16; CMSR; Boatner, *The Civil War Dictionary*, pp. 417–418; Cross, *They Sleep Beneath the Mockingbird*, pp. 36–38; *Rockingham Post-Dispatch*, Richmond County, North Carolina, November 30, 1949; "History of Itta Bena (Leflore County) Mississippi," History50States.com, internet; *The Delta General*, August 2010, vol. 13, issue 8, Brig. Gen. Benjamin G. Humphreys, Mississippi Division, Sons of Confederate Veterans.

70. Cross, *They Sleep Beneath the Mockingbird*, pp. 38–39.

71. Dinkins, *1861–1865, By An Old Johnnie*, p. 34.

72. Farwell, *Ball's Bluff*, pp. 33–34, 39, 75, 96, 108, 130, 146–47; Stephen W. Sears, *To The Gates of Richmond, The Peninsula Campaign* (New York: Ticknor & Fields, 1992), p. 332; Bell I. Wiley, *The Life of Johnny Reb, The Common Soldier of the Confederacy* (Baton Rouge, Louisiana: Louisiana State University Press, 1978), p. 56; Cross, *They Sleep Beneath the Mockingbird*, p. 12; Abernathy Manuscript, MDAH; CMSR, NA; Bettersworth, *Our Mississippi*, pp. 10–11; Thomas P. Lowry, *The Story The Soldiers Wouldn't Tell* (Mechanicsburg: Stackpole Books, 1994), pp. 70–71.

73. Joseph A. Miller Diary, FSNMP.

74. John F. Henley, "Winter Quarters at Leesburg," Fredericksburg and Spotsylvania National Military Park, Fredericksburg, Virginia.

75. Guy R. Everson and Edward W. Simpson, Jr., *"Far, Far from Home," The Wartime Letters of Dick and Tally Simpson, 3rd South Carolina Volunteers* (Oxford: Oxford University Press, 1994), p. 213; Stiles, *Four Years Under Marse Robert*, pp. 139, 143; *Annals of the War*, pp. 191–201; Joseph A. Miller Diary, FSNMP; CMSR, NA; Gottfried, *Brigades of Gettysburg*, p. 410.

76. Piston, *Lee's Tarnished Lieutenant*, p. 40.

77. Ibid; Davis, *Jefferson Davis*, pp. 154–159; Gottfried, *Brigades of Gettysburg*, p. 410.

78. Wert, *A Glorious Army*, p. 65.

79. William Cowper Nelson to Maria, January 15, 1863, UM.

80. St. Clair A .Mulholland, *The Story of the 116th Regiment, Pennsylvania Infantry* (Gaithersburg: Old Soldier Books, Inc., n.d.), p. 54.

81. CMSR, NA.

82. Oscar Ewell Stuart to Ann L. Hardeman, February 20, 1862, Trammell Family Papers.

83. Ibid.

84. Nye, *Here Come The Rebels!*, pp. 6–20; Davis, *Jefferson Davis*, pp. 504–505.

85. Davis, *Jefferson Davis*, pp. 503–505.

86. Wert, *A Glorious Army*, pp. 212–213.

87. Dick Stanley, "13th Mississippi Infantry Regiment, Correspondence," August 12, 2011, internet.

88. Wert, *A Glorious Army*, pp. 213–214, 219; Nye, *Here Come The Rebels!*, pp. 6–20; Davis, *Jefferson Davis*, pp. 504–505; Henley, "On the Way to Gettysburg," FSNMP.

89. Dick Stanley, "13th Mississippi Infantry Regiment, Correspondence," August 20, 2011, internet.

90. Wert, *A Glorious Army*, p. 204; Thomas, *Robert E. Lee*, p. 289; McWhiney and Jamieson, *Attack and Die*, pp. 1–88.

91. Thomas, *Robert E. Lee*, pp. 292–293.

92. Ibid; Wert, *A Glorious Army*, p. 212.

93. Ibid., p. 223.

94. Dick Stanley, "13th Mississippi Infantry Regiment, Correspondence," September 6, 2011, internet; Gottfried, *Brigades of Gettysburg*, p. 410.

95. Wert, *A Glorious Army*, pp. 225–228; Sears, *Gettysburg*, p. 502.

96. Ken Allers, Jr., *The Fog of Gettysburg: The Myths and Mysteries of the Battle* (Naperville: Cumberland House, 2008), pp. 43–44; CMSR, NA; Wert, *A Glorious Army*, pp. 230–231.

97. Allers, *The Fog of Gettysburg*, pp. 43–44; Coddington, *The Gettysburg Campaign*, pp. 180–181; Thomas, *Robert E. Lee*, p. 292; Wert, *A Glorious Army*, pp. 230–231.

98. Dick Stanley, "13th Mississippi Infantry Regiment, Correspondence," August 28, 2011, internet.

99. Thomas, *Robert E. Lee*, p. 293.

100. Walter Harrison, *Pickett's Men, A Fragment of War History* (Baton Rouge: Louisiana State University Press, 2000), pp. 23, 103; Kathy Georg Harrison and John W. Busey, *Nothing But Glory: Pickett's Division at Gettysburg* (Gettysburg: Thomas Publications, 1993), pp. 259.

101. Dick Stanley, "13th Mississippi Infantry Regiment, Correspondence," September 6, 2011, internet.

102. Allers, *The Fog of Gettysburg*, pp. 45, 47, 58–59; Wert, *A Glorious Army*, pp, 231–232; Thomas, *Robert E. Lee*, pp. 292–294.

103. Jones, *Civil War Command and Strategy*, p. 168; Sandburg, *Abraham Lincoln: The War Years*, vol. 2, pp. 280–282, 351–354; Thomas, *Robert E. Lee*, p. 293; Wert, *A Glorious Army*, pp.232–233; Allers, *The Fog of Gettysburg*, pp.43–44.

104. Sears, *Gettysburg*, pp. 506–507; Thomas, *Robert E. Lee*, p. 293; Jones, *Civil War Command and Strategy*, p. 168.

105. Early, *Narrative of the War Between the States*, p. 269; Hunt, "The First Day at Gettysburg," in *Battles and Leaders*, Vol. III, p. 282; Wert, *A Glorious Army*, pp. 245, 250.

106. Hood, *Advance and Retreat*, p. 57; Wert, *A Glorious Army*, p. 251.

107. Gottfried, *Brigades of Gettysburg*, p. 411; Henley, "On the Way to Gettysburg," GNMP.

108. Frank Aretas Haskell, *The Battle of Gettysburg* (Boston: Houghton Mifflin Company, 1969), pp. 2–3, 59; Noah Andre Trudeau, *Gettysburg, A Testing of Courage* (New York: Harper Collins, 2002), pp. 279–282.

109. Haskell, *The Battle of Gettysburg*, pp. 2–3, 59; Trudeau, *Gettysburg*, p. 279; Sears, *Gettysburg*, pp. 501–504, 236–237; Thomas, *Robert E. Lee*, pp. 288–289, 296–297; Wert, *A Glorious Army*, pp. 247, 249.

110. Haskell, *The Battle of Gettysburg*, pp. 5–6.

111. Ibid., p. 18.

112. Ibid.

113. Ibid., pp. 2–6; Wert, *A Glorious Army*, pp. 247, 251, 257; Trudeau, *Gettysburg*, p. 279.

114. Harry W. Pfanz, *The Battle of Gettysburg*, National Park Civil War Series (Washington, D.C.: Eastern National Park and Monument Association, 1994), pp. 33–34.

115. Henley, "On the Way to Gettysburg," GNMP; Wert, *A Glorious Army*, pp. 251, 253–254; Harry W. Pfanz, *Gettysburg: The Second Day* (Chapel Hill: University of North Carolina Press, 1987), p. 82.

116. Henley, "On the Way to Gettysburg," GNMP; Wert, *A Glorious Army*, pp. 254–256; Trudeau, *Gettysburg*, pp. 297, 312, 321; James I. Robertson, Jr., *General A.P. Hill, The Story of a Confederate Warrior* (New York: Random House, 1992), pp. 8–17; Pfanz, Gettysburg, The Second Day, pp. 113, 115; Gottfried, *Brigades of Gettysburg*, p. 411.

117. Humphreys to McLaws, January 6, 1875, UNCL; Henley, "On the Way to Gettysburg," GNMP; Haskell, *The Battle of Gettysburg*, pp. 35–36; Trudeau, *Gettysburg*, pp. 292–293, 318, 321; Pfanz, *Gettysburg: The Second Day*, pp. 82, 94, 151; Gottfried, *Brigades of Gettysburg*, pp. 411, 696.

118. Trudeau, *Gettysburg*, p. 318; Wert, *A Glorious Army*, p. 257.

119. Edward Porter Alexander, *Fighting for the Confederacy* (Chapel Hill: University of North Carolina Press, 1989), pp. 236–237; Trudeau, *Gettysburg*, p. 297; Wert.

120. *Annuals of the War* (Edison: The Blue & Grey Press, 1996), p. 457; Wert, *A Glorious Army*, pp. 255–257; Trudeau, *Gettysburg*, pp. 279; 297.

121. CMSR, NA; Henley, "On the Way to Gettysburg," GNMP; Dinkins, *Personal Recollections and Experiences in the Confederate Army*, p. 42; McNeily, "Barksdale's Mississippi Brigade at Gettysburg," *PMSH*; p. 233; Trudeau, *Gettysburg*, pp. 314, 321; Earl S. Miers and Richard A. Brown, *Gettysburg* (Armonk: M. E. Sharpe, Inc., 1996), pp. 41, 68–69, 84; Wert, *A Glorious Army*, pp. 256–257; Gottfried, *Brigades of Gettysburg*, p. 411; Pfanz, Gettysburg, The Second Day, pp. 94, 500–505.

122. Trudeau, *Gettysburg*, p. 321.

123. Wert, *A Glorious Army*, p. 234; Trudeau, *Gettysburg*, p. 112.

124. Humphreys to McLaws, January 6, 1878, UNCL; Trudeau, *Gettysburg*, p. 321; CMSR, NA.

125. Dinkins, *Personal Recollections and Experiences in the Confederate Army*, pp. 47, 49–50; Moore, *A Life For The Confederacy*, p. 69; Humphreys to McLaws, January 6, 1878, UNCL; Miers and Brown, *Gettysburg*, p. 89; CMSR, NA.

126. Henry Robinson Berkeley Diary, Virginia Historical Society, Richmond, VA.

127. Oscar Ewing Stuart to Annie E. Stuart, December 17, 1861, Trammell Family Papers.

128. Dinkins, *Personal Recollections and Experiences in the Confederate Army*, pp. 70–71.

129. Ibid., pp. 56, 70–71.

130. Ibid., p. 78; Moore, *A Life for the Confederacy*, p. 134; A.P. Andrews, "Gallantry At Gettysburg: An Act of Courageous Deeds of the Mississippi Brigades Commanded by William Barksdale and Joseph R. Davis," Gettysburg National Military Park Archives, Gettysburg, Pennsylvania; Trudeau, *Gettysburg*, p. 112; Pfanz, *Gettysburg: The Second Day*, p. 301.

131. Dinkins, *Personal Recollections and Experiences in the Confederate Army*, p. 78.

132. Harrison, *Pickett's Men*, p. 73.

133. Dinkins, *Personal Recollections and Experiences in the Confederate Army*, p. 78; John B. Gordon, *Reminiscences of the Civil War* (New York: Charles Scribner's Sons, 1904), p. 142.

134. Ibid., pp. 52–53.

135. Ibid., p. 78.

136. Dick Stanley, "13th Mississippi Infantry Regiment, Correspondence," August 20, 2011, internet.

137. *Rockingham Post-Dispatch*, November 30, 1949; Moore, *A Life For The Confederacy*, pp. 133, 146–147; Edwin C. Bearss, *Grant Strikes a Fatal Blow: The Campaign for Vicksburg*, vol. 2 (3 vols: Dayton: Morningside Bookshop, 1986), pp. 348–349

138. Dick Stanley, "13th Mississippi Infantry Regiment, Correspondence," August 8, 2011, internet.

139. Ibid., pp. 588–595; CMSR, NA; Trudeau, *Gettysburg*, p. 321.

140. Dick Stanley, "13th Mississippi Infantry Regiment, Correspondence," August 20, 2011.

141. Trudeau, *Gettysburg*, p. 321; Haskell, *The Battle of Gettysburg*, p. 35; Thomas Keneally, *American Scoundrel: The Life of the Notorious Civil War General Dan Sickles* (New York: Doubleday, 2002), p. 279.

142. Haskell, *The Battle of Gettysburg*, pp. 22, 35–36; Trudeau, *Gettysburg*, pp. 294, 313–314.

143. Allers, *The Fog of Gettysburg*, pp. 96–97; Trudeau, *Gettysburg*, pp. 294, 301; Wert, *A Glorious Army*, pp. 256–257; Pfanz, *Gettysburg, The Second Day*, pp. 124–125.

144. Trudeau, *Gettysburg*, pp. 294, 313–314; Wert, *A Glorious Army*, pp. 256–257; Keneally, *American Scoundrel*, 264.

145. Keneally, *American Scoundrel*, pp. 12–59, 280; Haskell, *The Battle of Gettysburg*, pp. 35–36; Pfanz, *Gettysburg, The Second Day*, p. 93.

146. Keneally, *American Scoundrel*, p. 280; Trudeau, *Gettysburg*, p. 367.

147. Haskell, *The Battle of Gettysburg*, p. 6.

148. Ibid., p. 36.

149. Wert, *A Glorious Army*, p. 257.

150. Trudeau, *Gettysburg*, pp. 295, 301.

151. Haskell, *The Battle of Gettysburg*, pp. 25–26; Thomas, *Robert E. Lee*, p. 288; Allers, *The Fog of Gettysburg*, p. 97.

152. Wert, *A Glorious Army*, p. 257.
153. Gordon, *Reminiscences of the Civil War*, p. 141; Alexander, *Fighting for the Confederacy*, p. 229; Nye, *Here Come The Rebels!*, pp. 3-6; Pfanz, *Gettysburg: The Second Day*, pp. 72, 128.
154. Dick Stanley, "13th Mississippi Infantry Regiment, Correspondence," September 6, 2011.
155. William Henry Hill Diary, Mississippi Department of Archives and History, Jackson, MS.
156. CMSR, NA; J.W. Duke, "Mississippians at Gettysburg," *Confederate Veteran*, vol. 14, p. 216; Pfanz, *Gettysburg, The Second Day*, p. 320.
157. Duke, "Mississippians at Gettysburg," *CV*, p. 216; Sears, *Gettysburg*, p. 51; Pfanz, *Gettysburg, The Second Day*, p. 304.
158. Wert, *A Glorious Army*, p. 260; Duke, "Mississippians at Gettysburg," *CV*, p. 216; Pfanz, *Gettysburg, The Second Day*, p. 320.
159. Duke, "Mississippians at Gettysburg," *CV*, p. 216; Pfanz, *Gettysburg, The Second Day*, p. 304.
160. Pfanz, *Gettysburg, The Second Day*, p. 320.
161. Duke, "Mississippians at Gettysburg," *CV*, p. 216.
162. Ibid.
163. Ibid; Pfranz, *Gettysburg, The Second Day,* pp. 304, 320; CMSR, NA.
164. Duke, "Mississippians at Gettysburg," *CV*, p. 216; Trudeau, *Gettysburg*, p. 294.
165. Allers, *The Fog of Gettysburg*, p. 97; Keneally, *American Scoundrel*, pp. 278–279; Trudeau, *Gettysburg*, pp. 301, 313–314.
166. Johnson and Buel, eds., *Battles and Leaders*, vol. 3, pp. 296, 333; Trudeau, *Gettysburg*, pp. 314, 326; Pinchon, *Dan Sickles*, p. 198; Sears, *Gettysburg*, pp. 250–251, 507; Mac Wyckoff, *AHistory of the 2nd South Carolina Infantry: 1861–1865* (Fredericksburg, Va.: Sergeant Kirkland's, 1994), p. 78; Keneally, *American Scoundrel*, pp. 52–53, 71, 73; Edwin B. Coddington, *The Gettysburg Campaign, A Study in Command* (New York: Charles Scribner's Sons, 1968), pp. 397–398, 415; Miers and Brown, Gettysburg, p. 95; O.R., vol. 27, ser. 1, pt. 1, pp. 234–35, 558, 569; Edward Longacre, "'The Soul of Our Artillery': General Henry J. Hunt," *Civil War Times Illustrated*, vol. 12, no. 3 (June 1973), pp. 42–43; Pfanz, *Gettysburg, The Second Day*, pp. 130–131, 133–135, 304–305.
167. Alexander, *Fighting for the Confederacy*, p. 238; Trudeau, *Gettysburg*, p. 20; Jeffery Wert, *General James Longstreet, The Confederacy's Most Controversial Soldier* (New York: Touchstone Books, 1993), p. 274.
168. Love, William A., "Mississippi At Gettysburg," *Publications of the Mississippi Historical Society*, vol. ix (1906), pp. 25–51; Pinchon, *Dan Sickles*, p. 200; Coddington, *The Gettysburg Campaign*, pp. 397–398; Carol Reardon, *Pickett's Charge in History and Memory* (Chapel Hill: University of North Carolina Press, 1997), pp. 1–10, 154–213; Pfanz, *Gettysburg, The Second Day*, pp. 147–148,.

169. Gordon, Reminiscences Of The Civil War, p. 154.

170. Johnson and Buel, eds., *Battles and Leaders*, vol. 3, pp. 300–301; Haskell, The Battle of Gettysburg, pp. 35–36; Wert, A Glorious Army, p. 257; Trudeau, Gettysburg, p. 359.

171. William Henry Hill Diary, MDAH.

172. McNeily, "Barksdale's Mississippi Brigade at Gettysburg," *PMHS*, pp. 233–234, 256.

173. Dick Stanley, "13th Mississipi Infantry Regiment, Correspondence," September 6, 2011.

174. Ibid; CMSR, NA.

175. ood, *Advance and Retreat*, p. 58; Longstreet, *From Mannassas to Appomattox*, p. 368; Wyckoff, *A History of the 2nd South Carolina Infantry*, p. 78; Johnson and Buel, eds., *Battlesand Leaders*, vol. 3, pp. 331–337.

176. Gerald J. Smith, *"One of the Most Daring of Men," The Life of Confederate General William Tatum Wofford* (Murfreesboro: Confederate Heritage Press, 1997), pp. 1–21, 23–75, 81; Boatner, *The Civil War Dictionary*, p. 945; Wyckoff, *A History of the 2nd South Carolina Infantry*, p. 78; Alexander, *Fighting for the Confederacy*, p. 238; Humphreys to McLaws, UNCL; J. B. Polley, *Hood's Texas Brigade* (Dayton: Morningside, 1988), pp. 19, 98, 101, 106, 117, and 122; Trudeau, *Gettysburg*, pp. 377, 379; Dowdey, *Death of a Nation*, p. 220; Pfanz, *Gettysburg, The Second Day*, p. 328

177. Alexander, *Fighting for the Confederacy*, pp. 238–239; Pfanz, *Gettysburg, The Second Day*, p. 303; Johnson and Buel, eds., *Battles and Leaders*, vol. 3, pp. 303-04; Jay Jorgensen, " . . . I'll go my arm, leg, or death on it": Edward Porter Alexander, Confederate Cannoneer at Gettysburg, *Gettysburg Magazine*, no. 17 (n.d.), pp. 41–45; Trudeau, *Gettysburg*, p. 273.

178. Pfranz, *Gettysburg, The Second Day*, p. 320; Freeman, *Lee's Lieutenants*, p. 117; Alexander, *Fighting for the Confederacy*, p. 238–249; W. C. Storrick, *Gettysburg* (Harrisburg: J. Horace McFarland Company, 1932), pp. 48–49; Wert, *A Glorious Army*, p. 258.

179. John S. Henley, "Career of a Veteran," Fredericksburg and Spotsylvania National Military Park, Fredericksburg, Virginia; Pfranz, *Gettysburg, The Second Day*, pp. 152, 320.

180. Alexander, *Fighting for the Confederacy*, p. 240; Abernathy Manuscript, MDAH; Pfanz, *Gettysburg, The Second Day*, pp. 155–156, 303, 309–310; Jorgensen, Alexander, *GM*, p. 44; Trudeau, *Gettysburg*, pp. 328–329; Henry Woodhead, editor, *Echoes of Glory*, Arms and Equipment of the Confederacy (Alexandria: Time-Life Books, 1991), pp. 116–117.

181. Henley, "On the Way to Gettysburg," FSNMP.

182. Owen, *In Camp and Battle with the Washington Artillery*, p. 244; Pfanz, *Gettysburg, The Second Day*, pp. 155, 309, 459; Jorgensen, Alexander, *GM*, pp. 44–46.

183. Alexander, "Artillery Fighting at Gettysburg," in *Battles and Leaders of the Civil War*, Vol. III, pp. 359–60. Owen, *In Camp and Battle with the Washing-*

ton Artillery, p. 244; Smith, "One of the Most Daring of Men," pp. 82–83; Pfanz, *Gettysburg: The Second* Day, pp. 117, 310; Paul Johnson, *Napoleon, A Life* (New York: Penguin Books, 2002), pp. 66–68.

184. Kershaw, "Kershaw's Brigade at Gettysburg," in *Battles and Leaders*, Vol. III, p. 334; *OR*, Series 1, Vol. XXVII. Gottfried, *Brigades of Gettysburg*, p. 412.

185. Petruzzi and Stanley, *The Gettysburg Campaign in Numbers and Losses*, p. 122; Joseph A. Miller Diary, FSNMP; CMSR, NA.

186. Ibid.

187. Ibid; CMSR, NA.

188. Joseph A. Miller, FSNMP; CMSR, NA.

189. CMSR, NA; Joseph A. Miller, FSNMP.

190. Joseph A. Miller, FSNMP.

191. McNeily, "Barksdale's Mississippi Brigade at Gettysburg," *PMHS*, p. 235; Pfranz, *Gettysburg, The Second Day*, p. 152.

192. Henley, "On the Way to Gettysburg," FSNMP.

193. Brian C. Pohanka, *Don Troiani's Civil War* (Mechanicsburg, Pa.: Stackpole Books, 1995), pp. 114; Foote, *The Civil War*, vol. 2, p. 508; McNeily, "Barksdale's Mississippi Brigade At Gettysburg," *PMHS*, pp. 235, 237; Smith, *"One of the Most Daring of Men,"* p. 81; McElfresh Map Company, Gettysburg Battlefield Map, The Second and Third Days' Battlefield; Duke, "Mississippians at Gettysburg, CV, p. 216; Pfanz, *Gettysburg, The Second Day*, pp. 72, 152; William Allen, Ordnance Officer of the Mississippi Brigade, Ordnance Reports, April 1863, CMSR, NA; Earl J. Coates, Michael J. McAfee, and Don Troiani, *Don Troiani's Regiments and Uniforms of the Civil War* (Mechanicsburg, Pa: Stackpole Books, 2002), pp. 138.

194. William Allen Ordnance Reports, September 1862 to April 1863, CMSR, NA; Trudeau, *Gettysburg*, p. 359; Coats, McAfee, and Troiani, *Don Troiani's Regiments and Uniforms of the Civil War*, pp. 111, 138.

195. Ezekiel Armstrong Diary, MDAH; CMSR, NA.

196. CMSR, NA.

197. Ezekiel Armstrong Diary, MDAH; CMSR, NA.

198. CMSR, NA; Davis, *Jefferson Davis*, p. 8; Coco, *Confederates Killed in Action*, pp. 84–87.

199. Coco, *Confederates Killed in Action*, pp. 84–87.

200. Duke, "Mississippians at Gettysburg," *CV*, p. 216.

201. Ibid; CMSR, NA.

202. Charles W. Squires Manuscript, Library of Congress, Washington, D.C; CMSR, NA; Dinkins, *Personal Recollections and Experiences in the Confederate Army*, pp. 86–87.

203. Dinkins, *Personal Recollections and Experiences in the Confederate Army*, p. 87.

204. Owen, *In Camp And Battle with the Washington Artillery*, p. 245; McNeily, "Barksdale's Mississippi Brigade At Gettysburg," *PMHS*, p. 236; Pfanz, *Gettysburg: The Second Day*, pp. 310–311, 320.

205. *History of the 57th Pennsylvania Veteran Volunteers* (Kearny: Belle Grove Publishing Company, 1995), p. 90; Pfanz, *Gettysburg: The Second Day*, p. 96.

206. Gottfried, *Brigades of Gettysburg*, p. 412; Pfanz, *Gettysburg: The Second Day*, pp. 310–311, 500–505; Dowdey, *Death of a Nation*, pp. 219–220.

207. McNeily, "Barksdale's Mississippi Brigade At Gettysburg," *PMHS*, pp. 235–236; Gottfried, *Brigade of Gettysburg*, p. 412; Wert, *A Glorious Army*, p. 261; Pfanz, *Gettysburg: The Second Day*, pp. 310–311.

208. Duke, "Mississippians at Gettysburg," *CV*, p. 216; Pfanz, *Gettysburg: The Second Day*, p. 149; Dowdey, *Death of a Nation*, pp. 220–221.

209. Gottfield, *Brigades of Gettysburg*, p. 412; Pfanz, *Gettysburg, The Second Day*, pp. 310–311.

210. Freeman, *Lee's Lieutenants*, vol. 3, p. 122; Love, "Mississippi At Gettysburg," *SHSP*, pp. 31–32; Foote, *The Civil War*, vol. 2, p. 506; McNeily, "Barksdale's Mississippi Brigade at Gettysburg," *PMHS*, p. 235; Gottfield, *Brigades of Gettysburg*, pp. 410, 412; Piston, *Lee's Tarnished Lieutenant*, pp. 17–18.

211. McNeily, "Barksdale's Mississippi Brigade At Gettysburg," *PMHS*, p. 236; Pfanz, *Gettysburg, The Second Day*, p. 303.

212. Gregory A. Coco, *Wasted Valor: The Confederate Dead at Gettysburg* (Gettysburg, Pa: Thomas Publications, 1990), p. 147; E.P. Harman to W.S. Decker, August 16, 1886 letter, Charles A. Richardson Papers, Ontario County Historical Society, Ontario, New York.

213. McNeily, "Barksdale's Mississippi Brigade At Gettysburg," *PMHS*, p. 236; Lavass and Nelson, eds., *Guide to the Battle of Gettysburg*, p. 62; Gottfried, *Brigades of Gettysburg*, p. 412; Wert, *A Glorious Army*, p. 257.

214. Owen, *In Camp and Field with the Washington Artillery*, p. 245; Pfanz, *Gettysburg: The Second Day*, p. 320.

215. Dinkins, *Personal Recollections and Experiences in the Confederate Army*, p. 86.

216. Dinkins, *Personal Recollections and Experiences in the Confederate Army*, p. 88; CMSR, NA; *The Calhoun Monitier*, Pittsboro, Mississippi, April 28, 1904; Davis, *Jefferson Davis*, pp. 154–159.

217. Oscar Ewell Stuart to Ann L. Hardeman, September 25, 1861 and to William Hardeman, January 18, 1863; Trammell Family Papers; McNeily, "Barksdale's Mississippi Brigade At Gettysburg," *PMHS*, pp. 236, 241, 243–46; Coddington, *The Gettysburg Campaign*, pp. 402–403; CMSR, NA; Abernathy Manuscript, MDAH; Pfanz, *Gettysburg, The Second Day*, pp. 302–304, 320–321, 335; *The Aberdeen Examiner*, Aberdeen, Mississippi, August 22, 1913; Duke Account, GNMPA; "Biographical Sketch of William Barksdale," pp, 29–30; John Francis Hamtramck Claiborne Papers, 1797–1884, Southern Historical Collection, Louis Round Wilson Special Collections, University of North Carolina, Chapel Hill, North Carolina; Boatner, *The Civil War Dictionary*, p. 270; John A. Crow, Spain, *The Root and The Flower* (Los Angeles: University of California Press, 2005), pp. 139–141; Gottfried, *Brigades of Gettysburg*, pp. 410–416; Piston, *Lee's Tarnished Lieutenant*, pp. 16, 110; Compiled Military

Service Records of Confederate Soldiers Who Served in Organizations from the State of Georgia, National Archives, Washington, D.C.; McWhiney and Jamieson, *Attack and Die*, pp. 170–191; Ethelbert Barksdale Papers, Mississippi Department of Archives and History, Jackson, Mississippi; Dick Stanley, "Mississippi Infantry Regiment, The Mississippi Brigade Attacks," September 18, 2001, internet; Compiled Military Service Records of Confederate Soldiers Who Served in Organizations From the State of Virginia, Washington, D.C.; Trudeau, *Gettysburg*, p. 377; Dowdey, *Death of a Nation*, pp. 220–221; Smith, "One of the Most Daring of Men," pp. 81-83, 85; Harrison, *Pickett's Men*, pp. 33–35; John A. Barksdale, *Barksdale Family History and Genealogy* (Richmond: private printer, 1940), 1–25.

218. Trudeau, *Gettysburg*, p. 367; Pfanz, *Gettysburg, The Second Day*, pp. 304, 310–311, 318–321; Barksdale, *Barksdale Family History and Genealogy*, pp. 1–25; B.J. Jordan, *One Final Charge! The Life and Times of Mississippi General William Barksdale, C.S.A.* (Denver: Outskirts Press, Inc, 2008), p. 104.

219. "Biographical Sketch of William Barksdale," pp. 29–30, Claiborne Papers, SHC.

220. Stanley, "Mississippi Infantry Regiment, The Mississippi Brigade Attacks," internet.

221. CMSR, NA.

222. Humphreys to McLaws, January 6, 1878, UNCL; Time-Life editors, *Gettysburg*, p. 109; Harman to Decker, August 16, 1886, OCHS; *The Aberdeen Examiner*, August 22, 1913; Pfanz, *Gettysburg: The Second Day*, pp. 310–311, 322

223. Henley, "On the Way to Gettysburg," FSNMP.

224. Ibid; Trudeau, *Gettysburg*, p. 367; Joseph A. Miller Diary, FSNMP; Freeman, *Lee's Lieutenants*, vol. 3, p. 124; Humphreys, General Barksdale Biographical Sketch, UNL; Foote, *The Civil War*, vol. 2, p. 508; McNeily, "The Mississippi Brigade At Gettysburg," *PMHS*, p. 236; Woodhead, editor, *Echoes of Glory*, pp. 116–117.

225. Henley, "On the Way to Gettysburg," FSNMP.

226. Catalog of the Flags of the 13th, 17th, 18th and 21st Mississippi Regiments, Mississippi Department of Archives and History, Jackson, MS; Exhibit of the Burt Rifles Flag, Mississippi Department of Archives and History.

227. Trudeau, *Gettysburg*, p. 368.

228. McNeily, "Barksdale's Mississippi Brigade At Gettysburg," *PMHS*, p. 241; *The Aberdeen Examiner*, August 22, 1913.

229. McNeily, "Barksdale's Mississippi Brigade At Gettysburg," *PMHS*, p. 241; *The Aberdeen Examiner*, August 22, 1913; Trudeau, *Gettysburg*, p. 296.

230. Pfanz, *Gettysburg: The Second Day*, p. 321; *The Aberdeen Examiner*, August 22, 1913; McNeily, "Barksdale's Mississippi Brigade at Gettysburg," *PMHS*, p. 241.

231. Henley, "On the Way to Gettysburg," FSNMP.

232. Ibid; Wert, *General James Longstreet*, p. 275; Trudeau, *Gettysburg*, p. 368;

Time-Life Editors, *Gettysburg*, p. 102; Owen, *In Camp and Battle with the Washington Artillery*, p. 245; Richard Wheeler, *Witness to Gettysburg* (New York: Meridan Books, 1987), p. 203; Trudeau, *Gettysburg*, p. 254; Tucker, *High Tide At Gettysburg*, pp. 276–277; Cross, *They Sleep Beneath the Mockingbird*, p. 12; Gottfried, *Brigades of Gettysburg*, pp. 410, 413, 416.

233. Pfanz, *Gettysburg, The Second Day*, p. 321.

234. McNeily, "Barksdale's Mississippi Brigade At Gettysburg," *PMHS*, p. 241.

235. Edward J. Hagerty, *Collis' Zouaves, The 114th Pennsylvania Volunteers in the Civil War* (Baton Rouge: Louisiana State University Press, 1997), p. 240; Trudeau, *Gettysburg*, p. 368; Pfanz, Gettysburg: The Second Day, pp. 130–132.

236. *History of the 57th Pennsylvania Veteran Volunteers*, p. 91; Haskell, *The Battle of Gettysburg*, p. 32.

237. *History of the 57th Pennsylvania Veteran Volunteers*, p. 91; Trudeau, *Gettysburg*, p. 368.

238. Ibid., p. 260.

239. William A. Fletcher, *Rebel Private: Front and Rear, Memoirs of a Confederate Soldier* (New York: Meridian Books, 1997), p. 84.

240. Wert, *A Glorious Army*, pp. 260–262; Pfanz, *Gettysburg, The Second Day*, pp. 302–304.

241. Foote, *The Civil War*, vol. 2, p. 508; Miers and Brown, *Gettysburg*, p. 42; Time-Life Editors, *Voices of Gettysburg*, p. 90; Gottfried, *Brigades of Gettysburg*, p. 412; *History of the 57th Pennsylvania Veteran Volunteers*, p. 90; Haskell, *The Battle of Gettysburg*, pp. 35–36; Hagerty, *Collis' Zouaves*, p. 240.

242. Haskell, *The Battle of Gettysburg*, p. 41.

243. Henley, "On the Way to Gettysburg," FSNMP; Trudeau, *Gettysburg*, p. 367.

244. McNeilly, "Barksdale's Mississippi Brigade At Gettysburg," *PMHS*, p. 231.

245. Humphrey to McLaws, January 6, 1878, UNCL; Gottfried, *Brigades of Gettysburg*, pp. 412–413; Pfanz, *Gettysburg: The Second Day*, pp. 310–311, 318.

246. McNeily, "Barksdale's Mississippi Brigade At Gettysburg," *PMHS*, p. 231; Dowdey, *The Death of a Nation*, p. 221; Tucker, *High Tide At Gettysburg*, p. 276; Humphreys to McLaws, January 6, 1878, UNCL; Clark, *Gettysburg*, p. 109.

247. General Barksdale Biographical Sketch, UNCL; Pfanz, *Gettysburg: The Second Day*, pp. 132, 322.

248. *History of the 57th Pennsylvania Veteran Volunteers*, p. 89; Pfanz, *Gettysburg: The Second Day*, p. 322.

249. *History of the 57th Pennsylvania Veteran Volunteers*, p. 91; Gottfried, *Brigades of Gettysburg*, p. 188.

250. *History of the 57th Pennsylvania Veteran Volunteers*, p. 91.

251. Ibid, pp. 11, 16–17, 22, 41–42, 57–58, 68, 74, 195; *Gottfried, Brigades of Gettysburg*, p. 190; Compiled Service Records of Soldiers from the State of Pennsylvania, Record Group, National Archives, Washington, D.C.; Robert

Fuhrman, "'Yes, I think we will go now': The 57th Pennsylvania Volunteer Infantry at Gettysburg," *Gettysburg Magazine*, no. 17 (n.d.), pp. 62–63; Laurence M. Hauptman, *Between Two Fires, American Indians in the Civil War* (New York: Free Press, 1996), pp. 72–73; Ray Raphael, Founders, *The People Who Brought You A Nation* (New York: MJF Books, 2009), pp. 366–367; Hargety, *Collis' Zouaves*, p. 240.

252. *History of the 57th Pennsylvania Veteran Volunteers*, pp. 56–58, 73, 87, 90, 95; Fuhrman, "The 57th Pennsylvania Volunteer Infantry at Gettysburg," *GM*, pp. 63–64; Joseph Wheelan, *Invading Mexico, America's Continental Dream and the Mexican War, 1846–1848* (New York: Carroll and Graf Publishers, 2007), p. 359; Pfanz, *Gettysburg: The Second Day*, pp. 310–313, 320.

253. *History of the 57th Pennsylvania Veteran Volunteers*, p. 57.

254. Hagerty, *Collis' Zouaves*, pp. 125–126, 239–230; Pfanz, *Gettysburg: The Second Day*, pp. 118, 132–133, 310–311, 320.

255. Pfanz, *Gettysburg: The Second Day*, pp. 132–133; Hagerty, *Collis' Zouaves*, pp. 1–33, 74-82, 126–127; CMSR, NA.

256. Gottfried, *Brigades of Gettysburg*, p. 410; Hagerty, *Collis' Zouaves*, p. 28.

257. Hagerty, *Collis' Zouaves*, pp. 127, 167.

258. Hagerty, *Collis' Zouaves*, pp. 109–110, 127, 167, 191, 226–227.

259. Jerry Thompson, editor, *Tejanos in Gray, Civil War Letters of Captains Joseph Rafael de la Garza and Manuel Yturri* (College Station: Texas A & M University Press, 2012), p. 12; Editors of Time-Life Books, *Voices of Gettysburg*, pp. 64, 97; Francis A. Lord, *Civil War Collector's Encyclopedia* (New York: Castle Books, 1965), pp. 63, 314–315; *Don Troiani's Civil War*, pp. 116–117; *Pennsylvania At Gettysburg*, Vol. 2 (2 vols., Harrisburg, Pa: William Stanley Ray, State Printer, 1904), pp. 606–611; *History of the 57th Pennsylvania Veteran Volunteers*, pp. 90–91; Oliver Wilson Davis, *Sketch of Frederic Fernandez Cavada* (Philadelphia, Pa: James B. Chandler Printer, 1871), pp. 7–14; Haskell, *The Battle of Gettysburg*, pp. 35–36; O.R., vol. 27, ser. 1, pt. 1, pp. 502, 585; Kent Gramm, *Gettysburg, A Meditation On War And Values* (Bloomington: Indiana University Press, 1994), p. 122; Hagerty, *Collis' Zouaves*, pp. 22–23, 59, 93, 192–193, 203–204, 205–220, 225–226, 233, 239–241; Gottfried, *Brigades at Gettysburg*, p. 188; Pfanz, *Gettysburg, The Second Day*, pp. 314, 322–323; Phillip Thomas Tucker, editor, *Cubans in the Confederacy: Jose Agustin Quintero, Ambrosio Jose Gonzales, and Loreta Janeta Velazquez* (Jefferson: McFarland and Company, Inc., Publishers, 2002), pp. 1–237; Frank de Varona, editor, *Hispanic Presence In the United States: Historical Beginnings* (Miami: Mnemosyne Publishing Company, 1993), pp. 165–168; National Park Service, *Hispanics and the Civil War, From Battlefield to Homefront* (Washington, D.C.: Department of the Interior, n.d.), pp. 1–40; Franklin W. Knight, *Slave Society in Cuba during the Nineteenth Century* (Madison: The University of Wisconsin Press, 1974), pp. 25–46, 59–120.

260. Hagerty, *Collis' Zouaves*, pp. 184–193, 199.

261. *History of the 57th Pennsylvania Veteran Volunteers*, pp. 89-91; *Don Troiani's*

Civil War, pp. 115–116; Gottfried, *Brigades of Gettysburg*, pp. 190–191; *Pennsylvania At Gettysburg*, pp. 606, 611-612; Roach, *Gettysburg*, p. 34; Fuhrman, "The 57th Pennsylvania Volunteer Infantry at Gettysburg," *GM*, p. 64; Pfanz, *Gettysburg, The Second Day*, p. 323;Given Diary, CWLM; Hagerty, *Collis' Zouaves*, pp. 61, 226, 241–242; Haskell, *The Battle of Gettysburg*, p. 32; Editors of Time-Life, *Voices of Gettysburg*, pp. 64, 90-91, 97; CPSR, NA.

262. Keneally, *American Scoundrel*, p. 220; Eric A. Campbell, "Hell in a Peach Orchard," *America'sCivil War* (July 2003), pp. 40–41.

263. Campbell, "Hell in a Peach Orchard," *ACW*, pp. 40–41; Pfanz, Gettysburg, The Second Day, p. 323.

264. Campbell, "Hell in a Peach Orchard," p. 41.

265. Ibid.

266. Editors of Time-Life, *Voices of Gettysburg*, pp. 64, 97.

267. Hagerty, *Collis' Zouaves*, pp. 203–204.

268. Ibid; Tucker, ed., *Cubans in the Confederacy*, pp. 1–237.

269. Hagerty, *Collis' Zouaves*, p. 242.

270. Campbell, "Hell in the Peach Orchard," *ACW*, pp. 40–41.

271. Henley, "On the Way to Gettysburg," FSNMP; *History of the 57th Pennsylvania Veteran Volunteers*, p. 91; McNeily, "Barksdale's Mississippi Brigade At Gettysburg," *PMHS*, p. 237; Wert, *Longstreet*, p. 275; Fuhrman, "The 57th Pennsylvania Volunteer Infantry at Gettysburg," *GM*, p. 64; Hagerty, *Collis' Zouaves*, p. 242; Gottfried, *Brigades of Gettysburg*, p. 413; Pfanz, *Gettysburg: The Second Day*, pp. 323, 327–328; Trudeau, *Gettysburg*, p. 377.

272. Hagerty, *Collis' Zouaves*, pp. 334; CPSR, NA; Pfanz, *Gettysburg: The Second Day*, p. 314.

273. Henley, "On the Way to Gettysburg," FSNMP.

274. Ibid; Gottfried, *Brigades of Gettysburg*, p. 190.

275. Gregory A. Coco, *Wasted Valor, The Confederate Dead at Gettysburg* (Gettysburg: Thomas Publications, 1990), p. 49; CMSR, NA.

276. Ibid; CMSR, NA.

277. Pfanz, *Gettysburg: The Second Day*, p. 118.

278. Abernathy Manuscript, MDAH; Henley, "On the Way to Gettysburg," FSNMP.

279. Henley, "On the Way to Gettysburg," FSNMP.

280. Gottfried, *Brigades of Gettysburg*, p. 191.

281. Ibid.

282. Ibid.

283. CMSR, NA; *Winston County Journal*, Louisville, Mississippi, March 4, 1898; Dick Stanley, "13th Mississippi Infantry Regiment, The Mississippi Brigade Attacks," September 18, 2011, internet.

284. *History of the 57th Pennsylvania Veteran Volunteers*, p. 91; Humphreys, General Barksdale Biographical Sketch, UNL; *Pennsylvania At Gettysburg*, p. 606; Love, Mississippi At Gettysburg, *SHSP*, p. 32; General Barksdale Biographical Sketch, UNCL; Gottfried, *Brigades of Gettysburg*, p. 413; Miers and Brown,

Gettysburg, pp. 135–138; Fuhrman, "The 57th Pennsylvania Volunteer Infantry at Gettysburg," *GM*, pp. 64-66; Pfanz, *Gettysburg, The Second Day*, pp. 314, 326–327; Harman to Decker, August 16, 1886, OCHS; *The Aberdeen Examiner*, August 22, 1913.

285. Henley, "On the Way to Gettysburg," FSNMP.

286. CMSR, NA; CPSR, NA; Hagerty, Collis' Zouaves, pp. xi, 6-7, 65, 77, 81, 226, 228.

287. Editors of Time-Life Books, *Voices of Gettysburg*, p. 91.

288. Ibid.

289. Henley, "On the Way to Gettysburg," FSNMP.

290. Thurman Early Hendricks Diary, Mississippi, Department of Archives and History, Jackson, MS.

291. Haskell, *The Battle of Gettysburg*, p. 42.

292. Henley, "On the Way to Gettysburg," FSNMP; CMSR, NA; *History of the 57th Pennsylvania Veteran Volunteers*, p. 91; *Don Troiani's Civil War*, p. 116; McNeily, "Barksdale's Mississippi Brigade At Gettysburg," *PMHS*, pp. 236, 238, 244; O.R., vol. 27, ser. 1, pt. 1, pp. 500–501, 503; Hagerty, *Collis'-Zouaves*, pp. 242–244, 320; Davis, *Jefferson Davis*, pp. 8, 40, 154–159; Coco, *Confederates Killed in Action at Gettysburg*, pp. 84–87, 132; Joseph A. Miller Diary, FSNMP; Pfanz, *Gettysburg, The Second Day*, pp. 131–132; 314, 326–327; Gottfried, *Brigades of Gettysburg*, pp. 191–192, 413; Luvaas and Nelson, eds., *Guide to the Battle of Gettysburg*, pp. 121–122.

293. Trudeau, *Gettysburg*, p. 368; Pfanz, *Gettysburg: The Second Day*, pp. 328–329.

294. CMSR, NA; Gottfried, *Brigades at Gettysburg*, p. 413; Lover, *Mississippi At Gettysburg*, SHSP, p. 32; Pfanz, *Gettysburg: The Second Day*, pp. 131–133, 314; Gottfield, *Brigades of Gettysburg*, p. 413.

295. Editors of Time-Life Books, *Voices of Gettysburg*, p. 91; Pfanz, *Gettysburg: The Second Day*, pp. 328–329; Hagerty, *Collis' Zouaves*, p. 242.

296. Gottfried, *Brigades of Gettysburg*, p. 220; Campbell, "Hell in a Peach Orchard," *CWT*, p. 41.

297. Editors of Time-Life Books, *Voices of Gettysburg*, p. 91; Gottfried, *Brigades of Gettysburg*, p. 220

298. Ibid.

299. Ibid., p. 43; Henley, "On the Way to Gettysburg," FSNMP; Gottfriend, *Brigades of Gettysburg*, pp. 220–221, 413.

300. Gottfried, *Brigades of Gettysburg*, p. 221.

301. Luvaas and Nelson, eds., *Guide to the Battle of Gettysburg*, p. 122; Trudeau, *Gettysburg*, p. 380; Pfanz, *Gettysburg: The Second Day*, p. 329

302. Gottfried, *Brigades of Gettysburg*, pp. 413–414; Lavaas and Nelson, eds., *Guide to the Battle of Gettysburg*, p. 122; Trudeau, *Gettysburg*, p. 380.

303. Lavaas and Nelson, eds., *Guide to the Battle of Gettysburg*, p. 123; Gottfried, *Brigades of Gettysburg*, p. 191.

304. *History of the 57th Pennsylvania Veteran Volunteers*, pp. 91–92, 195;

Fuhrman, "The 57th Pennsylvania Volunteer Infantry at Gettysburg," *GM*, pp. 66–68; Duke, "Mississippians at Gettysburg," *CV*, p. 216; Gottfried, *Brigades at Gettysburg*, p. 413; CMSR, NA; Pfanz, *Gettysburg: The Second Day*, p. 413; Editors of Time-Life Books, *Voices of Gettysburg*, p. 91; Hagerty, *Collis' Zouaves*, p. 235; Pfanz, *Gettysburg, The Second Day*, pp. 329–330

305. Hagerty, *Collis' Zouaves*, p. 248.

306. Ibid., p. 250; Harrison, *Pickett's Men*, pp. 90–104.

307. CPSR, NA; Hagerty, *Collis' Zouaves*, pp. 249–250.

308. Coddington, *The Gettysburg Campaign*, p. 405; CPSR, NA; Henley, "On the Way to Gettysburg," FSNMP; General Barksdale Biographical Sketch, UNCL; B. J. Jordan, *One Final Charge!*, p. 104.

309. Henley, "On the Way to Gettysburg," FSNMP; *Pennsylvania At Gettysburg*, p. 612; McNeily, "Barksdale's Mississippi Brigade At Gettysburg," *PMHS*, p. 236; CMSR, NA; Gottfried, *Brigades at Gettysburg*, p.413; Pfanz, *Gettysburg, The Second Day*, p. 314; Luvaas and Nelson, eds., *Guide to the Battle of Gettysburg*, pp. 121–122; Hagerty, *Collis' Zouaves*, pp. 248–249; Coates, McAfee, and Troiani, *Don Troiani's Regiments and Uniforms of the Civil War*, p. 89.

310. Campbell, "Hell in a Peach Orchard," *ACW*, p. 42; Pfanz, *Gettysburg, The Second Day*, p. 330.

311. Campbell, "Hell in a Peach Orchard," *ACW*, p. 42; CMSR, NA.

312. Trudeau, *Gettysburg*, p. 380.

313. Trudeau, *Gettysburg*, pp. 371–372; Gottfried, *Brigades of Gettysburg*, pp. 191–192.

314. Trudeau, *Gettysburg*, pp. 371–372.; CMSR, NA; Gottfried, *Brigades at Gettysburg*, p. 413; Luvaas and Nelson, eds., *Guide to the Battle of Gettysburg*, pp. 121–122.

315. Trudeau, *Gettysburg*, pp. 371–372, 380; CMSR, NA; Gottfried, *Brigades of Gettysburg*, p. 413.

316. Gottfried, *Brigades of Gettysburg*, p. 192; Pfanz, *Gettysburg: The Second Day*, p. 132.

317. Trudeau, *Gettysburg*, pp. 372, 380.

318. Campbell, "Hell in a Peach Orchard," *ACW*, p. 42.

319. Smith, *"One of the Most Daring of Men,"* p. 83.

320. Hagerty, *Collis' Zouaves*, pp. 235, 242–244, 248–249; Campbell, "Hell in a Peach Orchard," *ACW*, p. 42; Henley, "On the Way to Gettysburg," FSNMP; CPSR, NA; Trudeau, *Gettysburg*, p. 380.

321. Haskell, *The Battle of Gettysburg*, pp. 44–45.

322. Trudeau, *Gettysburg*, pp. 368 (note).

323. McNeily, "Barksdale's Mississippi Brigade at Gettysburg," *PMHS*, p. 237; Pfanz, *Gettysburg: The Second Day*, p. 330.

324. General Barksdale Biographical Sketch, UNCL; CMRS, NA; Oscar Ewing Stuart to Ann L. Hardeman, September 21, 1861, Trammell Papers.

325. McNeily, "Barksdale's Mississippi Brigade at Gettysburg," *PMHS*, pp. 236–237.

326. McNeily, "Barksdale's Mississippi Brigade at Gettysburg," *PMHS*, pp. 237–238; CMSR, NA; "Geralds' Theatrics—Florence Gerald and Judge G.B. Gerald," Waco History Project, Waco, Texas, internet; Gottfried, *Brigades of Gettysburg*, p. 413; Editors of Time-Life Books, *Voices of Gettysburg*, pp. 90–91.

327. Editors of Time-Life Books, *Voices of Gettysburg*, p. 91.

328. Ibid., p. 90; "Geralds' Theatrics—Florence Gerald and Judge G. B. Gerald," WHP.

329. Editors of Time-Life Books, *Voices of Gettysburg*, pp. 90-91; McNeilly, "Barksdale's Mississippi Brigade at Gettysburg," *PMHS*, pp. 90-91.

330. McNeily, "The Mississippi Brigade at Gettysburg," *PMHS*, pp.237–238; Editors of Time-Life Books, *Voices of Gettysburg*, p. 91..

331. Ibid.

332. Harman to Decker, August 16, 1886, OCHS.

333. Trudeau, *Gettysburg*, pp. 380–381; Gottfried, *Brigades of Gettysburg*, pp. 191–192, 413–414; Boatner, *Civil War Dictionary*, p. 638; *Don Troiani's Civil War*, p. 116; *Pennsylvania at Gettysburg*, pp. 685-686; Pfanz, *Gettysburg, The Second Day*, pp. 132, 329, 332–333, 347; Tucker, *High Tide at Gettysburg*, p. 278; Humphreys to McLaws, January 6, 1878, UNCL; Wert, *Longstreet*, p. 275; Luvaas and Nelson, eds., *Guide to the Battle of Gettysburg*, pp. 121–122; O.R., vol. 27, ser. 1, pt. 1, p. 505; *National Tribune*, August 25, 1921.

334. Luvaas and Nelson, eds., *Guide to the Battle of Gettysburg*, pp. 123–124; Campbell, "Hell in a Peach Orchard," *ACW*, pp. 41–42.

335. Luvaas and Nelson, eds., *Guide to the Battle of Gettysburg*, pp. 123–125; Pfanz, *Gettysburg; The Second Day*, p. 333

336. Coco, *Killed in Action*, pp. 65–66.

337. David Craft, *History of the One Hundred Forty-First Regiment, Pennsylvania Volunteers, 1862–1865* (Towanda: Reporter-Journal Printing Company, 1885), p. 128.

338. *Pennsylvania at Gettysburg*, p. 609; Davis, *Sketch of Frederic Fernandez Cavada*, pp. 3–5, 14–19; Editors of Time-Life Books, *Voices of Gettysburg*, pp. 64, 97; Kevin O'Brien, "'To Unflinchingly Face Danger And Death': Carr's Brigade Defends Emmitsburg Road," *Gettysburg Magazine*, no. 12 (January 1, 1995), pp. 16–17; Varona, ed., *Hispanic Presence in the United States*, pp. 168–170; Coddington, *The Gettysburg Campaign*, p. 405; CPSR, NA; General Barksdale Biographical Sketch, UNCL.

339. Editors of Time-Life Books, *Voices of Gettysburg*, pp. 64, 97.

340. Roach, *Gettysburg*, p. 34; Hagerty, *Collis' Zouaves*, pp. 37, 169; General Barksdale Biographical Sketch, UNCL; CMSR, NA; Pfanz, *Gettysburg, The Second Day*, p. 335.

341. Editors of Time-Life Books, *Voices of Gettysburg*, p. 91; General Barksdale Biographical Sketch, UNCL.

342. *History of the 57th Pennsylvania Veteran Volunteers*, pp. 95-96; *Don Troiani's*

Civil War, p. 116; Owen, *In Camp and Battlefield with the Washington Artillery*, p. 247; *Pennsylvania at Gettysburg*, p. 612; Gottfried, *Brigades of Gettysburg*, p. 191; Trudeau, *Gettysburg*, pp. 378; Luvaas and Nelson, eds., *Guide to the Battle of Gettysburg*, pp. 123–124; Pfanz, *Gettysburg: The Second Day*, p. 333

343. Campbell, "Hell in a Peach Orchard," *ACW*, pp. 42–43.

344. Bigelow, *The Peach Orchard*, p. 16; *Don Troiani's Civil War*, p. 116; Trudeau, *Gettysburg*, pp. 377–380; Tucker, *High Tide at Gettysburg*, p. 279; Pfanz, *Gettysburg, the Second Day*, pp. 131, 95, 135, 151, 314, 331–332; Wert, *Longstreet*, p. 275; Coddington, *The Gettysburg Campaign*, p. 405; General Barksdale Biographical Sketch, UNCL; McNeily, "Barksdale's Mississippi Brigade At Gettysburg," *PMHS*, pp. 246–47; Coco, *Killed In Action*, pp. 69-70; Miers and Brown, *Gettysburg*, p. 138; O.R., vol. 27, ser. 1, no. 1, p. 501; CMSR NA; Gottfried, *Brigades of Gettysburg*, pp. 188, 192, 413–414; Editors of Time-Life Books, *Voices of Gettysburg*, p. 91; Campbell, "Hell in a Peach Orchard," *ACW*, pp. 41–43; Smith, *"One of the Most Daring of Men,"* pp. 81-83, 85-89.

345. McNeily, "Barksdale's Mississippi Brigade At Gettysburg," *PMHS*, p. 237; Coddington, *The Gettysburg Campaign*, p. 414; Hagerty, *Collis' Zouaves*, pp. 242–243; Pfanz, *Gettysburg: The Second Day*, p. 314; Luvaas and Nelson, eds., *Guide to the Battle of Gettysburg*, pp. 124–125; Gottfried, *Brigades of Gettysburg*, pp. 413–414.

346. Trudeau, *Gettysburg*, p. 379.

347. Ibid.

348. John Heiser, "Action On The Emmitsburg Road," *Gettysburg Magazine*, No. 1, July 1, 1989, p. 81; *National Tribune*, New York, NY, November 6, 1890; Trudeau, *Gettysburg*, pp. 379, 572; Roach, *Gettysburg*, p. 36; CMSR, NA; Pfanz, Compiled Service Records of Soldiers Who Served in Organizations from the State of New York, Record Group. National Archives, Washington, D.C.; Hagerty, *Collis' Zouaves*, p. 176; Gottfried, *Brigades of Gettysburg*, pp. 188, 216, 219–222; Keneally, *American Scoundrel*, pp. 7, 219–220; Jordan, *One Final Charge!*, p. 104.

349. Henley, "The Career of a Veteran," FSNMP; Trudeau, *Gettysburg*, p. 379; Gottfried, *Brigades of Gettysburg*, pp. 219–221.

350. Trudeau, *Gettysburg*, p. 379; Gottfried, *Brigades of Gettysburg*, p. 221.

351. Campbell, "Hell in a Peach Orchard," *ACW*, p. 43.

352. Trudeau, *Gettysburg*, p. 380; Haskell, *The Battle of Gettysburg*, p. 42; Gottfried, *Brigades of Gettysburg*, pp. 413–414; Lavaas and Nelson, eds., *Guide to the Battle of Gettysburg*, p. 124

353. Haskell, *The Battle of Gettysburg*, p. 42; Trudeau, *Gettysburg*, p. 380.

354. Ibid; Gottfried, *Brigades of Gettysburg*, pp. 413–416; Smith, *"One of the Most Daring of Men,"* pp. 83, 86, 88-89; CMSR, NA; McNeily, "Barksdale's Mississippi Brigade at Gettysburg," *PMHS*, p. 237.

355. McNeily, "Barksdale's Mississippi Brigade at Gettysburg," *PMHS*, p. 237.

356. Humphreys to McLaws, January 6, 1878, UNCL.

357. Gottfield, *Brigades of Gettysburg*, p. 226; Tucker, *High Tide at Gettysyburg*, pp. 278–279; Boatner, *The Civil War Dictionary*, p. 350; Humphreys to McLaws, January 6, 1878, UNCL; McNeily, "Barksdale's Mississippi Brigade at Gettysburg," *PMHS*, p. 237; Trudeau, *Gettysburg*, p. 380; Foote, *The Civil War*, vol. 2, p. 508; General Barksdale Biographical Sketch, UNCL; Pfanz, *Gettysburg: The Second Day*, pp. 130–31, 338.

358. McNeily, "Barksdale's Mississippi Brigade At Gettysburg," *PMHS*, p. 237; Gottfried, *Brigades of Gettysburg*, p. 413; Trudeau, *Gettysburg*, p. 380; Pfanz, *Gettysburg: The Second Day*, pp. 130–131.

359. Trudeau, *Gettysburg*, p. 380.

360. Humphreys to McLaws, January 6, 1878, UNCL; Pfanz, *Gettysburg, The Second Day*, pp. 130–131, Gottfried, *Brigades of Gettysburg*, pp. 413–414; Trudeau, *Gettysburg*, p. 380; Tucker, *High Tide at Gettysburg*, p. 278; Owen, *In Camp And Battlefield with the Washington Artillery*, p. 246; Humphreys to McLaws, January 6, 1878, UNCL; McNeily, "Barksdale's Mississippi Brigade at Gettysburg," *PMHS*, p. 237; Wert, *Longstreet*, p. 276; Heiser, "Action on the Emmitsburg Road," *Gettysburg Magazine*, p. 80.

361. Gottfried, *Brigades of Gettysburg*, p. 413; Trudeau, *Gettysburg*, p. 380.

362. Gottfried, *Brigades of Gettysburg*, p. 413; Humphreys to McLaws, January 6, 1878, UNCL; Trudeau, *Gettysburg*, p. 380; Smith, *"One of the Most Daring of Men,"* p. 83.

363. Trudeau, *Gettysburg*, p. 384; Pfanz, *Gettysburg: The Second Day*, pp. 311–312, 329; Gottfried, *Brigades of Gettysburg*, p. 414.

364. Trudeau, *Gettysburg*, p. 380; Humphreys to McLaws, January 6, 1878, UNCL; B.T. Arrington, *The Medal of Honor at Gettysburg* (Gettysburg, PA: Thomas Publications, 1996), p. 11; Pfanz, *Gettysburg: The Second Day*, pp. 311, 338–41; O.R., vol. 27, ser. 1, no. 1, pp. 585–86; Gottfried, *Brigades of Gettysburg*, p. 190; Haskell, *The Battle of Gettysburg*, p. 45; Luvaas and Nelson, *Guide to the Battle of Gettysburg*, pp. 122–124; CMSR, NA.

365. Humphreys to McLaws, January 6, 1878, UNCL; Coddington, *The Gettysburg Campaign*, pp. 414–415; Trudeau, *Gettysburg*, pp. 376–381; Gottfried, *Brigades of Gettysburg*, pp. 221, 413–414.

366. Bradley M. Gottfried, *The Artillery of Gettysburg* (Nashville: Cumberland House, 2008), pp. 126–127; Gottfried, *Brigades of Gettysburg*, p. 221.

367. Humphreys to McLaws, Janury 6, 1878; UNCL; Martin Haynes, *A History of the Second Regiment, New Hampshire Volunteer Infantry in the War of the Rebellion* (Lakeport, NH: Republcian, 1896), p. 178; Trudeau, *Gettysburg*, pp. 380–381; Gottfried, *Brigades of Gettysburg*, pp. 413–414.

368. *Don Troiani's Civil War*, p. 116; Owen, *In Camp and Battlefield with the Washington Artillery*, p. 245; Humphreys to McLaws, January 6, 1878, UNCL; Gottfried, *Brigades of Gettysburg*, pp. 412–413; Wert, *Longstreet*, p. 275; McNeily, "Barksdale's Mississippi Brigade at Gettysburg," *PMHS*, pp. 246–47; Trudeau, *Gettysburg*, pp. 377, 380–381; Smith, *"One of the Most*

Daring of Men," pp. 83, 85–86.

369. Trudeau, *Gettysburg*, p. 389; Wheeler, *Witness to Gettysburg*, pp. 203–204

370. CMSR, NA; Trudeau, *Gettysburg*, pp. 380–381.

371. *Pennsylvania at Gettysburg*, pp. 612-613, 997; Humphreys to McLaws, January 6, 1878, UNCL; Wert, *Longstreet*, p. 275; O'Brien, "'To Unflinchingly Face Danger And Death': Carr's Brigade Defends Emmitsburg Road," *GM*, p. 17; Pfanz, *Gettysburg: The Second Day*, pp. 347, 349; O.R., vol. 27, series 1, pt. 1, pp. 503, 533; McNeily, "Barksdale's Mississippi Brigade at Gettysburg," *PMHS*, pp. 239, 245.

372. Abernathy Manuscript, MDAH; CMSR, NA.

373. CMSR, NA.

374. Winschel, "To Assuage The Grief," *GM*, pp. 77–81; CMSR, NA; *Historic Mobile: An Illustrated Guide* (Mobile: The Junior League of Mobile, Alabama, Inc., 1974), pp. xi-87.

375. Frank A. Haskell and William C. Oates, *Gettysburg* (New York: Bantam Books, 1992), pp. 170–175; McNeily, "Barksdale's Mississippi Brigade at Gettysburg," *PMHS*, p. 247; Trudeau, *Gettysburg*, p. 377.

376. Wheeler, *Witness to Gettysburg*, p. 204; Tucker, *High Tide at Gettysburg*, p. 276.

377. Henley, "The Career of a Veteran," FSNMP.

378. Gottfried, *Brigades of Gettysburg*, p. 416; McNeily, "Barksdale's Mississippi Brigade at Gettysburg," *PMHS*, p. 237; Wert, *Longstreet*, p. 278; CMSR, NA.

379. O'Brien, "'To Unflinchingly Face Danger and Death': Carr's Brigade Defends Emmitsburg Road," *Gettysburg Magazine*, no. 12 (January 1, 1995), p. 14–18; Abernathy Manuscript, MDAH; O.R., vol. 27, ser. 1, pt. 1, pp. 501, 553–54, 559; McNeily, "Barksdale's Mississippi Brigade at Gettysburg," *PMHS*, p. 239; Miers and Brown, *Gettysburg*, p. 138; Harman to Decker, August 16, 1886, OCHS; Roberts and Moneyhon, *Portraits of Conflict*, p. 89; Trudeau, *Gettysburg*, p. 571; Gottfried, *Brigades of Gettysburg*, pp. 25, 216.

380. Compiled Military Service Records of Soldiers from Organizations of the State of New Hampshire, Washington, D.C.; James A. Burns, "The 12th New Hampshire Regiment at Gettysburg and Beyond," *Gettysburg Magazine*, no. 20, pp. 113–117; Trudeau, *Gettysburg*, p. 571.

381. Burns, "The 12th New Hampshire at Gettysburg and Beyond," *GM*, p. 115.

382. Ibid., 115–116; CNHSR, NA; Willard Sterne Randall, *Benedict Arnold, Patriot and Traitor* (New York: Quill/William Morrow, 1990), pp. 92–99.

383. Burns, "The 12th New Hampshire at Gettysburg and Beyond, *GM*, pp. 117–118.

384. Henley, "On the Way to Gettysburg," FSNMP; Trudeau, *Gettysburg*, p. 571; Compiled Service Records of Men Who Served from the State of Massachusetts, National Archives, Washington, D.C.; Eleventh Regiment Massachusetts Regiment, Acton Memorial Library, Civil War Archives, Acton, Massachusetts.

385. Trudeau, *Gettysburg*, p. 571; Henley, "On the Way to Gettysburg," FSNMP;

Eleventh Regiment Massachusetts Regiment, AML.

386. Gottfried, *Brigades of Gettysburg*, p. 416; Hagerty, *Collis' Zouaves*, p. 240; Henley, "On the Way to Gettysburg," FSNMP; Henley, "The Career of a Veteran," FSNMP; Pfanz, *Gettysburg: The Second Day*, p. 361; CMSR, NA.

387. Haskell, *The Battle of Gettysburg*, pp. 35–36; Hagerty, *Collis' Zouaves*, p. 240; Gottfried, *Brigades of Gettysburg*, pp. 410, 414.

388. Haskell, *The Battle of Gettysburg*, pp. 35–47; Burns, "The 12th New Hampshire Regiment at Gettysburg And Beyond," *GM*, pp. 114, 117–117; Editors of Time-Life Books, *Voices of Gettysburg*, p. 92; Gottfried, *Brigades of Gettysburg*, pp. 412–416; Hagerty, *Collis' Zouaves*, p. 240; Henley, "On the Way to Gettysburg," FSNMP; Henley, "The Career of a Veteran," FSNMP.

389. Hagerty, *Collis' Zouaves*, p. 240; Haskell, *The Battle of Gettysburg*, p. 35–36.

390. Editors of Time-Life Books, *Voices of Gettysburg*, p. 92; Wert, *A Glorious Army*, p. 262.

391. George G. Meade Collection, Historical Society of Pennsylvania, Philadelphia, Pennsylvania: Trudeau, *Gettysburg*, pp. 351–352, 377, 379–381; Tucker, *High Tide at Gettysburg*, p. 275; Humphreys to McLaws, January 6, 1878, UNCL; McWhiney and Jamieson, *Attack and Die*, p. 24; Miers and Brown, *Gettysburg*, p. 142; Harman to Decker, August 16, 1886, OCHS; Wert, *A Glorious Army*, p. 262; Editors of Time-Life Books, *Voices of Gettysburg*, p. 92; Burns, "The 12th New Hampshire Regiment at Gettysburg and Beyond," *GM*, p. 114; Haskell, *The Battle of Gettysburg*, pp 35–47; Smith, *"One of the Most Daring of Men,"* pp. 85, 90-91.

392. Haskell, *The Battle of Gettysburg*, p. 45; Hagerty, *Collis' Zouaves*, p. 240; Haskell, *The Battle of Gettysburg*, pp. 35–47.

393. Burns, "The 12th New Hampshire Regiment at Gettysburg and Beyond," *GM*, pp. 117–118; Gottfried, *Brigades of Gettysburg*, pp. 413–416.

394. Thomas, *Robert E. Lee*, pp. 288, 292; Longstreet, *From Manassas to Appomattox*, p. 371.

395. Love, "Mississippi At Gettysburg," *SHSP*, p. 32; Trudeau, *Gettysburg*, pp. 380–381.

396. David Craft, *History of the One Hundred Forty-First Regiment, Pennsylvania Volunteers, 1862–1865* (Towanda, PA: Reporter-Journal Printing Company, 1885), p. 128; Gottfried, Brigades of Gettysburg, pp. 413–416; Burns, "The 12th New Hampshire Regiment at Gettysburg and Beyond," *GM*, pp. 117–118..

397. McNeily, "Barksdale's Mississippi Brigade At Gettysburg," *PMHS*, pp. 238–239; Editors of Time-Life Books, *Voices of Gettysburg*, p. 91.

398. Ibid.

399. CMSR, NA; Lauderdale County, Mississippi, Census Records for 1860, Mississippi Department of Archives and History, Jackson, Mississippi; Charles A. Earp, "The Seven McElroys of the 13th Mississippi Infantry C.S.A.," *Confederate Veteran* (September-October 1993), pp. 36–42; McWhiney and

Jamieson, *Attack and Die*, p. 4; Jordan, *One Final Charge!*, p. 77.

400. CMSR, NA.

401. William H. Hill Diary, MDAH; Dick Stanley, "13th Mississippi Infantry Regiment, Gen. Barkdale's New Horse," August 6, 2011, internet.

402. William H. Hill Diary, MDAH.

403. William H. Hill Diary, MDAH; Stanley, "13th Mississippi, Infantry Report, Gen. Barksdale's New Horse," internet.

404. Stanley, "Mississippi Infantry Regiment, The Mississippi Brigade Attacks," internet.

405. Haskell, *The Battle of Gettysburg*, pp. 46–47.

406. Bigelow, *The Peach Orchard*, p. 31.

407. Bigelow, *The Peach Orchard*, p. 39.

408. Pfanz, *Gettysburg: The Second Day*, pp. 117, 336; Alexander, *Fighting for the Confederacy*, p. 240.

409. Alexander, *Fighting for the Confederacy*, p. 240.

410. Ibid.

411. Humphreys to McLaws, January 6, 1878, UNCL; Pfanz, *Gettysburg: The Second Day*, p. 336.

412. Pfanz, *Gettysburg, The Second Day*, pp. 117, 337.

413. Alexander, *Fighting for the Confederacy*, p. 244.

414. lexander, "The Great Charge and Artillery Fighting at Gettysburg," in *Battles and Leaders*, Vol. III, p. 360; Cowell, *Tactics at Gettysburg*, p. 57; Haskell, *The Battle of Gettysburg*, p. 32; *Pennsylvania At Gettysburg*, pp. 612–613.

415. Alexander, *Fighting For the Confederacy*, p. 240; Humphreys to McLaws, January 6, 1878, UNCL.

416. Alexander, *Fighting For the Confederacy*, p. 240.

417. Ibid.

418. Wert, *A Glorious Army*, pp. 263–265; Bigelow, *The Peach Orchard*, pp. 32, 39; Humphreys to McLaws, January 6, 1878, UNCL; Pfanz, *Gettysburg: The Second Day*, p. 336.

419. Haskell, *The Battle of Gettysburg*, p. 27; Bigelow, *The Peach Orchard*, pp. 32, 39; Humphreys to McLaws, January 6, 1878, UNCL.

420. Haskell, *The Battle of Gettysburg*, pp. 35–36; Thomas, *Robert E. Lee*, pp. 288, 292; Hagerty, *Collis' Zouaves*, p. 240; Wert, *A Glorious Army*, pp. 262–265; Bigelow, *The Peach Orchard*, pp. 32, 39, Humphreys to McLaws, January 6, 1878, UNCL.

421. Thomas, *Robert E. Lee*, p. 288.

422. Hagerty, *Collis' Zouaves*, p. 240; Wert, *A Glorious Army*, pp. 262–265; Bigelow, *The Peach Orchard*, pp. 32, 39; Humphreys to McLaws, January 6, 1878, UNCL.

423. Wert, *A Glorious Army*, pp. 262–265; Bigelow, *The Peach Orchard*, pp. 32, 39; Humphreys to McLaws, January 6, 1878, UNCL; Sears, *Gettysburg*, p. 506.

424. Bigelow, *The Peach Orchard*, p. 39.

425. Haskell and Oates, *Gettysburg*, p. 175; Miers and Brown, *Gettysburg*, p. 134; Gottfried, *Brigades of Gettysburg*, pp. 410–416.

426. Trudeau, *Gettysburg*, p. 381.

427. Sears, *Gettysburg*, p. 503.

428. Ibid., pp. 302; 503; Trudeau, *Gettysburg*, pp. 377, 379.

429. Sears, *Gettysburg*, pp. 500–505.

430. Trudeau, *Gettysburg*, p. 381; Alexander, *Fighting for the Confederacy*, p. 240; Thomas, *Robert E. Lee*, pp. 296–298; Smith, *"One of the Most Daring of Men,"* pp. 85, 90–91; Jordan, *One Final Charge!*, pp. 106–107.

431. Trudeau, *Gettysburg*, pp. 377, 379, 380–381; Gottfried, *Brigades of Gettysburg*, p. 420; Tucker, *High Tide at Gettysburg*, p. 279; Bailey George McClelen, *I Saw the Elephant* (Shippensburg, Pa: White Mane Publishing Company, 1995), pp. 41–42; Sears, *Gettysburg*, pp. 303–304; Humphreys to McLaws, January 6, 1878, UNCL; Coddington, *The Gettysburg Campaign*, pp. 405–406; McNeily, "Barksdale's Mississippi Brigade at Gettysburg," *PMHS*, p. 243; Hagerty, *Collis' Zouaves*, p. 250; Smith, *"One of the Most Daring of Men,"* pp. 81, 83, 85–86.

432. Smith, *"One of the Most Daring of Men,"* p. 86.

433. Coddington, *The Gettysburg Campaign*, p. 416; Humphreys to McLaws, January 6, 1878, UNCL; Trudeau, *Gettysburg*, pp. 380–381, 572; Coddington, *The Gettysburg Campaign*, pp. 415–416; David M. Jordan, *Winfield Scott Hancock, A Soldier's Life* (Indianapolis, IN: University Press, 19), p. 92; Pfanz, *Gettysburg: The Second Day*, pp. 128–129; Paul J. Lader, "The 7th New Jersey in the Gettysburg Campaign," *Gettysburg Magazine*, no. 16 (1997), pp. 46–65; O.R., vol. 27, ser. 1, pt. 1, p. 587; McNeily, "Barksdale's Mississippi Brigade at Gettysburg," *PMHS*, pp. 246–47; CMSR, NA; John B. Hood, "Tribute of Gen. Barksdale," Gettysburg National Military Park Archives, Gettysburg, PA; Gottfried, *Brigades of Gettysburg*, p. 413; Pfanz, *Gettysburg: The Second Day*, pp. 129, 263–264; *The Aberdeen Examiner*, August 22, 1913; Wert, *A Glorious Army*, pp. 262–265.

434. Trudeau, *Gettysburg*, p. 384; Pfanz, *Gettysburg: The Second Day*, pp. 339–340; CMSR, NA.

435. Humphreys to McLaws, January 6, 1878, UNCL; Pfanz, *Gettysburg: The Second Day*, p. 336.

436. Humphreys to McLaws, January 6, 1878, UNCL; Wheeler, *Witness to Gettysburg*, p. 204; McNeily, "Barksdale's Mississippi Brigade at Gettysburg," *PMHS*, p. 239.

437. McNeily, "Barksdale's Mississippi Brigade at Gettysburg," *PMHS*, p. 239.

438. Humphreys to McLaws, January 6, 1878, UNCL; Coddington, *The Gettysburg Campaign*, pp. 406–407, 413.

439. Smith, *"One of the Most Daring of Men,"* pp. 85, 90–91; Humphreys to McLaws, January 6, 1878.

440. Wheeler, *Witness to Gettysburg*, p. 204; Coddington, *The Gettysburg Cam-*

paign, pp. 414–415; Humphreys to McLaws, January 6, 1878, UNCL; Pfanz, *Gettysburg, The Second Day*, p. 333; Trudeau, *Gettysburg*, p. 376.

441. Trudeau, *Gettysburg*, p. 376.
442. Ibid.
443. Alexander, *Fighting For The Confederacy*, p. 240.
444. Ibid; Coddington, *The Gettysburg Campaign*, pp. 416.
445. Humphreys to McLaws, January 6, 1878, UNCL; Trudeau, pp. 277, 279; Wheeler, *Witness to Gettysburg*, p. 209; Coddington, *The Gettyburg Campaign*, pp. 414–415; Harman to Decker, August 16, 1886, OCHS; Wert, *A Glorious Army*, pp. 262–265; Dowdey, *Death of a Nation*, pp. 220–222; Smith, "*One of the Most Daring of Men*," pp. 81, 85–86, 90–91; Sears, *Gettysburg*, pp. 500–505.
446. Pfanz, *Gettysburg: The Second Day*, pp. 358, 367; CMSR, NA; Henley, "On the Way to Gettysburg," FSNMP.
447. Coddington, *The Gettysburg Campaign*, p. 416.
448. Abernathy Manuscript, MDAH.
449. Pfanz, *Gettysburg*, p. 367; Gottfried, *Brigades of Gettysburg*, p. 222.
450. Henley, "On the Way to Gettysburg," FSNMP; CMSR, NA.
451. Henley, "On the Way to Gettysburg," FSNMP.
452. Roach, *Gettysburg*, p. 35.
453. Dick Stanley, "13th Mississippi Infantry, Night on the Battlefield," September 2011, internet.
454. CMSR, NA; Henley, "On the Way to Gettysburg," FSNMP.
455. Bigelow, *The Peach Orchard*, p. 56.
456. William A. Frassanito, *Gettysburg: A Journey In Time* (New York: Macmillan Publishing Company, 1975), p. 149; Trudeau, *Gettysburg*, pp. 275, 286, 384–385; Coddington, *The Gettysburg Campaign*, pp. 415–416; Bigelow, *The Peach Orchard*, pp. 55–56; Trudeau, *Gettysburg*, p. 385; CMSR, NA; Eric Campbell, "We Saved the Line from Being Broken: Freeman McGilvery, John Bigelow, Charles Reed and the Battle of Gettysburg," Gettysburg National Park Service, Unsung Heroes of Gettysburg, Programs of the Fiftieth Annual Gettysburg Seminar (Gettysburg: National Park Service, 1996), pp. 43–45, 53–55; Levi W. Baker, *The History of the Ninth Massachusetts Battery* (Lancaster: Vanberg Publishing, 1996), pp. vii, 60, 66, 195, 201, 213–14; McNeily, "Barksdale's Mississippi Brigade at Gettysburg," *PMHS*, pp. 249, 262; Thomas, *Robert E. Lee*, p. 288; Sears, *Gettysburg*, p. 507; Gottfried, *Brigades of Gettysburg*, p. 417; Wert, *A Glorious Army*, pp. 262–265; Pfanz, *Gettysburg: The Second Day*, pp. 341–345; 367, 455; Lowry, *The Story The Soldiers Wouldn't Tell*, pp. 72–75.
457. Haskell, *The Battle of Gettysburg*, p. 45.
458. Coddington, *The Gettysburg Campaign*, p. 416.
459. Frank Putnam Deane, editor, "*My Dear Wife*," *The Civil War Letters Of David Brett, 9th Massachusetts Battery, Union Cannoneer* (Little Rock, Arkansas: Pioneer Press, 1964), pp. 1–4, 8, 14, 22, 24, 32; Coddington, *The Gettysburg*

Campaign, pp. 416–417; Bigelow, *The Peach Orchard*, pp. 39, 42; Trudeau, *Gettysburg*, pp. 384–385; Campbell, "We Saved the Line from Being Broken," Unsung Heroes of Gettysburg, pp. 43, 54–55; Levi W. Baker, *History of the Ninth Massachusetts Battery*, pp. ii–iii, ix–x, 8-9, 11, 17, 19, 214, 259–260; Bigelow, *The Peach Orchard*, pp. 24, 31–32, 39, 42.

460. Deane, ed, *"My Dear Wife,"* pp. 33, 38–39; Baker, *History of the Ninth Massachusetts Battery*, pp. iii, 23, 44, 46, 48–50, 56–57, 60–61, 214, 219–21; Trudeau, *Gettysburg*, pp. 385–386; Coddington, *The Gettysburg Campaign*, p. 416.

461. Deane, ed., *"My Dear Wife,"* pp. 33, 67, 122; Trudeau, *Gettysburg*, pp. 385–386; Coddington, *The Gettysburg Campaign*, p. 416; Pfanz, *Gettysburg: The Second Day*, p. 344; Bigelow, *The Peach Orchard*, pp. 57–59; Baker, *History of the Ninth Massachusetts Battery*, pp. 8, 17, 60-61, 76-77, 214–15, 220–21, 223–26; Augustus Hesse to Deborah Weston, July 12, 1863, Boston Public Library, Boston, MA; Campbell, "We Saved the Line from Being Broken," Unsung Heroes of Gettysburg, pp. 56–57.

462. Deane, *"My Dear Wife,"* pp. 59, 121; Pfanz, *Gettysburg: The Second Day*, p. 344; Bigelow, *The Peach Orchard*, pp. 59-60; Campbell, "We Saved the Line from Being Broken," Unsung Heroes of Gettysburg, pp. 56–57; CMSR, NA.

463. McNeily, "The Mississippi Brigade at Gettysburg," *PMHS*, pp. 247–48.

464. Ibid., pp. 33–34; Coddington, *The Gettysburg Campaign*, p. 417; Bigelow, *The Peach Orchard*, pp. 57-61; Deane, *"My Dear Wife,"* pp. xvii, 60-61, 63, 73; Survivors' Association, *History of the Corn Exchange Regiment, 118th Pennsylvania Volunteers* (Philadelphia, PA: J.L. Smith Publishers, 1888), p. 249; McWhiney and Jamieson, *Attack and Die*, pp. 170–191; Trudeau, *Gettysburg*, p. 385; CMSR, NA; McNeily, "Barksdale's Mississippi Brigade At Gettysburg," *PMHS*, pp. 244, 247–48; Baker, *History of the Ninth Massachusetts Battery*, pp. iii, 9, 60–62, 66, 76–77, 96, 196, 200, 215–216, 229–233, 247–248; Cunliffe, *The Ancient Celts*, pp. 93–104; Campbell, "We Saved The Line From Being Broken," Unsung Heroes of Gettysburg, pp. 56–57.

465. Arrington, *The Medal of Honor at Gettysburg*, p. 22; Deane, *"My Dear Wife,"* p. 61; Eric Campbell, "Baptism of Fire: The Ninth Massachusetts Battery at Gettysburg, July 2, 1863," *Gettysburg Magazine*, No. 5 (July 1, 1991), pp. 74–76; Trudeau, *Gettysburg*, pp. 385–386; Campbell, "We Saved the Line from Being Broken," Unsung Heroes of Gettysburg, pp. 44–45, 56–57; Pfanz, *Gettysburg: The Second Day*, p. 345; Baker, *The History of the Ninth Massachusetts Battery*, pp. 62, 69-70, 80, 189–192, 200, 226–228, 254–256; Chandler, *The Campaigns of Napoleon*, pp. 81-84, 290–296.

466. McNeily, "Barksdale's Mississippi Brigade at Gettysburg," *PMHS*, p. 249; CMSR, NA.

467. Ibid.

468. Ibid.

469. Ibid; Henley, "On the Way to Gettysburg," FSNMP; Henley, "The Career of a Veteran," FSNMP; McWhiney and Jamieson, *Attack and Die*, p. 115;

Humphreys to McLaws, January 6, 1878, UNCL; Wert, *A Glorious Army*, p. 263; Time-Life editors, *Gettysburg*, pp. 107–108; Coddington, *The Gettysburg Campaign*, pp. 416–418; Trudeau, *Gettysburg*, pp. 275, 377–379; Luvaas and Nelson, *Guide to the Battle of Gettysburg*, pp. 136–137; Baker, *The History of the Ninth Massachusetts Battery*, pp. v, 62-65, 200–203; Gottfried, *Brigades of Gettysburg*, pp. 415–417; Dowdey, *Death of a Nation*, p. 284; Campbell, "We Saved the Line from Being Broken," Unsung Heroes of Gettysburg, pp. 57–59.

470. Trudeau, *Gettysburg*, p. 387; Pfanz, *Gettysburg:The Second Day*, p. 346.

471. Trudeau, *Gettysburg*, pp. 300, 383, 377–378, 385–386; Gottfried, *Brigades of Gettysburg*, p. 415; Wert, *A Glorious Army*, pp. 262–263; Henley, "On the Way to Gettysburg," FSNMP; Humphreys to McLaws, January 6, 1878, UNCL; Time-Life Editors, *Gettysburg*, p. 108; Letters Home: A Collection of Original Civil War Soldiers' Letters (Gettysburg, Pa: Alan Sessarego, 1990), p. 21; Coddington, *The Gettysburg Campaign*, pp. 401–402, 411, 416–417; McWhiney and Jamieson, *Attack and Die*, p. 115; Michael Aikey, "'Boys, Remember Harper's Ferry'!" *Civil War Magazine*, vol. 17 (1989), pp. 31–33; McNeily, "Barksdale's Mississippi Brigade At Gettysburg," *PMHS*, p. 249; Haskell, *The Battle of Gettysburg*, pp. 45–46; Hood, "Tribute to Gen. Barksdale," GNMPA.

472. Wayne, Mahood, *'Written in Blood': A History of the 126th New York Infantry in the Civil War* (Hightstown: Longstreet House, 1997), p. 129; Trudeau, *Gettysburg*, pp. 383–384.

473. Trudeau, *Gettysburg*, p. 384.

474. Henley, "The Career of a Veteran," FSNMP.

475. Trudeau, *Gettysburg*, p. 388.

476. John Saunders Henley, "Battle of Harpers Ferry and Sharpsburg," Fredericksburg and Spotsylvania National Military Park, Fredericksburg, Virginia; Murray, *The Redemption of the Harpers Ferry Cowards*, pp. 44, 46, 49, 51, 61, 88-89, 93, 95, 99; Gottfried, *Brigades of* Gettysburg, p. 177; Trudeau, *Gettysburg*, pp. 299, 388; Mahood, *"Written in Blood,"* pp. 27–46, 129–130.

477. Trudeau, *Gettysburg*, p. 299.

478. Ibid.

479. Ibid., p. 300

480. Ibid.

481. Ibid, p. 388; Gottfried, *Brigades of Gettysburg*, p. 178.

482. Trudeau, *Gettysburg*, pp. 388, 570; Coddington, *The Gettysburg Campaign*, pp. 417–418; Mahood, *"Written In Blood,"* pp. 129–131, 135; Murray, *The Redemption of the "Harpers Ferry Cowards,"* pp. 101–102; Abernathy Manuscript, MDAH; Baker, *History of the Ninth Massachusetts Battery*, p. 198; Mahood, *"Written In Blood,"* pp. 129–131, 135; Gottfried, *Brigades of Gettysburg*, pp. 177–178; Miers and Brown, *Gettysburg*, p. 138; Henley, "On the Way to Gettysburg," FSNMP; Henley, "The Career of a Veteran," FNSMP; McNeily, "Barksdale's Mississippi Brigade at Gettysburg," *PMHS*, p. 250;

Crandell Diary, GNMPA; Trudeau, *Gettysburg*, p. 299..

483. Murray, *The Redemption of the "Harpers Ferry Cowards,"* pp. 102–112; Love, "Mississippi At Gettysburg," *SHSP*, pp. 32–33; Trudeau, *Gettysburg*, p. 388; Gottfried, *Brigades of Gettysburg*, p. 178; Miers and Brown, *Gettysburg*, pp. 95–97; Crandell Diary, GNMPA; Mahood, *"Written In Blood,"* pp. 132–133.

484. Charles A. Richardson Papers, Ontario County, New York, Historical Society, Canandaigua, NY; Abernathy Manuscript, MDAH; Trudeau, *Gettysburg*, p. 388; Crandell Diary, GNMPA; Mahood, *"Written In Blood,"* pp. 131–132, 135; CMSR, NA; Gottfried, *Brigades of Gettysburg*, pp. 177–178.

485. McNeily, "Barksdale's Mississippi Brigade at Gettysburg," PMHS, p. 230; Henley, "On the Way to Gettysburg," FSNMP; Trudeau, *Gettysburg*, p. 388.

486. *The Mississippi Index*, June 13, 1866; Trudeau, *Gettysburg*, p. 388; CMSR, NA.

487. Coddington, *The Gettysburg Campaign*, pp. 417–418; Abernathy Manuscript, MDAH; McNeily, "Barksdale's Mississippi Brigade at Gettysburg," *PMHS*, p. 250; CMSR, NA; Trudeau, *Gettysburg*, p. 388; Crandell Diary, GNMPA; Mahood, *"Written In Blood,"* pp. 130–131.

488. Haskell and Oates, *Gettysburg*, p. 175; Wert, *Longstreet*, p. 277; Dowdey, *Death of a Nation*, pp. 224–225; Foote, *The Civil War*, vol. 2, p. 509; McNeily, "Barksdale's Mississippi Brigade at Gettysburg," *PMSH*, p. 250; Crandell Diary, GNMPA; CMSR, NA; Trudeau, *Gettysburg*, pp. 388, 570.

489. McNeily, "Barksdale's Mississippi Brigade at Gettysburg," *PMHS*, pp. 250; Mahood, *"Written In Blood,"* p. 134; Crandell Diary, GNMPA; Trudeau, *Gettysburg*, p. 388; CMSR, NA;

490. Coddington, *The Gettysburg Campaign*, pp. 370–384; Wert, *A Glorious Army*, pp. 255, 263; Dowdey, *Death of a Nation*, pp. 220–221.

491. Coddington, *The Gettysburg Campaign*, pp. 370–384; CMSR, NA; Dowdey, *Death of a Nation*, pp. 220–221; Wert, *A Glorious Army*, pp. 255, 263.

492. Harrison, *Pickett's Men*, p. 88; Hood, *Advance and Retreat*, p. 57.

493. Gottfried, *Brigades of Gettysburg*, pp. 222, 410–416, 420–421; Henley, "On the Way to Gettysburg," FSNMP; *The Mississippi Index*, June 13, 1866, MDAH; Coddington, *The Gettysburg Campaign*, pp. 370–384;Foote, *The Civil War*, vol. 2, pp. 508–509; Tucker, *High Tide at Gettysburg*, pp. 280–281; Cross, *They Sleep Beneath the Mockingbird*, p. 12; Samuel Toombs, *New Jersey Troops in the Gettysburg Campaign* (Orange, New Jersey: Evening Mail Publishing House, 1888), p. 239; Murray, *The Redemption of the "Harpers Ferry Cowards,"* p. 102; Pfanz, *Gettysburg: The Second Day*, p. 348; O.R., vol. XXVII, ser. 1, pt. 1, p. 436; Wert, *A Glorious Army*, pp. 248–263; Richardson Papers, OCHS; General Barksdale Biographical Sketch, UNCL; McNeily, "The Mississippi Brigade at Gettysburg," *PMHS*, p. 243; Roach, *Gettysburg*, p. 36; Henry Stevens Willey, "The Story of My Experiences During the Civil War," Collections of the Manuscript Division, Library of Congress, Washington, D.C.; CMSR, NA; Dowdey, *Death of a Nation*, pp. 220–221; Mahood, *"Written In*

Blood," pp. 133–134; Trudeau, *Gettysburg*, pp. 377, 381, 388–379, 572; Hood, "Tribute to Gen. Barksdale," GNMPA; Wert, *A Glorious Army*, pp. 262–265.

494. Mahood, *"Written In Blood,"* pp. 133–134; Wert, *A Glorious Army*, p. 251; Trudeau, *Gettysburg*, p. 572.

495. *The Mississippi Index*, June 13, 1866, William Barksdale Subject File, Mississippi Department Archives and History, Jackson, Mississippi.

496. *The Mississippi Index*, June 13, 1866, MDAM; Mahood, *"Written In Blood,"* pp. 35–46, 133–134; Henley, "On the Way to Gettysburg," FSNMP; Pfanz, *Gettysburg: The Second Day*, p. 435; CMSR, NA.

497. *The Mississippi Index*, June 13, 1866, MDAH; Henley, "On the Way to Gettysburg," FSNMP; Coco, Wasted Valor, pp. 147–148; Cross, They Sleep Beneath the Mockingbird, p. 12; Love, "Mississippi at Gettysburg," *SHSP*, p. 33; General Barksdale Biographical Sketch, UNCL; William Youngblood, "Unwritten History of the Gettysburg Campaign," *Southern Historical Society Papers*, vol. 38 (1907), pp. 316, 318; Trudeau, *Gettysburg*, p. 388; CMSR, NA; *The Aberdeen Examineer*, August 22, 1913; Mahood, *"Written In Blood,"* pp. 133–134.

498. *The Mississippi Index*, June 13, 1866.

499. McNeilly, "Barksdale's Mississippi Brigade At Gettysburg," *PMHS*, p. 239; Aikey, "'Boys, Remember Harpers Ferry!',", *CWM*, p. 33; Harman to Decker, August 16, 1886, OCHS; The Mississippi Index, June 13, 1866, MDAH; Pfanz, *Gettysburg: The Second Day*, p. 435.

500. Hill Diary, MDAH; CMSR; CMSR, NA; Luvaas and Nelson, eds., *Guide to the Battle of Gettysburg*, p. 137; Gottfried, *Brigades of Gettysburg*, pp. 410–416; "Henley," On the Way to Gettysburg," FSNMP.

501. General Barksdale Biographical Sketch, UNCL; Aikey, "'Boys, Remember Harpers Ferry!',", *CWM*, p. 33; Baker, *History of the Ninth Massachusetts Battery*, p. 198; CMSR, NA; Mahood, *"Written in Blood,"* p. 131.

502. Richardson Papers, OCHS; Campbell, "We Saved the Line from Being Broken," Unsung Heroes of Gettsyburg, p. 59.

503. Dick Stanley, "13th Mississippi Infantry Regiment, The Death of Private Nash," September 26, 2011, internet; CMSR, NA.

504. Arrington, *The Medal of Honor at Gettysburg*, p. 15.

505. General Barksdale Biographical Sketch, UNCL.

506. Mahood, *"Written in Blood,"* pp. 133–134.

507. Ibid.

508. Ibid., p. 471, note 69; *The Mississippi Index*, June 13, 1866, DMAH.

509. Trudeau, *Gettysburg*, p. 391; Gottfried, *Brigades of Gettysburg*, pp. 410–416.

510. Charles W. Squires Manuscript, LC.

511. Ibid; CMSR, NA; Joseph A. Miller Diary, FSNMP.

512. Arrington, *The Medal of Honor at Gettysburg*, p. 15; Lavaas and Nelson, eds., *Guide to the Battle of Gettysburg*, p. 136; Bigelow, *The Peach Orchard*, pp. 24, 31–32, 39, 42; Baker, *History of the Ninth Massachusetts Battery*, pp. 71,

198–199; Campbell, "We Saved The Line From Being Broken," Unsung Heroes at Gettysburg, pp. 58–59; McNeily, "Barksdale's Mississippi Brigade At Gettysburg," *PMHS*, p. 249; *The Wilkes-Barre Record*, July 17, 1925; Catalog of the Flags of the 13th, 17th, 18th, and 21st Mississippi Regiments, MDAH; CMSR, NA; Trudeau, *Gettysburg*, pp. 372, 390–391; Hood, "Tribute to Gen. Barksdale," GNMPA; "Major Malbone Francis 'Peggy" Watson (1939–1891), Find A Grace," internet; Wert, *A Glorious Army*, pp. 262–265; Gottfried, *Brigades of Gettysburg*, pp. 178, 410–416; Pfanz, *Gettysburg: The Second Day*, pp. 317, 346–347.

513. CMSR, NA; Trudeau, *Gettysburg*, p. 390.

514. CMSR, NA; *Confederate Veteran*, vol. 33 (1925), p. 185.

515. Eric Campbell, "'Remember Harpers Ferry': The Degradation, Humiliation, and Redemption of Col. George L. Willard's Brigade," *Gettysburg Magazine*, no. 7 (July 1, 1992), p. 52; Michael Bacarella, *Lincoln's Foreign Legion: The 39th New York Infantry, The Garibaldi Guard* (Shippensburg, Pa: White Mane Publishing Company, 1996), p. 69; Trudeau, *Gettysburg*, p. 390; Gottfried, *Brigades of Gettysburg*, p. 178.

516. Bacarella, *Lincoln's Foreign Legion*, pp. 20, 26, 28, 44–45.

517. CMSR, NA; Bigelow, *The Peach Orchard*, pp. 24, 31–32, 39, 42.

518. Humphreys to McLaws, January 6, 1878, UNCL.

519. Alexander, *Fighting for the Confederacy*, p. 242; McNeily, "Barksdale's Mississippi Brigade at Gettysburg," *PMHS*, p. 249.

520. Trudeau, *Gettysburg*, pp. 390–391; CMSR, NA; Humphreys to McLaws, January 6, 1878, UNCL; Garrison, *Civil War Stories*, p. 179

521. Bigelow, *The Peach Orchard*, pp. 24, 31–32, 39, 42; Gottfried, *Brigades of Gettysburg*, p. 415.

522. Arrington, *The Medal of Honor at Gettysburg*, p.15; Bacarella, *Lincoln's Foreign Legion*, p. 138; McNeily, *Barksdale's Mississippi Brigade at Gettysburg*, p. 249; CMSR, NA; CNYSR, NA.

523. CMSR, NA; Trudeau, *Gettysburg*, p. 390; Gottfried, *Brigades of Gettysburg*, p. 178.

524. Alexander, "Artillery Fighting at Gettysburg," in *Battles and Leaders*, Vol. III, p. 367; Luvaas and Nelson, eds., *Guide to the Battle of Gettysburg*, p. 137.

525. Trudeau, *Gettysburg*, p. 391.

526. Humphreys to McLaws, January 6, 1878, UNCL; O.O. Howard's Commencement Address to Syracuse University, *Gettysburg Magazine*, no. 11 (July 1, 1994), p. 76; Gottfried, *Brigades of Gettysburg*, p. 415; McNeily, "Barksdale's Mississippi Brigade at Gettysburg," *PMHS*, p. 249.

527. Humphreys to McLaws, January 6, 1878, UNCL; Baker, *History of the Ninth Massachusetts Battery*, pp. 203-04; McNeily, "Barksdale's Mississippi Brigade at Gettysburg," *PMHS*, pp. 244–251, 262; CMSR, NA; Hood, "Tribute to Gen. Barksdale," GNMPA; Andrews, "Gallantry at Gettysburg," GNMPA; Trudeau, *Gettysburg*, pp. 377, 379; Gottfried, *Brigades of Gettysburg*, pp. 410–416, 419.

528. Humphreys to McLaws, January 6, 1878, UNCL; Trudeau, *Gettysburg*, p. 380; Cross, *They Sleep Beneath the Mockingbird*, pp. 38–39.

529. Trudeau, *Gettysburg*, p. 551.

530. Wert, *A Glorious Army*, pp. 262–265; Gottfried, *Brigades of Gettysburg*, pp. 410–416.

531. Sears, *Gettysburg*, pp. 504–505.

532. Ibid., p. 506.

533. Ibid., pp. 506, 508.

534. Ibid., p. 498; Trudeau, *Gettysburg*, p. 529..

535. Sears, *Gettysburg*, p. 498.

536. Coco, *Wasted Valor*, p. 107; McNeily, "Barksdale's Mississippi Brigade at Gettysburg," *PMHS*, pp. 257, 260; Trudeau, *Gettysburg*, p. 551.

537. Love, "Mississippi at Gettysburg," *SHSP*, p. 33.

538. Cross, *They Sleep Beneath the Mockingbird*, pp. 12–13; Coco, *Wasted Valor*, p. 147.

539. Willey, "The Story of My Experiences During the Civil War," LC; Trudeau, *Gettysburg*, p. 417.

540. Willey, "The Story of My Experiences During the Civil War," LC.

541. Coco, *Wasted Valor*, p. 147; Time-Life Editors, *Gettysburg*, p. 108; Hill Diary, MDAH; McNeily, "Barksdale's Mississippi Brigade at Gettysburg," *PMHS*, p. 241.

542. Clark, *Gettysburg*, p. 108.

543. *Harpers Weekly*, New York, New York, February 2, 1861.

544. Cross, *They Sleep Beneath the Mockingbird*, p. 13; General Barksdale Biographical Sketch, UNCL.

545. *The Mississippi Index*, June 13, 1866, MDAH.

546. Ibid.

547. Ibid.

548. Ibid; Pfanz, *Gettysburg*, p. 435.

549. *Letters Home*, p. 24; O.R., vol. 27, ser. 1, pt. 1, p. 371; Wert, *A Glorious Army*, p. 265.

550. Coco, *Wasted Valor*, p. 148; O.R., vol. XXVII, ser. 1, pt. 1, pp. 74, 260. 596; Clark, Gettysburg, p. 109; Trudeau, *Gettysburg*, p. 321; Jordan, *One Final Charge!*, p. 104.

551. Dinkins, *Personal Recollections and Experiences in the Confederate Army*, p. 86; CMSR, NA.

552. Moore, *A Life for the Confederacy*, p. 162.

553. Moore, *A Life for the Confederacy*, p. 153; Cross, *They Sleep Beneath the Mockingbird*, pp. 13–14; CMSR, NA.

554. Humphreys to McLaws, January 6, 1878, UNCL; CMSR, NA; McNeily, "Barksdale's Mississippi Brigade at Gettysburg," *PMHS*, p. 243; Gottfried, *Brigades of Gettysburg*, pp. 410–416; Wert, *A Glorious Army*, p. 262; Trudeau, *Gettysburg*, p. 381; Dowdey, *Death of a Nation*, pp. 220–221; John C. Oeffinger, *A Soldier's General: The Civil War Letters of Major General*

Lafayette McLaws (Chapel Hill: University of North Carolina Press, 2002), 197.

555. General Barksdale Biographical Sketch, UNCL; McNeily,"Barksdale's Mississippi Brigade at Gettysburg," *PMHS*, pp. 243–244, 251; Trudeau, *Gettysburg*, pp 371–391; Sears, *Gettysburg*, pp. 297–319; Coddington, *The Gettysburg Campaign*, p. 405; CPSR, NA; CNYSR, NA; Gottfried, *Brigades of Gettysburg*, pp. 410–416; Humphreys to McLaws, January 6, 1878, UNCL; Jordan, *One Final Charge!*, p. 104.

556. Duke, "Mississippians at Gettysburg," CV, p. 216.

557. Ibid; CMSR, NA.

558. CMSR, NA.

559. CMSR, NA; William Burton Owen to Luman Baker, Greene County Historical Society, Coxsackie, New York.

560. "13th Mississippi Infantry Regiment, Correspondence," September 6, 2011, internet.

561. Longstreet, From Manassas to Appomattox, p. 373

562. Coddington, *The Gettysburg Campaign*, pp. 421–422.

563. Trudeau, *Gettysburg*, pp. 332–333; Harrison, *Pickett's Men*, p. 146.

564. Ibid.

565. Baker, *History of the Ninth Massachusetts Battery*, p. 261.

566. McNeily, "Barksdale's Mississippi Brigade at Gettysburg," *PMHS*, p. 261; Hood, "Tribute to Gen. Barksdale," GNMPA.

567. Keneally, *American Scoundrel*, p. 291.

568. Bigelow, *The Peach Orchard*, p. 32, 39.

569. Coddington, *The Gettysburg Campaign*, p. 443.

570. Ibid.

Ϛᐂᔓ

Bibliography

Manuscript and Unpublished Sources

William Meshack Abernathy, *Our Mess: Southern Army Gallantry and Privations, 1851–1865* (Jackson, MS: Department of Archives and History).

_____, Edward Porter Alexander Papers (Chapel Hill, NC: Wilson Library, Southern Historical Collection, University of North Carolina).

William Allen, *Ordnance Reports, September 1862–April 1863*, Compiled Service Records of Confederate Soldiers Who Served From the State of Mississippi (Washington, D.C.: Record Group 94, National Archives).

A.P. Andrews, *Gallantry at Gettysburg: An Act of Courageous Deeds of the Mississippi Brigades Commanded by William Barksdale and Joseph R. Davis* (Gettysburg, PA: Gettysburg National Military Park Archives).

Ezekiel Armstrong, *Armstrong (Ezekiel) Diary* (Jackson, MS: Mississippi Department of Archives and History).

_____, *Barksdale (Ethelbert) Papers* (Jackson, MS: Mississippi Department of Archives and History).

_____, *Barksdale Family Papers* (Jackson, MS: Department of Archives and History).

John A. Barksdale, *To Oscar J.E. Stuart, June 29, 1863* (Jackson, MS: J.E.B. Stuart Family Papers).

_____, *William Barksdale Subject File* (Jackson, MS: Mississippi Department of Archives and History).

Henry Robinson Berkeley, *The Diary of Henry Robinson Berkeley* (Richmond, VA: Virginia Historical Society).

_____, *Biographical Files of Mississippi Soldiers* (Jackson, MS: Mississippi Department of History and Archives).

_____, *Biographical Sketch of William Barksdale* (Chapel Hill, NC: John Francis Hamtramck Claiborne Papers 1797–1884, Louis Round Wilson Special Collections, Southern Historical Collection, University of North Carolina).

295

Robert L. Brandon, *To Mrs. Perry, June 2, 1896* (Jackson, MS: Catalog no. Z1699, Mississippi Department of Archives and History).

———, Catalog of the Flags of the 13th, 17th, 18th, and 21st Mississippi Regiments (Jackson, MS: Mississippi Department of Archives and History).

———, Compiled Military Service Records of Soldiers Who Served from the State of Alabama (Washington, D.C.: Record Group 94, National Archives).

———, Compiled Military Service Records of Soldiers Who Served from the State of Georgia (Washington, D.C.: Record Group 94, National Archives).

———, Compiled Military Service Records of Soldiers Who Served from the State of Massachusetts (Washington, D.C.: Record Group 94, National Archives).

———, Compiled Military Service Records of Soldiers Who Served from the State of New Hampshire (Washington, D.C.: Record Group 94, National Archives).

———, Compiled Military Service Records of Soldiers Who Served from the State of New York (Washington, D.C.: Record Group 94, National Archives).

———, Compiled Military Service Records of Soldiers Who Served from the State of Pennsylvania (Washington, D.C.: Record Group 94, National Archives).

———, Compiled Military Service Records of Soldiers Who Served from the State of Virginia (Washington, D.C.: Record Group 94, National Archives).

———, *John Francis Hamtramck Claiborne Papers 1797–1884* (Chapel Hill, NC: Louis Round Wilson Special Collection, Southern Historical Collection, University of North Carolina).

Lewis H. Crandell, *Lewis H. Crandell Civil War Diary* (Gettysburg, PA: Gettysburg National Military Park Archives).

James T. Downs, *Letter to Mother, June 9, 1862* (Jackson, MS: James Tickell Downs and Family Papers, Mississippi Department of Archives and History).

James W. Duke, *James W. Duke Account* (Gettysburg, PA: Gettysburg National Military Park Archives).

———, *Eleventh Regiment Massachusetts Regiment* (Acton, MA: Acton Memorial Library, Civil War Archives).

Alexander W. Given, *Diary of Alexander W. Given*, (Philadelphia, PA: Alexander W. Given Collection, Civil War Library Museum).

George K. Griggs, *Diary of George K. Griggs* (Richmond, VA: Eleanor S. Brockenbrough Library, Museum of the Confederacy).

E.P. Harman, *Letter to W.S. Decker, August 16, 1886* (Ontario, NY: Charles A. Richardson Papers, Ontario County Historical Society).

Thurman Hendricks, *Thurman Hendricks Early Memoir* (Jackson, MS: Mississippi Department of Archives and History).

John S. Henley, undated articles (Aberdeen, MS and Fredericksburg, VA: *Aberdeen Examiner*, Fredericksburg and Spotsylvania National Military Park).

John S. Henley, *Battle of Harpers Ferry and Sharpsburg* (Fredericksburg, VA: Fredericksburg and Spotsylvania National Military Park).

John S. Henley, *Drove the Enemy Back* (Fredericksburg, VA: Fredericksburg and Spotsylvania National Military Park).

John S. Henley, *On the Way to Gettysburg* (Fredericksburg, VA: 17th Mississippi File, Gettysburg National Military Park, Fredericksburg, and Spotsylvania National Military Park).

John S. Henley, *The Career of a Soldier* (Fredericksburg, VA: Fredericksburg and Spotsylvania National Military Park).

John S. Henley, *Winter Quarters at Leesburg* (Fredericksburg, VA: Fredericksburg and Spotsylvania National Military Park).

Augustus Hesse, *Letter to Deborah Weston, July 12, 1863* (Boston, MA: Boston Public Library).

William Henry Hill, *Diary of William Henry Hill* (Jackson, MS: John C. Rietti Papers, Mississippi Department of Archives and History).

John B. Hood, *Tribute of General Barksdale* (Gettysburg, PA: Gettysburg National Park Archives).

Benjamin G. Humphreys, *General Barksdale Biographical Sketch* (Chapel Hill, NC: University of North Carolina Library).

Benjamin G. Humphreys, *Letter to Lafayette McLaws, January 6, 1878* (Chapel Hill, NC: Lafayette McLaws' Papers, Southern Historical Society Collection, University of North Carolina Library).

_____, *Lauderdale County, Mississippi Census Records for 1860* (Jackson, MS: Mississippi Department of Archives and History).

Pinkney M. Lewis, *Letter to Family, May 13, 1864* (icollector.com live auction, item no. 3098, internet).

_____, *McAlister Papers* (Jackson, MS: Mississippi Department of Archives and History).

_____, *Lafayette McLaws Papers* (Chapel Hill, NC: Southern Historical Collection, University of North Carolina).

George G. Meade, *George G. Meade Collection* (Philadelphia, PA: Historical Society of Pennsylvania).

Ezekiel Miller, *Pickens Diary* (Fredericksburg, VA: Fredericksburg and Spotsylvania National Military Park).

Joseph A. Miller, *Joseph A. Miller Diary* (Fredericksburg, VA: Fredericksburg and Spotsylvania National Military Park).

Henry H. Mitchell, "Lt. Col. John Hampton Sims, Jr.," "Robert Gill Sims," and "William Edward Sims," (internet).

J.E.B. Trammell, *Narrative of Berkeley Green, June 27, 1863* (Jackson, MS: Trammell Family Papers).

William C. Nelson, *William C. Nelson Collection* (Jackson, MS: Special Collections, University of Mississippi).

William C. Nelson, *Letter to Maria, January 15, 1863* (Jackson, MS: William C. Nelson Collection, Special Collections, University of Mississippi).

Chaplain William Burton Owen, *Letter to Luman Baker* (Coxsackie, NY: Greene

County Historical Society).

Charles A. Richardson, *Charles A. Richardson Papers* (Canandaigua, NY: Ontario County, New York, Historical Society).

Charles W. Squires, *Charles W. Squires Manuscript* (Washington, D.C.: Library of Congress).

Mary Stamps, *Mary Stamps Papers* (Chapel Hill, NC: Southern Historical Collection, University of North Carolina).

Oscar Ewing Stuart, *Letter to Sisters, September 6, 1861* (Jackson, MS: Trammel Family Papers).

Oscar Ewing Stuart, *Letter to Ann L. Hardeman, September 21, 1861* (Jackson, MS: Trammel Family Papers).

Oscar Ewing Stuart, *Letter to Ann L. Hardeman, September 25, 1861* (Jackson, MS: Trammel Family Papers).

Oscar Ewing Stuart, *Letter to Anne L. Hardeman, February 20, 1862* (Jackson, MS: Trammel Family Papers).

Oscar Ewing Stuart, *Letter to Sister, March 6, 1862* (Jackson, MS: Trammel Family Papers).

Oscar Ewing Stuart, *Letter to Annie E. Stuart, December 17, 1862* (Jackson, MS: J.E.B. Trammel Family Papers).

Oscar Ewing Stuart, *Letter to Father, February 4, 1863* (Jackson, MS: Trammel Family Papers).

Oscar Ewing Stuart, *Letter to Father, April 17, 1863* (Jackson, MS: Trammel Family Papers).

_____, *The Mississippi Index, June 13, 1866* (Jackson, MS: William Barksdale Subject File, Mississippi Department of Archives and History).

Thurman E. Hendricks, *Early Hendricks Diary* (Jackson, MS: Mississippi Department of Archives and History).

J.E.B. Trammell, "Emails to Author" (Jackson, MS: internet, 2012).

J.E.B. Trammell, *Trammell Family Papers* (Jackson, MS: Miscellaneous Documents, Trammell Family).

Thomas D. Wallace, *Thomas D. Wallace Diary* (Jackson, MS: Special Collections, Mississippi State University Press).

Henry Stevens Willey, *The Story of my Experiences During the Civil War* (Washington, D.C.: Collections of the Manuscript Division, Library of Congress).

NEWSPAPERS

Aberdeen Examiner, Aberdeen MS
Harper's Weekly, New York NY
National Tribune, New York NY
Philadelphia Inquirer, Philadelphia PA
Rockingham Post-Dispatch, Richmond County NC
The Calhoun Monitor, Pittsboro MS

The Wilkes-Barre Record, Wilkes-Barre PA
Winston County Journal, Louisville MS
Woodville Republican, Woodville MS

PUBLISHED SOURCES

Michael Aikey, "'Boys, Remember Harper's Ferry!'" (*Civil War Magazine*, vol. 17, 1989).

Edward Porter Alexander, *Fighting For the Confederacy* (Chapel Hill: University of North Carolina Press, 1989).

Ken Allers Jr., *The Fog of Gettysburg: The Myths and Mysteries of the Battle* (Naperville: Cumberland House, 2008).

_____, *Annals of the War* (Edison: The Blue and Grey Press, 1996).

B.T. Arrington, *The Medal of Honor At Gettysburg* (Gettysburg: Thomas Publications, 1996).

_____, *Autobiography of Jefferson Davis* (Biloxi: The Beauvoir Press, 1998).

Michael Bacarella, *Lincoln's Foreign Legion: The 39th New York Infantry, the Garibaldi Guard* (Shippensburg: White Mane Publishing Company, 1996).

Levi W. Baker, *The History of the Ninth Massachusetts Battery* (Lancaster: Vanberg Publishing, 1996).

Charles K. Barrow (ed.), J. H. Segars (ed.), and R.B. Rosenburg (ed.), "Forgotten Confederates: An Anthology about Black Southerners" (*Journal of Confederate History Series*, vol. 14, 1995).

Edwin C. Bearss, *Grant Strikes a Fatal Blow: The Campaign for Vicksburg* (Dayton: Morningside Bookshop, 3 vols., 1986).

Stephen Berry, *House of Lincoln: Lincoln and the Todds, A Family Divided by War* (New York: Mariner Books, 2009).

John K. Bettersworth, *Mississippi: The Land and the People* (Austin: Steck-Vaughn Company, 1981).

John K. Bettersworth, *Your Mississippi* (Austin: Steck-Vaughn Company, 1975).

John Bigelow, *The Peach Orchard* (Gaithersburg: Old Soldier Books, 1987).

Mark Mayo Boatner, *The Civil War Dictionary* (New York: David McKay Company, 1959).

B. A. Botkin, *A Civil War Treasury of Tales, Legends and Folklore* (New York: Random House, 1960).

George A. Bruce, *The Twentieth Regiment of Massachusetts Volunteer Infantry, 1861–1865* (Boston: Houghton, Mifflin and Company, 1906).

James A Burns, "The 12th New Hampshire Regiment at Gettysburg And Beyond" (*Gettysburg Magazine*, no. 20).

Eric A. Campbell, "Baptism of Fire: The Ninth Massachusetts Battery at Gettysburg, July 2, 1863" (*Gettysburg Magazine*, no. 5, July 1991).

Eric A. Campbell, "Hell in a Peach Orchard" (*America's Civil War*, July 2003).

Eric A. Campbell, "Remember Harper's Ferry": The Degradation, Humiliation, and Redemption of Col. George L. Willard's Brigade" (*Gettysburg Magazine*, no. 7, July 1992).

Eric A. Campbell, "We Saved the Line from Being Broken: Freeman McGilvery, John Bigelow, Charles Reed and the Battle of Gettysburg" (Gettysburg: Unsung Heroes of Gettysburg, Programs of the Fifty Annual Gettysburg Seminar, Gettysburg National Military Park, Service 1966).

_____, *Campfires and Battlefields: A Pictorial Narrative of the Civil War* (New York: The Civil War Press, 1967).

Tom Carhart, *Lost Triumph: Lee's Real Plan at Gettysburg—And Why It Failed* (Mechanicsburg: Stackpole Books, 2005).

Samuel Carter III, *The Final Fortress: The Campaign for Vicksburg, 1862–1863* (New York: St. Martin's Press, 1980).

The Century Magazine, *Battles and Leaders of the Civil War, Vol. III; The Tide Shifts* (Reprint ed., New York, Castle Books, 1996).

David A. Clary, *Eagles and Empire: The United States, Mexico, and the Struggle for a Continent* (New York: Bantam Books, 2009).

Gregory A. Coco, *Killed in Action* (Gettysburg: Thomas Publications, 1992).

_____, *Wasted Valor: The Confederate Dead at Gettysburg* (Gettysburg: Thomas Publications, 1990).

Edwin B. Coddington, *The Gettysburg Campaign: A Study in Command* (New York: Charles Scribner's Sons, 1979).

James Lee Conrad, *The Young Lions: Confederate Cadets at War* (Mechanicsburg: Stackpole Books, 1997).

A.T. Cowell, *Tactics at Gettysburg* (Gaithersburg: Old Soldier Books, 1987).

David Craft, *History of the One Hundred Forty-First Regiment: Pennsylvania Volunteers, 1862–1865* (Towanda: Reporter-Journal Printing Company, 1885).

Harold A. Cross, "They Sleep Beneath the Mockingbird: Mississippi Burial Sites and Biographies of Confederate Generals" (*Journal of Confederate History*, vol. 12, 1994).

John A. Crow, *The Root and The Flower* (Los Angeles: University of California Press, 2005).

Wilson Oliver Davis, *Sketch of Frederic Fernandez Cavada* (Philadelphia: James B. Chandler Printer, 1871).

William C. Davis, *Jefferson C. Davis: The Man and His Hour: A Biography* (New York: HarperCollins Publishers, 1992).

Frank Putnam Deane (ed.), "My Dear Wife: The Civil War Letters of David Brett, 9th Massachusetts Battery, Union Cannoneer" (Little Rock: *Pioneer Press*, 1964).

Frank Allen Dennis (ed.), *Kemper County Rebel: The Civil War Diary of Robert Masten Holmes, C.S.A.* (Jackson: University and College press of Mississippi, 1973).

David Detzer, *Donnybrook: The Battle of Bull Run, 1861* (New York: Harcourt, Inc., 2004).

James Dinkins, "1861–1865, By An Old Johnnie: Personal Recollections and Experiences in the Confederate Army" (Dayton: Morningside Bookshop, 1975).

Clifford Dowdey, *Death of A Nation: The Story of Lee and His Men at Gettysburg* (New York: Knopf Publishers, 1958).

J. W. Duke, "Mississippians at Gettysburg" (*Confederate Veteran*, vol. 14, 1906).

Charles A. Earp, "The Seven McElroys of the Thirteenth Mississippi Infantry, C.S.A." (*Confederate Veteran*, Sep.-Oct. 1993).

Clement Eaton, *Jefferson Davis* (New York: The Free Press, 1977).

Editors of Time-Life Books, *Voices of Gettysburg* (Alexandria: Time-Life Books, 1995).

Guy R. Everson and Edward W. Simpon, Jr., *"Far, Far from Home: The Wartime Letters of Dick and Tally Simpson, 3rd South Carolina Volunteers* (New York: Oxford University Press, 1994).

Byron Farwell, *Ball's Bluff: A Small Battle and Its Long Shadow* (McLean: EPM Publications, Inc., 1990).

William A. Fletcher, *Rebel Private: Front and Rear: Memoirs of a Confederate Soldier* (New York: Meridian Books, 1997).

Shelby Foote, *The Civil War: A Narrative: Fredericksburg to Meridian* (New York: Random House, 3 vols., 1963).

Frank A. Haskell and William C. Oates, *Gettysburg* (New York: Bantam Books, 1992).

William A. Frassanito, *Gettysburg: A Journey in Time* (New York: Macmillan Publishing Company, 1975).

Douglas Southall Freeman, *Lee's Lieutenants: Cedar Mountain to Chancellorsville* (New York: Charles Scribner's Sons, 3 vols., 1971).

Robert Fuhrman, "'Yes, I think we will go now': The 57th Pennsylvania Volunteer Infantry at Gettysburg" (*Gettysburg Magazine*, no. 17, n.d.).

Gary W. Gallagher, *The Third Day at Gettysburg and Beyond* (Chapel Hill: The University of North Carolina Press, 1994).

The Second and Third Day's Battlefield (Olean: McElfresh Map Company, Gettysburg Battlefield Map).

George Alphonso Gibbs, "'War is . . . a dirty, bloody mess': With a Mississippi Private in a Little Known Part of the Battle of First Bull Run and at Ball's Bluff" (*Civil War Times Illustrated*, vol. 4, no. 1 April 1965).

Grady T. Gleeson, *The Irish in the South, 1815–1877* (Chapel Hill: University of North Carolina Press, 2001).

Terry Golway, *For the Cause of Liberty: A Thousand Years of Ireland's Heroes* (New York: Simon and Schuster, 2000).

John B. Gordon, *Reminiscences of the Civil War* (New York: Charles Scribner's Sons, 1904).

Bradley M. Gottfried, *The Brigades of Gettysburg: The Union and Confederate Brigades at the Battle of Gettysburg* (New York: Skyhorse Publishing, 2012).

_____, *The Artillery of Gettysburg* (Nashville: Cumberland House, 2008).

_____, *The Maps of Gettysburg: An Atlas of the Gettysburg Campaign, June 3–July 13, 1863* (El Dorado Hills, CA: Savas-Beatie, 2007).

Kent Graham, *Gettysburg: A Meditation on War and Values* (Bloomington: Indiana University Press, 1994).

Dale Greenwell, *The Third Mississippi, C.S.A.* (Pascagoula, MS: Lewis Printing Services, 1972).

Edward J. Hagerty, *Collis' Zouaves: The 114th Pennsylvania Volunteers in the Civil War* (Baton Rouge: Louisiana State University Press, 1997).

Kathy Georg Harrison and John W. Busey, *Nothing but Glory: Pickett's Division at Gettysburg* (Gettysburg: Thomas Publications, 1993).

Walter Harrison, *Pickett's Men: A Fragment of War History* (Baton Rouge: Louisiana State University Press, 2000).

Richard B. Harwell, *The Confederate Reader: How the South Saw the War* (New York: Dorset Press, 1992).

Frank Aretas Haskell, *The Battle of Gettysburg* (Boston: Houghton Mifflin Company, 1969).

Laurence M. Hauptman, *Between Two Fires: American Indians in the Civil War* (New York: Free Press, 1996).

Steve C. Hawley, "Barksdale's Mississippi Brigade at Fredericksburg" (*Civil War History*, vol. 40, no. 1, March 1994).

Martin Haynes, *A History of the Second Regiment: New Hampshire Volunteer Infantry in the War of the Rebellion* (Lakeport: Republican, 1896).

John Heiser, "Action on the Emmitsburg Road" (*Gettysburg Magazine*, no. 1, July 1989).

_____, *Historic Mobile: An Illustrated Guide* (Mobile: The Junior League of Mobile, Alabama, Inc., 1974).

"History of Itta Bena, (Leflore County) Mississippi" (History50States. com, internet).

_____, *History of the Fifty-Seventh Pennsylvania Veteran Volunteers* (Kearny: Belle Grove Publishing Company, 1995).

"Holder, Bowles, Limerick, Stuart and Related Families" (Rootsweb, internet).

John Bell Hood, *Advance and Retreat* ((Lincoln: University of Nebraska Press, 1996).

Clint Johnson, *Civil War Blunders* (Winston-Salem: John F. Blair Publishers, 1997).

Archer Jones, *Civil War Command and Strategy: The Process of Victory and Defeat* (New York: The Free Press, 1992).

David M. Jordan, *Winfield Scott Hancock: A Soldier's Life* (Indianapolis: Indiana University Press, 1995).   .

Jay Jorgensen, "'...I'll go my arm, leg, or death on it': Edward Porter Alexander, Confederate Cannoneer at Gettysburg" (*Gettysburg Magazine*, no. 17, n.d.).

Thomas Keneally, *American Scoundrel: The Life of the Notorious Civil War*

General Dan Sickles (New York: Doubleday, 2002).

Franklin W. Knight, *Slave Societies in Cuba during the Nineteenth Century* (Madison: The University of Wisconsin Press, 1974).

Robert K. Krick, *Lee's Colonels: A Biographical Register of the Field Officers of the Army of Northern Virginia* (Dayton: Morningside Bookshop, 1992).

Paul J. Lader, "The 7th New Jersey in the Gettysburg Campaign" (*Gettysburg Magazine*, no. 16, 1997).

_____, "Lafayette McLaws at Gettysburg," (*North and South Magazine*, N & S Document, no. 1 November 1997).

Richard M. Lee, *Mr. Lincoln's City: An Illustrated Guide to the Civil War Sites of Washington* (McLean: EPM Publications, Inc., 1981).

Alan Sessarego, *Letters Home: A Collection of Original Civil War Soldiers' Letters: Antietam-Gettysburg-Chancellorsville* (Gettysburg: private printing, 1990).

Kevin M. Levin, *Remembering the Battle of the Crater* (Lexington: University of Kentucky Press, 2012).

Edward Longacre, "The Soul of Our Artillery: General Henry J. Hunt" (*Civil War Times Illustrated*, vol. 12, no. 3 June 1973).

James Longstreet, *From Manassas to Appomattox* (New York, Da Capo Press, 1992).

Francis A. Lord, *Civil War Collector's Encyclopedia* (New York: Castle Books, 1965).

William A. Love, "Mississippi at Gettysburg" (*Publications of the Mississippi Historical Society*, vol. 9, 1906).

Thomas P. Lowry, *The Story the Soldiers Wouldn't Tell* (Mechanicsburg: Stackpole Books, 1994).

Jay Luvass and Harold W. Nelson, *A Guide to the Battle of Gettysburg* (Lawrence: University Press of Kansas, 1994).

Wayne Mahood, *Written in Blood: A History of the 126th New York Infantry in the Civil War* (Hightstown: Longstreet House, 1997).

Robert E. May, *John A Quitman: Old South Crusader* (Baton Rouge: Louisiana State University Press, 1985).

"Major Malbone Francis 'Peggy' Watson, (1839–1891)" (Find a Grave, internet).

Bailey George McClelen, *I Saw the Elephant* (Shippensburg: White Mane Publishing Company, 1995).

John S. McNeily, "Barksdale's Mississippi Brigade at Gettysburg" (*Publications of the Mississippi Historical Society*, vol. 14, 1914).

Grady McWhiney, *Cracker Culture: Celtic Ways in the Old South* (Tuscaloosa: University of Alabama Press, 1988).

Grady McWhiney and Perry D. Jamieson, *Attack and Die: Civil War Military Tactics and the Southern Heritage* (Tuscaloosa: University of Alabama Press, 1990).

Earl S. Miers and Richard A. Brown, *Gettysburg* (Armonk: M. E. Sharpe, 1996).

Robert A. Moore, *A Life for the Confederacy: From the War Diary of Robert A. Moore* (Dayton: Morningside Bookshop, 1977).

St. Clair A. Mulholland, *The Story of the 116th Regiment: Pennsylvania Infantry* (Gaithersburg: Old Soldier Books, Inc., n.d.).

R. L. Murray, *The Redemption of the 'Harper's Ferry Cowards'* (R. L. Murray, 1994).

_____, *Hispanics and the Civil War: From Battlefield to Homefront* (Washington, D.C.: Department of the Interior, National Park Service, n.d.).

Wilbur Sturtevant Nye, *Here Come the Rebels!* (Dayton: Morningside Bookshop, 1988).

O.O. Howard, "Commencement Address to Syracuse University" (*Gettysburg Magazine*, no. 11, July 1994).

William C. Oates, *The War between the Union and the Confederacy* (Dayton: Morningside Bookshop, 1985).

Kevin O'Brien, "'To Unflinchingly Face Danger and Death': Carr's Brigade Defends Emmitsburg Road" (*Gettysburg Magazine*, no. 12, January 1, 1995).

Seward R. Osborne, "New York in Confederate Gray: Pvt. Edgar Bakers, 21st Mississippi" (*North South Trader's Civil War*, vol. 34, no. 6, 2010).

William Miller Owen, *In Camp and Battle with the Washington Artillery* (Dayton: Morningside Bookshop, 1972).

Nell Irvin Painter, *Creating Black Americans: African-American History and its Meaning, 1619 to the Present* (New York: Oxford University Press, 2006).

_____, *Pennsylvania at Gettysburg* (Harrisburg: William Stanley Ray, State Printer, vol. 2., 1904).

Mark Perry, *Conceived in Liberty: Joshua Chamberlain, William Oates and the American Civil War* (New York: Viking, 1997).

Harry W. Pfanz, *Gettysburg: The Second Day* (Chapel Hill: University of North Carolina Press, 1987).

Harry W. Pfanz, *The Battle of Gettysburg* (Washington, D.C.: Eastern National Park and Monument Association, National Park Civil War Series, 1994).

Edgcumb Pinchon, *Dan Sickles: Hero of Gettysburg and Yankee King of Spain* (Garden City: Doubleday, Doran and Company, Inc., 1945).

James J. Pillar, *The Catholic Church in Mississippi, 1837–1865* (New Orleans: The Hauser Press, 1964).

William Garret Piston, *Lee's Tarnished Lieutenant: James Longstreet and His Place in Southern History* (Athens: University of Georgia Press, 1987).

J.B. Polley, *Hood's Texas Brigade* (Dayton: Morningside Bookshop, 1988).

Perry Lee Rainwater (ed.), "The Autobiography of Benjamin Grubb Humphreys" (*Mississippi Valley Historical Review*, vol. 20, September 1934).

Carol Reardon, *Pickett's Charge in History and Memory* (Chapel Hill: University of North Carolina Press, 1997).

Harry Roach, *Gettysburg: Hour By Hour* (Gettysburg: Thomas Publications, 1994).

Bobby Roberts and Carl Moneyhon, *Portraits of Conflict: A Photographic History of Mississippi in the Civil War* (Fayetteville: The University of Arkansas Press, 1993).

James Robertson, *General A.P. Hill: The Story of a Confederate Warrior* (New York: Random House, 1992).

Jay Rubenstein, *Armies of Heaven: The First Crusade and the Quest for Apocalypse* (New York: Basic Books, 2011).

Carl Sandberg, *Abraham Lincoln: The War Years, 1861–1864* (New York: Dell Publishing Company, 1960).

Robert Garth Scott (ed.), *Fallen Leaves: The Civil War Letters of Major Henry Livermore Abbot* (Kent: Kent State University Press, 1991).

Stephen W. Sears, *Gettysburg* (New York: Houghton Mifflin Company, 2004).

_____, *To the Gates of Richmond: The Peninsula Campaign* (New York: Ticknor & Fields, 1992).

Gerald J. Smith, *One of the Most Daring of Men: The Life of Confederate General William Tatum Wofford* (Murfreesboro: Confederate Heritage Press, 1997).

Dick Stanley, "13th Mississippi Infantry Regiment, Correspondence" (August 6, 8, 12, 20, 28, 30 and September 6, 18, 22, 24, and 26, 2011, internet).

Robert Stiles, *Four Years under Marsh Robert* (Marietta: R. Bemis Publishing Company, 1995).

W.C. Storrick, *Gettysburg* (J. Horace McFarland Company, 1932).

Charles L. Sullivan, *The Mississippi Gulf Coast: Portrait of a People* (Northbridge: Windsor Publications, 1985).

Survivors' Association, *History of the Corn Exchange Regiment: 118th Pennsylvania Volunteers* (Philadelphia: J. L. Smith Publishers, 1888).

Marcus Tanner, *Ireland's Holy War's: The Struggle for a Nation's Soul* (New Haven: Yale University Press, 2001).

_____, *The Delta General* (vol. 13, no. 8, August 2010).

_____, *The War of the Rebellion: A Compilation of the Official Records of the Union and Confederate Armies* (Washington, D.C.: Government Printing Office, 138 vols., 1880–1901).

Emory Thomas, *Robert E. Lee: A Biography* (New York: W. W. Norton and Company, 1995).

Jerry Thompson (ed.), *Tejanos in Gray: Civil War Letters of Captains Joseph Rafael de la Garza and Manuel Yturri* (College Station: Texas A & M University Press, 2012).

Samuel Toombs, *New Jersey Troops in the Gettysburg Campaign* (Orange: Evening Mail Publishing House, 1888).

Don Troiani and Brian Pohanka, *Don Troiani's Civil War* (Mechanicsburg: Stackpole Books, 1999).

Noah Andre Trudeau, *Gettysburg: A Testing of Courage* (New York: Harper Collins, 2002).

Glenn Tucker, *High Tide at Gettysburg* (Dayton: Morningside Bookshop, 1983).

Phillip Thomas Tucker (ed.), *Cubans in the Confederacy: Jose Agustin Quintero, Ambrosio Jose onzales, and Loreta Janeta Velazquez* (Jefferson: McFarland and Company, Inc., Publishers, 2002).

Jeffry D. Wert, *A Glorious Army: Robert E. Lee's Triumph, 1862-1863* (New York: Simon and Schuster, 2011).

Jeffry D. Wert, *General James Longstreet: The Confederacy's Most Controversial Soldier* (New York: Touchstone Books, 1993).

Joseph Wheelan, *Invading Mexico: America's Continental Dream and the Mexican War, 1846–1848* (New York: Carroll and Graf Publications, 2007).

Richard Wheeler, *Witness to Gettysburg* (New York: Penguin Books, 1989).

Bell Irvin Wiley, *Embattled Confederates: An Illustrated History of Southerners at War* (New York: Harper and Row, 1964).

Bell Irvin Wiley, *The Life of Johnny Reb: The Common Soldier of the Confederacy* (Baton Rouge: Louisiana State University Press, 1978).

Terrence J. Winschel "To Assuage the Grief: The Confederate Saga of Isaac and Mary Stamps" (*Gettysburg Magazine*, no. 7, July 1992).

C. Vann Woodward and Elisabeth Muhlenfeld, *The Private Mary Chesnut: The Unpublished Civil War Diaries* (New York: Oxford University Press, 1984).

Mac Wyckoff, *A History of the 2nd South Carolina Infantry, 1861–1865* (Fredericksburg: Sergeant Kirkland's Museum, 1994).

Henry Woodhead (ed.), *Echoes of Glory: Arms and Equipment of the Confederacy* (Alexandria: Time-Life Books, 1991).

William Youngblood, "Unwritten History of the Gettysburg Campaign" (*Southern Historical Society Papers*, vol. 38. n.d.).

Index

Abernathy, William Meshack (17th Mississippi) 24, 26, 158, 160, 161, 167, 186, 218, 220, 251–252

Alexander, Edward Porter (Colonel, artillery) action at Gettysburg 61, 67, 68, 73, 76, 78, 89, 99, 107, 110, 170, 184, 213, 229, 230, 231, 236, 244

advance toward Peach Orchard 170–174

Anderson, Richard (Major General) 41, 144–145, 153, 214–215, 255

Armstrong, Ezekiel (Private, 17th Mississippi) 8, 22, 26, 83

Army of the Cumberland 39

Army of Northern Virginia 2, 4, 7, 17, 33, 36, 39, 40, 41, 43, 89, 93, 95, 99, 103, 175, 181, 224, 229, 237, 244

Army of the Potomac 4, 16, 39, 41–42, 43, 44, 45, 49, 64, 70, 71, 86, 93, 147, 185, 186, 191, 194, 213, 214, 224, 235, 236

artillery 58, 59, 64, 65, 77, 95, 97, 104, 115, 117–118, 124, 161, 184–187, 212, 235–236

1st New Jersey Light 150–152, 179

1st Rhode Island Light 68, 80, 97, 104, 107, 108, 110, 112, 117, 118

1st Volunteer Light 66

5th Massachusetts Light 153, 182, 192, 212, 213

6th Maine 188, 212–213, 242

9th Massachussets Light 153, 189–210, 213–214, 233, 235, 242

15th New York Light 64, 66, 150, 234

assaults by Humphreys on Union batteries, 130–132, 139–140, 143–146, 147–155

Confederate 61, 64, 70, 71, 73, 76, 78, 89, 99, 107, 110, 152, 170, 184, 213, 229, 230, 231, 236, 244

Confederate, guns ineffective 85–86

Pennsylvania Light 150, 152–153

Union, guns out-shoot Confederate 77, 98

Union, positioned at Peach Orchard 66–67, 73–74, 76–77, 79–80

Union, regroup to form Plum Run Line 212–214

Bailey, Edward L. (Colonel, 2nd New Hampshire) 121–122, 127

Ball's Bluff, Virginia, battle of 7–8, 16, 22, 27, 108

Barksdale, Harris (Captain) 91–92,

307